PandoraHearts

Jun Mochizuki

CONTENTS

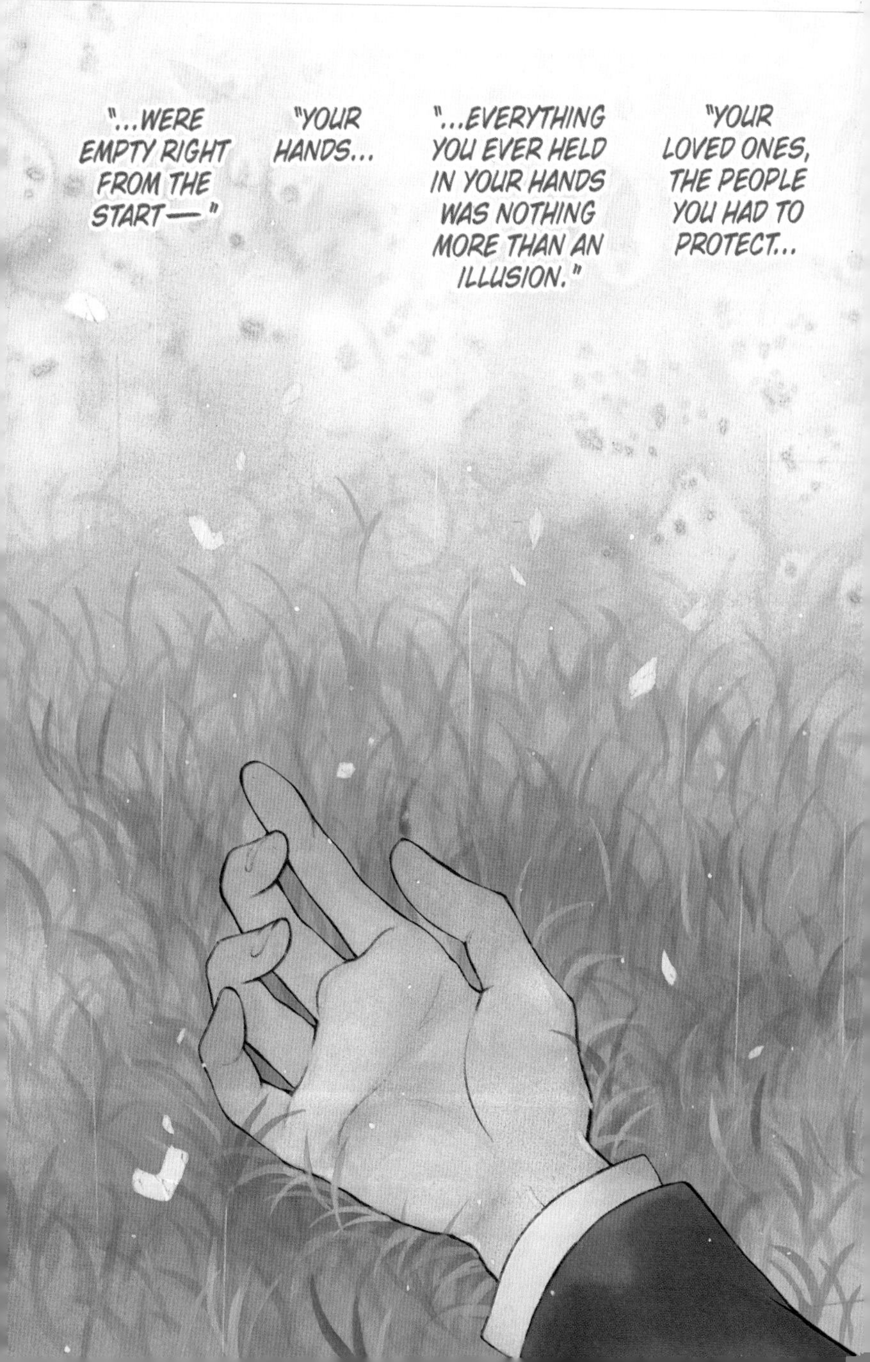
"YOUR LOVED ONES, THE PEOPLE YOU HAD TO PROTECT...
"...EVERYTHING YOU EVER HELD IN YOUR HANDS WAS NOTHING MORE THAN AN ILLUSION."
"YOUR HANDS...
"...WERE EMPTY RIGHT FROM THE START—"

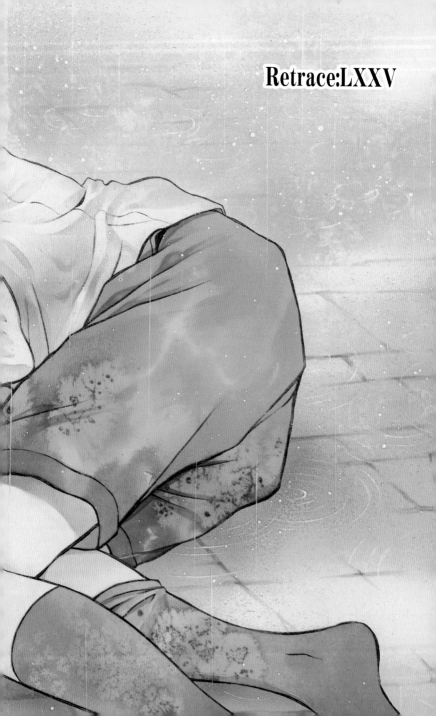

Retrace:LXXV

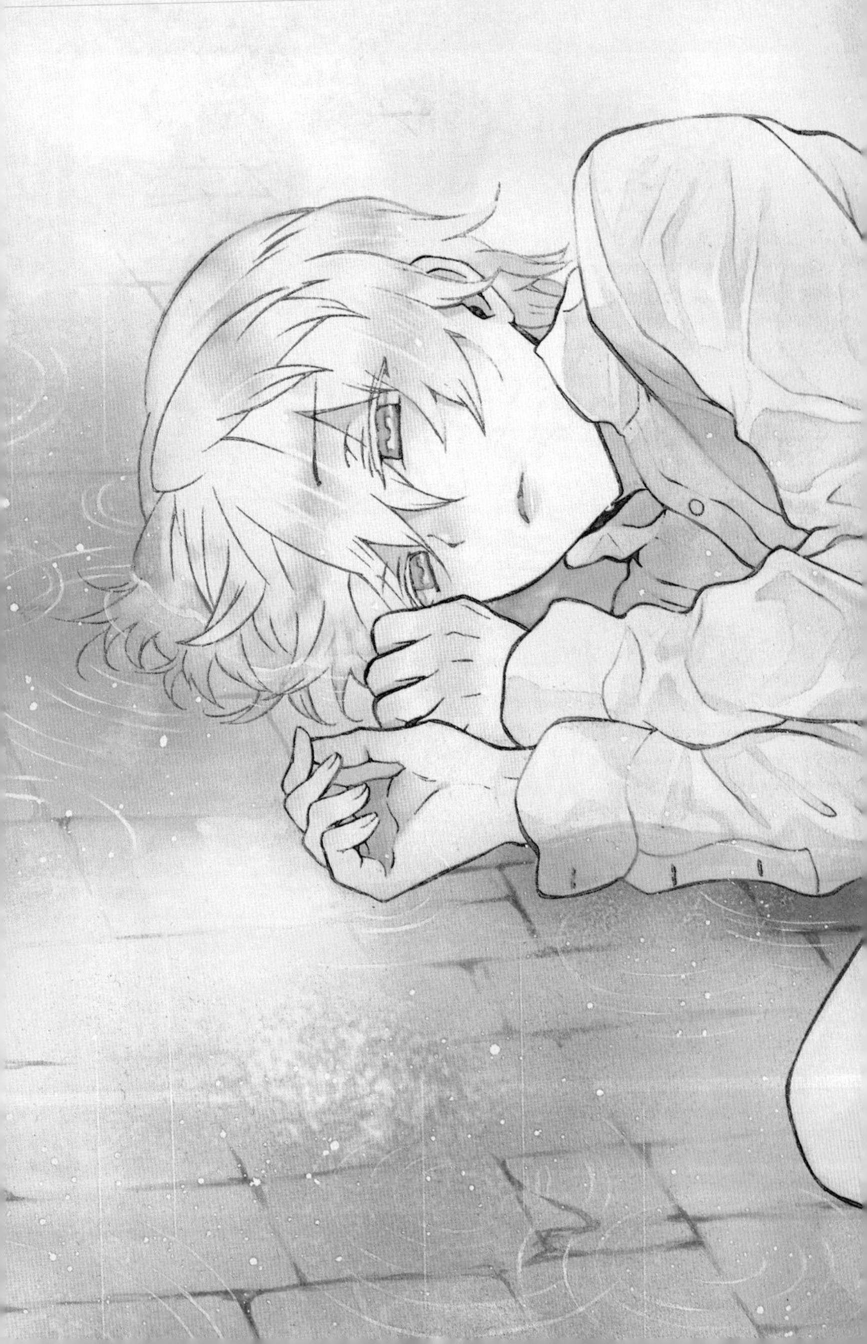

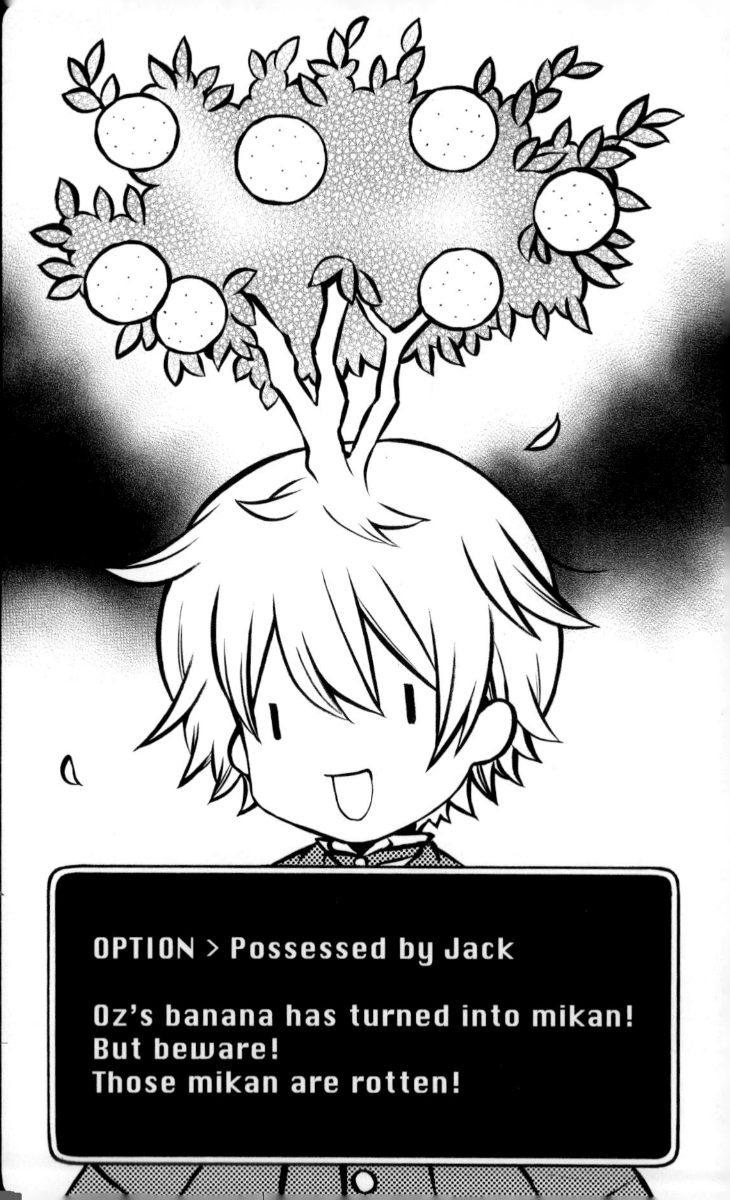
OPTION > Possessed by Jack
Oz's banana has turned into mikan!
But beware!
Those mikan are rotten!

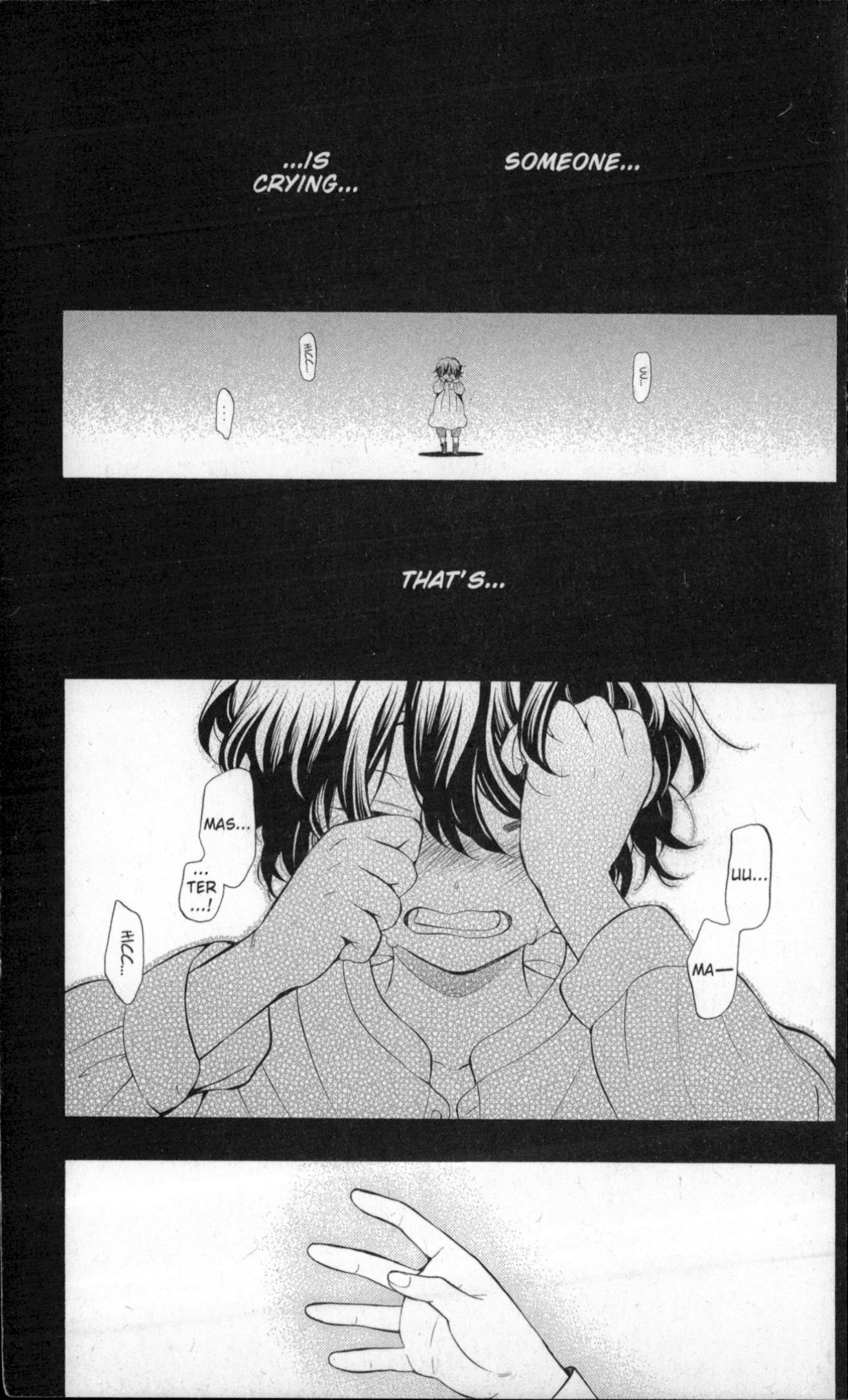
SOMEONE...
...IS CRYING...
UU...
HICC...
...
THAT'S...
UU...
MA—
MAS...
...TER...!
HICC...

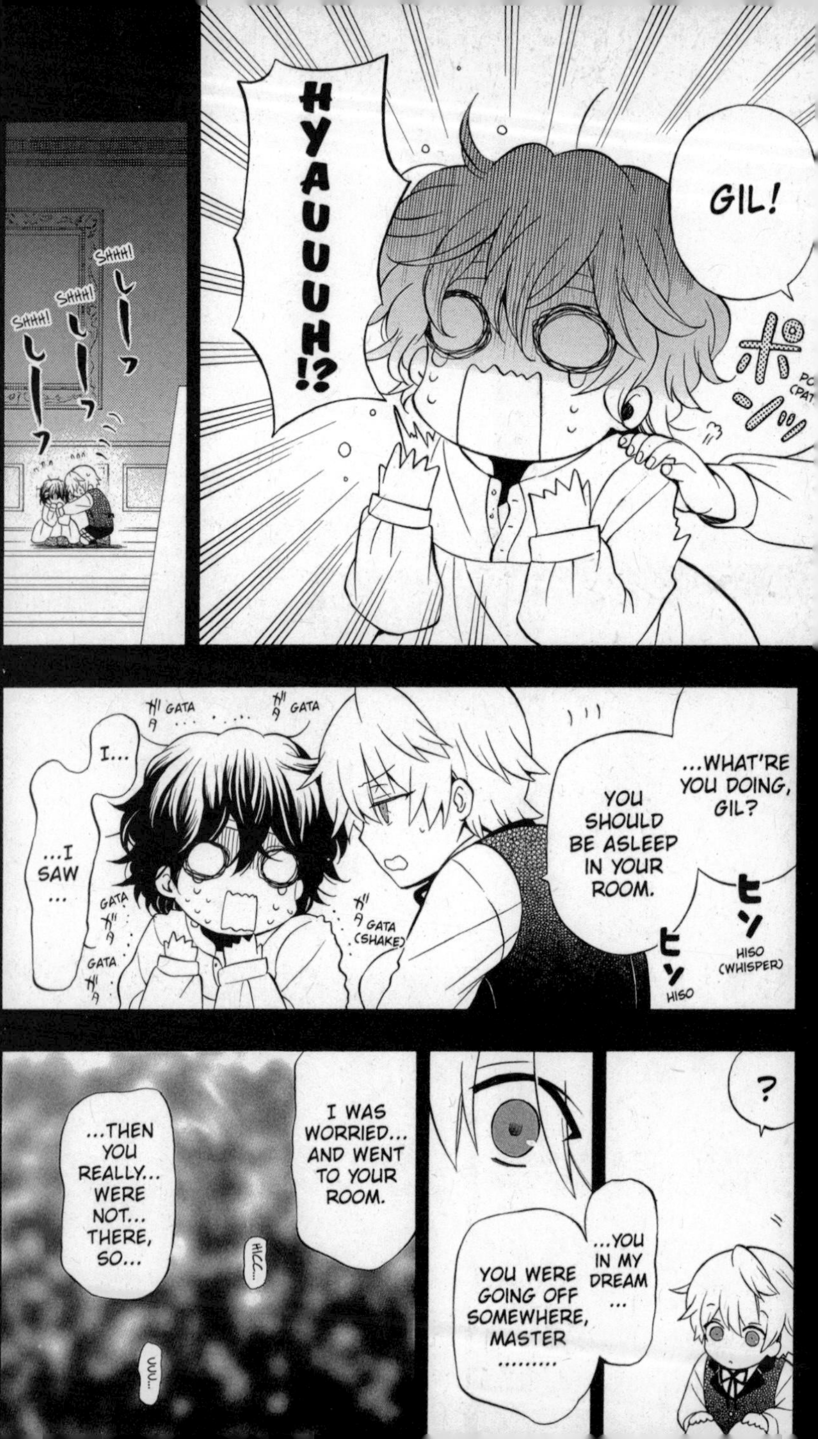
GIL!
HYAUUUH!?
SHHH!
SHHH!
SHHH!
...WHAT'RE YOU DOING, GIL?
YOU SHOULD BE ASLEEP IN YOUR ROOM.
HISO (WHISPER)
HISO
GATA
GATA
I...
...I SAW ...
GATA (SHAKE)
GATA
GATA
?
...YOU IN MY DREAM ...
YOU WERE GOING OFF SOMEWHERE, MASTER ....
I WAS WORRIED... AND WENT TO YOUR ROOM.
...THEN YOU REALLY... WERE NOT... THERE, SO...
HICC...
UUU...

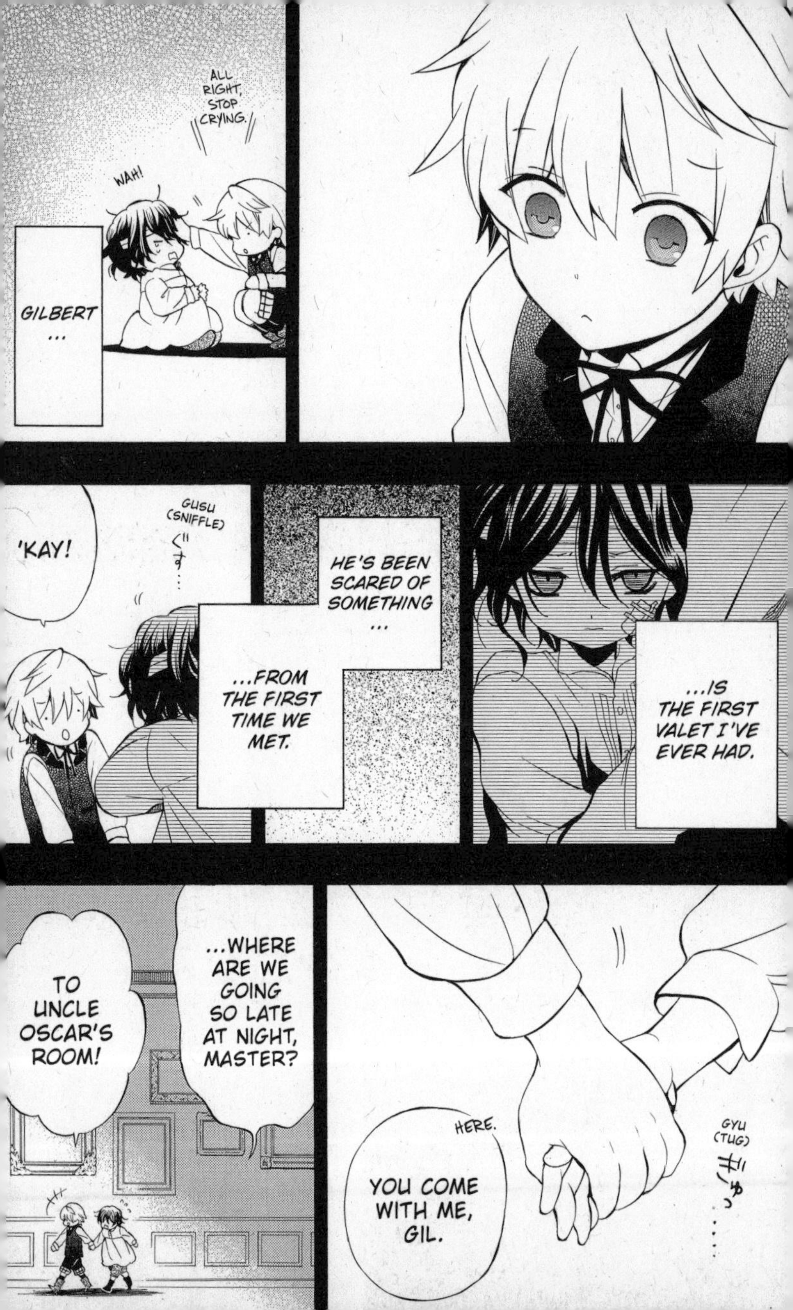
ALL RIGHT, STOP CRYING.
WAH!
GILBERT ...
...IS THE FIRST VALET I'VE EVER HAD.
HE'S BEEN SCARED OF SOMETHING ...
...FROM THE FIRST TIME WE MET.
GUSU (SNIFFLE)
ぐす…
'KAY!
HERE.
YOU COME WITH ME, GIL.
GYU (TUG)
ぎゅっ……
...WHERE ARE WE GOING SO LATE AT NIGHT, MASTER?
TO UNCLE OSCAR'S ROOM!

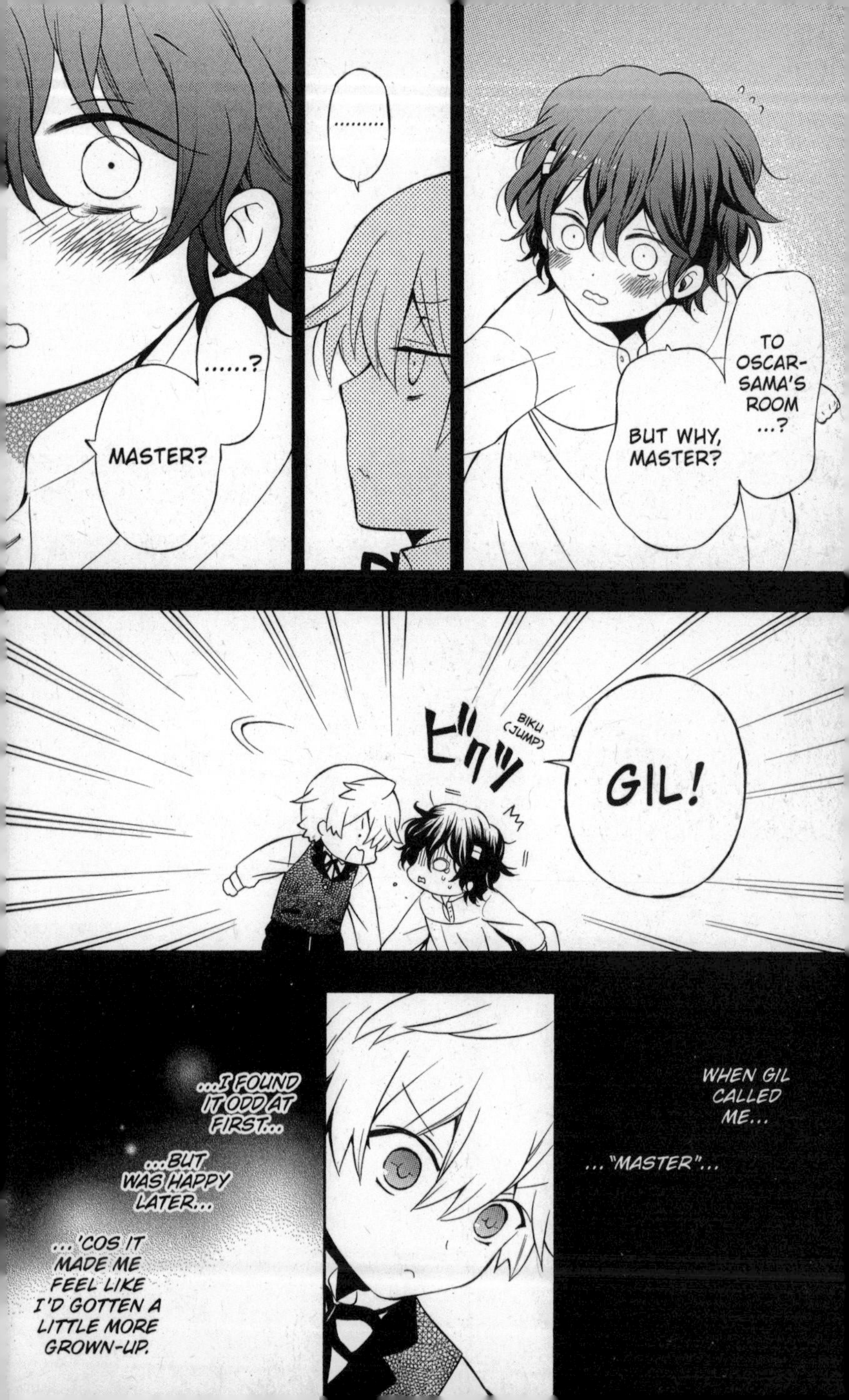
TO OSCAR-SAMA'S ROOM ...?
BUT WHY, MASTER?
....
......?
MASTER?
GIL!
BIKU (JUMP)
ビクッ
WHEN GIL CALLED ME...
..."MASTER"...
...I FOUND IT ODD AT FIRST...
...BUT WAS HAPPY LATER...
...'COS IT MADE ME FEEL LIKE I'D GOTTEN A LITTLE MORE GROWN-UP.

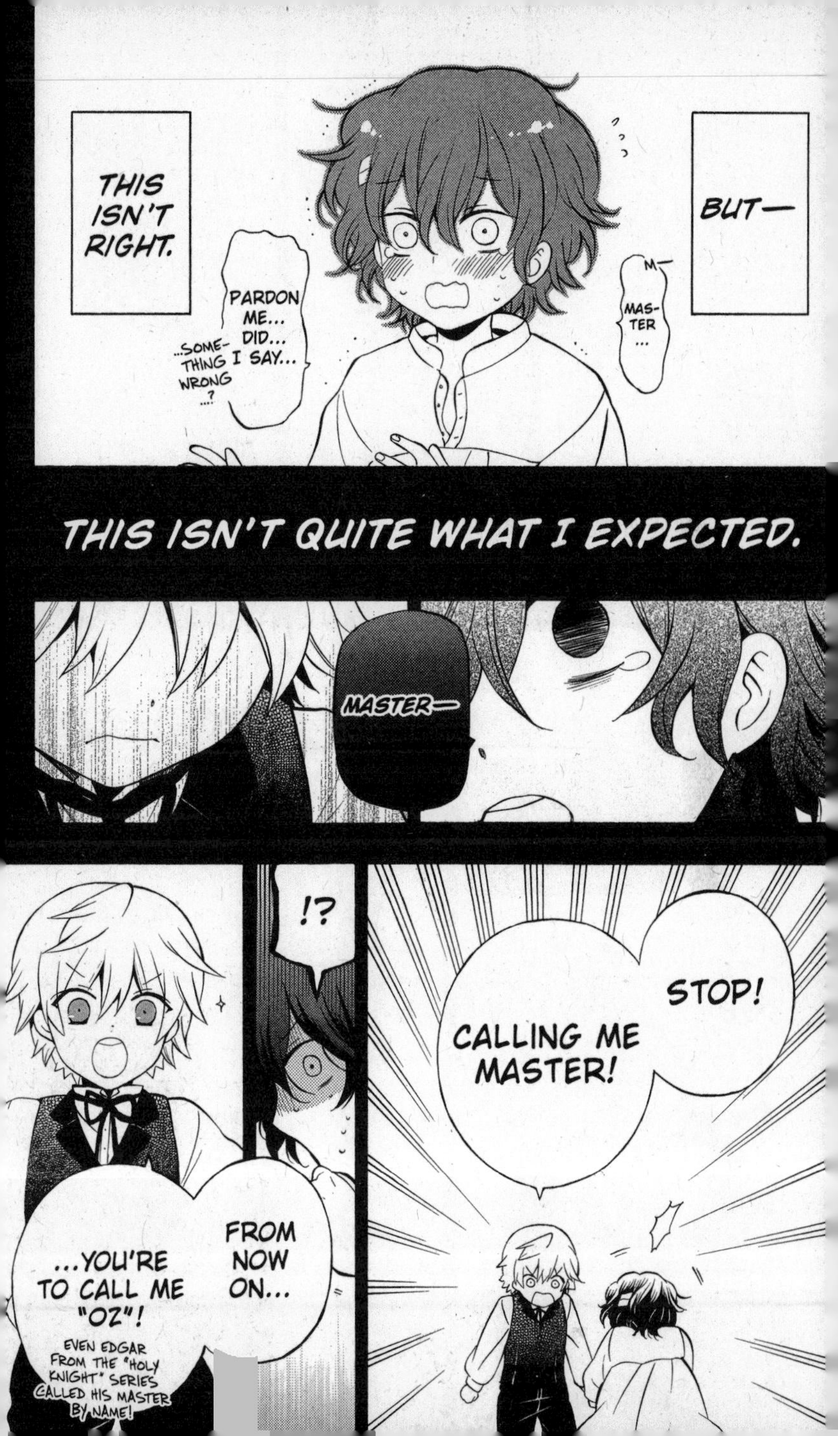
BUT—
M— MASTER...
PARDON ME... DID... I SAY... ...SOMETHING WRONG...?
THIS ISN'T RIGHT.
THIS ISN'T QUITE WHAT I EXPECTED.
MASTER—
STOP! CALLING ME MASTER!
!?
FROM NOW ON... ...YOU'RE TO CALL ME "OZ"!
EVEN EDGAR FROM THE "HOLY KNIGHT" SERIES CALLED HIS MASTER BY NAME!

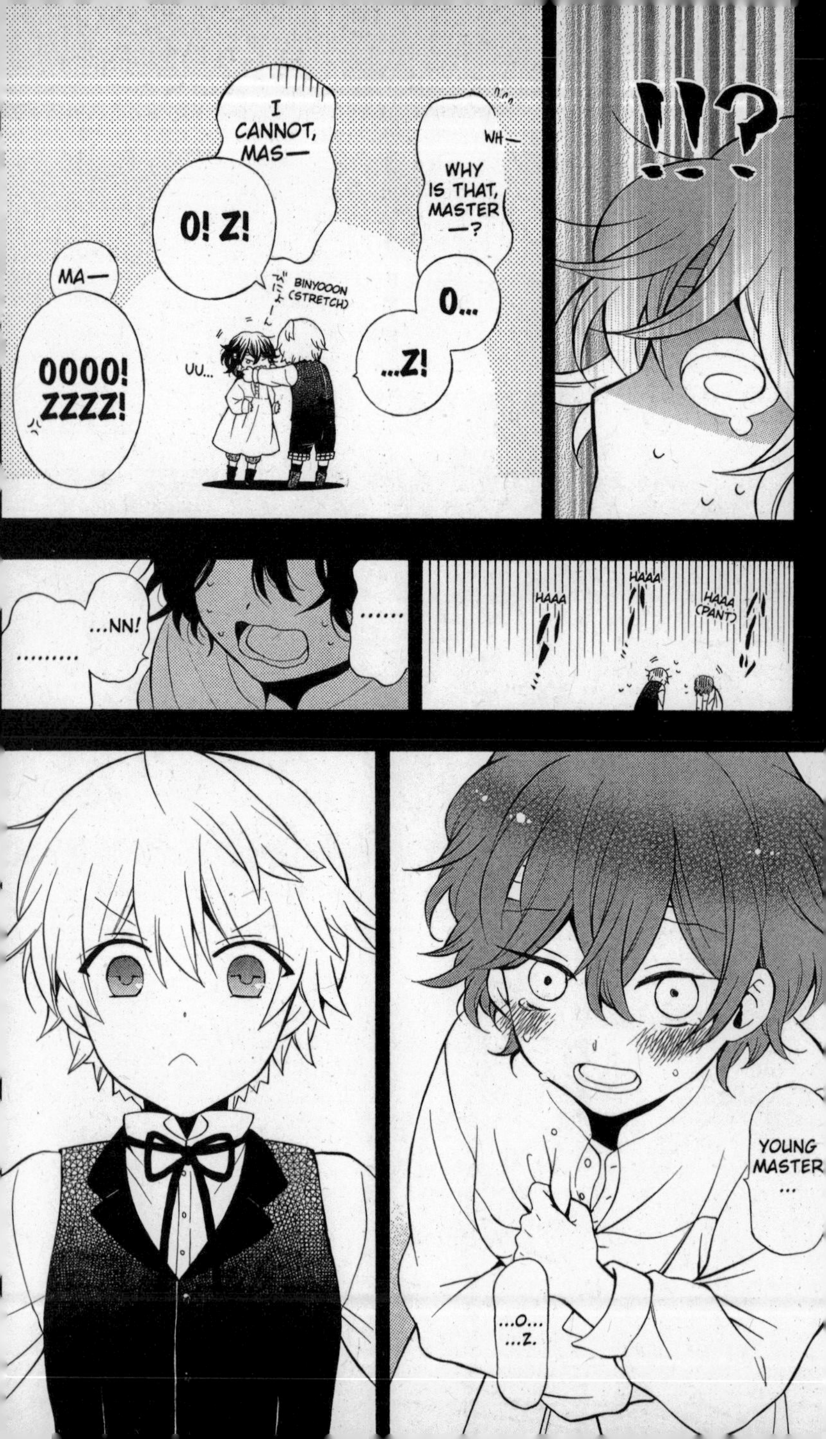

!!?
WH—
WHY IS THAT, MASTER—?
O...
...Z!
I CANNOT, MAS—
O! Z!
BINYOOON (STRETCH)
UU...
MA—
OOOO! ZZZZ!
HAAA
HAAA
HAAA (PANT)
......
...NN!
....
YOUNG MASTER...
...O... ...Z.

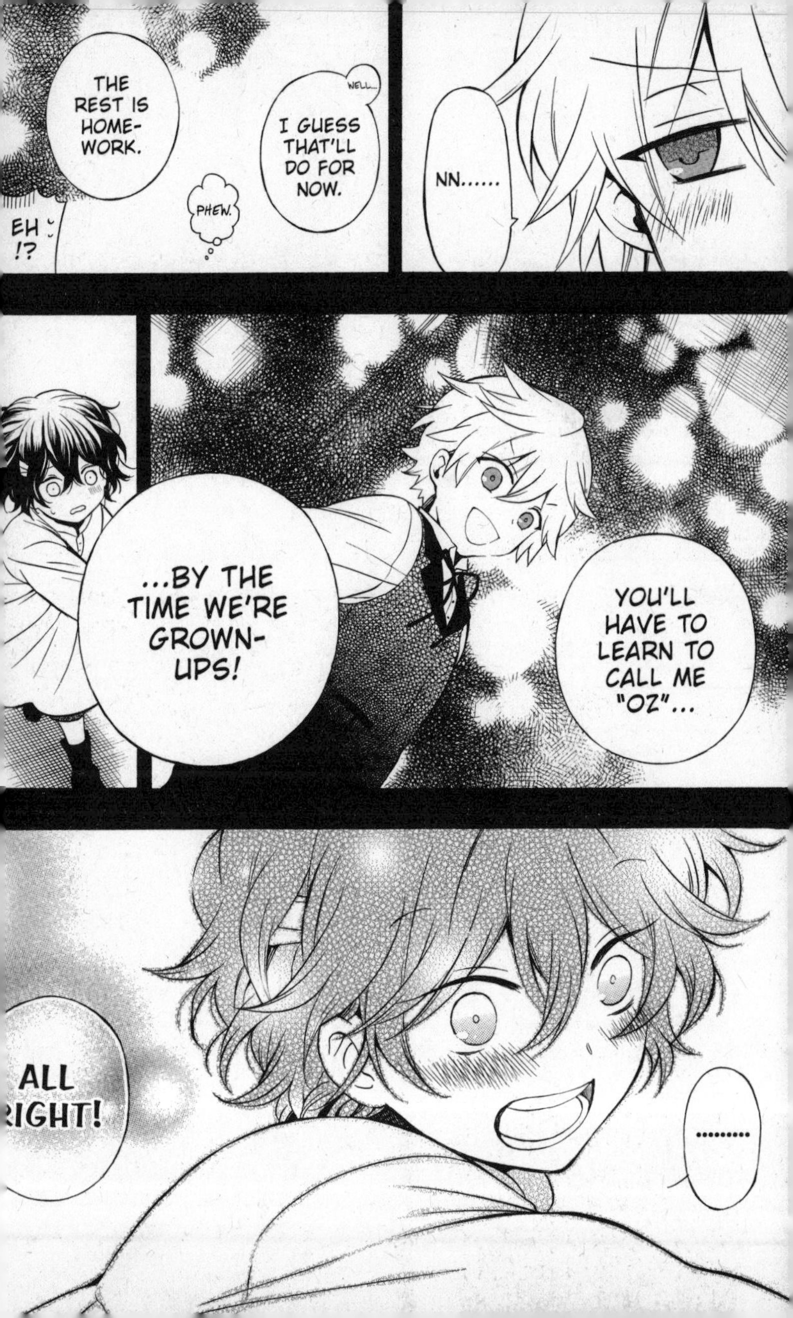
NN......
WELL...
I GUESS THAT'LL DO FOR NOW.
THE REST IS HOME-WORK.
PHEW.
EH!?
YOU'LL HAVE TO LEARN TO CALL ME "OZ"...
...BY THE TIME WE'RE GROWN-UPS!
....
ALL RIGHT!

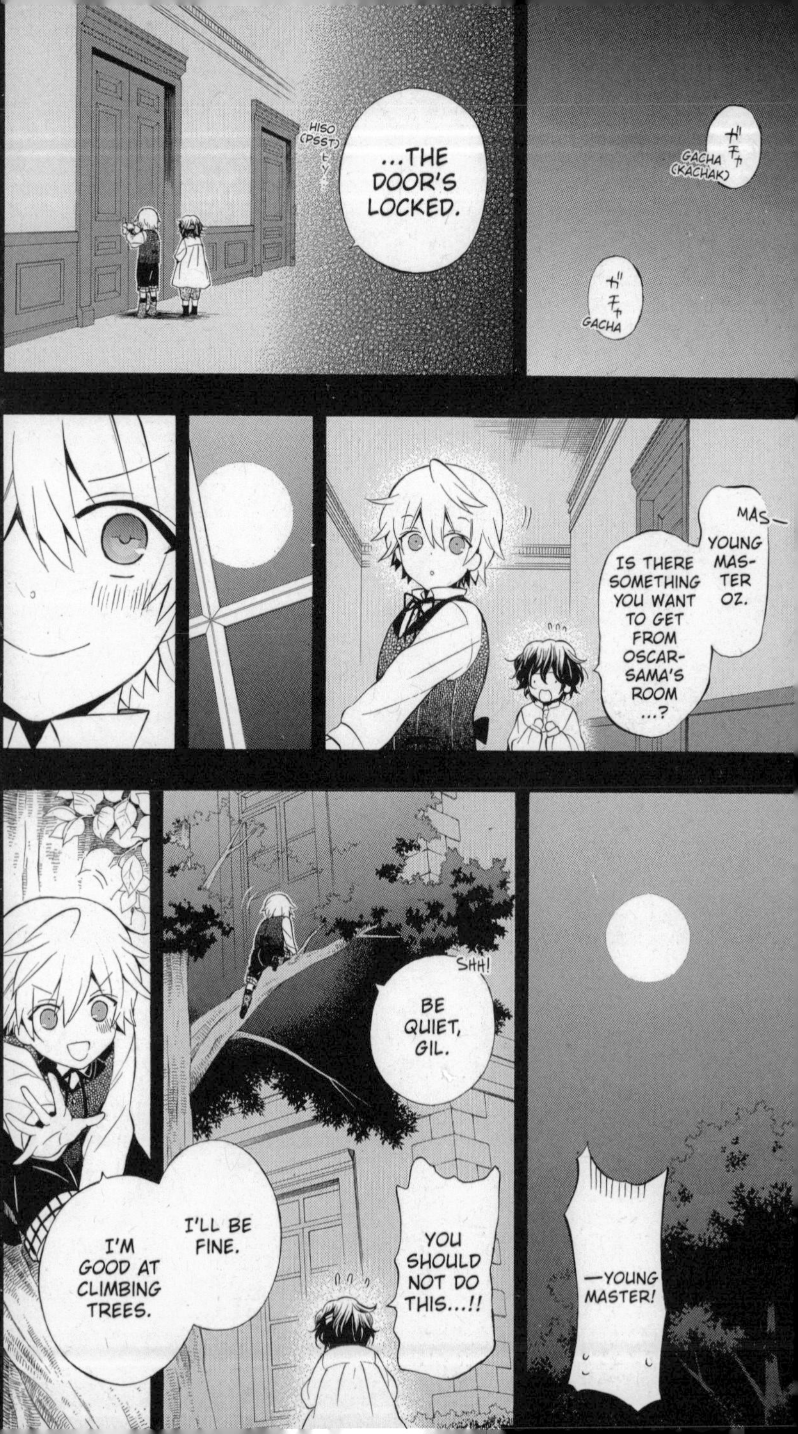
ガチャ
GACHA (KACHAK)
ガチャ
GACHA
ヒソ
HISO (PSST)
...THE DOOR'S LOCKED.
MAS—
YOUNG MAS-TER OZ.
IS THERE SOMETHING YOU WANT TO GET FROM OSCAR-SAMA'S ROOM ...?
—YOUNG MASTER!
YOU SHOULD NOT DO THIS...!!
SHH!
BE QUIET, GIL.
I'LL BE FINE.
I'M GOOD AT CLIMBING TREES.

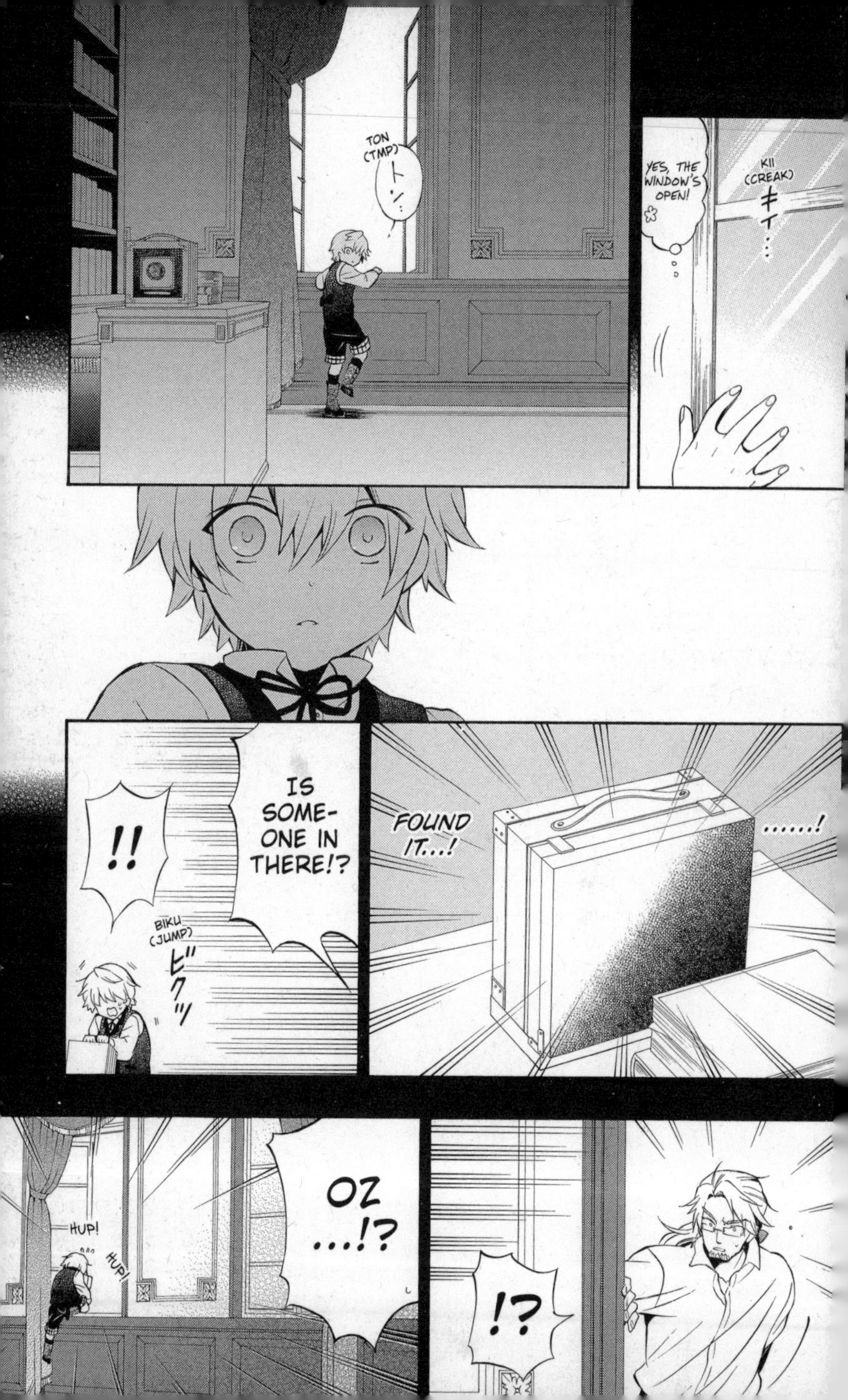
KII (CREAK)
キイ…
YES, THE WINDOW'S OPEN!
TON (TMP)
トンッ…
FOUND IT...!
......!
IS SOME-ONE IN THERE!?
!!
BIKU (JUMP)
ビクッ
!?
OZ ...!?
HUP!
HUP!

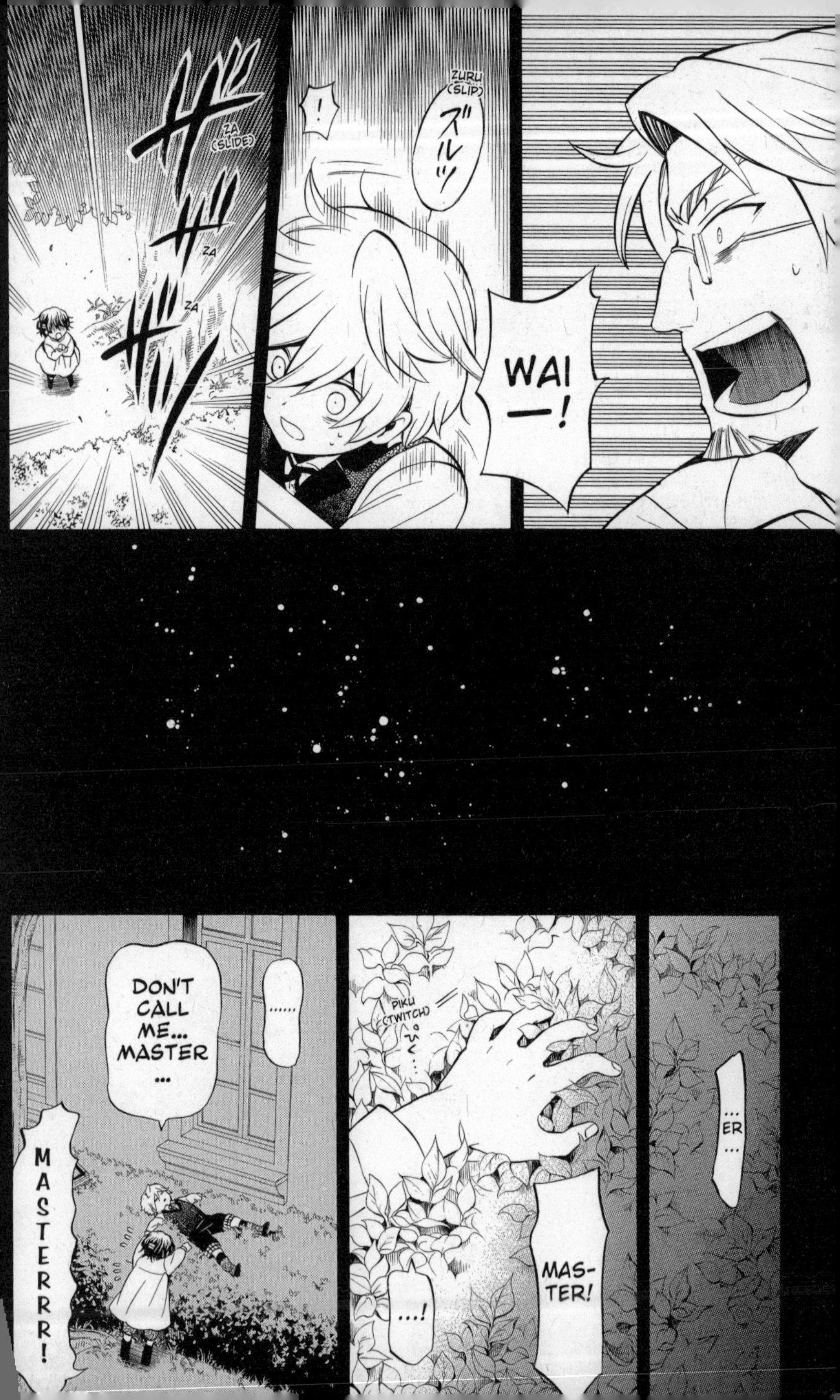
WAI—!
!
ZURU (SLIP)
ズルッ
ZA (SLIDE)
ZA
ZA
...ER...
PIKU (TWITCH)
ぴく…
MAS-TER!
...!
......
DON'T CALL ME... MASTER ...
MASTERRR!

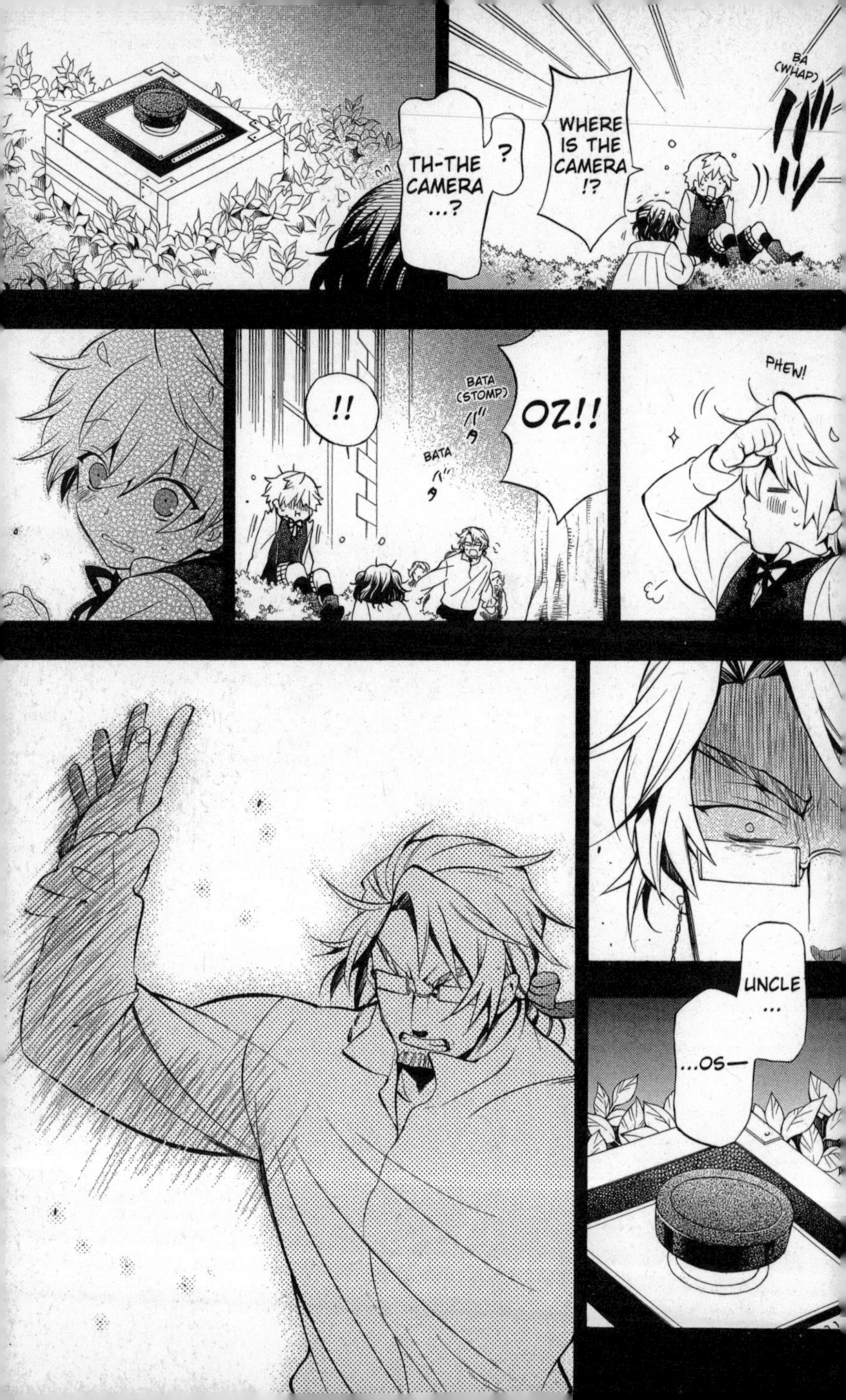
BA (WHAP)
WHERE IS THE CAMERA !?
?
TH-THE CAMERA ...?
PHEW!
OZ!!
BATA (STOMP)
BATA
!!
UNCLE ...
...OS—

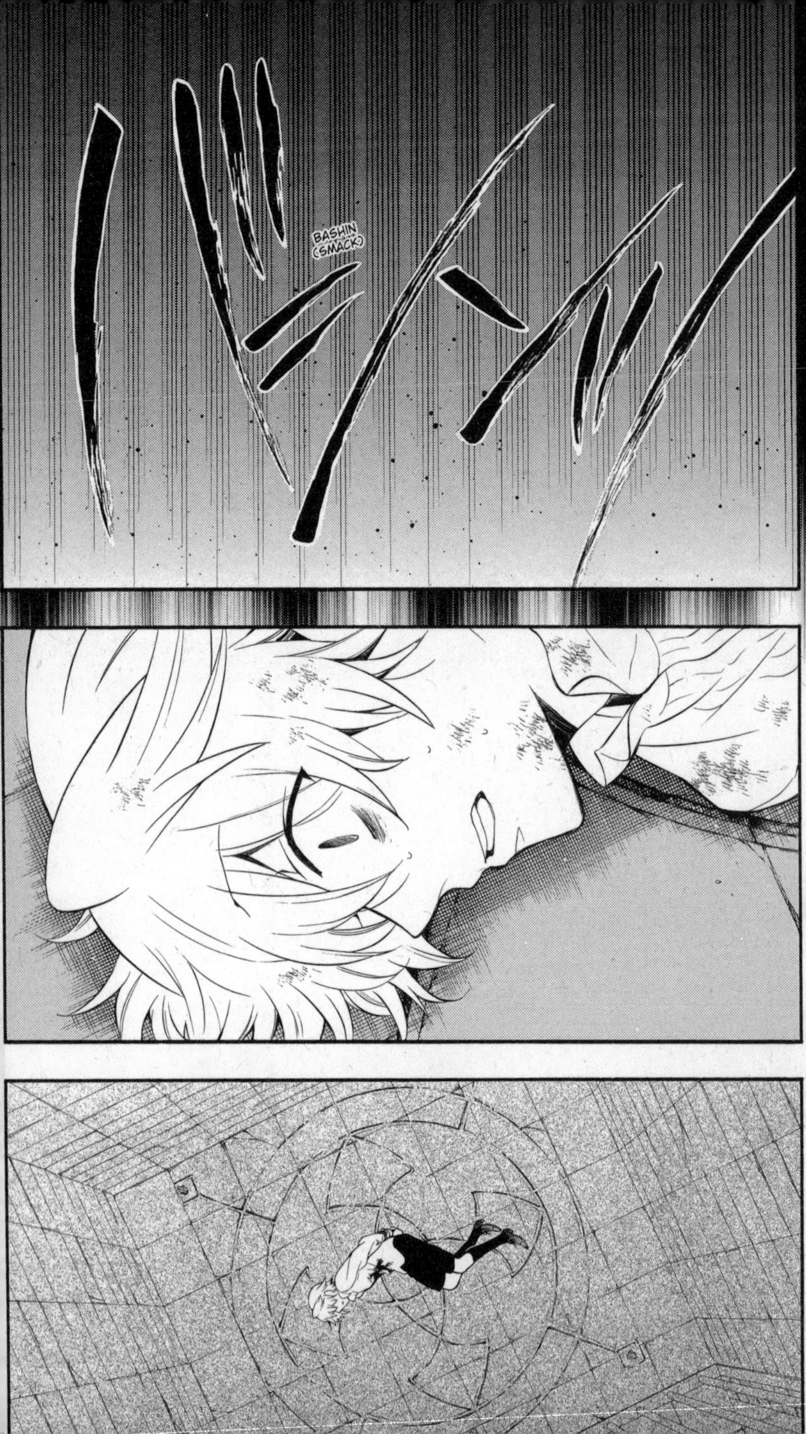
BASHIN
(SMACK)

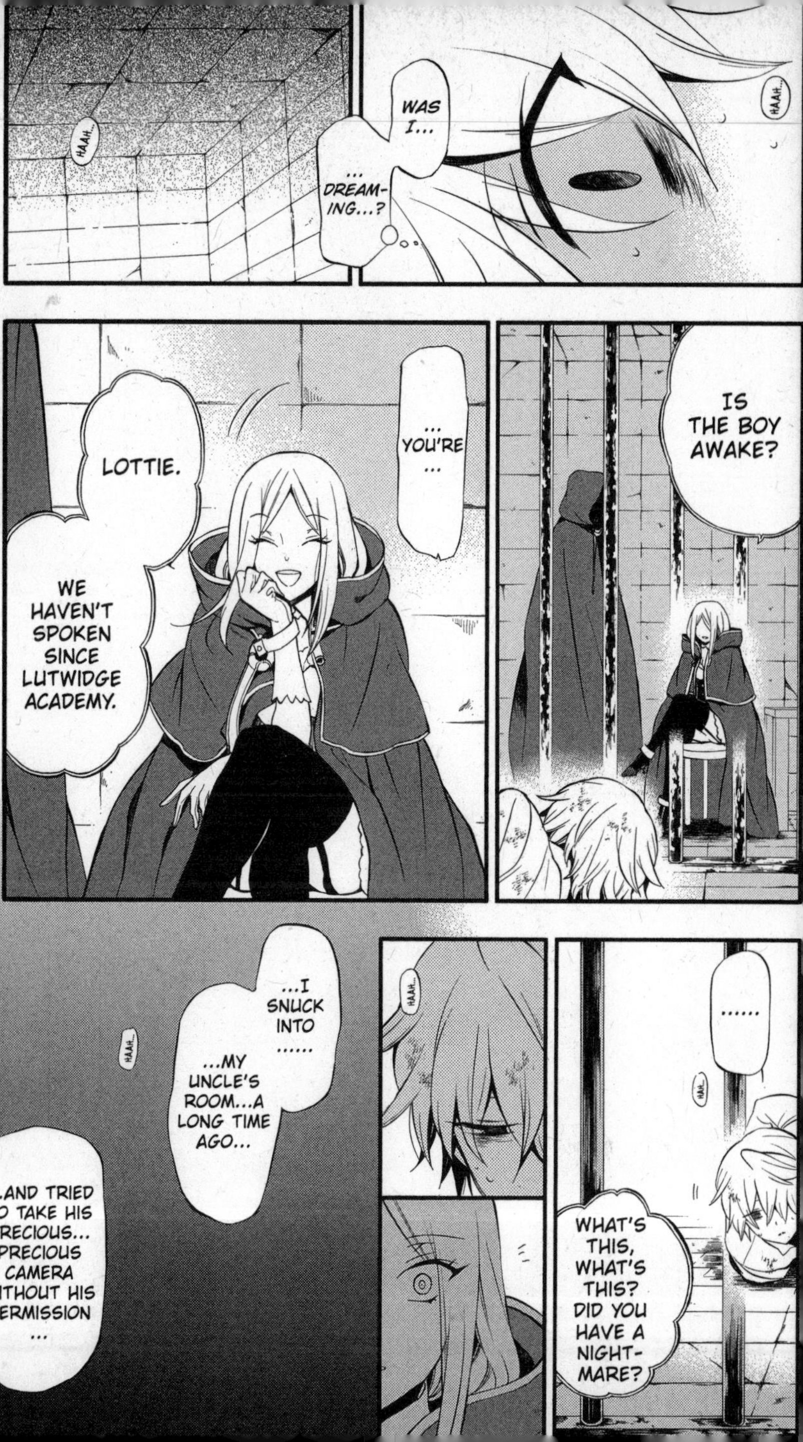
HAAH...
WAS I... ...DREAMING...?
HAAH...
IS THE BOY AWAKE?
...YOU'RE...
LOTTIE.
WE HAVEN'T SPOKEN SINCE LUTWIDGE ACADEMY.
......
HAAH...
WHAT'S THIS, WHAT'S THIS? DID YOU HAVE A NIGHTMARE?
HAAH...
...I SNUCK INTO ......
HAAH...
...MY UNCLE'S ROOM...A LONG TIME AGO...
...AND TRIED TO TAKE HIS PRECIOUS... PRECIOUS CAMERA WITHOUT HIS PERMISSION ...

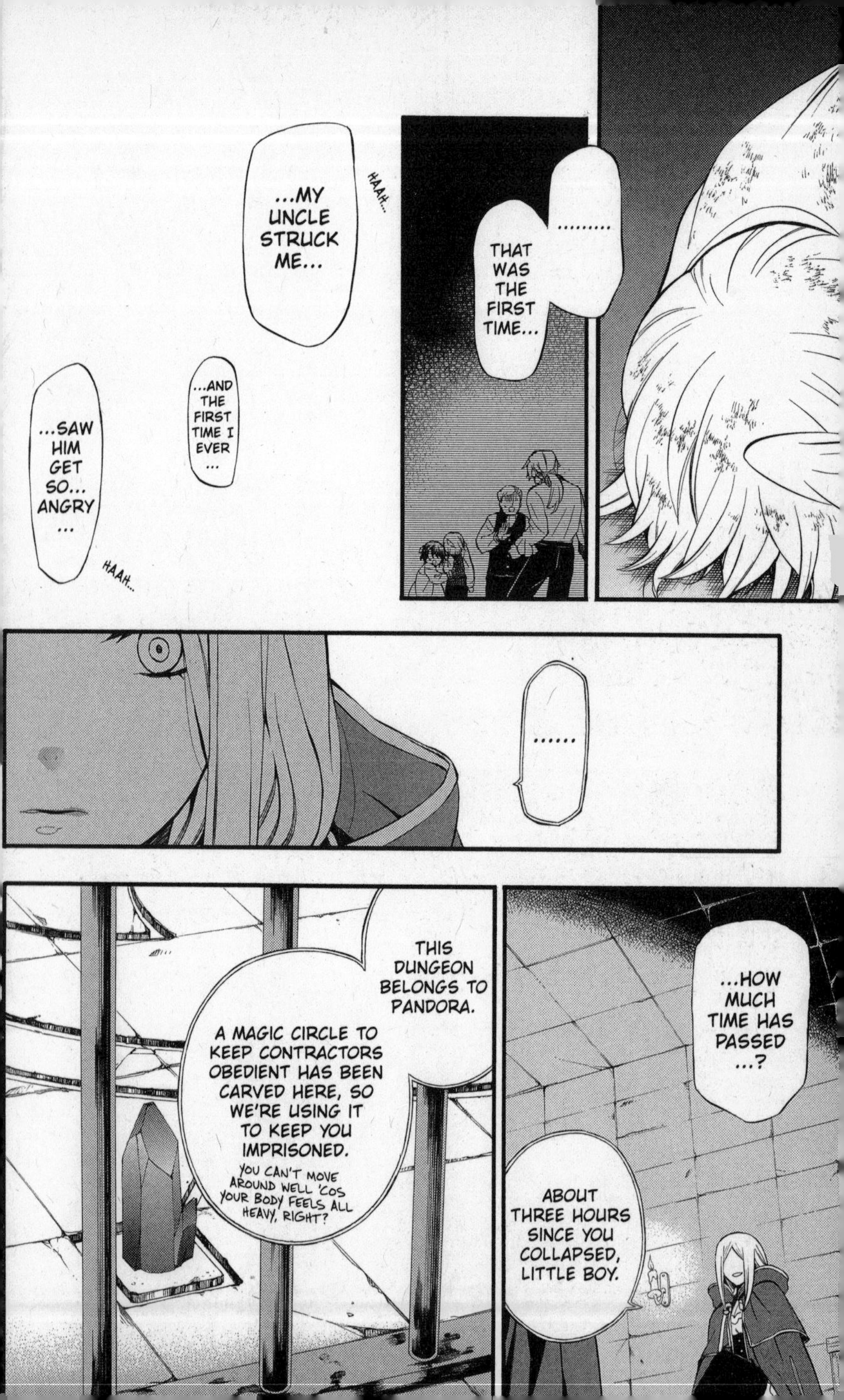
....
THAT WAS THE FIRST TIME...
...MY UNCLE STRUCK ME...
HAAH...
...AND THE FIRST TIME I EVER ...
...SAW HIM GET SO... ANGRY ...
HAAH...
......
...HOW MUCH TIME HAS PASSED ...?
ABOUT THREE HOURS SINCE YOU COLLAPSED, LITTLE BOY.
THIS DUNGEON BELONGS TO PANDORA.
A MAGIC CIRCLE TO KEEP CONTRACTORS OBEDIENT HAS BEEN CARVED HERE, SO WE'RE USING IT TO KEEP YOU IMPRISONED.
YOU CAN'T MOVE AROUND WELL 'COS YOUR BODY FEELS ALL HEAVY, RIGHT?

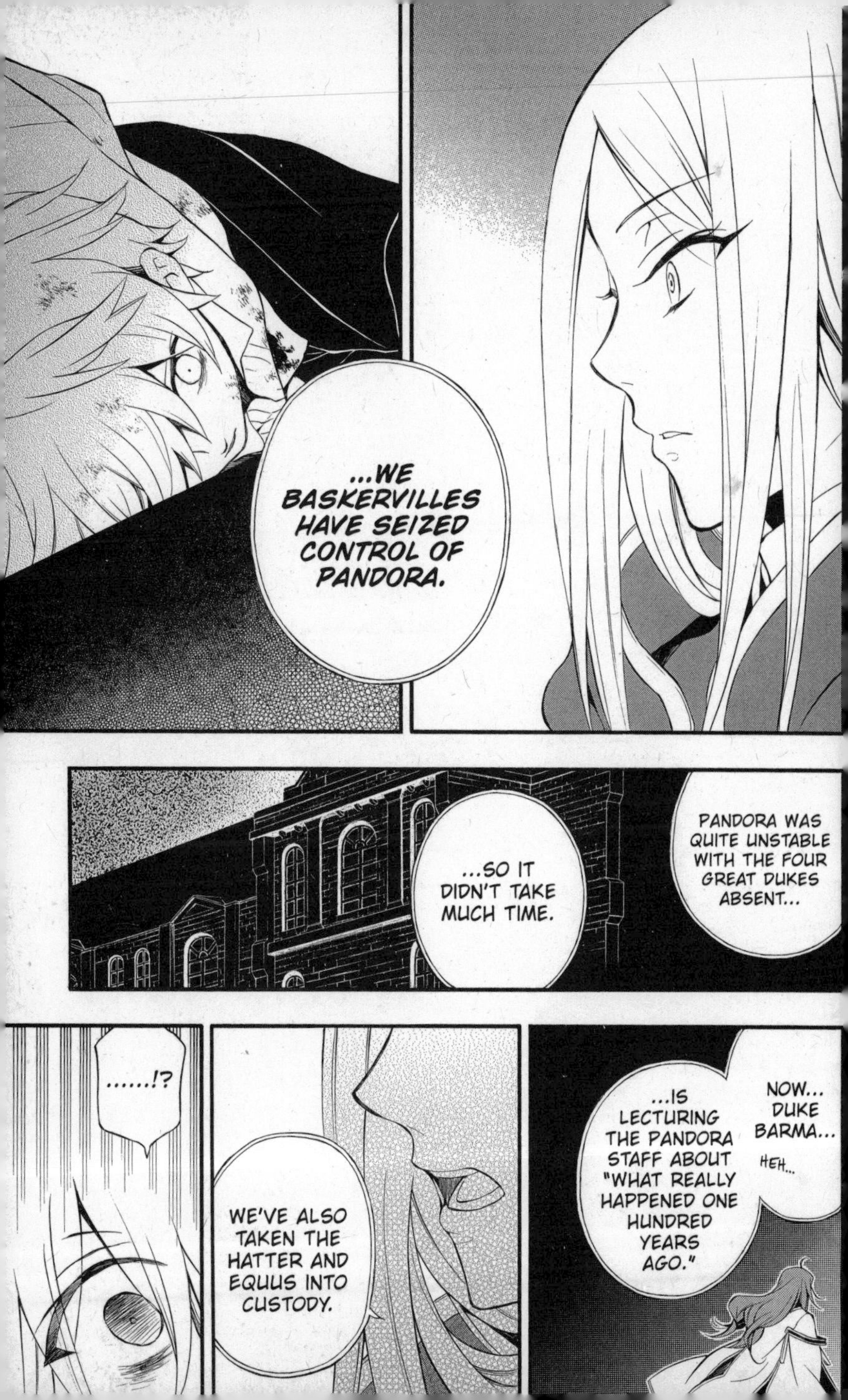
...WE BASKERVILLES HAVE SEIZED CONTROL OF PANDORA.
PANDORA WAS QUITE UNSTABLE WITH THE FOUR GREAT DUKES ABSENT...
...SO IT DIDN'T TAKE MUCH TIME.
NOW... DUKE BARMA...
...IS LECTURING THE PANDORA STAFF ABOUT "WHAT REALLY HAPPENED ONE HUNDRED YEARS AGO."
HEH...
WE'VE ALSO TAKEN THE HATTER AND EQUUS INTO CUSTODY.
......!?

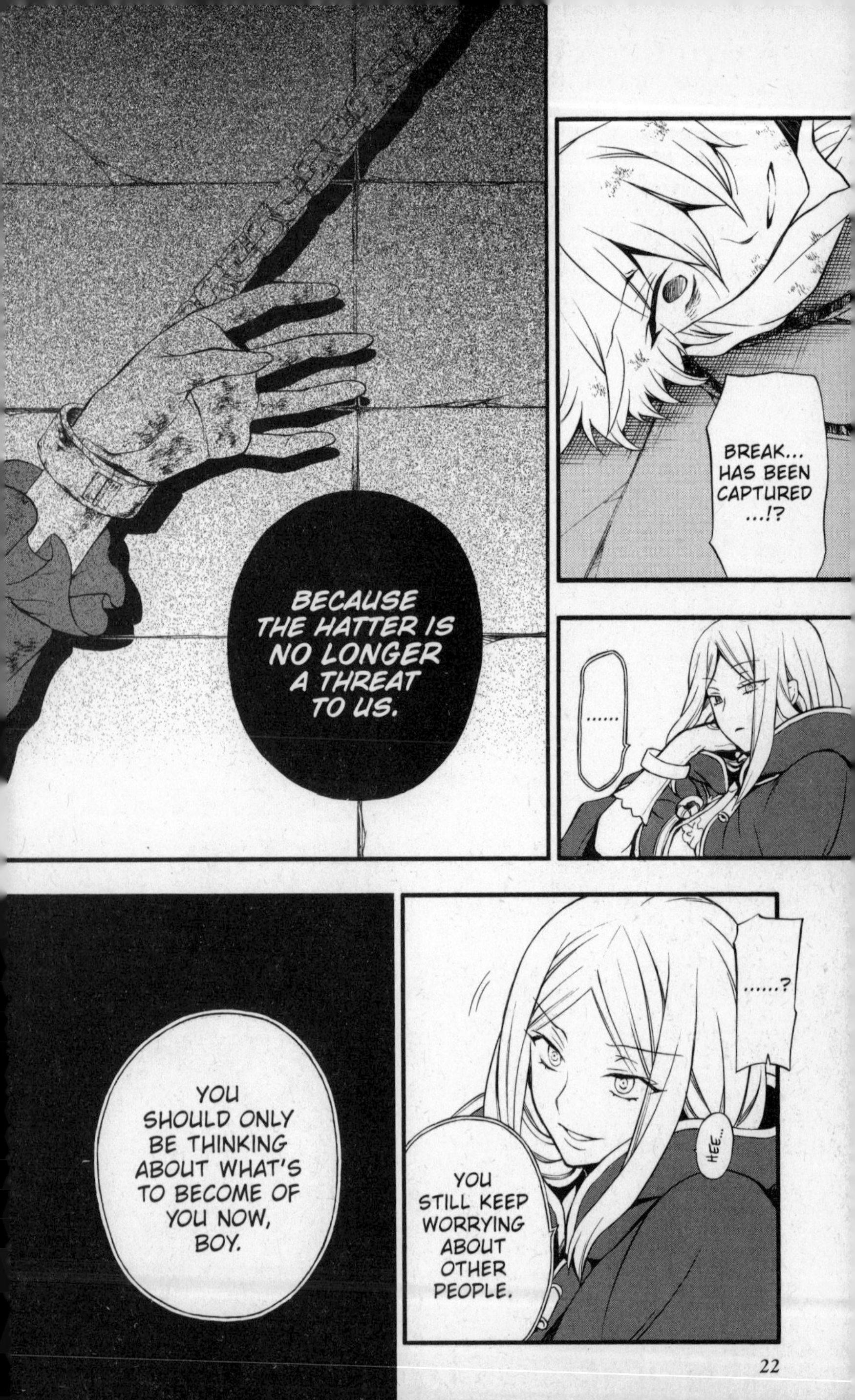
BREAK... HAS BEEN CAPTURED ...!?
......
BECAUSE THE HATTER IS NO LONGER A THREAT TO US.
......?
HEE...
YOU STILL KEEP WORRYING ABOUT OTHER PEOPLE.
YOU SHOULD ONLY BE THINKING ABOUT WHAT'S TO BECOME OF YOU NOW, BOY.

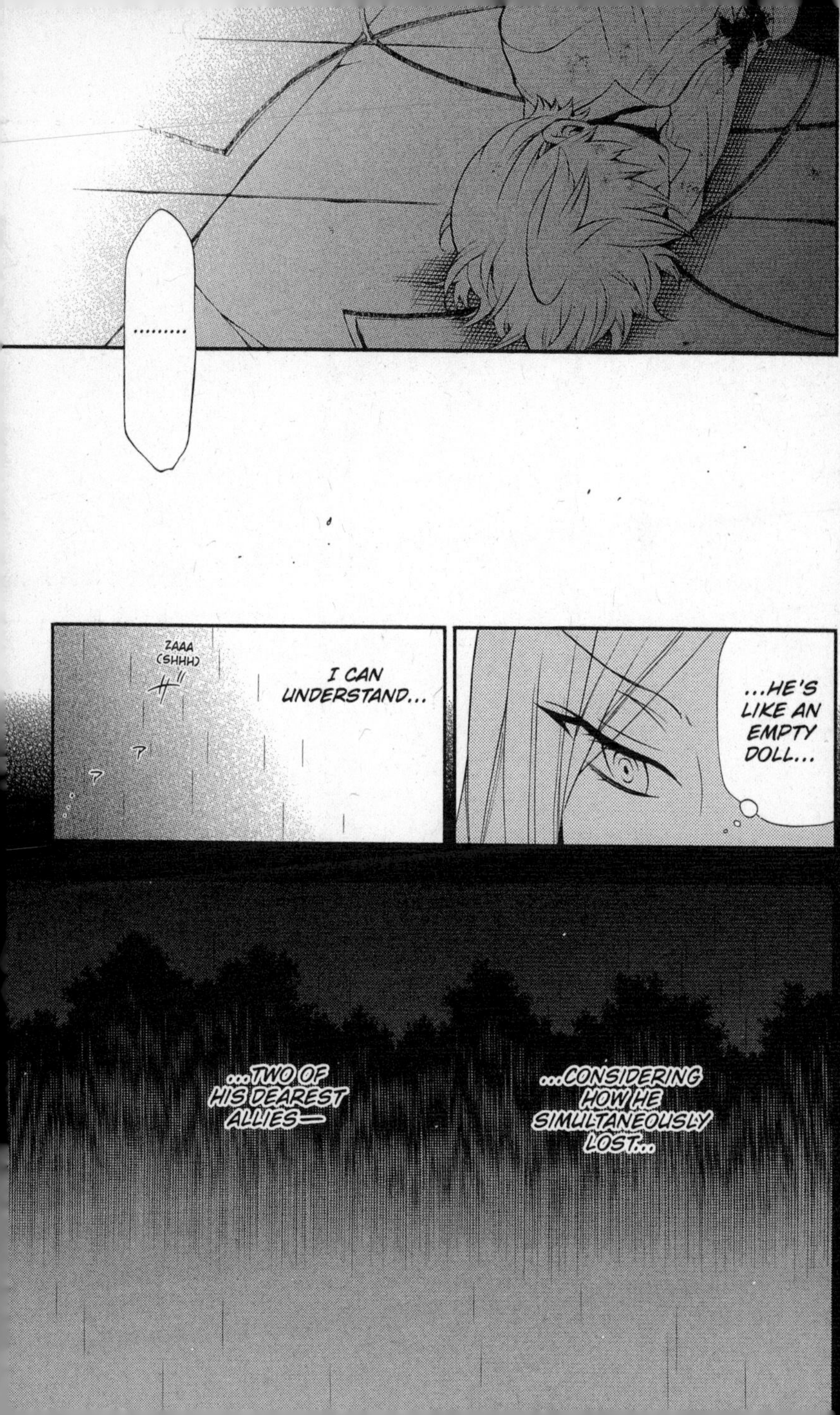
....
...HE'S LIKE AN EMPTY DOLL...
I CAN UNDERSTAND...
ZAAA (SHHH)
...CONSIDERING HOW HE SIMULTANEOUSLY LOST...
...TWO OF HIS DEAREST ALLIES—

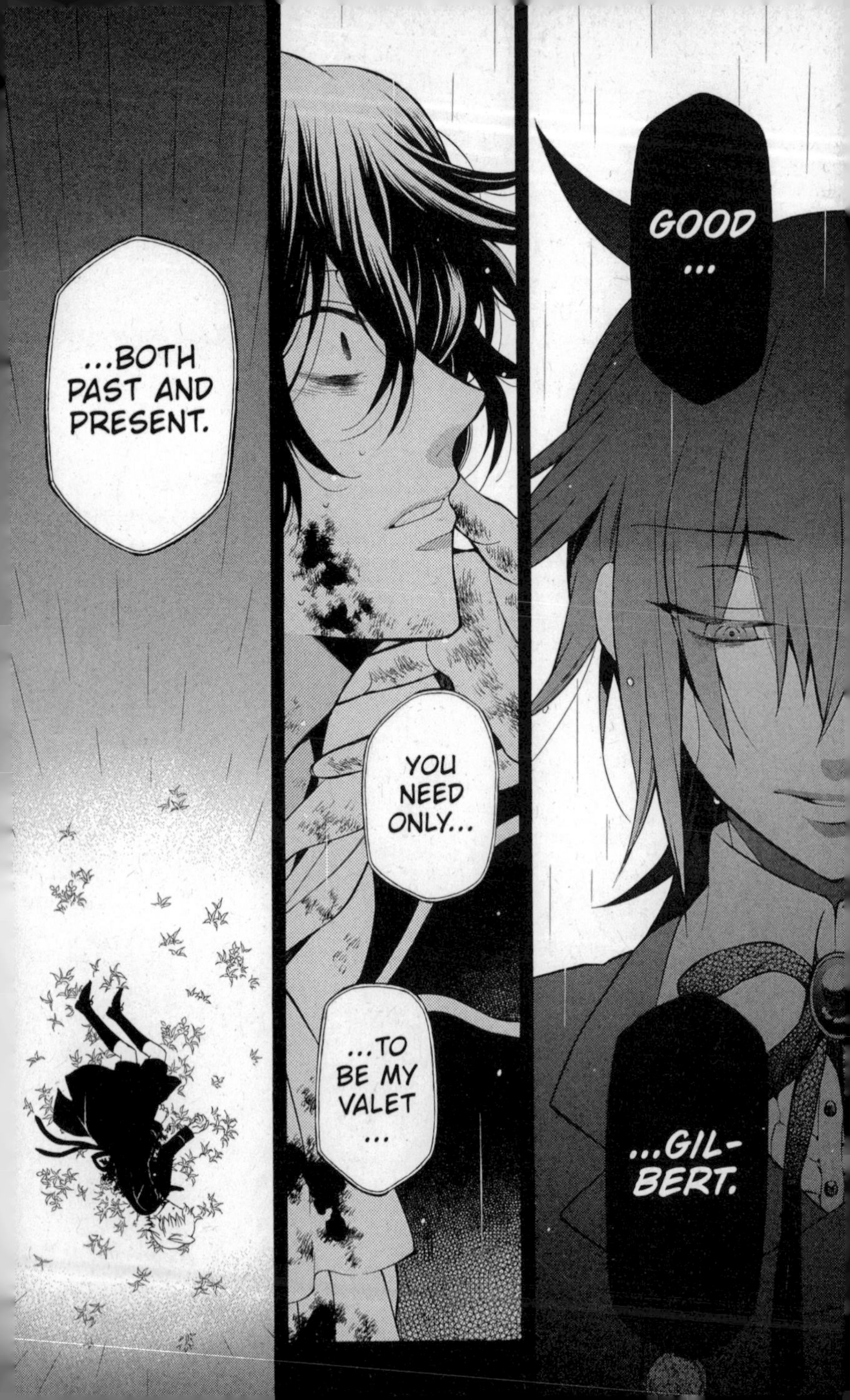
GOOD ...
...GIL-BERT.
YOU NEED ONLY...
...TO BE MY VALET ...
...BOTH PAST AND PRESENT.

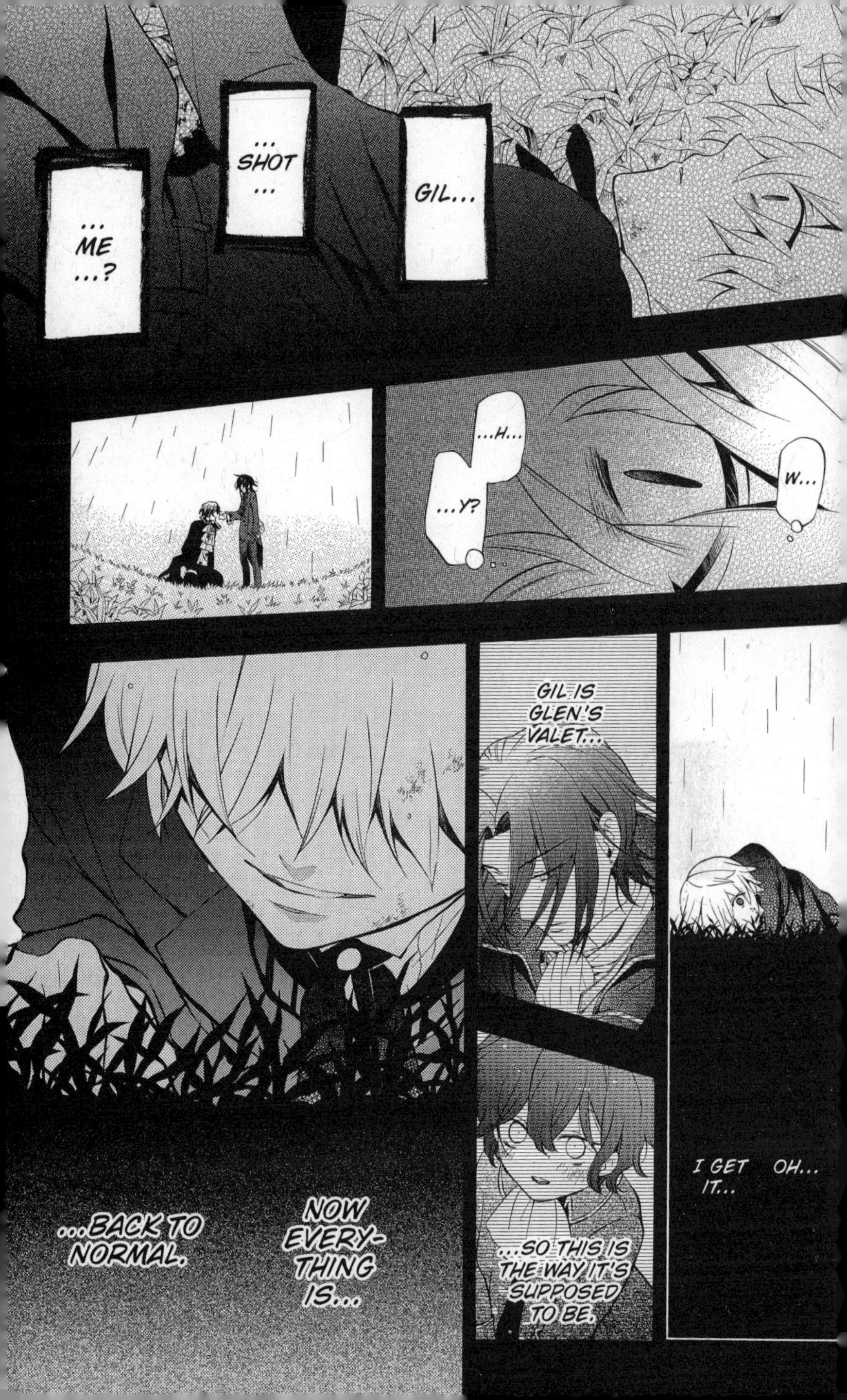
GIL...
...SHOT...
...ME...?
W...
...H...
...Y?
OH...
I GET IT...
GIL IS GLEN'S VALET...
...SO THIS IS THE WAY IT'S SUPPOSED TO BE.
NOW EVERY-THING IS...
...BACK TO NORMAL.

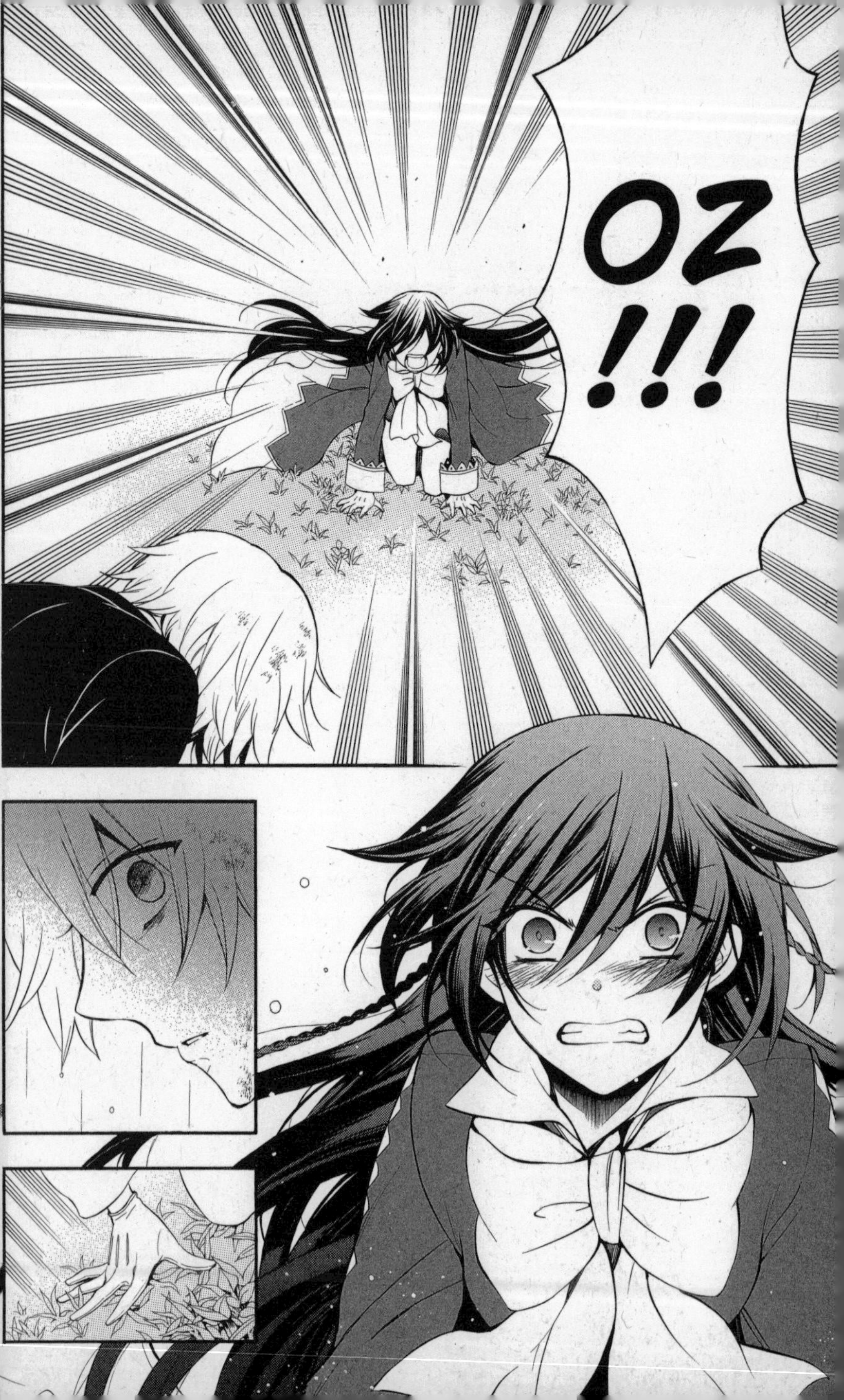
OZ
!!!

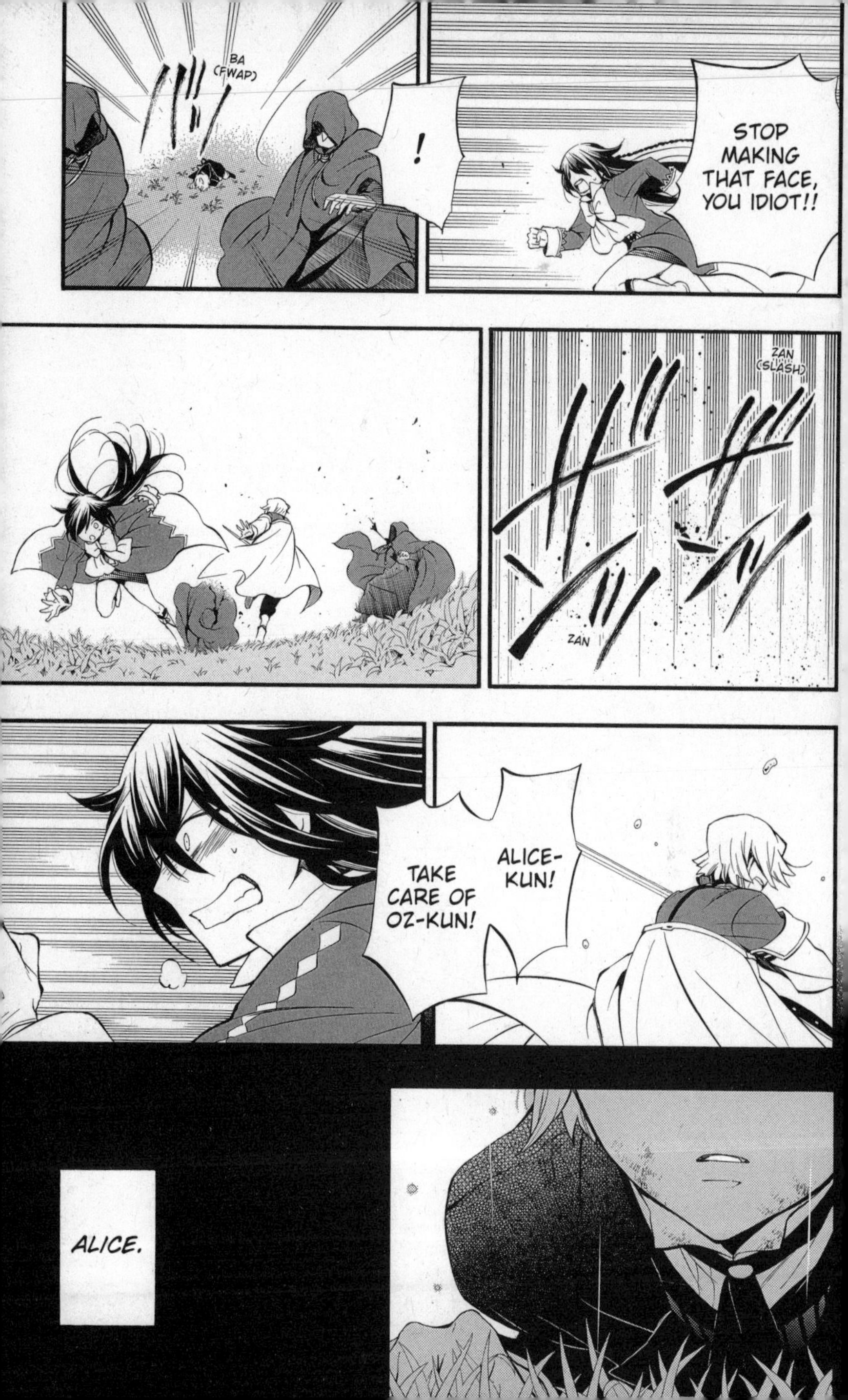
STOP MAKING THAT FACE, YOU IDIOT!!
!
BA (FWAP)
ZAN (SLASH)
ZAN
ALICE-KUN!
TAKE CARE OF OZ-KUN!
ALICE.

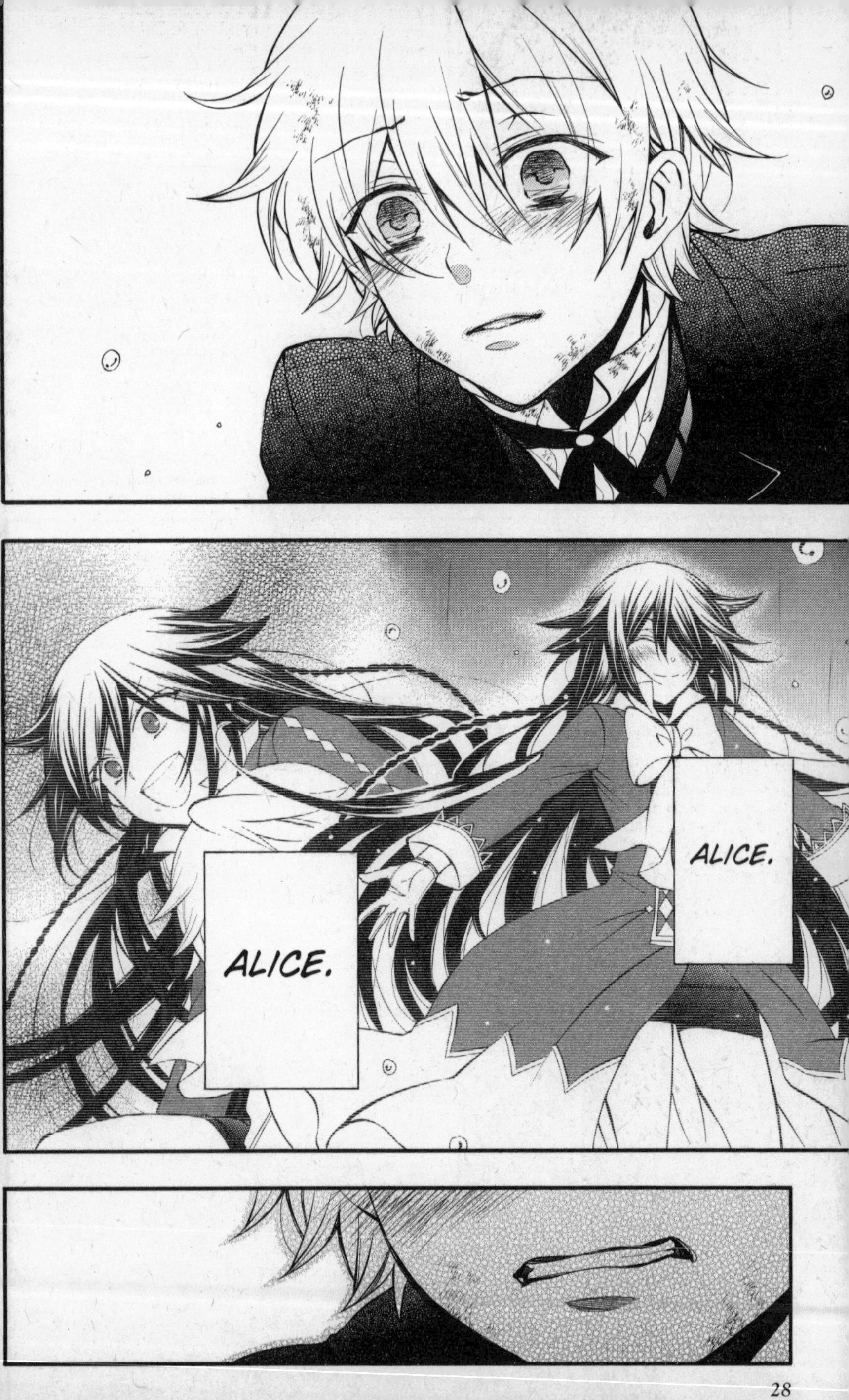
ALICE.
ALICE.

...YOU'VE DONE ENOUGH FOR ME, ALICE ......

YOU...

......

...THAT YOU...

IT'S 'COS I EXISTED...

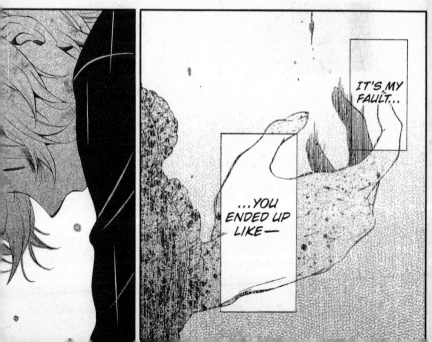

IT'S MY FAULT...

...YOU ENDED UP LIKE—

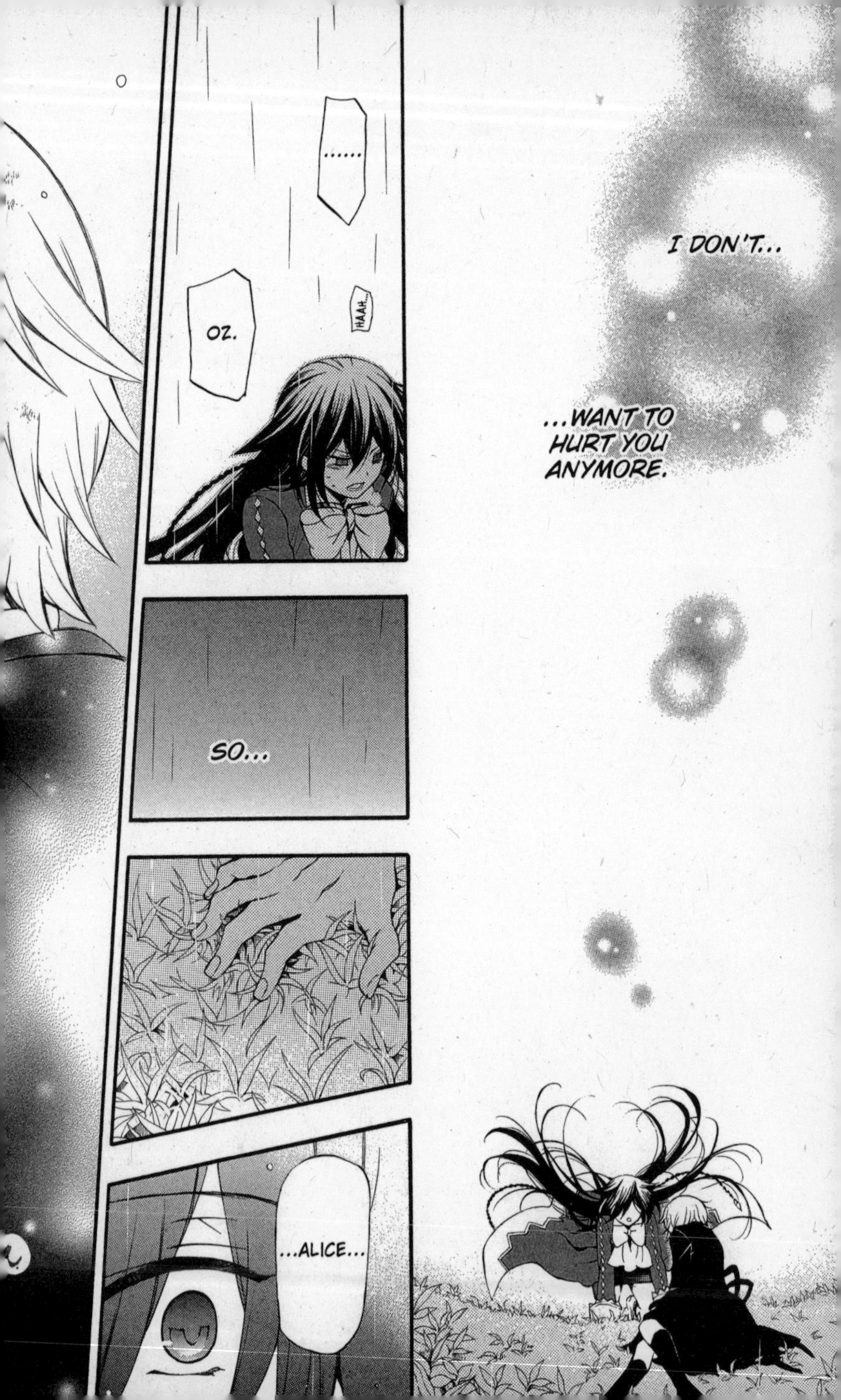
I DON'T...
...WANT TO HURT YOU ANYMORE.
......
HAAH...
OZ.
SO...
...ALICE...

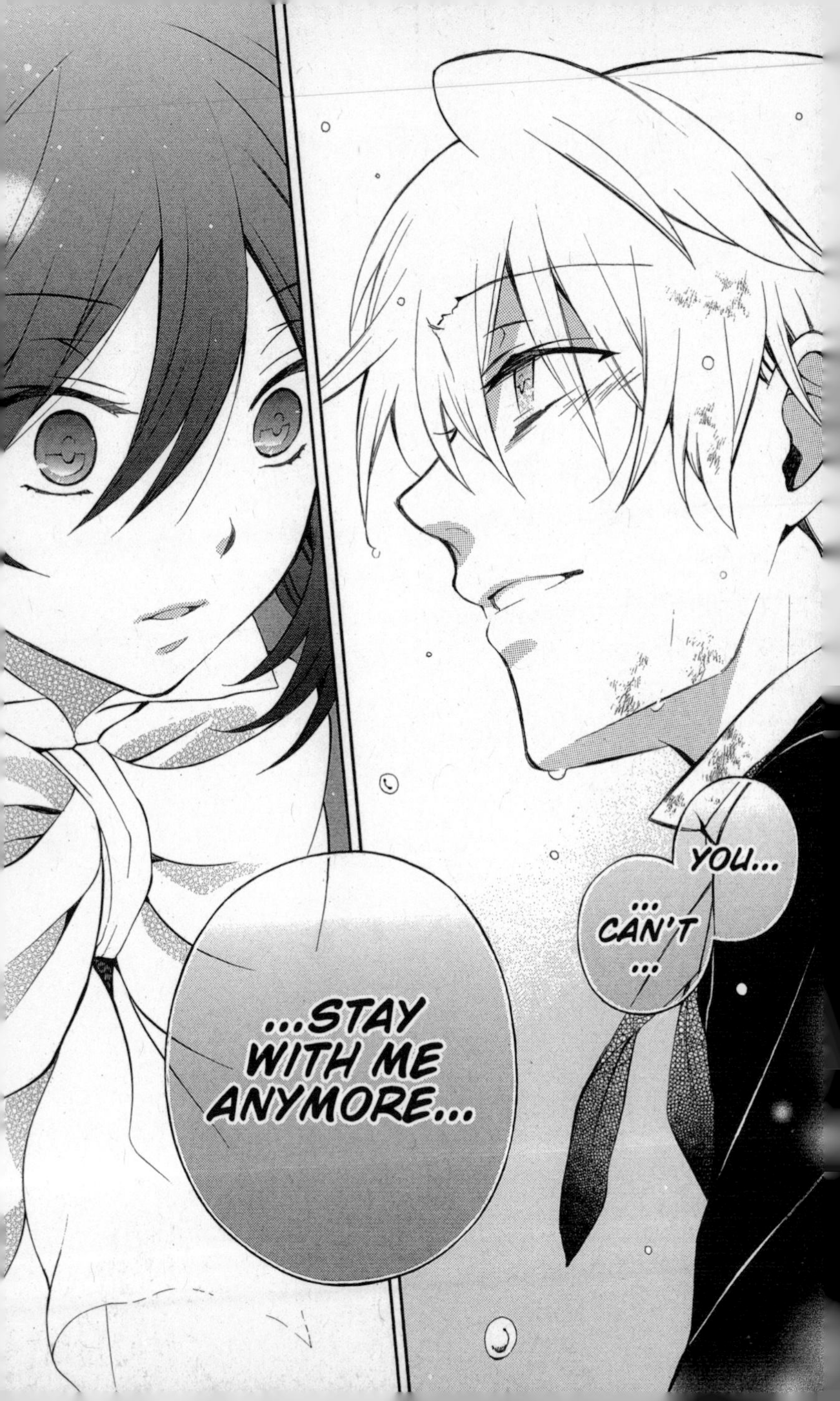
YOU...
...CAN'T...
...STAY WITH ME ANYMORE...

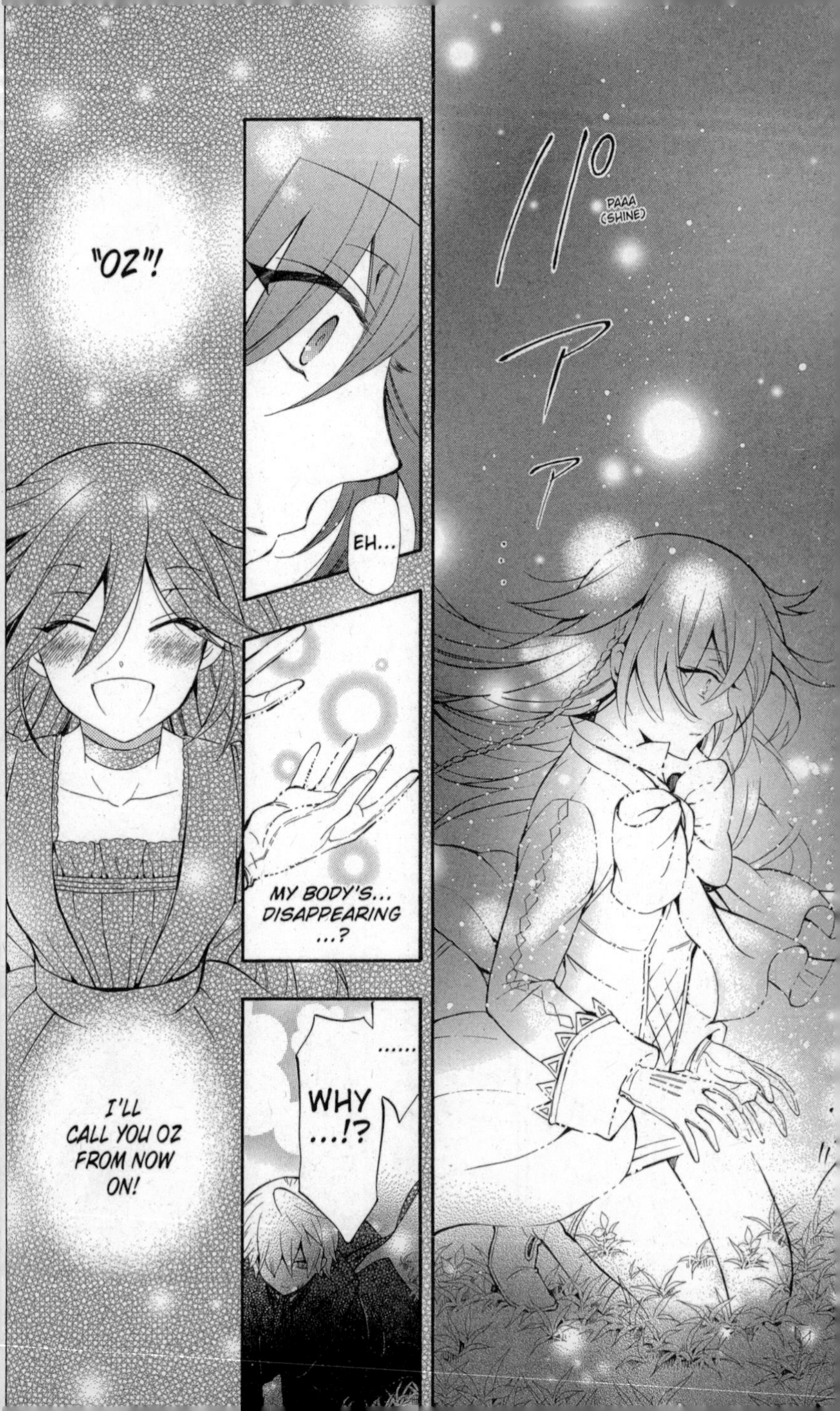
PAAA (SHINE)
EH...
MY BODY'S... DISAPPEARING ...?
......
WHY ...!?
"OZ"!
I'LL CALL YOU OZ FROM NOW ON!

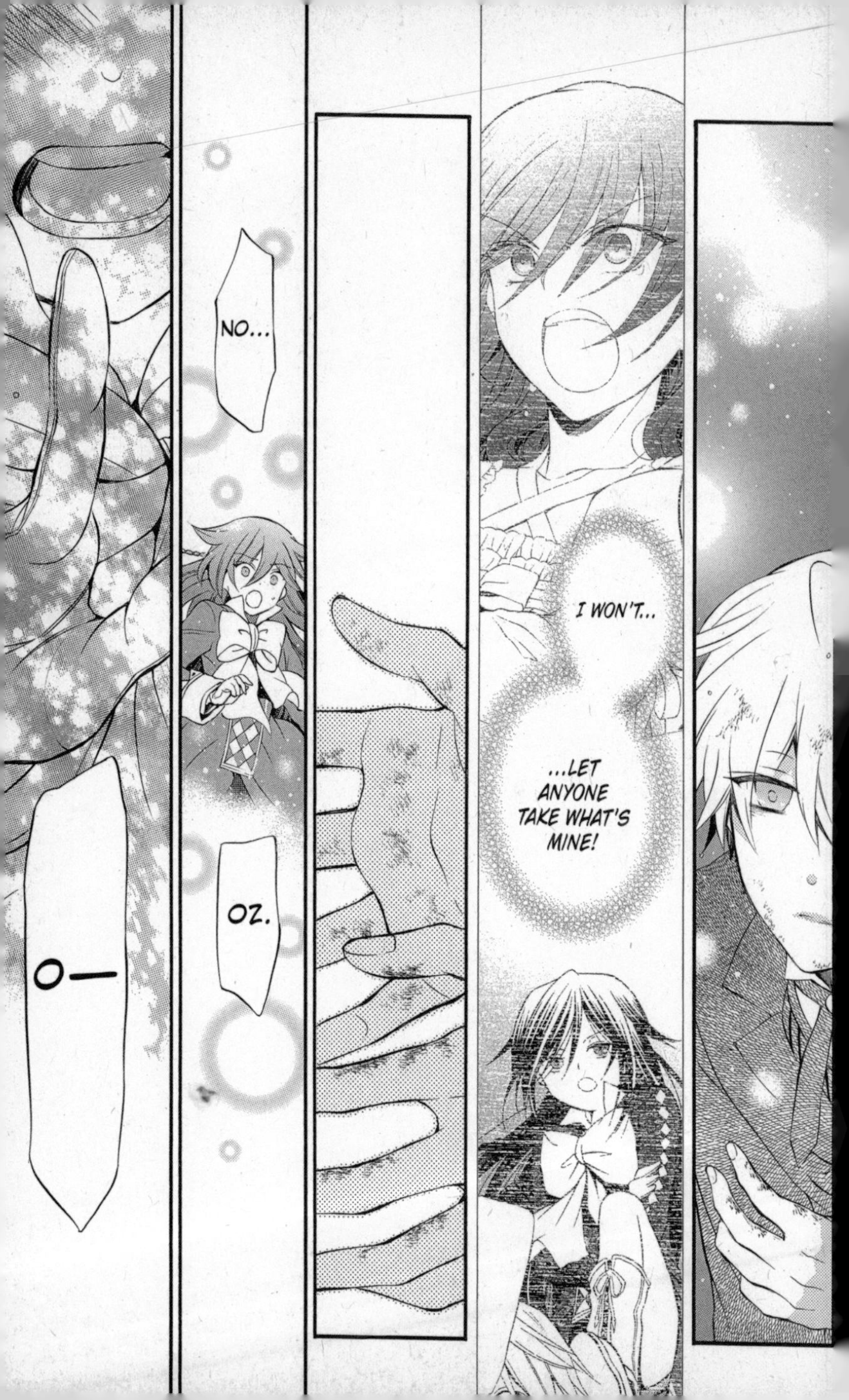
I WON'T...
...LET ANYONE TAKE WHAT'S MINE!
NO...
OZ.
O—

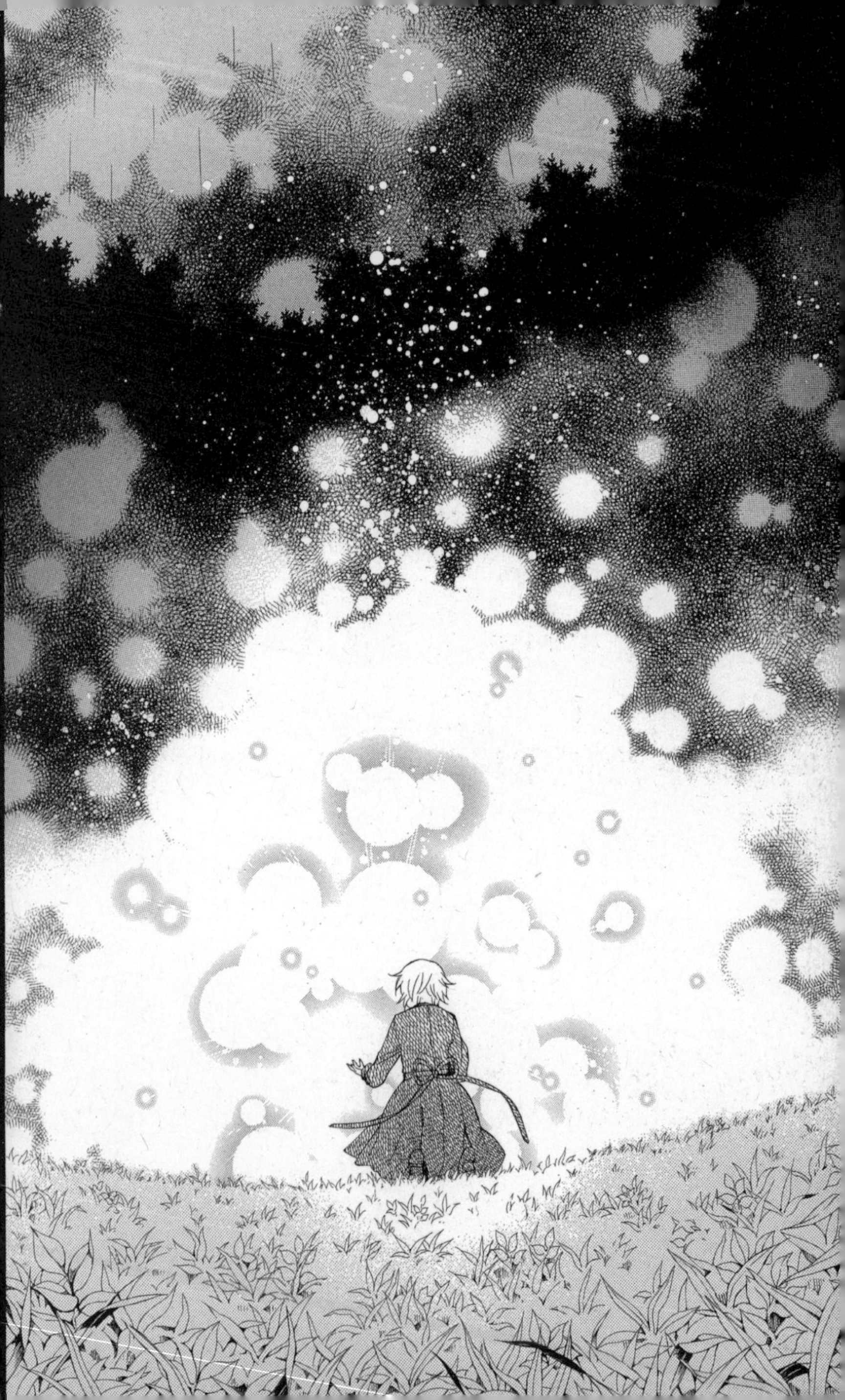

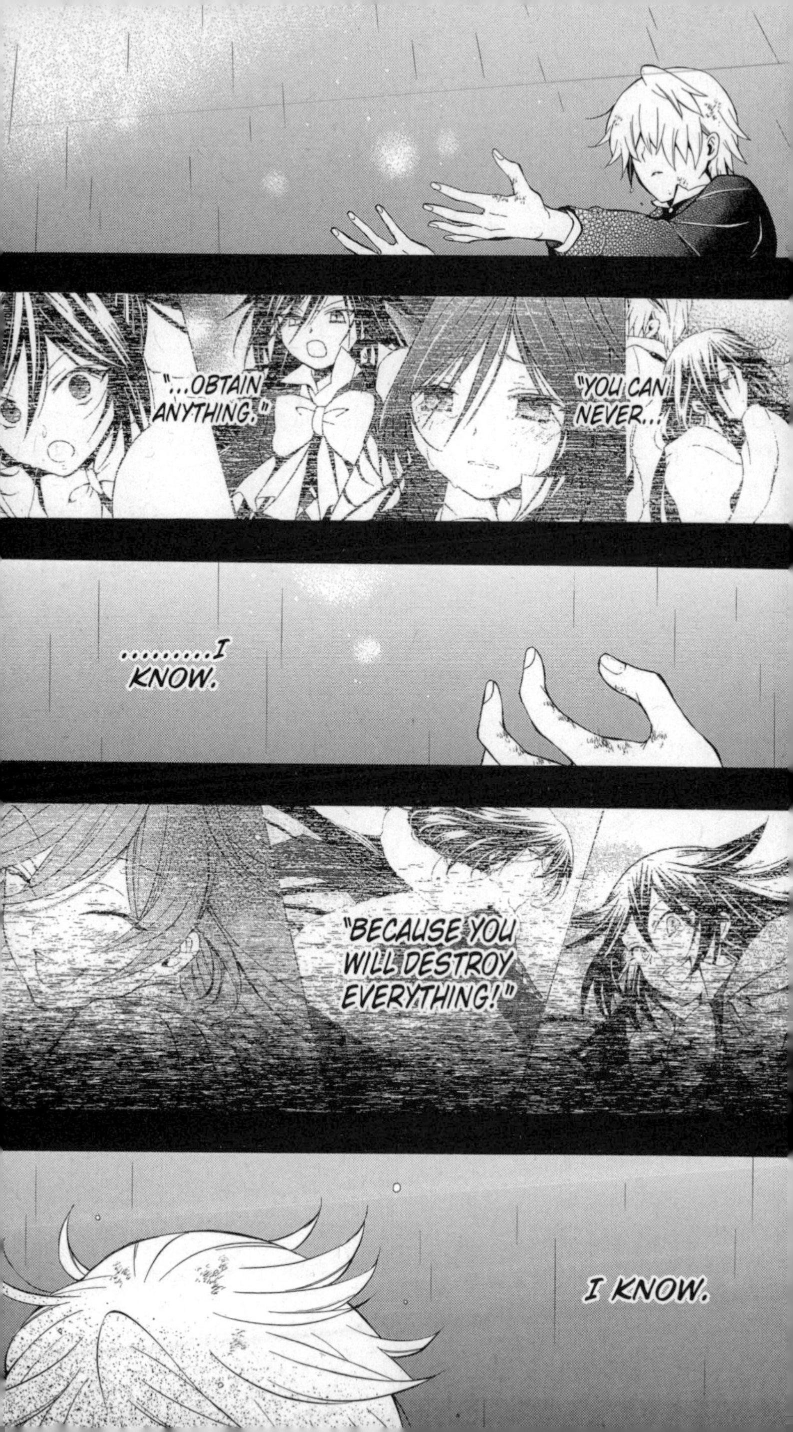
"YOU CAN NEVER...
"...OBTAIN ANYTHING."
..........I KNOW.
"BECAUSE YOU WILL DESTROY EVERYTHING!"
I KNOW.

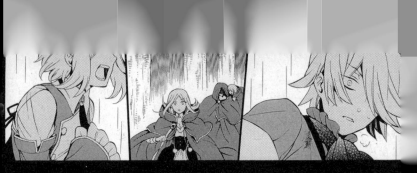

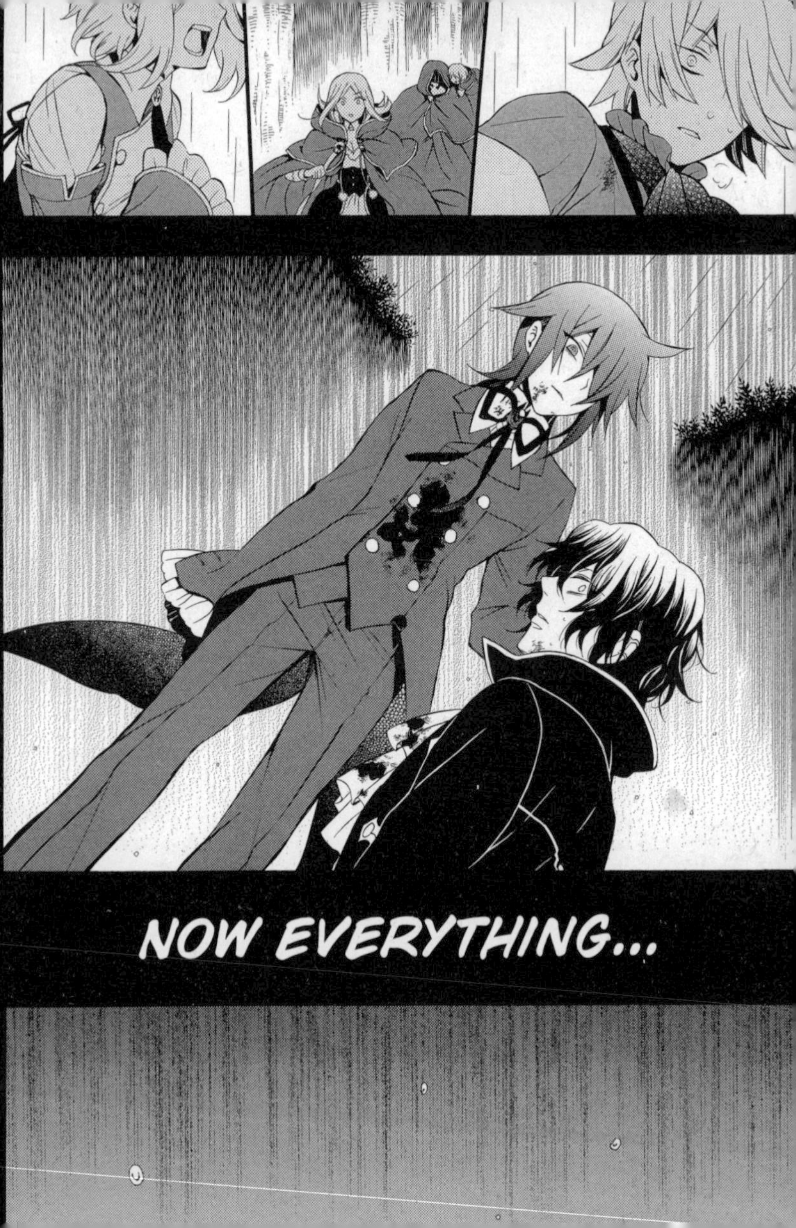
NOW EVERYTHING...

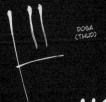
DOSA
(THUD)

...HAS GONE BACK
TO THE WAY IT
USED TO BE.

PARIN
(CRACKLE)

PARIN

PARIN

UNCLE...
WAIT!

UNCLE
...

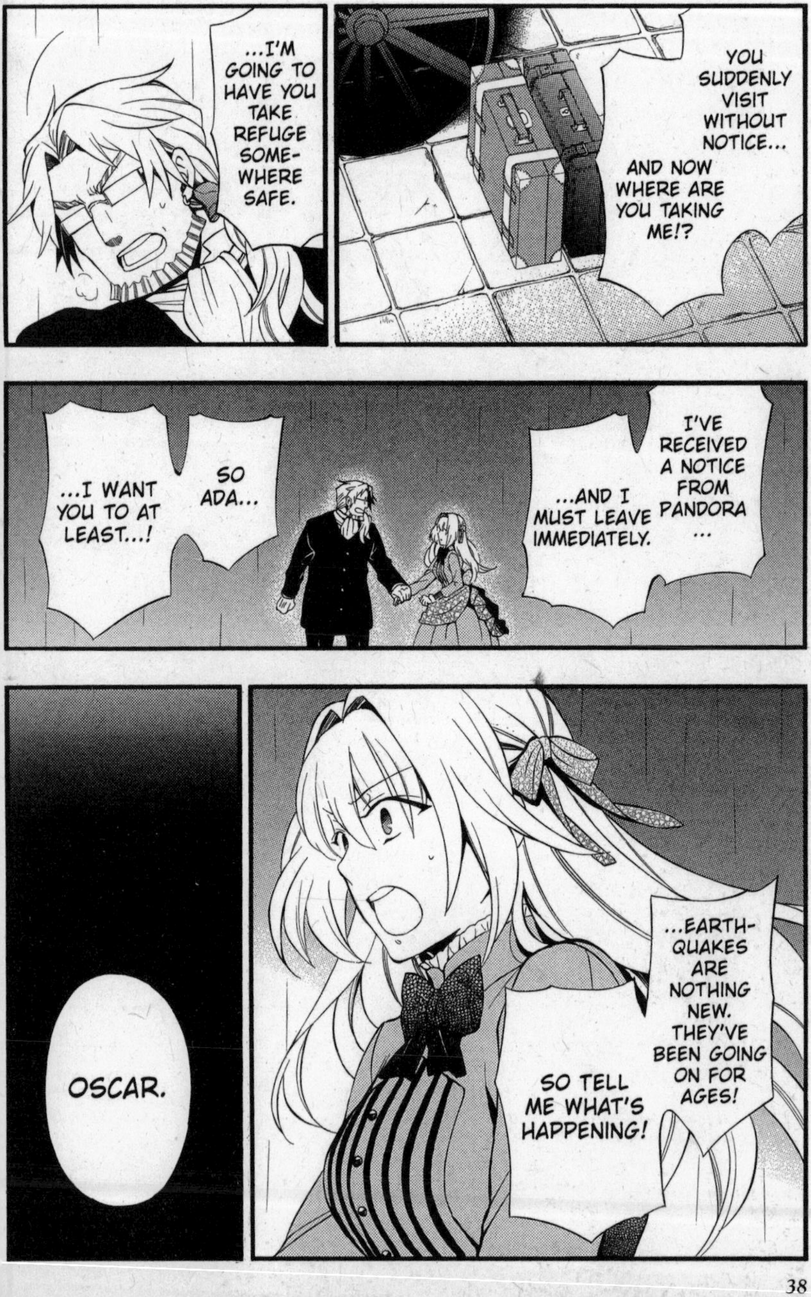
YOU SUDDENLY VISIT WITHOUT NOTICE...
AND NOW WHERE ARE YOU TAKING ME!?
...I'M GOING TO HAVE YOU TAKE REFUGE SOME-WHERE SAFE.
I'VE RECEIVED A NOTICE FROM PANDORA...
...AND I MUST LEAVE IMMEDIATELY.
SO ADA...
...I WANT YOU TO AT LEAST...!
...EARTH-QUAKES ARE NOTHING NEW. THEY'VE BEEN GOING ON FOR AGES!
SO TELL ME WHAT'S HAPPENING!
OSCAR.

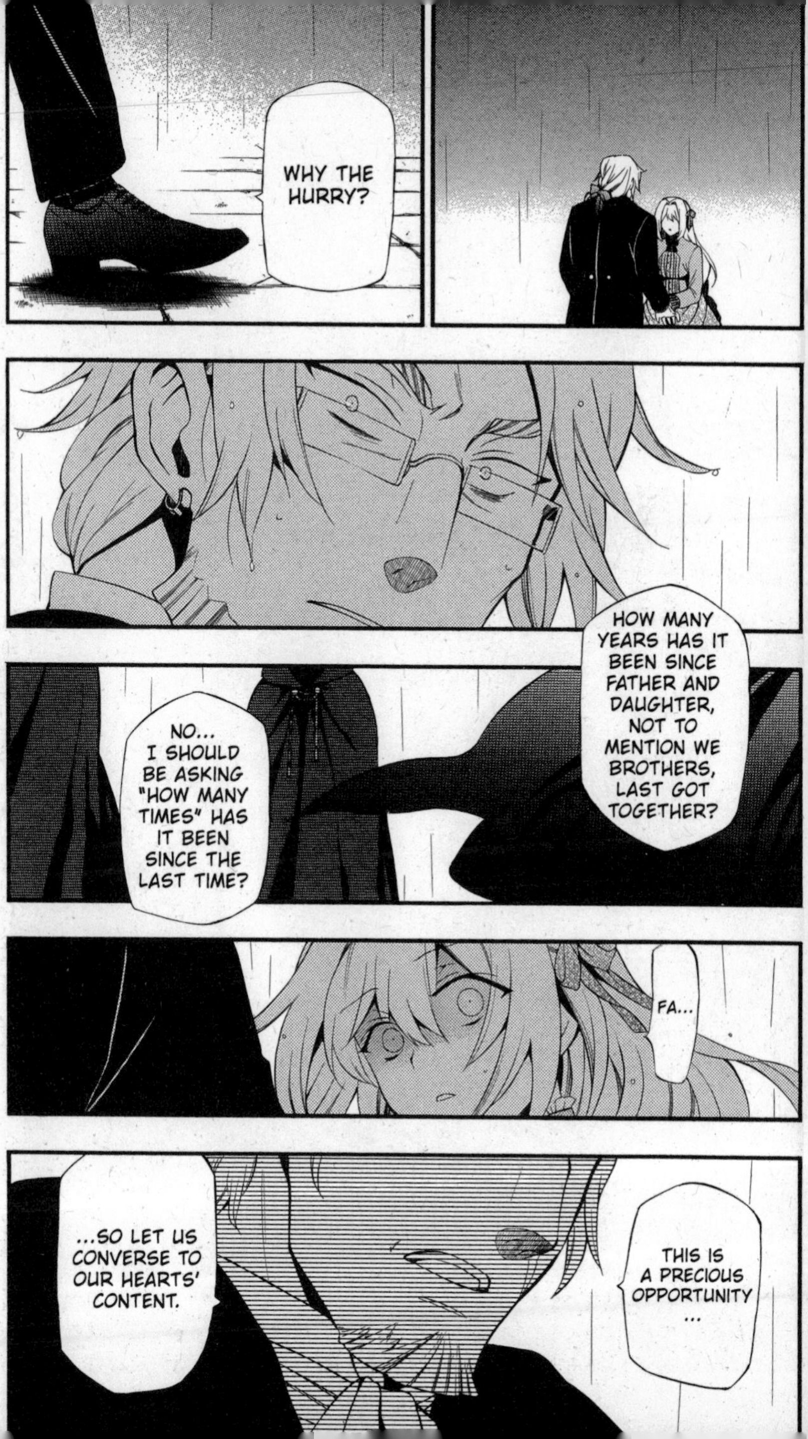
WHY THE HURRY?
HOW MANY YEARS HAS IT BEEN SINCE FATHER AND DAUGHTER, NOT TO MENTION WE BROTHERS, LAST GOT TOGETHER?
NO... I SHOULD BE ASKING "HOW MANY TIMES" HAS IT BEEN SINCE THE LAST TIME?
FA...
THIS IS A PRECIOUS OPPORTUNITY ...
...SO LET US CONVERSE TO OUR HEARTS' CONTENT.

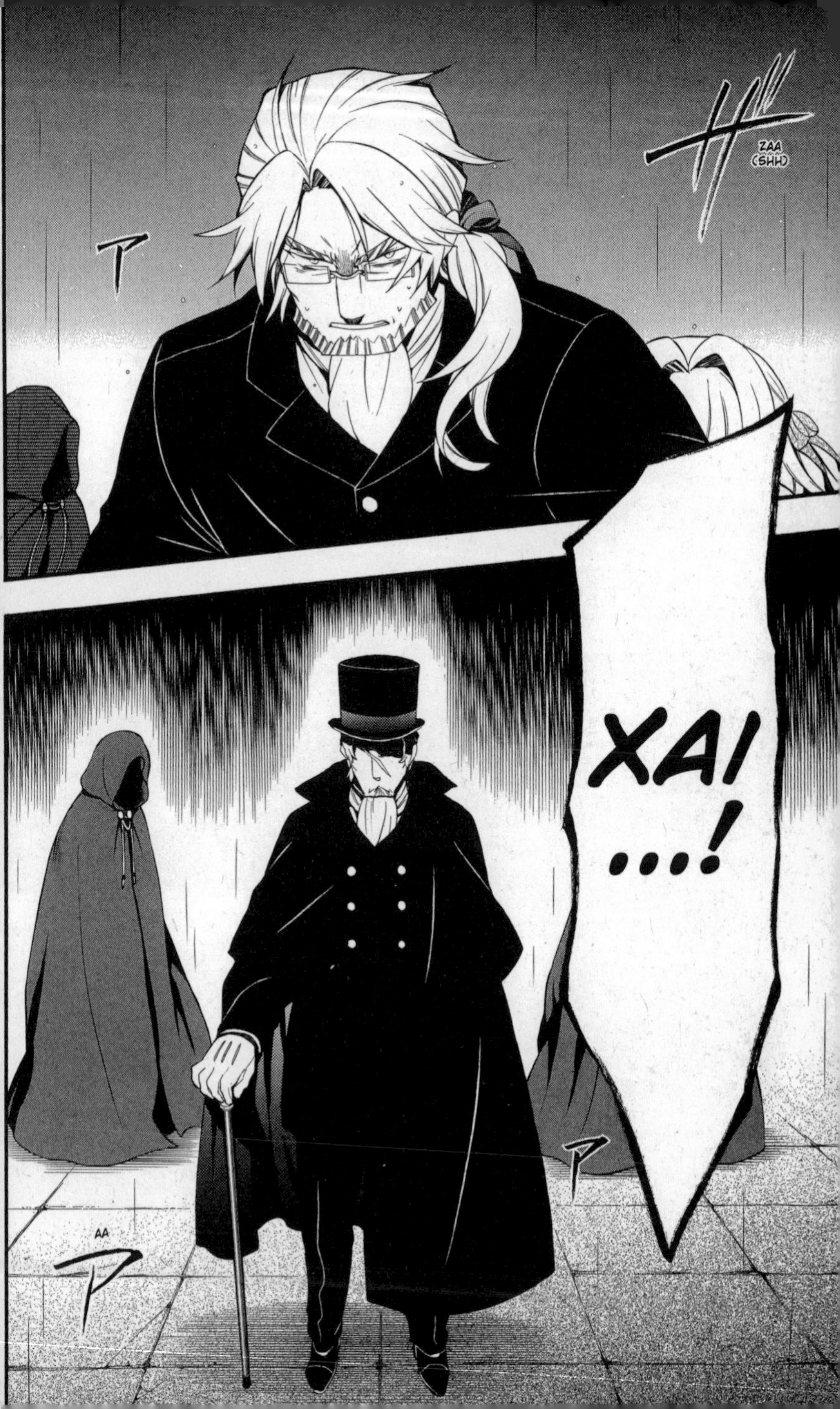
ZAA
(SHH)
XAI...!
AA

Retrace:LXXV   Alone

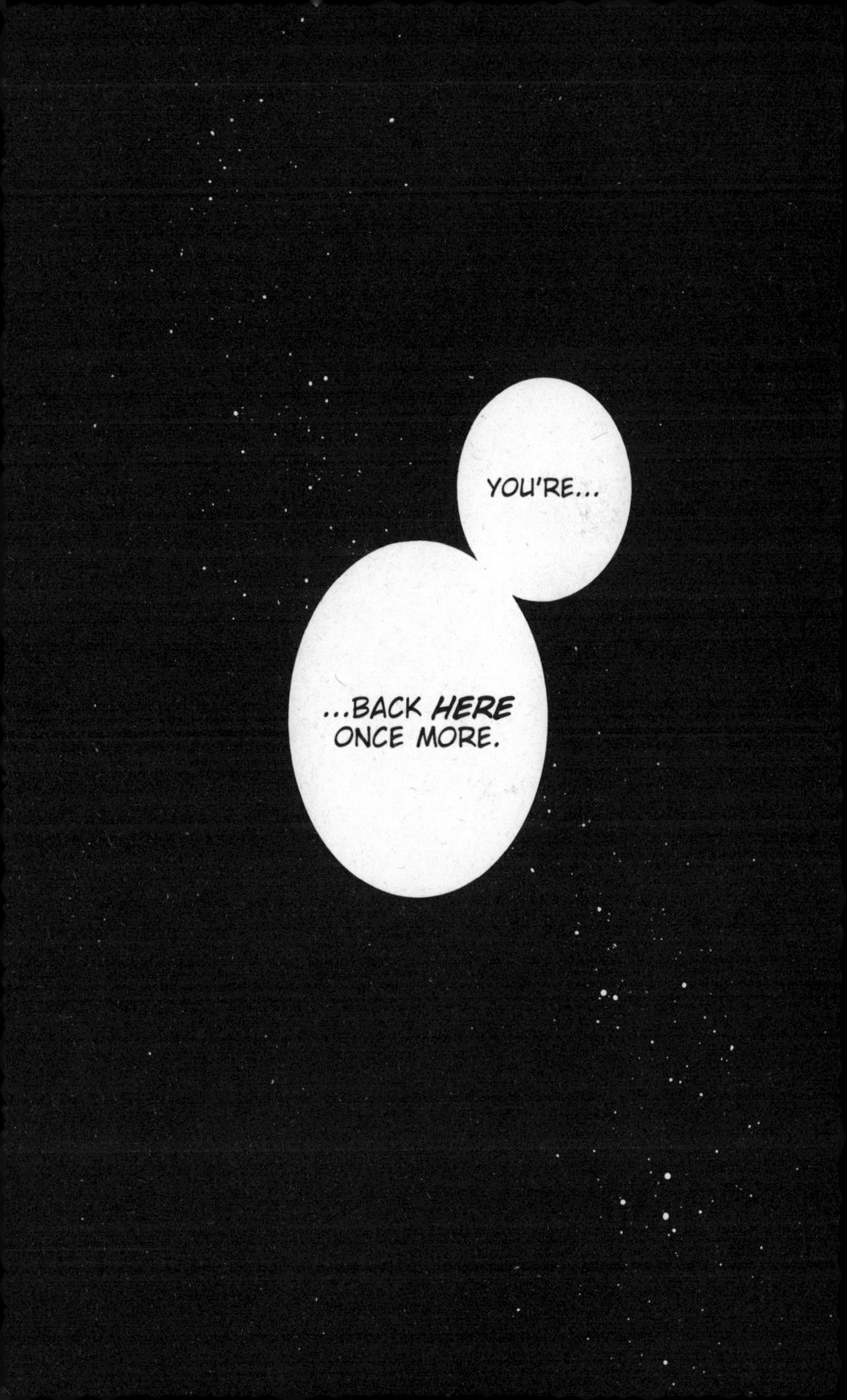
YOU'RE...
...BACK *HERE* ONCE MORE.

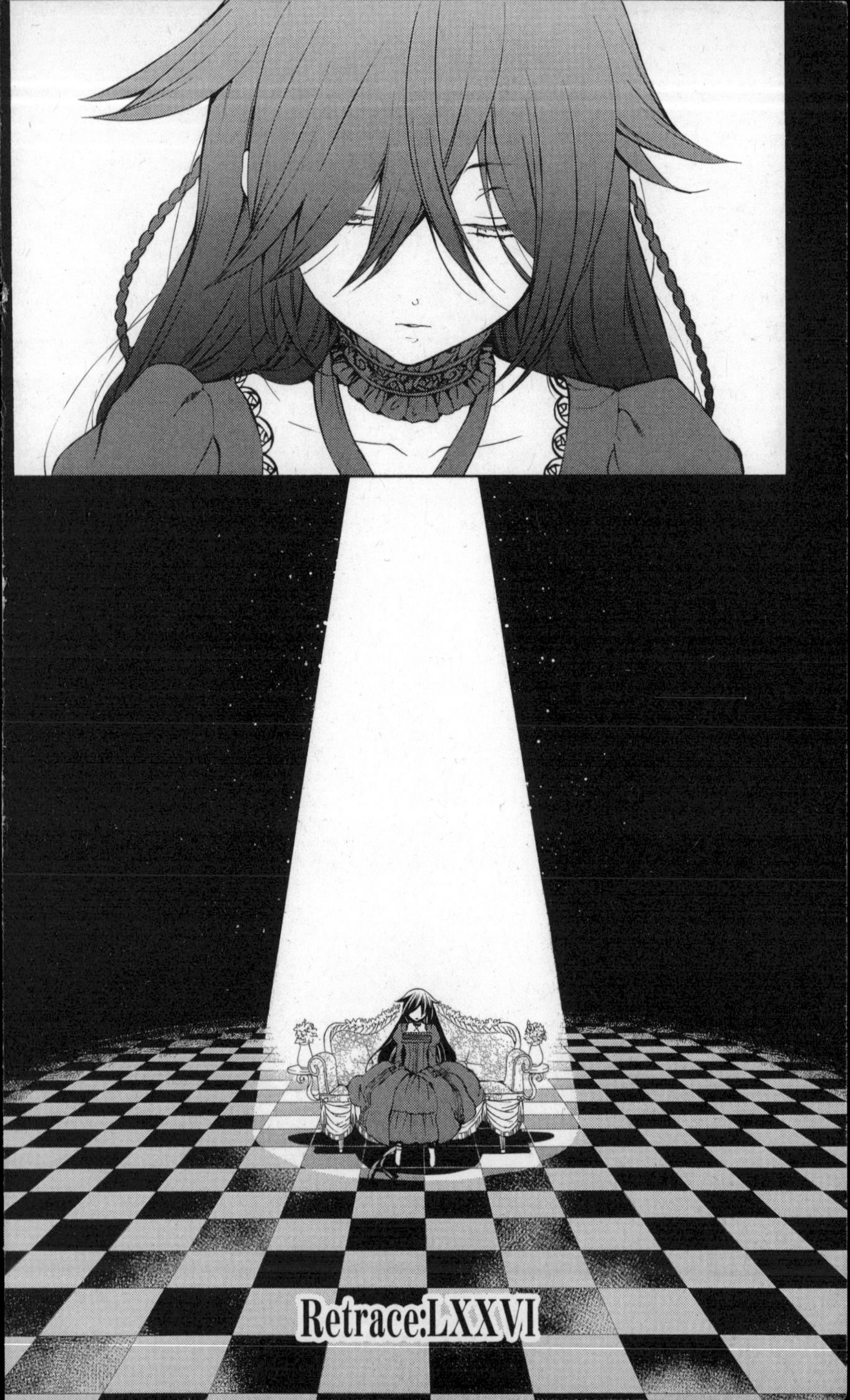
Retrace:LXXVI

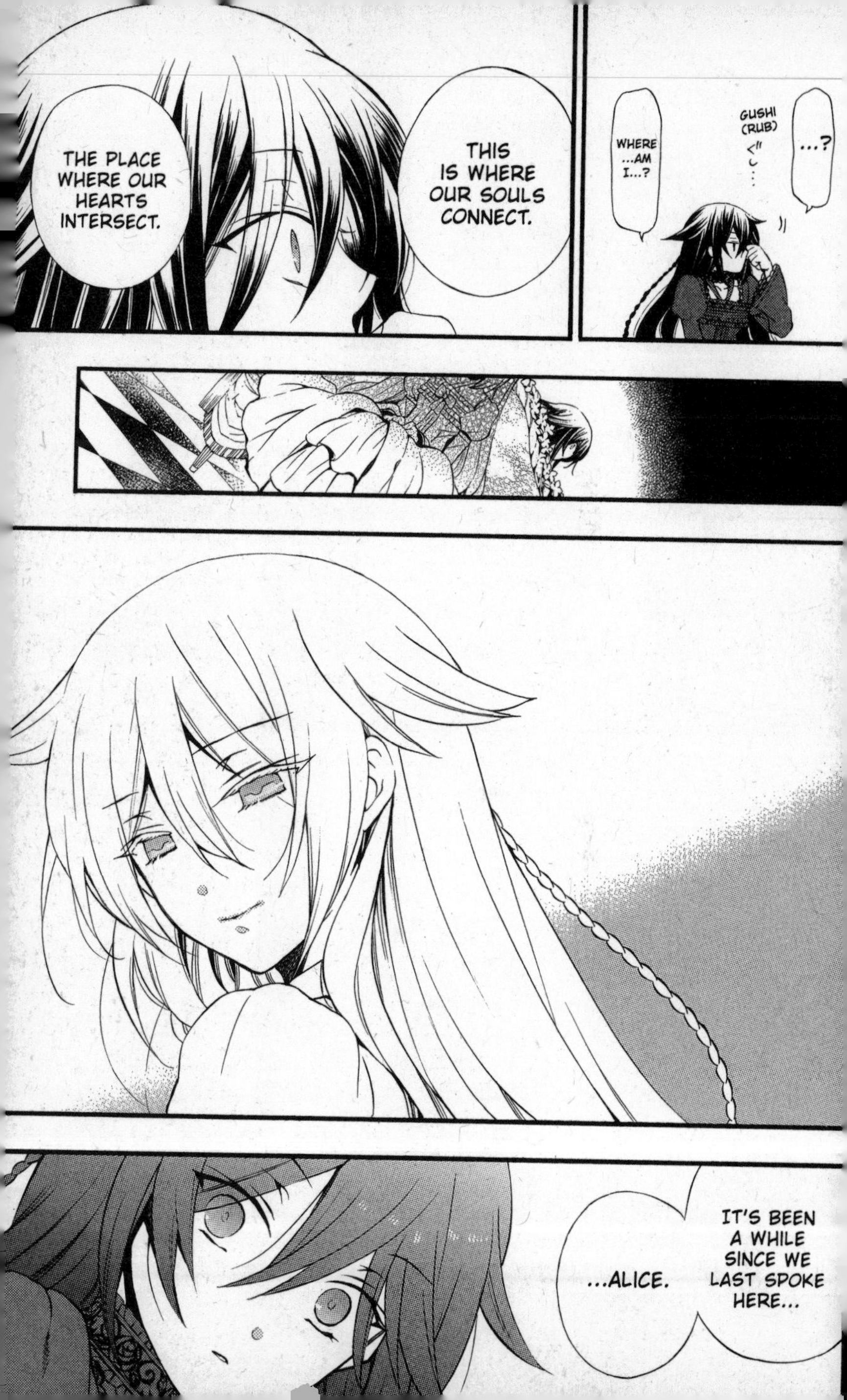
...?
GUSHI (RUB)
WHERE ...AM I...?
THIS IS WHERE OUR SOULS CONNECT.
THE PLACE WHERE OUR HEARTS INTERSECT.
IT'S BEEN A WHILE SINCE WE LAST SPOKE HERE...
...ALICE.

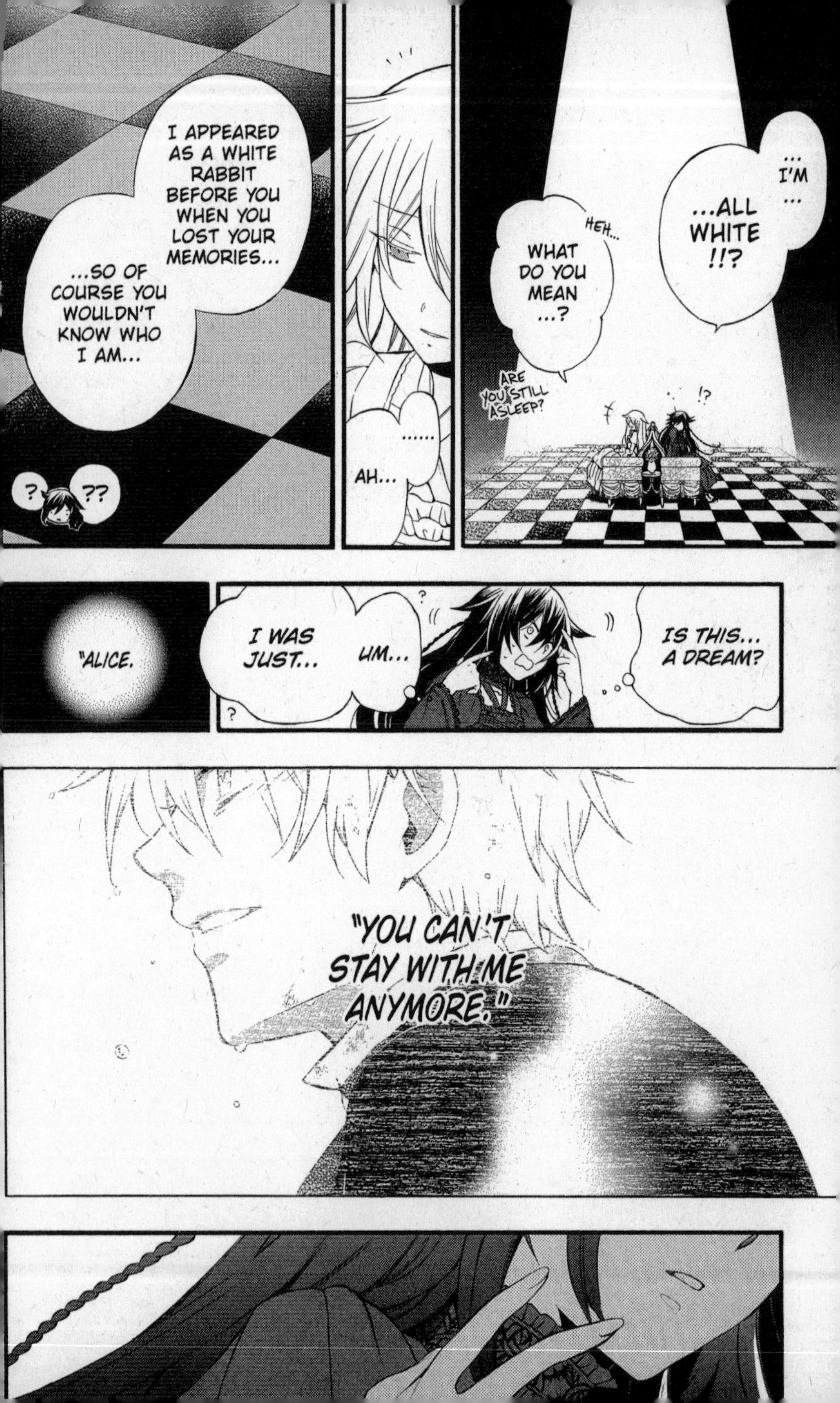
...I'M...
...ALL WHITE!!?
HEH... WHAT DO YOU MEAN...?
ARE YOU STILL ASLEEP?
!?
......
AH...
I APPEARED AS A WHITE RABBIT BEFORE YOU WHEN YOU LOST YOUR MEMORIES...
...SO OF COURSE YOU WOULDN'T KNOW WHO I AM...
??
?
IS THIS... A DREAM?
I WAS JUST... UM...
"ALICE.
"YOU CAN'T STAY WITH ME ANYMORE."

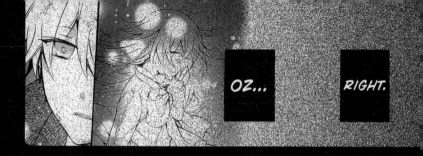

OZ... RIGHT.

...DENIED MY EXISTENCE.

...!
...

UGH...

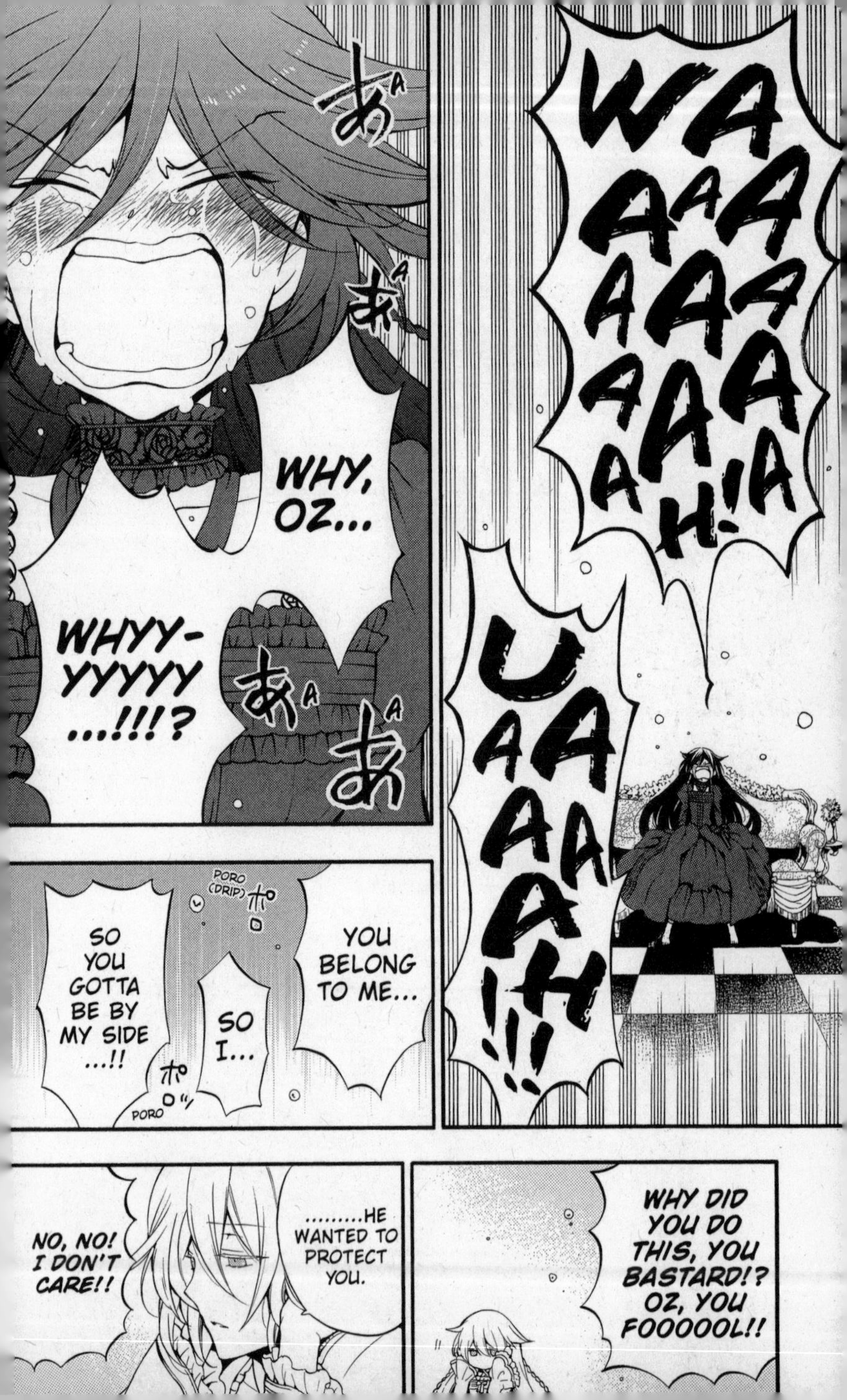

WAAAAAAAAAAAAH!!
UAAAAAH!!!
あ A
あ A
WHY, OZ...
WHYY-YYYYY...!!!?
あ A
あ A
YOU BELONG TO ME...
SO I...
SO YOU GOTTA BE BY MY SIDE...!!
PORO (DRIP) ポロ
ポロッ PORO
WHY DID YOU DO THIS, YOU BASTARD!? OZ, YOU FOOOOOL!!
.........HE WANTED TO PROTECT YOU.
NO, NO! I DON'T CARE!!

SFX: ZUBI (SNRRT)

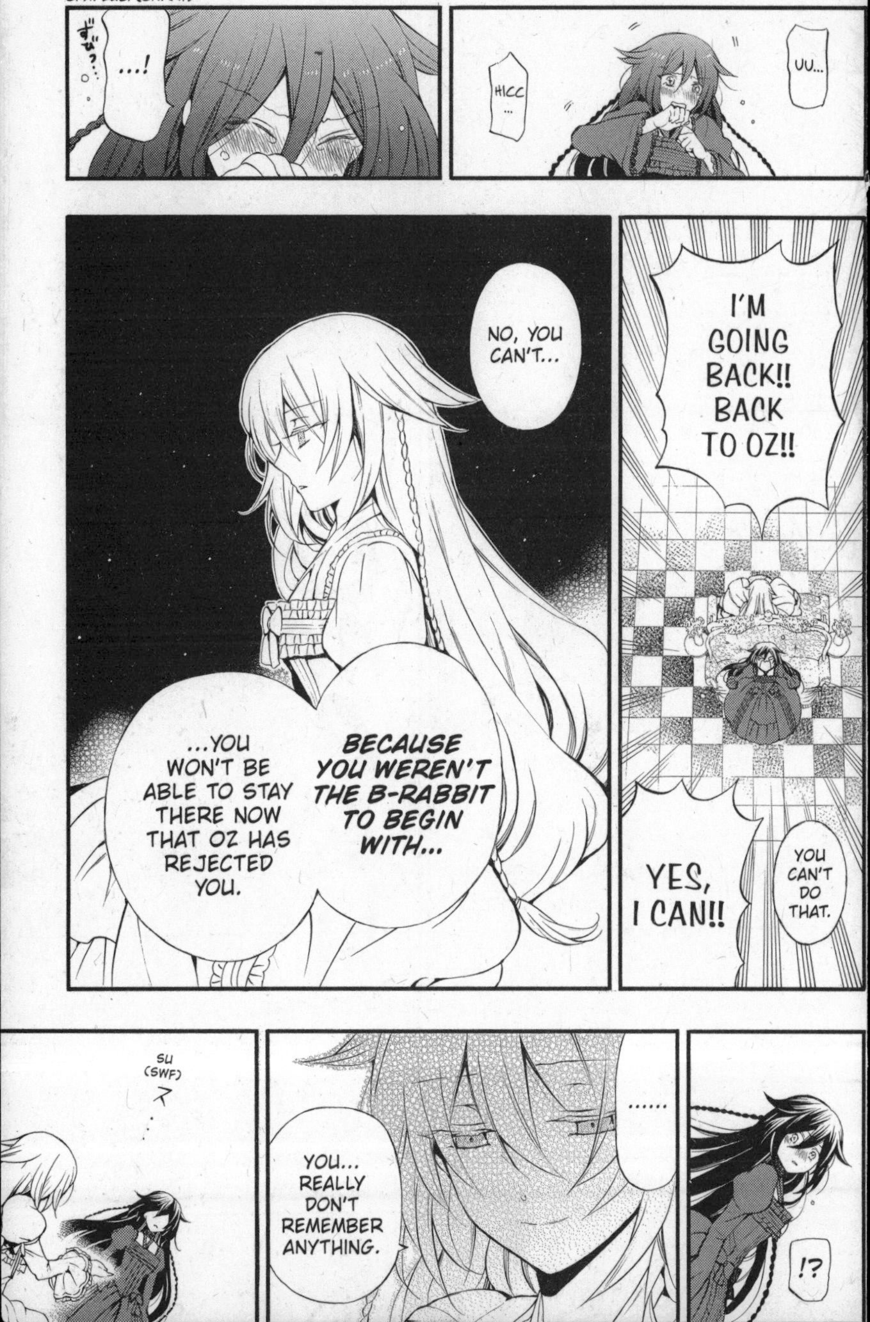
UU...
HICC...
ずびっ…
...!
I'M GOING BACK!! BACK TO OZ!!
YOU CAN'T DO THAT.
YES, I CAN!!
NO, YOU CAN'T...
BECAUSE YOU WEREN'T THE B-RABBIT TO BEGIN WITH...
...YOU WON'T BE ABLE TO STAY THERE NOW THAT OZ HAS REJECTED YOU.
!?
......
YOU... REALLY DON'T REMEMBER ANYTHING.
SU (SWF)
ス

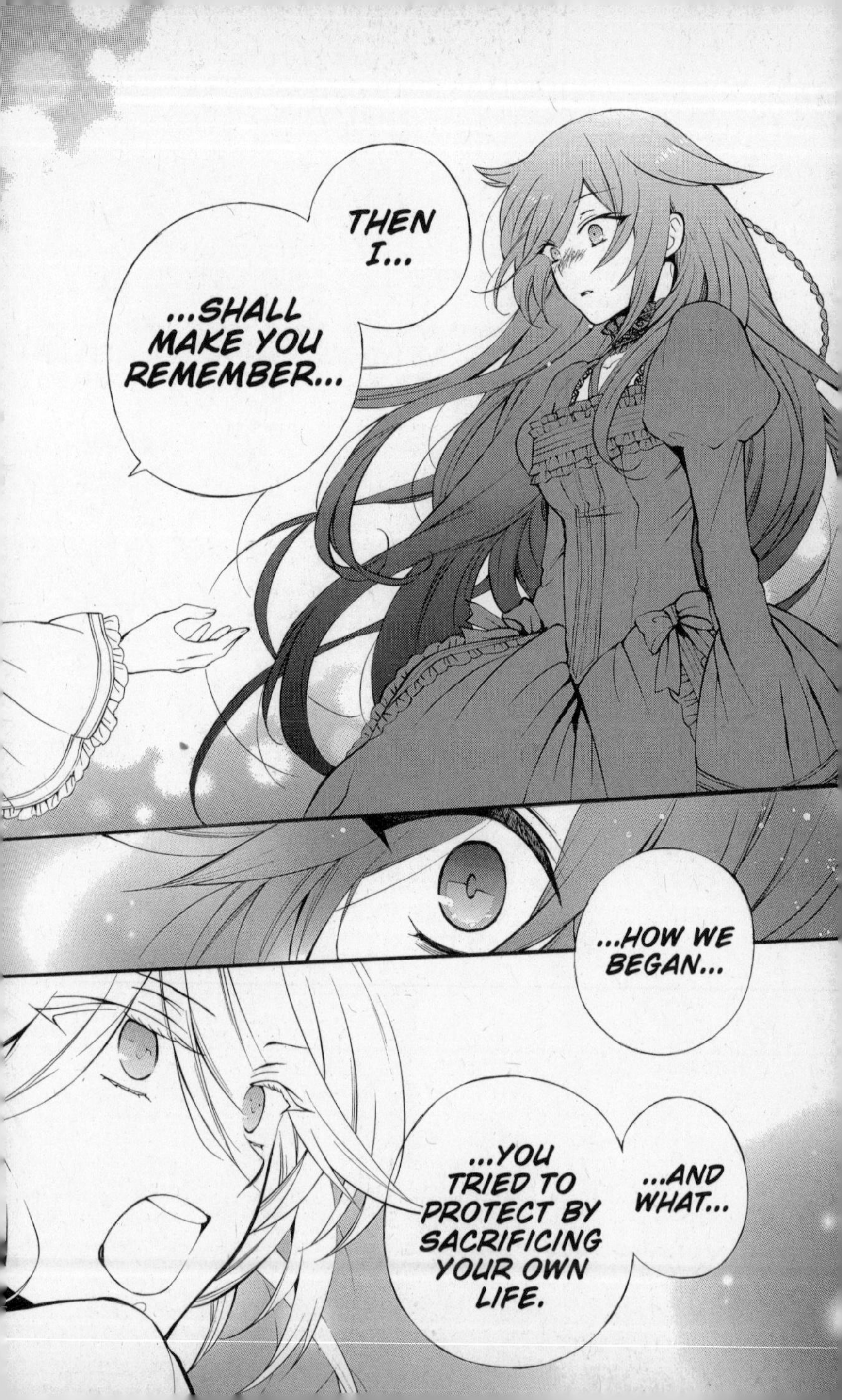
THEN I...
...SHALL MAKE YOU REMEMBER...
...HOW WE BEGAN...
...AND WHAT...
...YOU TRIED TO PROTECT BY SACRIFICING YOUR OWN LIFE.

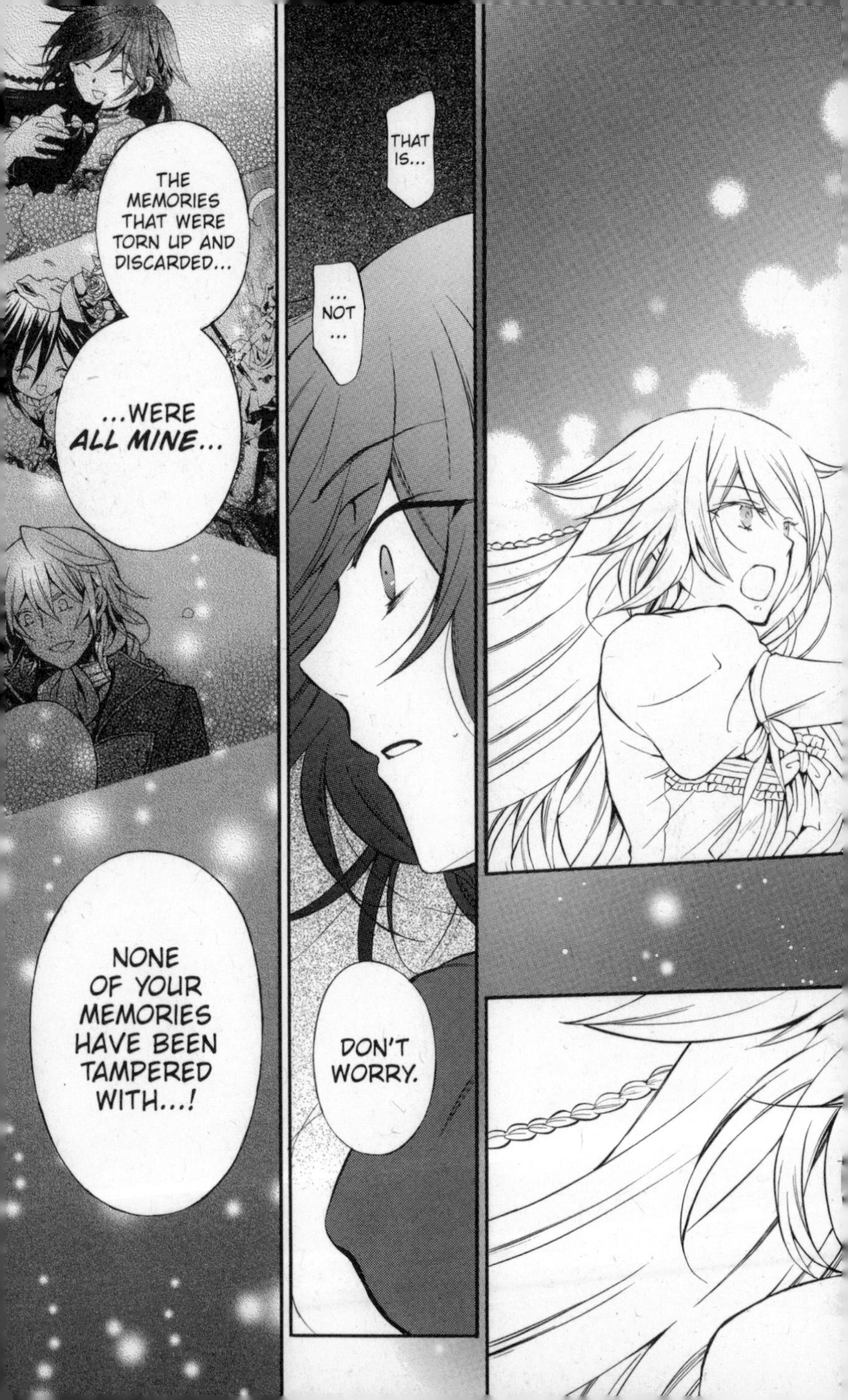
THAT IS...
...NOT...
DON'T WORRY.
THE MEMORIES THAT WERE TORN UP AND DISCARDED...
...WERE ALL MINE...
NONE OF YOUR MEMORIES HAVE BEEN TAMPERED WITH...!

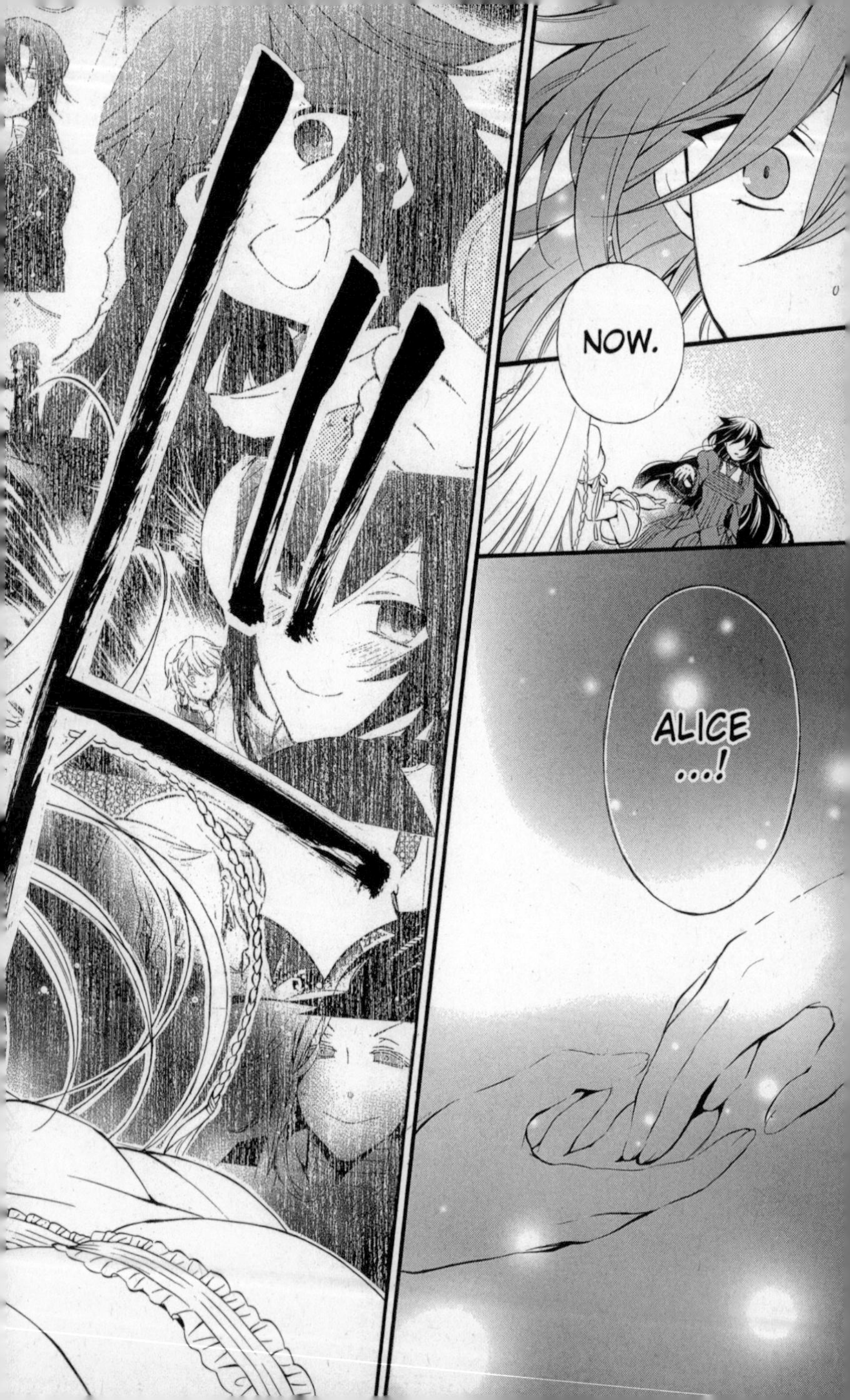
NOW.
ALICE ...!

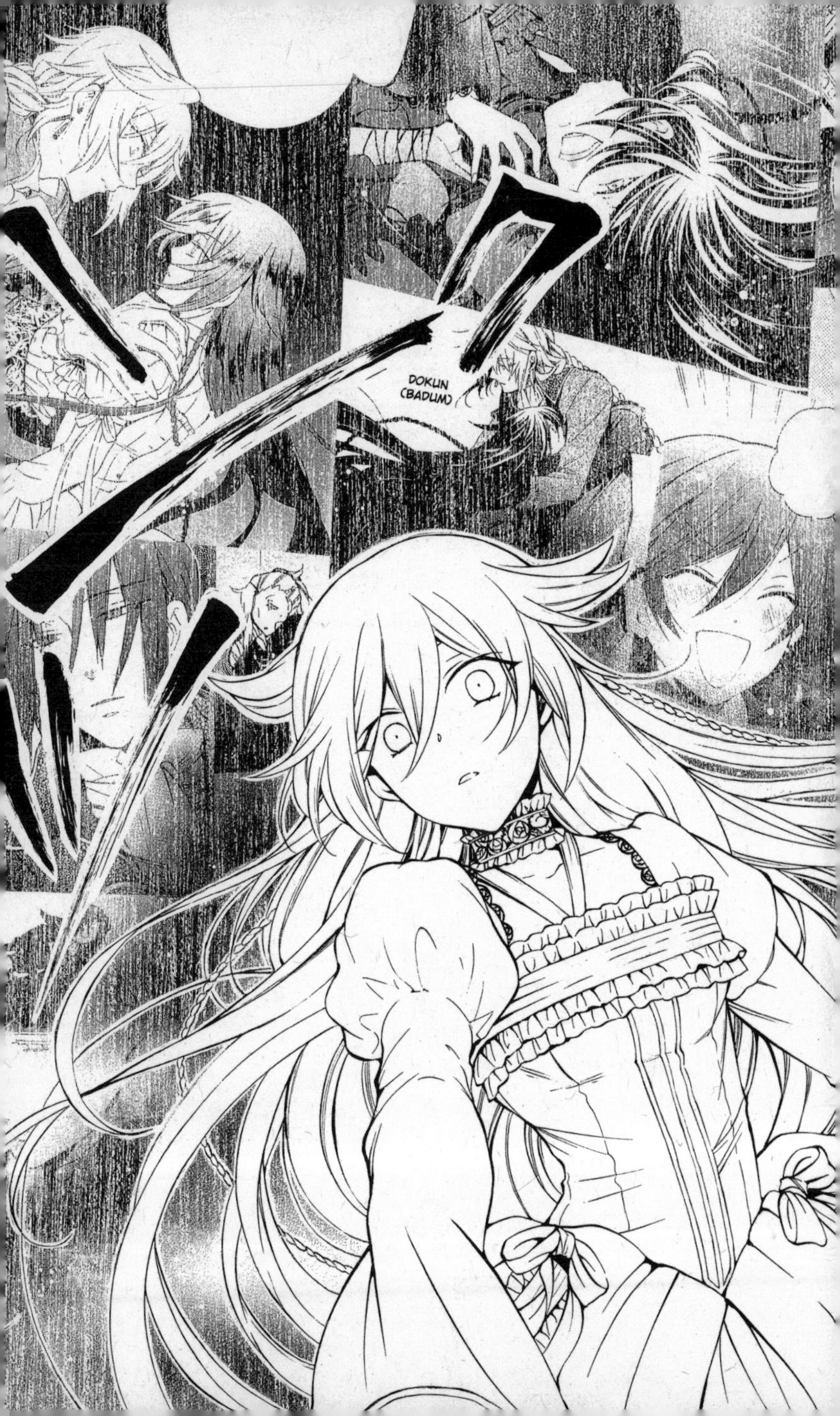
DOKUN (BADUM)

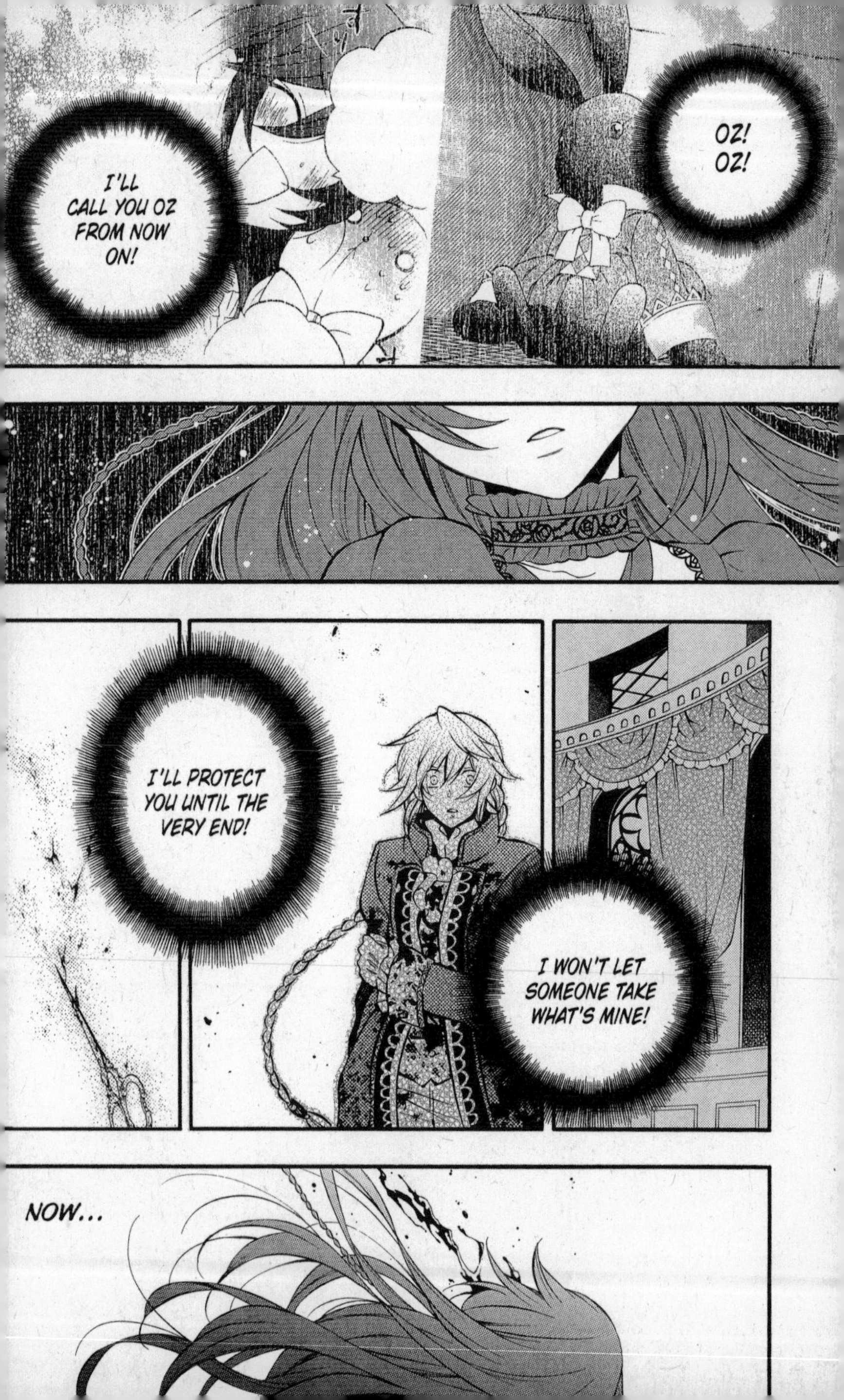
OZ! OZ!
I'LL CALL YOU OZ FROM NOW ON!
I'LL PROTECT YOU UNTIL THE VERY END!
I WON'T LET SOMEONE TAKE WHAT'S MINE!
NOW...

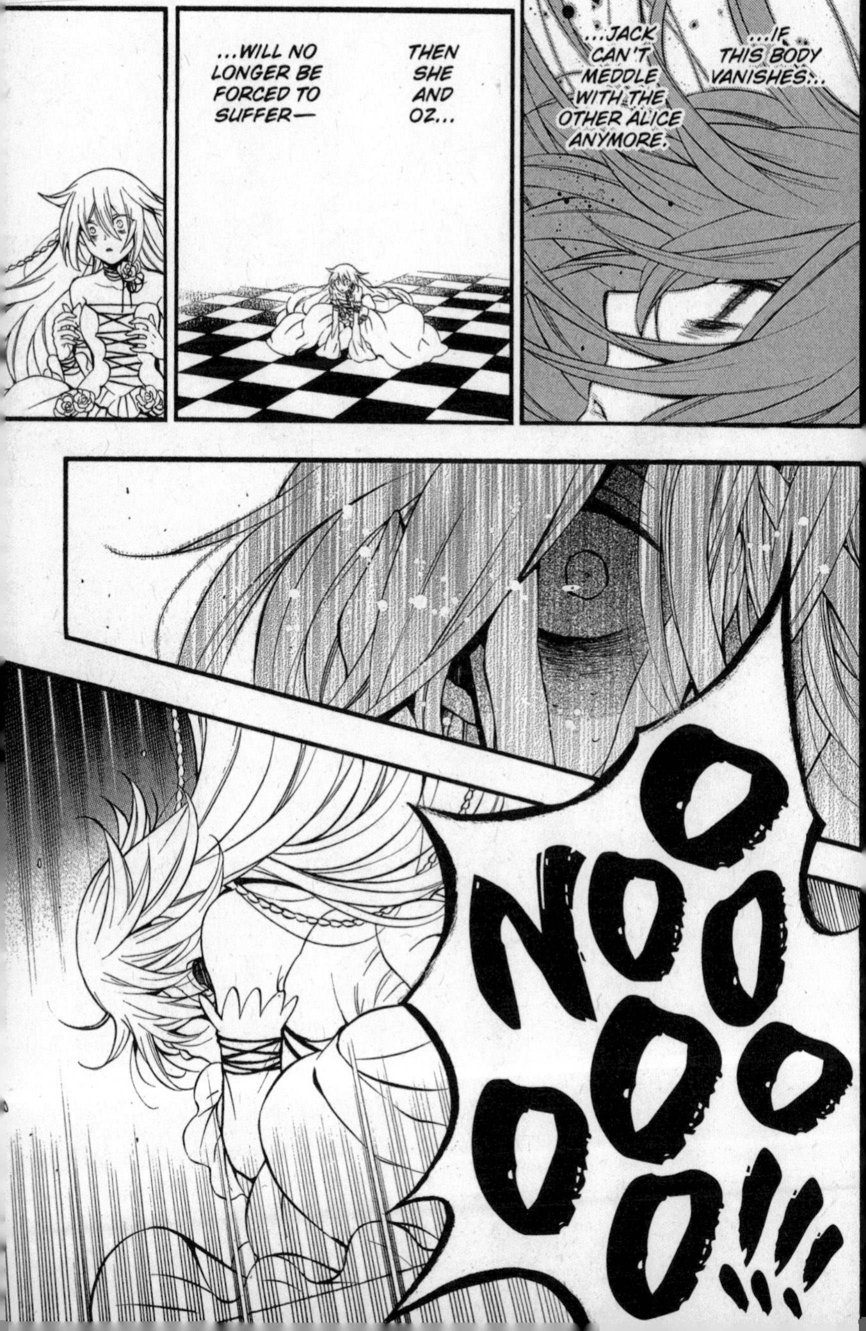
...IF THIS BODY VANISHES...
...JACK CAN'T MEDDLE WITH THE OTHER ALICE ANYMORE.
THEN SHE AND OZ...
...WILL NO LONGER BE FORCED TO SUFFER—
NOOOOOOOOOO!!

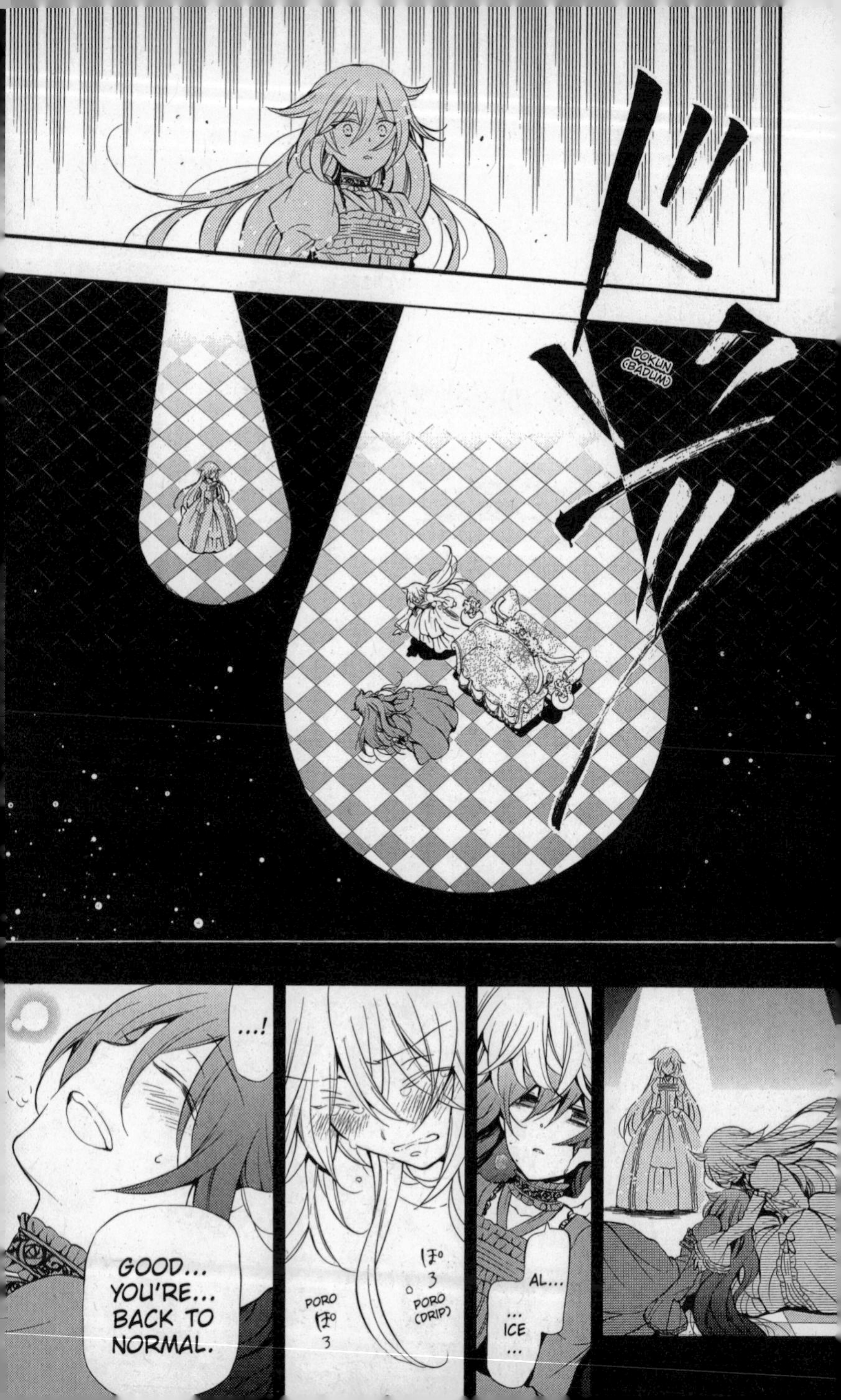
DOKLIN (BADUMP)
AL...
...ICE...
ぽろ
PORO (DRIP)
PORO
ぽろ
...!
GOOD... YOU'RE... BACK TO NORMAL.

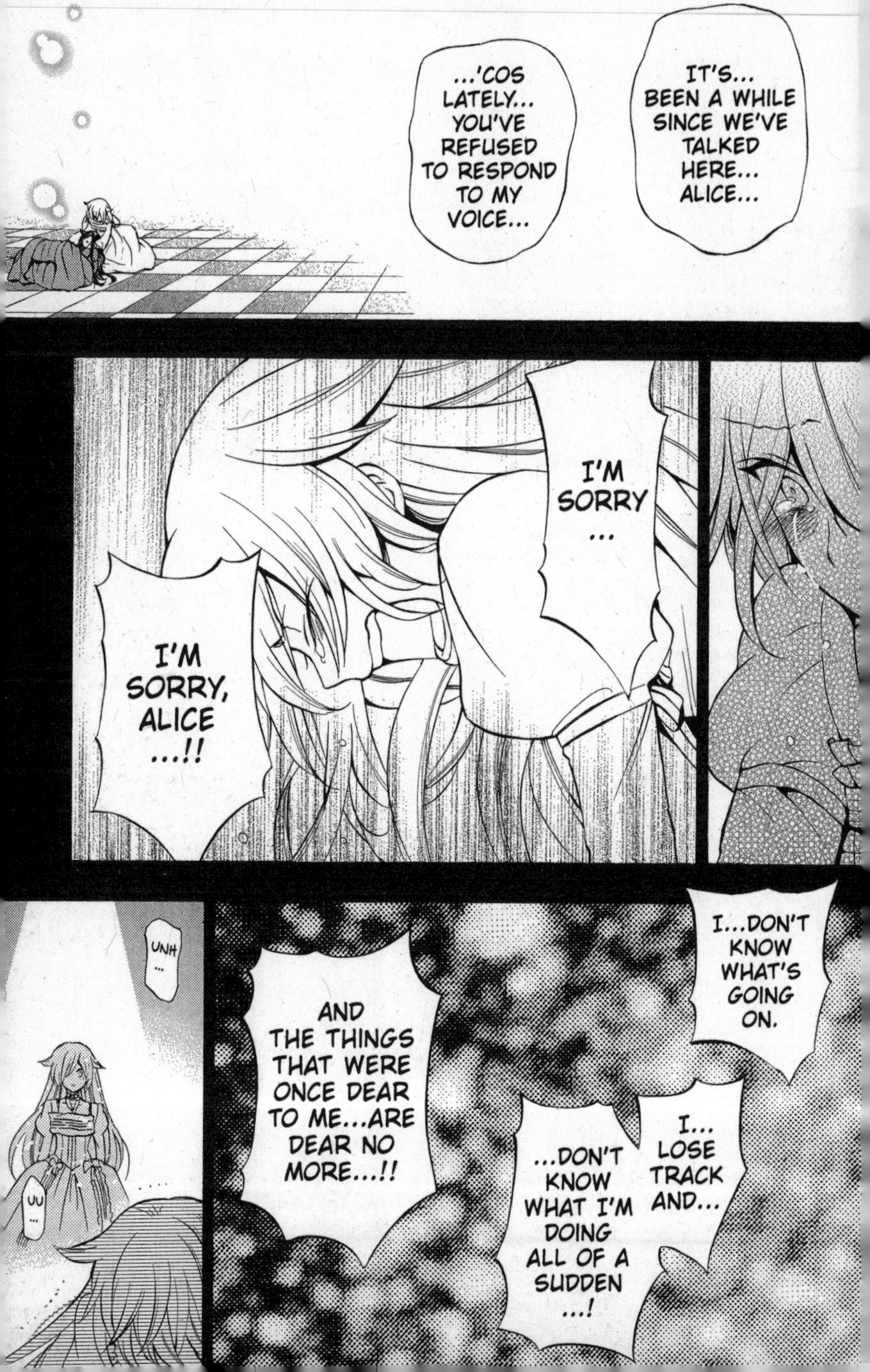
IT'S... BEEN A WHILE SINCE WE'VE TALKED HERE... ALICE...
...'COS LATELY... YOU'VE REFUSED TO RESPOND TO MY VOICE...
I'M SORRY...
I'M SORRY, ALICE...!!
I...DON'T KNOW WHAT'S GOING ON.
I... LOSE TRACK AND...
...DON'T KNOW WHAT I'M DOING ALL OF A SUDDEN...!
AND THE THINGS THAT WERE ONCE DEAR TO ME...ARE DEAR NO MORE...!!
UNH...
UU...
.....

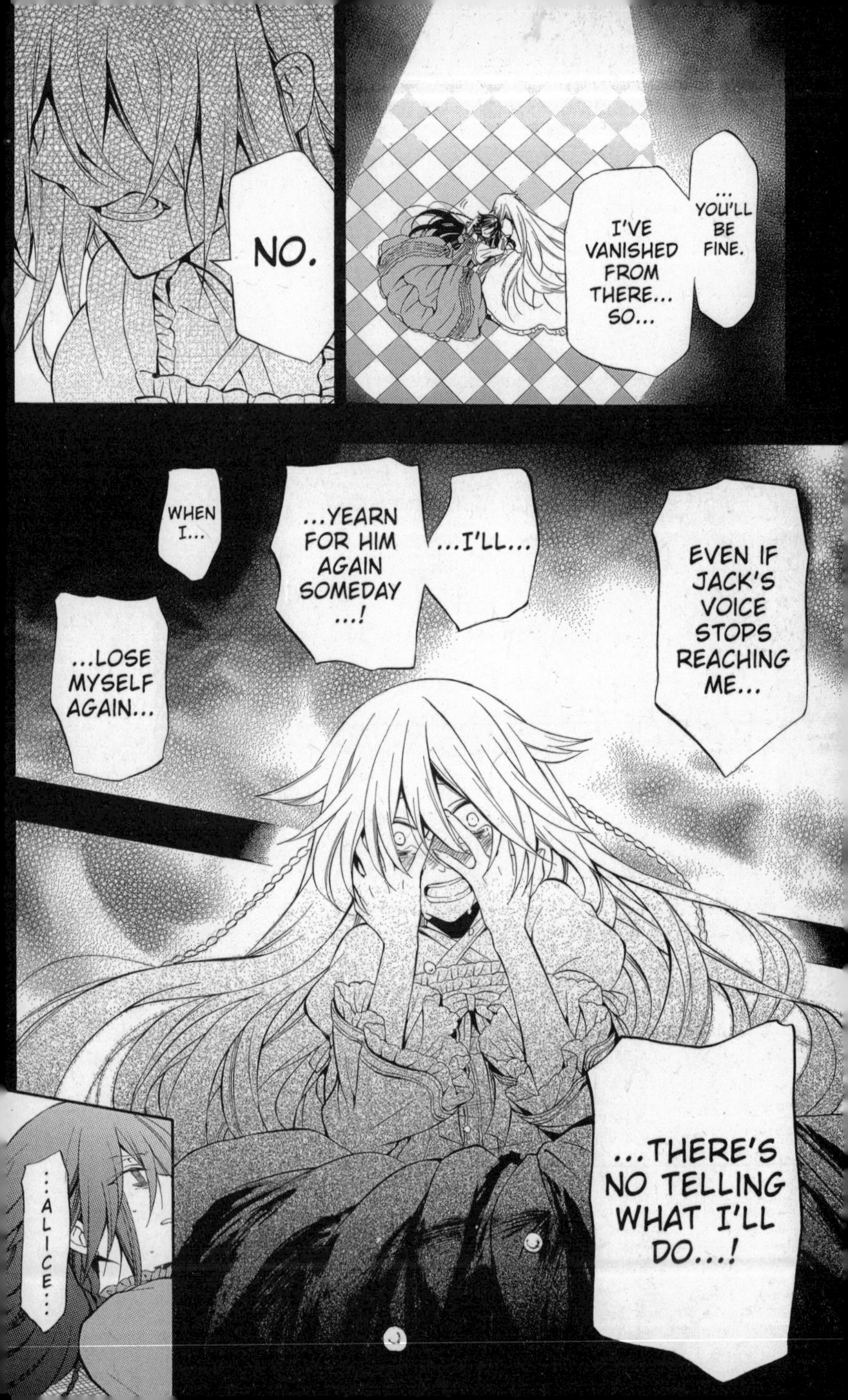
...YOU'LL BE FINE.
I'VE VANISHED FROM THERE... SO...
NO.
EVEN IF JACK'S VOICE STOPS REACHING ME...
...I'LL...
...YEARN FOR HIM AGAIN SOMEDAY ...!
WHEN I...
...LOSE MYSELF AGAIN...
...THERE'S NO TELLING WHAT I'LL DO...!
...ALICE...

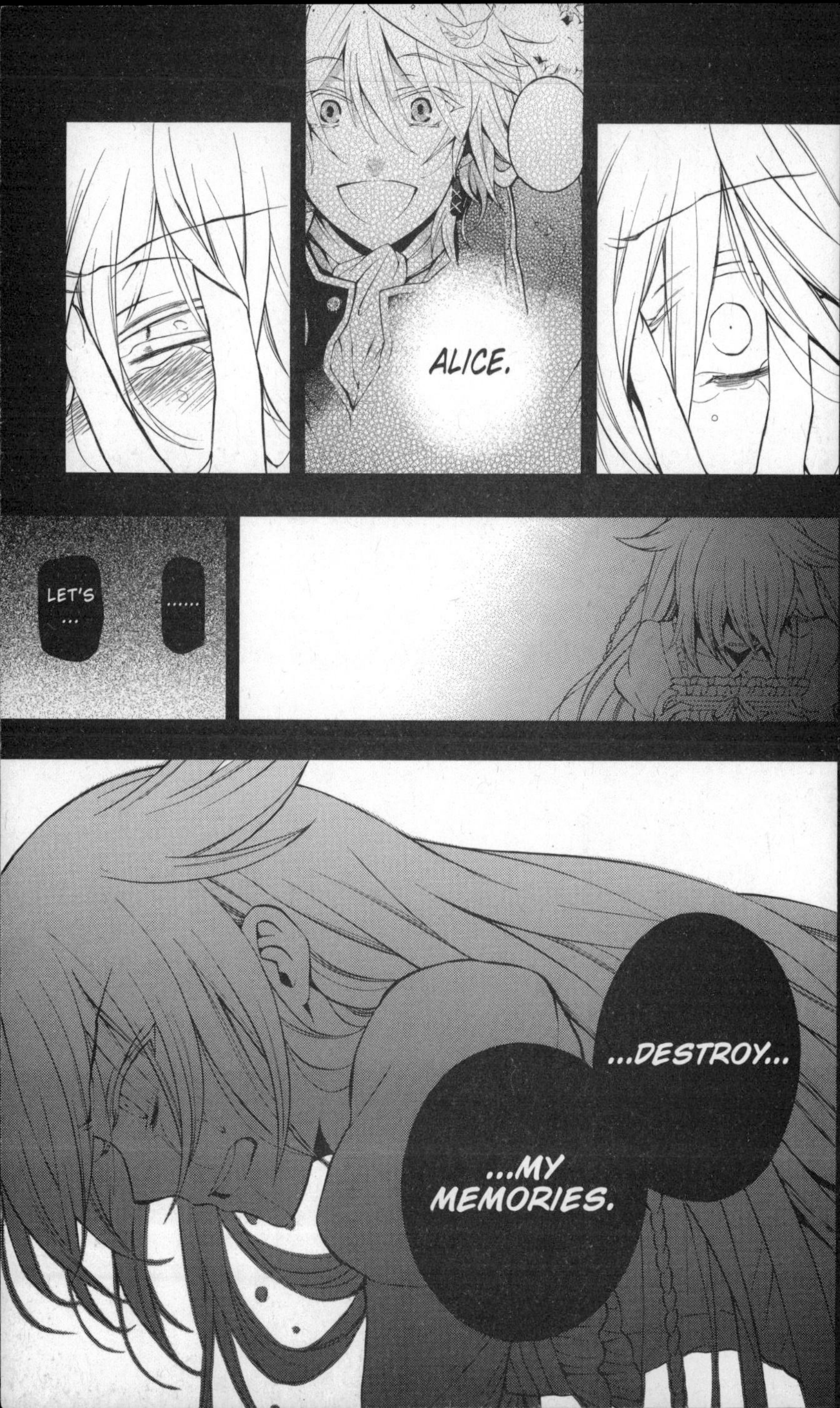
ALICE.
......
LET'S ...
...DESTROY...
...MY MEMORIES.

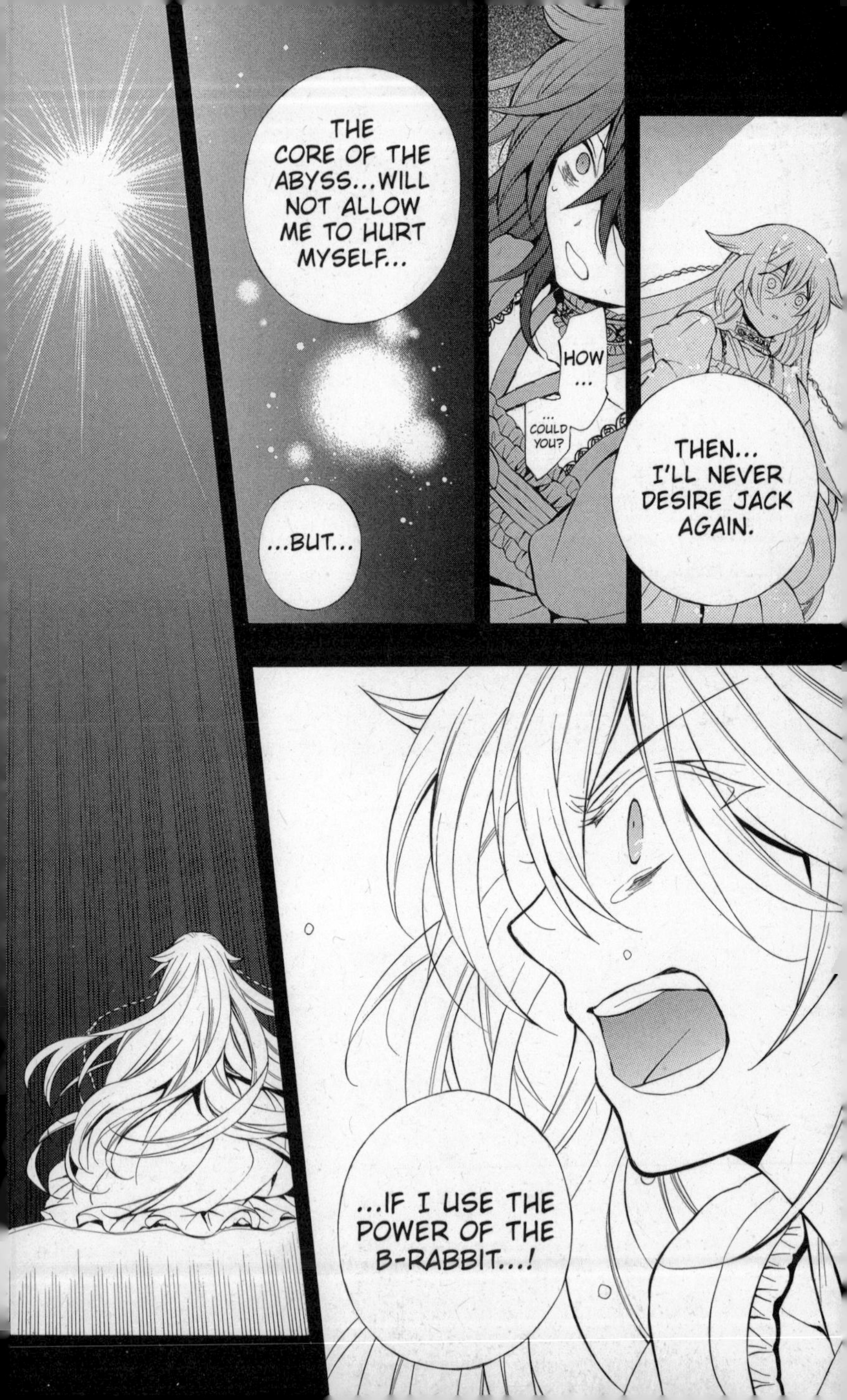
THEN... I'LL NEVER DESIRE JACK AGAIN.
HOW...
...COULD YOU?
THE CORE OF THE ABYSS...WILL NOT ALLOW ME TO HURT MYSELF...
...BUT...
...IF I USE THE POWER OF THE B-RABBIT...!

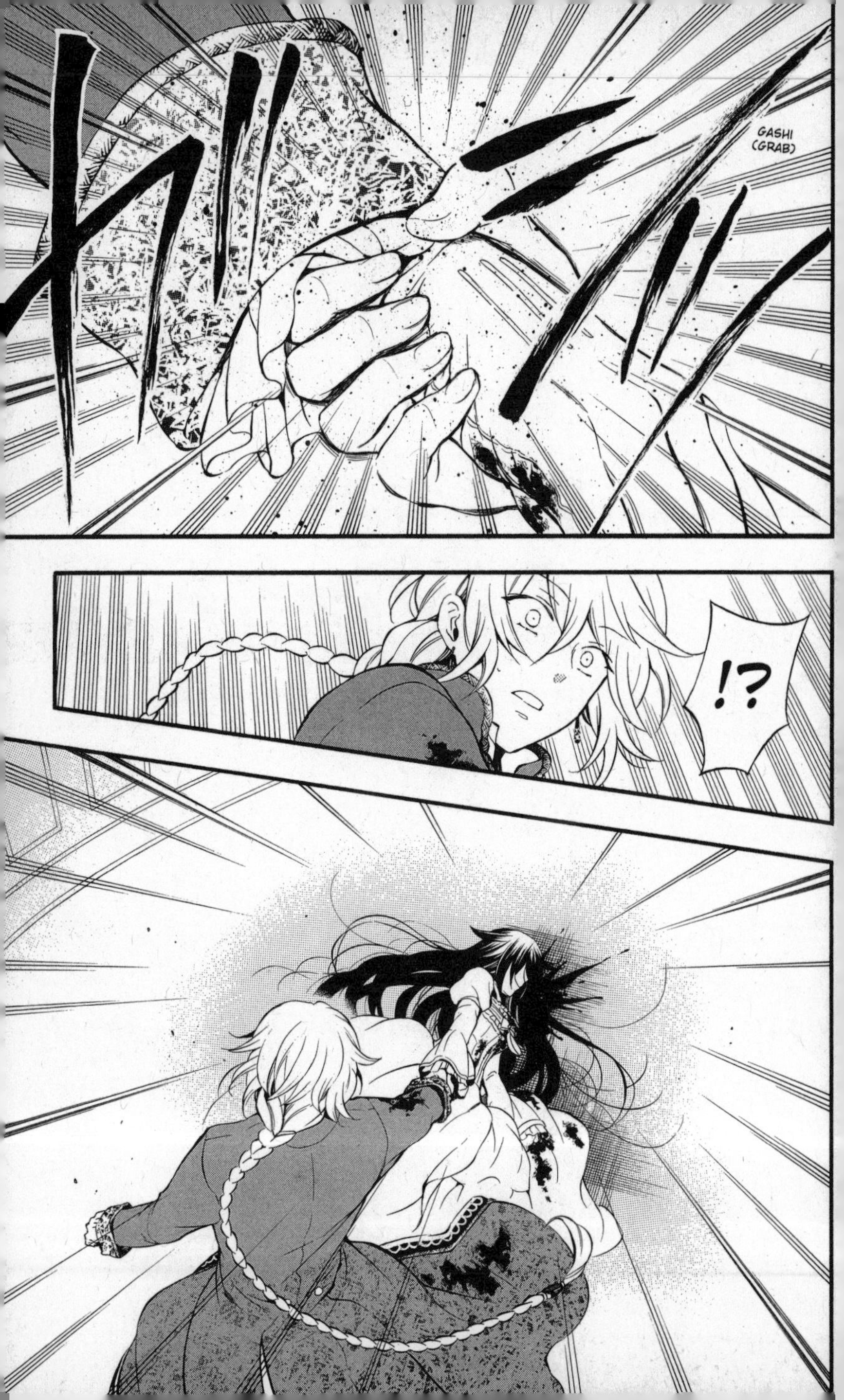
GASHI
(GRAB)
!?

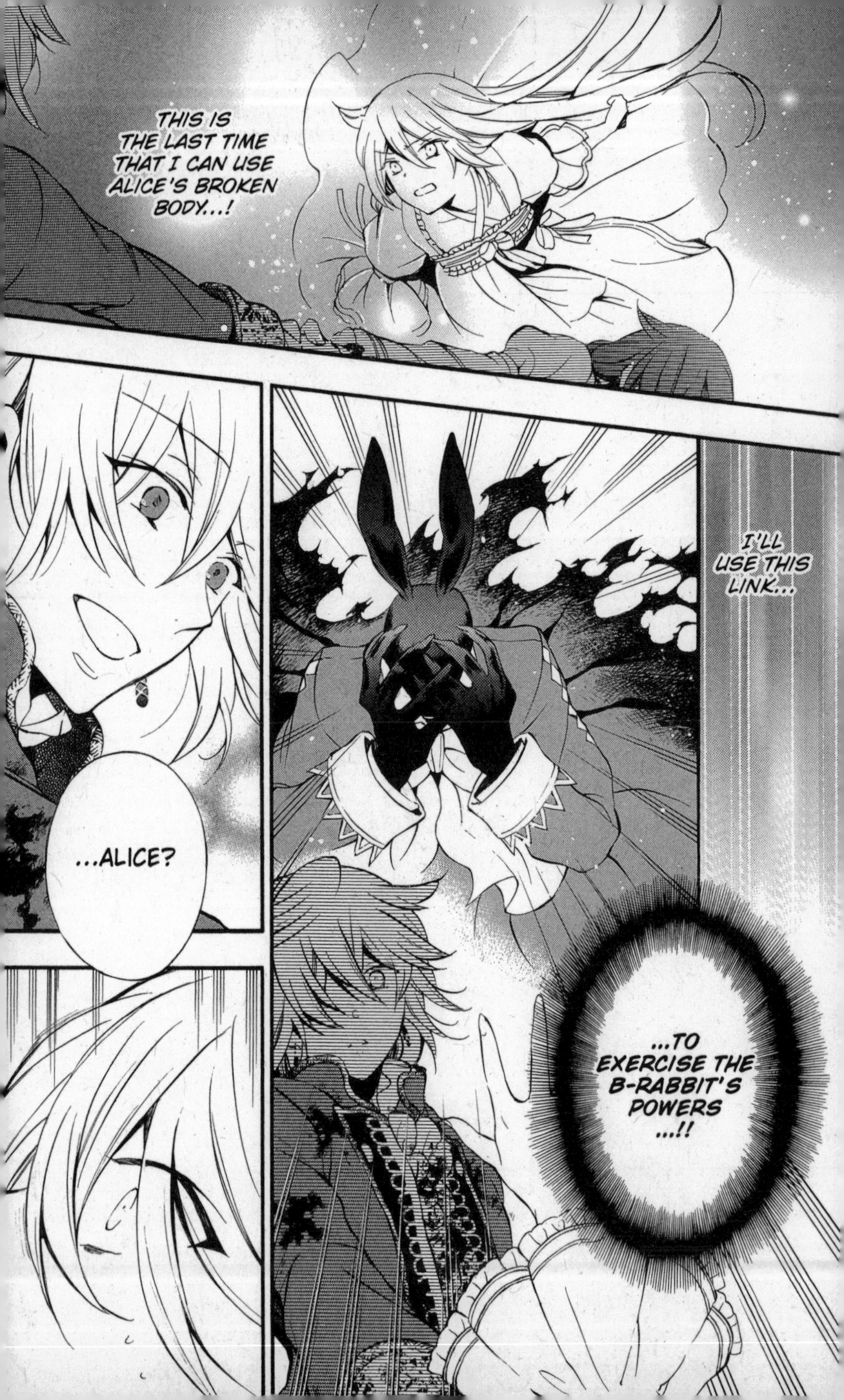
THIS IS THE LAST TIME THAT I CAN USE ALICE'S BROKEN BODY...!
I'LL USE THIS LINK...
...TO EXERCISE THE B-RABBIT'S POWERS ...!!
...ALICE?

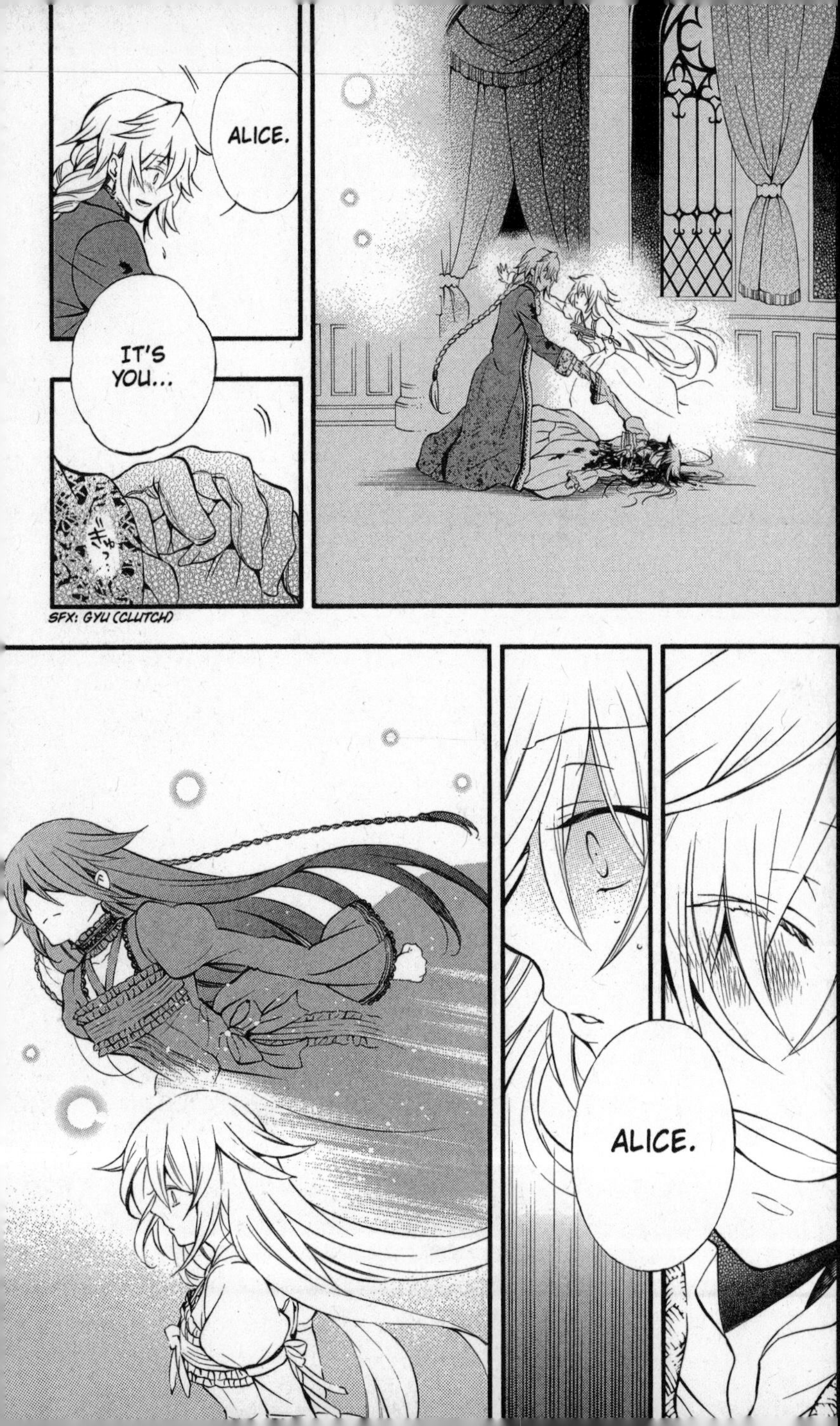
ALICE.
IT'S YOU...
ぎゅっ
SFX: GYU (CLUTCH)
ALICE.

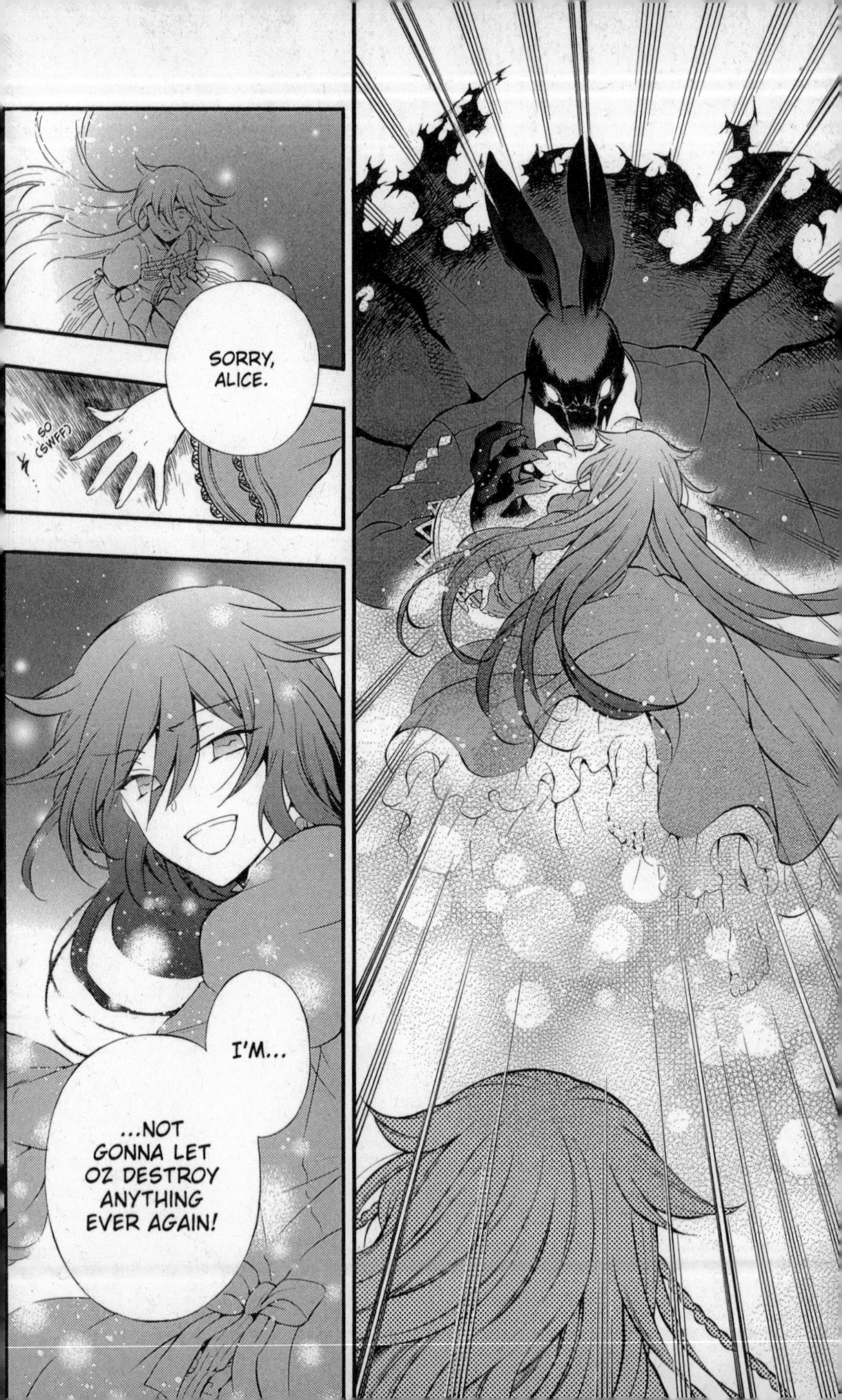
SORRY, ALICE.
SO (SWFF)
I'M...
...NOT GONNA LET OZ DESTROY ANYTHING EVER AGAIN!

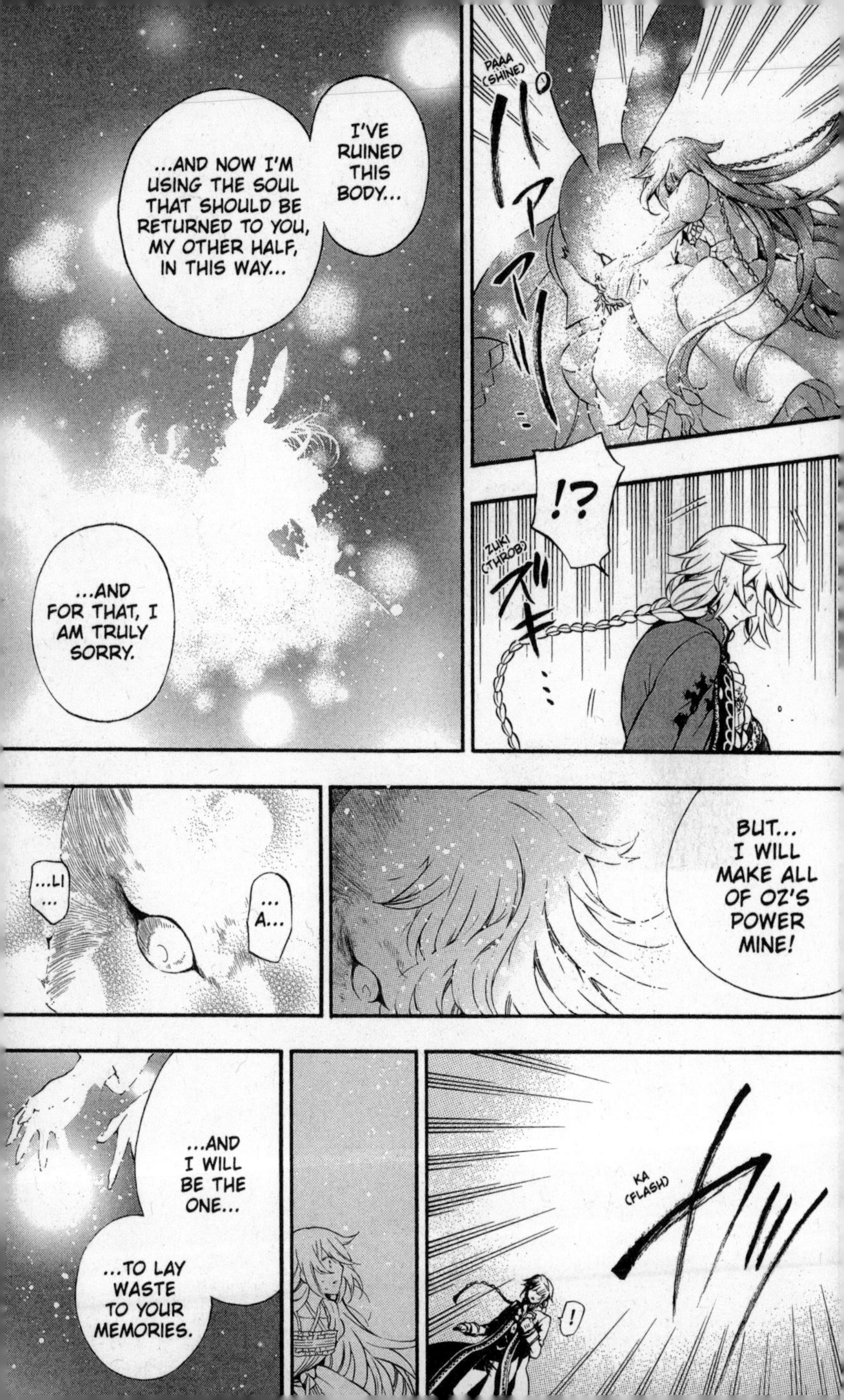
PAAA (SHINE)
!?
ZUKI (THROB)
I'VE RUINED THIS BODY...
...AND NOW I'M USING THE SOUL THAT SHOULD BE RETURNED TO YOU, MY OTHER HALF, IN THIS WAY...
...AND FOR THAT, I AM TRULY SORRY.
BUT... I WILL MAKE ALL OF OZ'S POWER MINE!
...A...
...LI...
KA (FLASH)
!
...AND I WILL BE THE ONE...
...TO LAY WASTE TO YOUR MEMORIES.

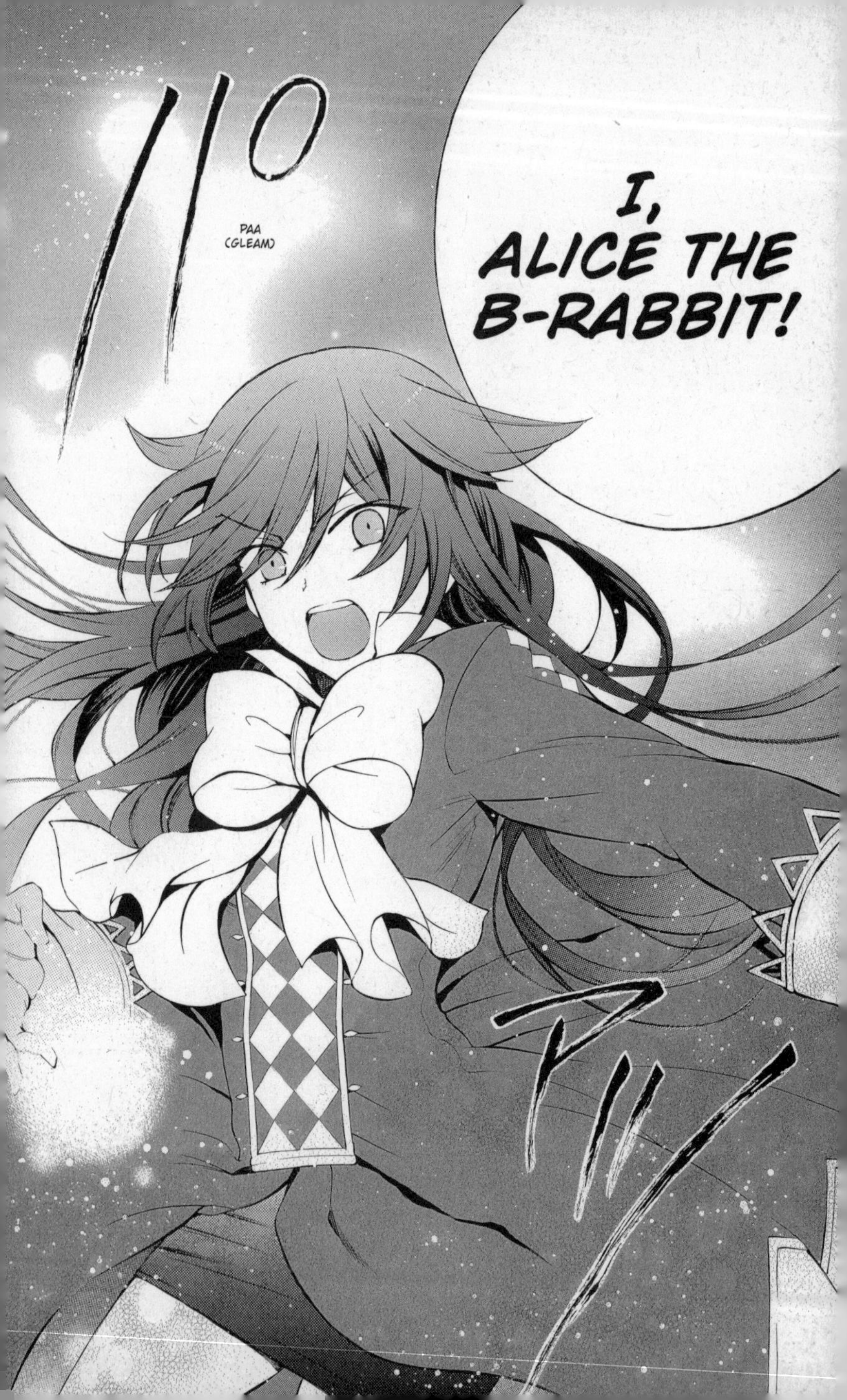
I, ALICE THE B-RABBIT!
PAA (GLEAM)

Retrace:LXXVI Alice & Oz

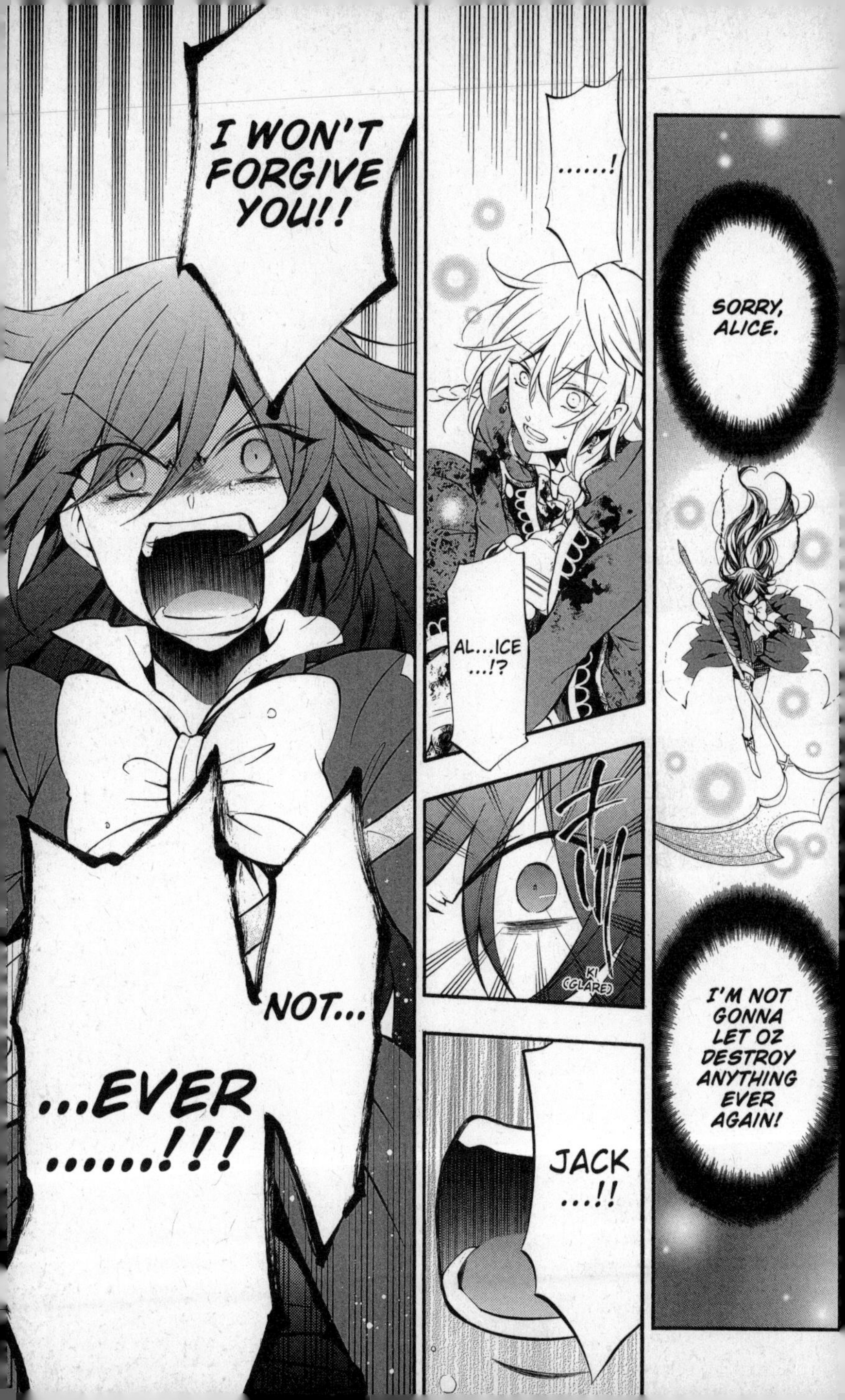
SORRY, ALICE.
I'M NOT GONNA LET OZ DESTROY ANYTHING EVER AGAIN!
......!
AL...ICE ...!?
KI (GLARE)
JACK ...!!
I WON'T FORGIVE YOU!!
NOT...
...EVER ......!!!

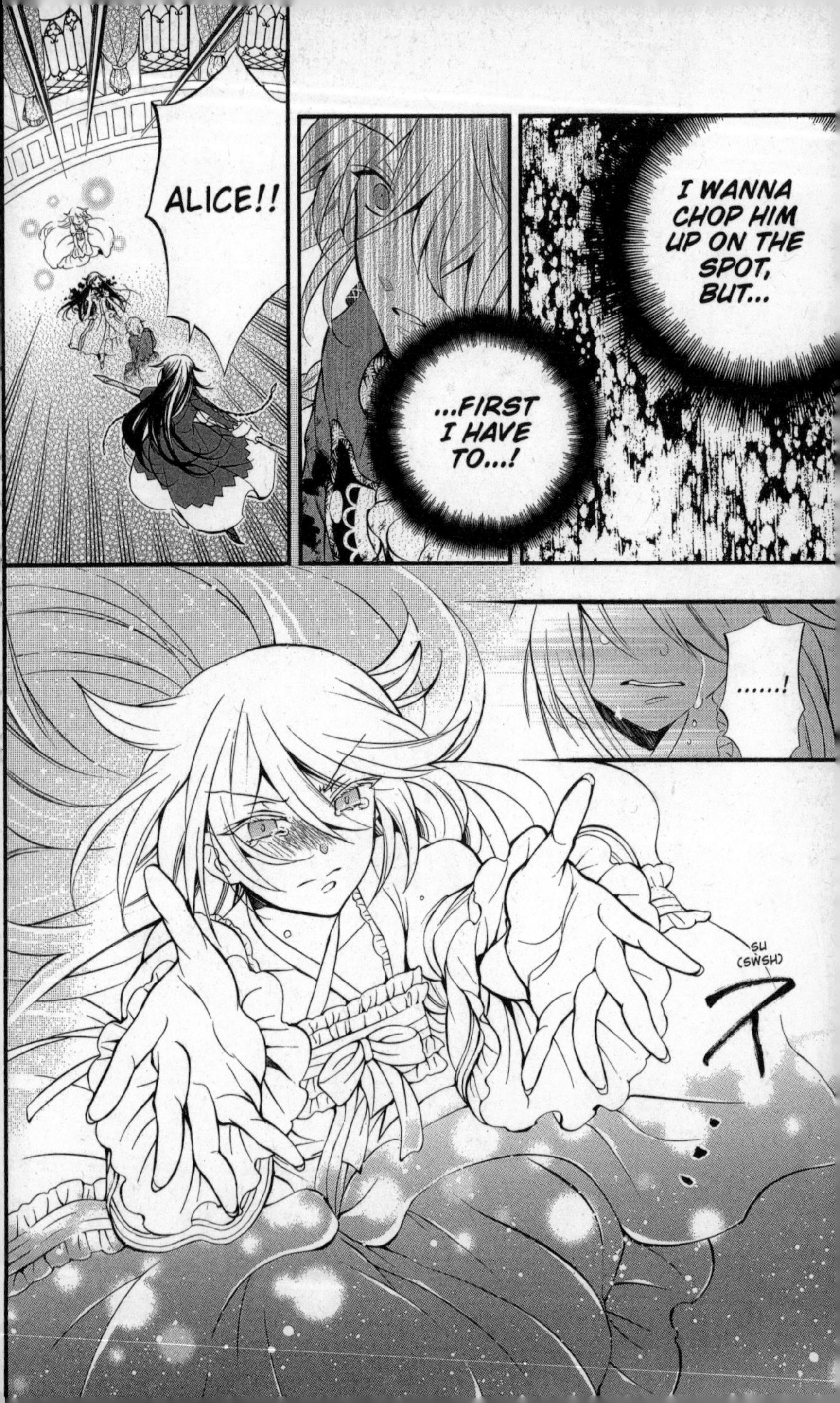
I WANNA CHOP HIM UP ON THE SPOT, BUT...
...FIRST I HAVE TO...!
ALICE!!
......!
SU (SWSH)

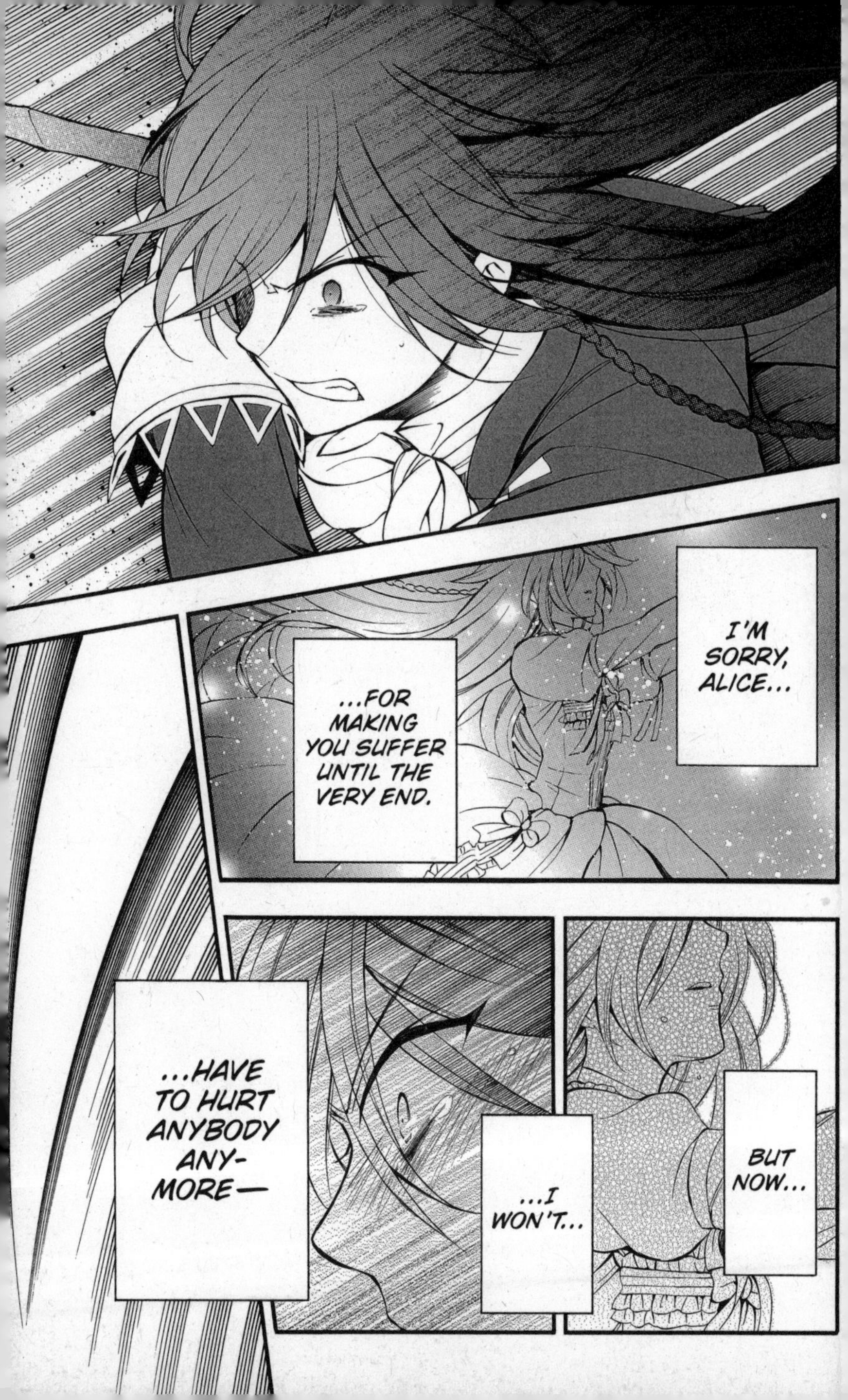
I'M SORRY, ALICE...
...FOR MAKING YOU SUFFER UNTIL THE VERY END.
BUT NOW...
...I WON'T...
...HAVE TO HURT ANYBODY ANY-MORE—

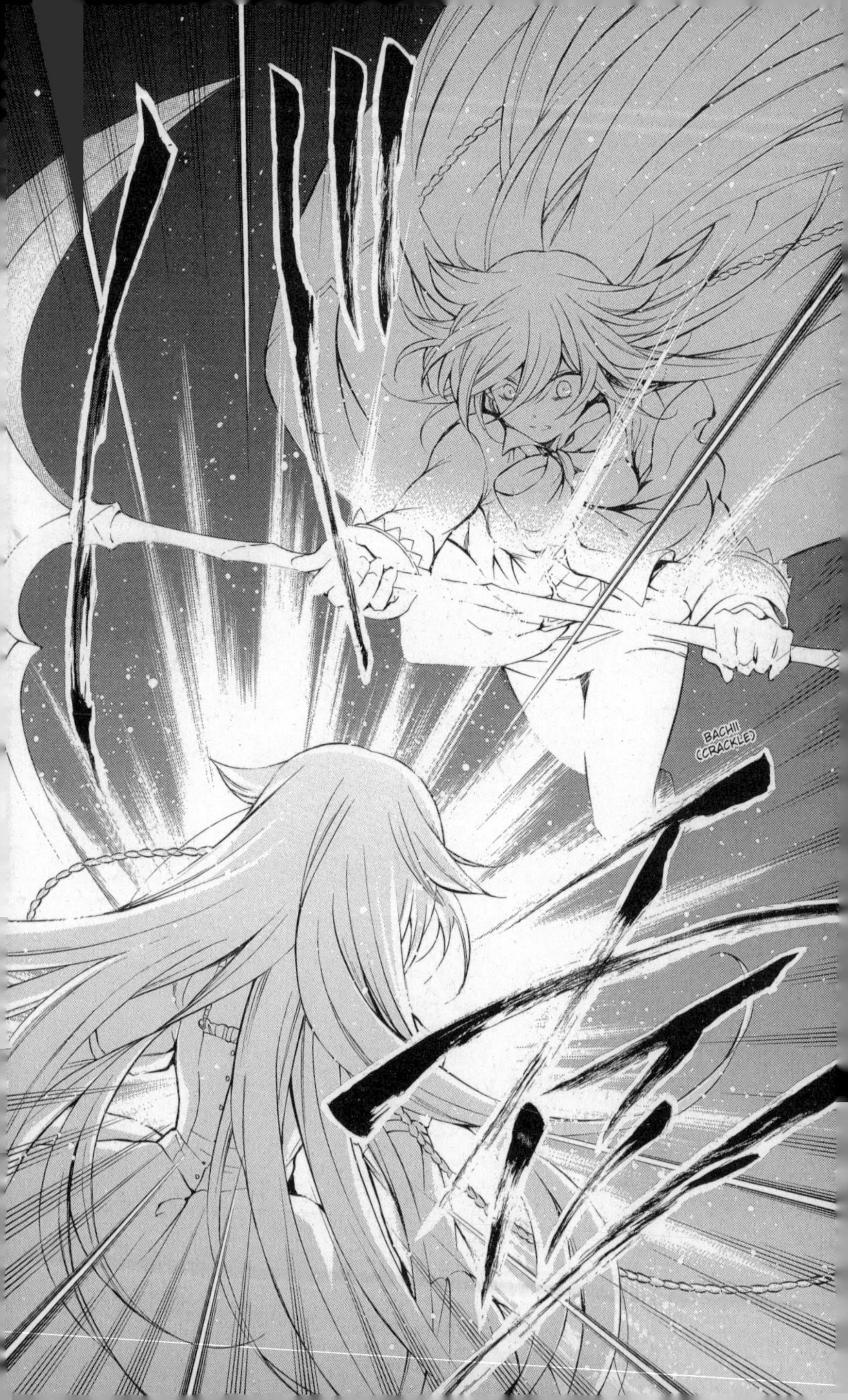
BACHI!
(CRACKLE)

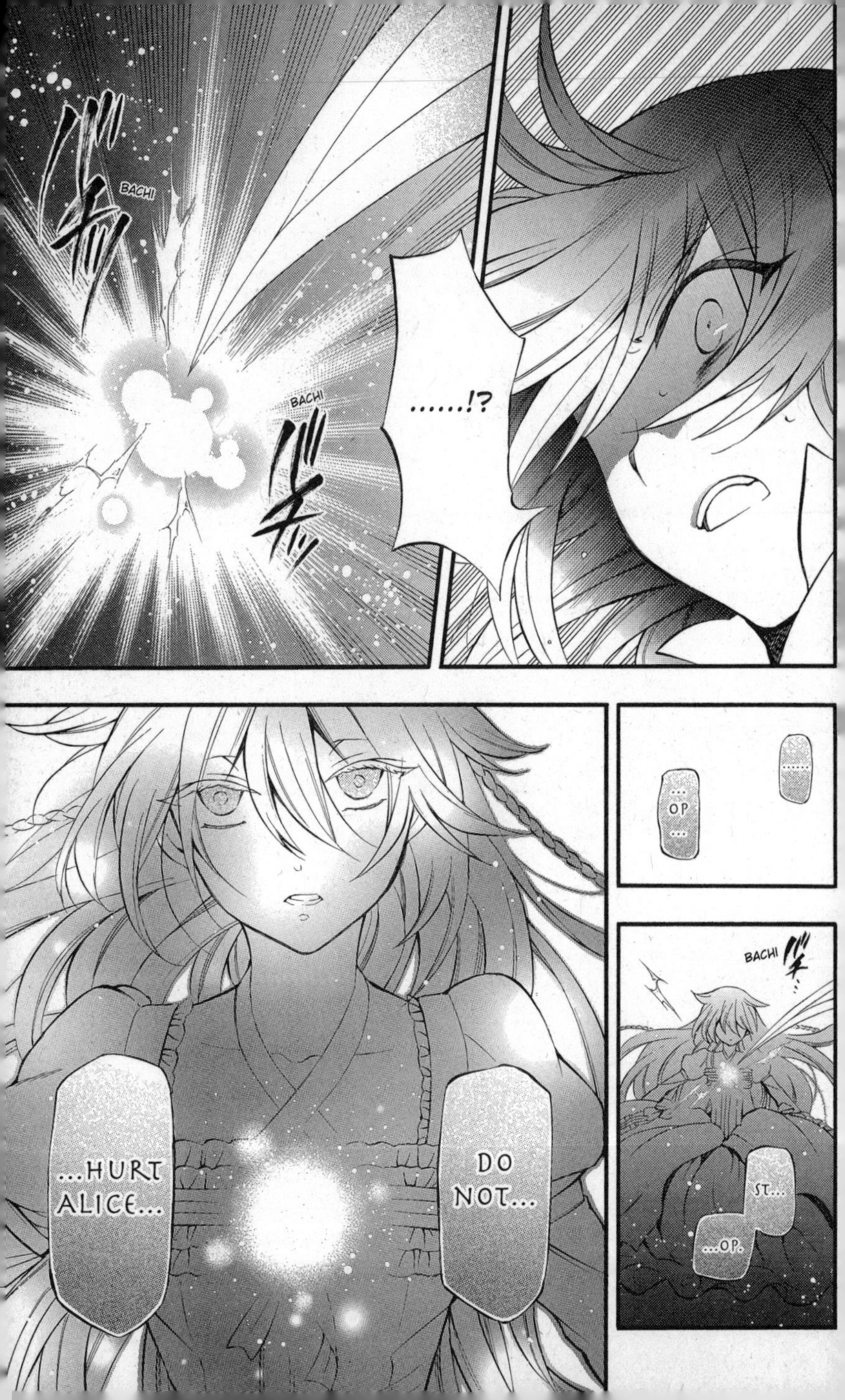
......!?
BACHI
BACHI
......
...OP...
BACHI
ST...
...OP.
DO NOT...
...HURT ALICE...

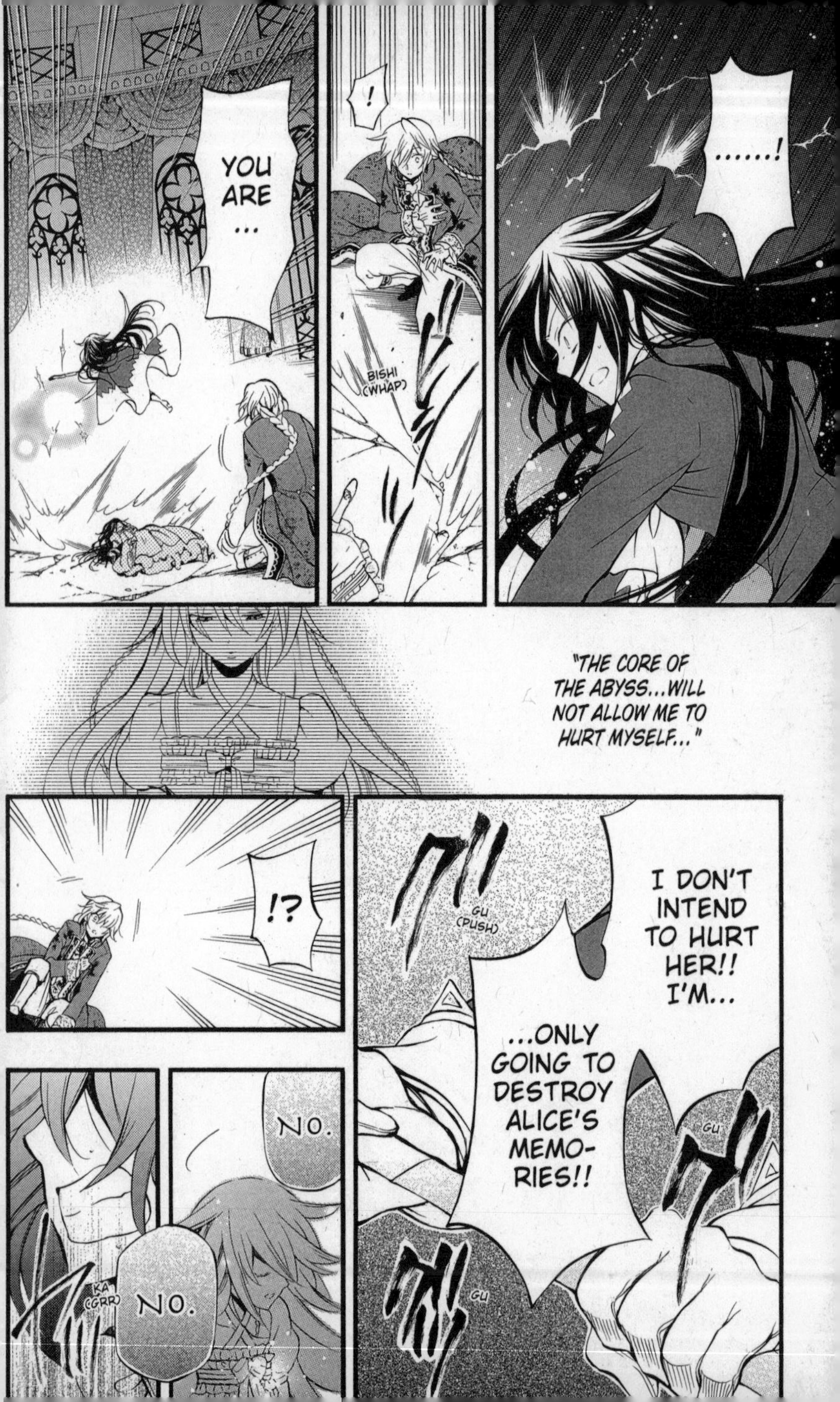
......!
!
BISHI (WHAP)
YOU ARE ...
"THE CORE OF THE ABYSS...WILL NOT ALLOW ME TO HURT MYSELF..."
I DON'T INTEND TO HURT HER!! I'M...
GU (PUSH)
...ONLY GOING TO DESTROY ALICE'S MEMO-RIES!!
GU
GU
!?
NO.
KA (GRR)
NO.

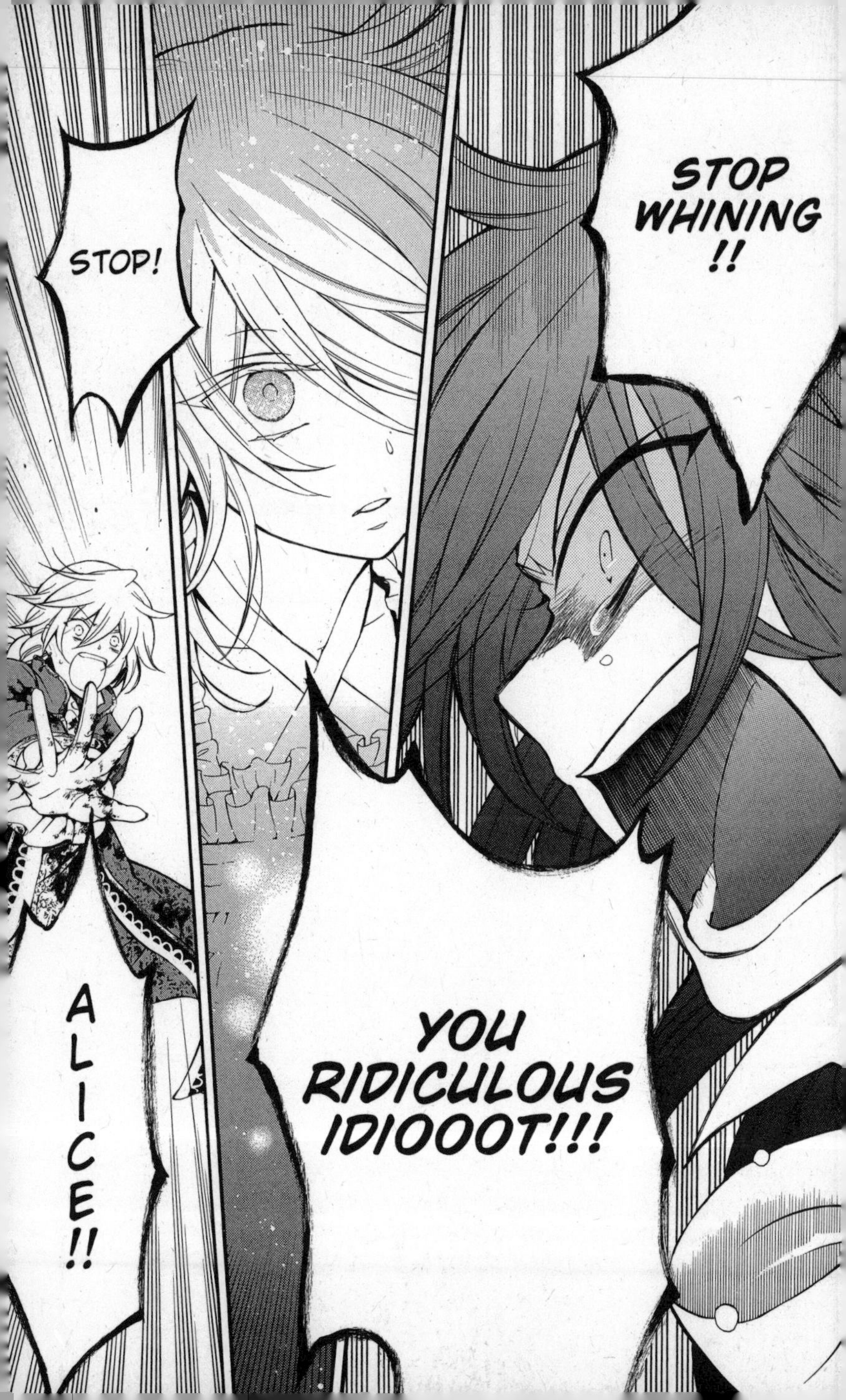
STOP WHINING!!
YOU RIDICULOUS IDIOOOT!!!
STOP!
ALICE!!

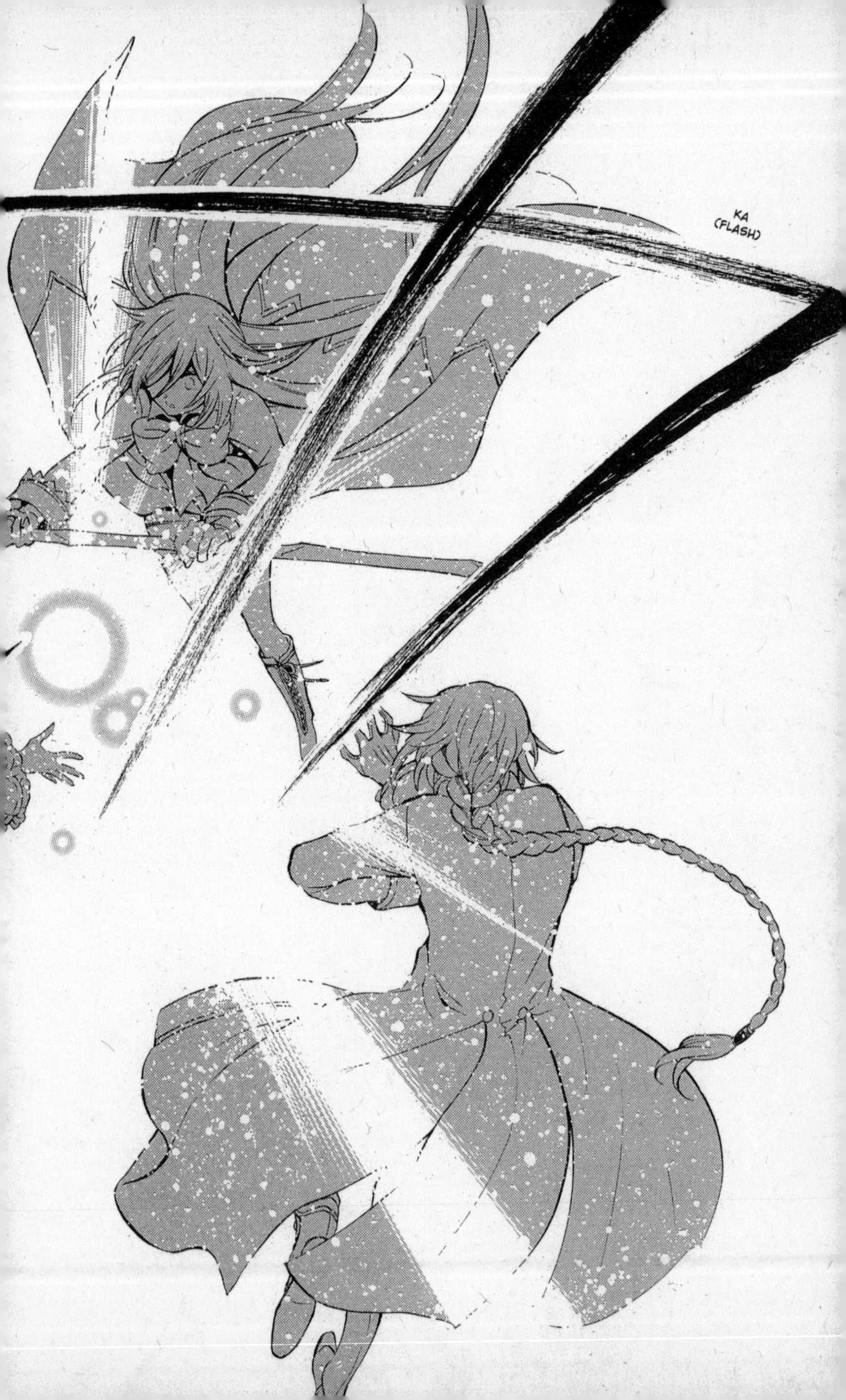
KA
(FLASH)

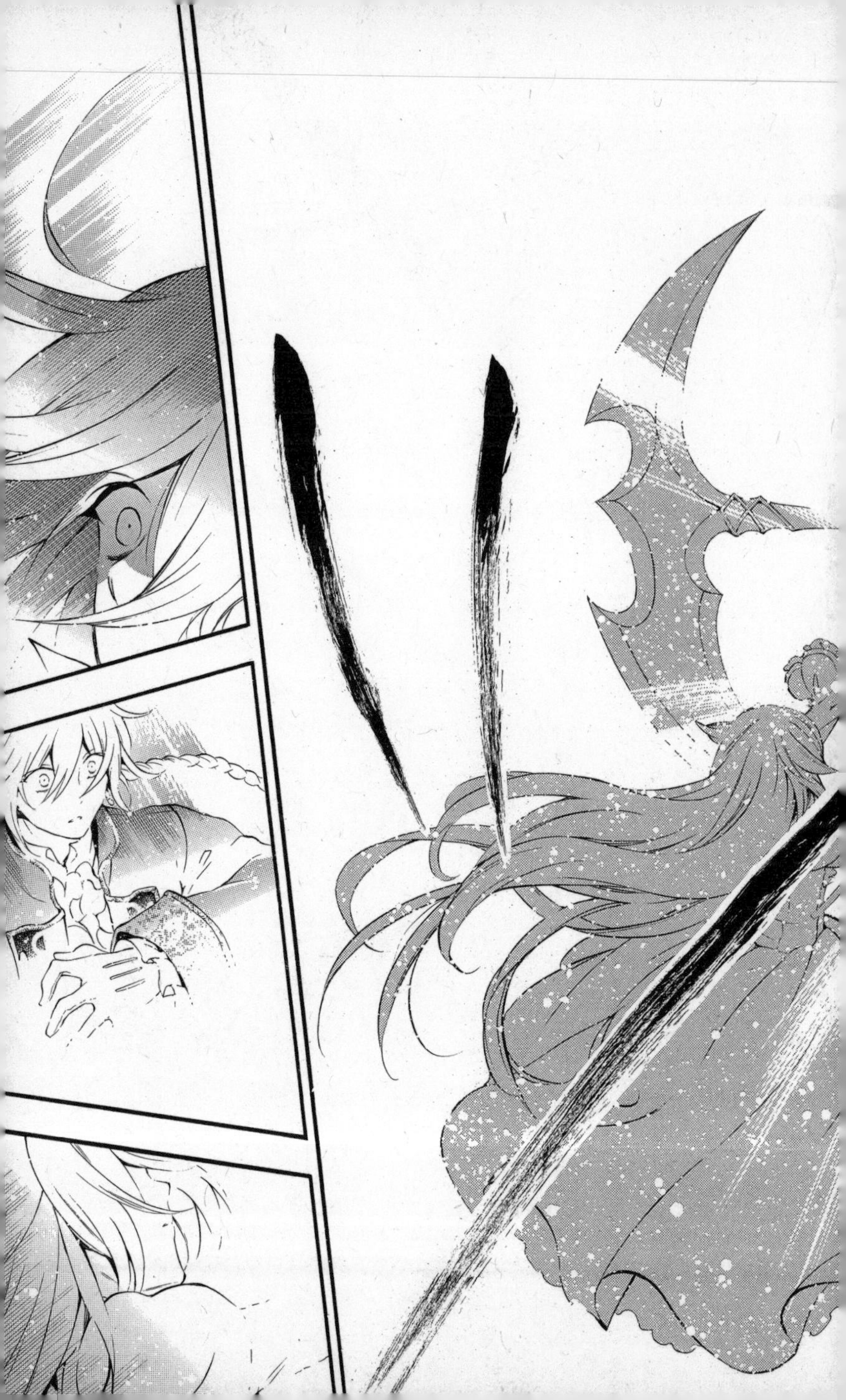

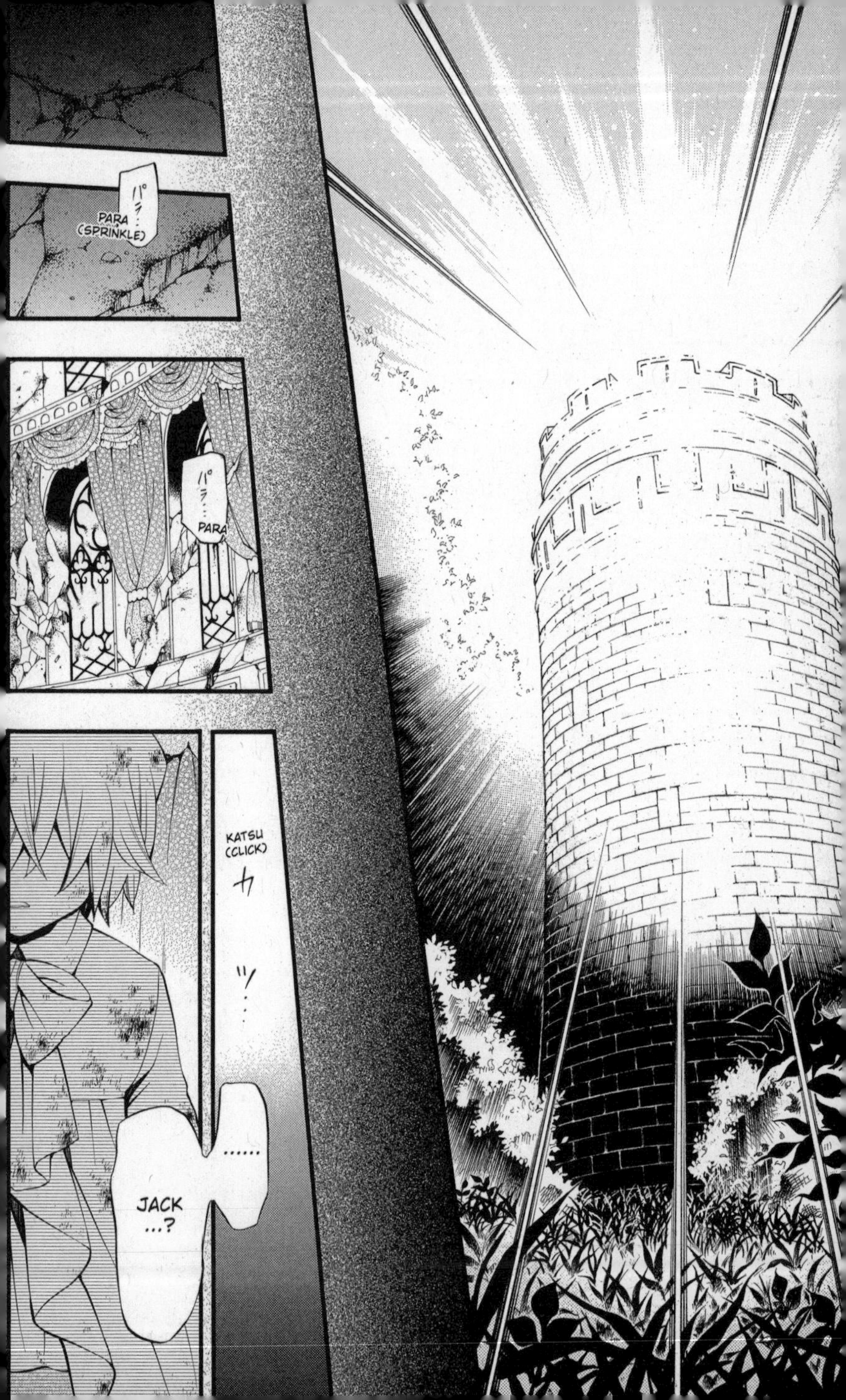
パラ…
PARA (SPRINKLE)
パラ…
PARA
KATSU (CLICK)
カ
ッ!…
……
JACK …?

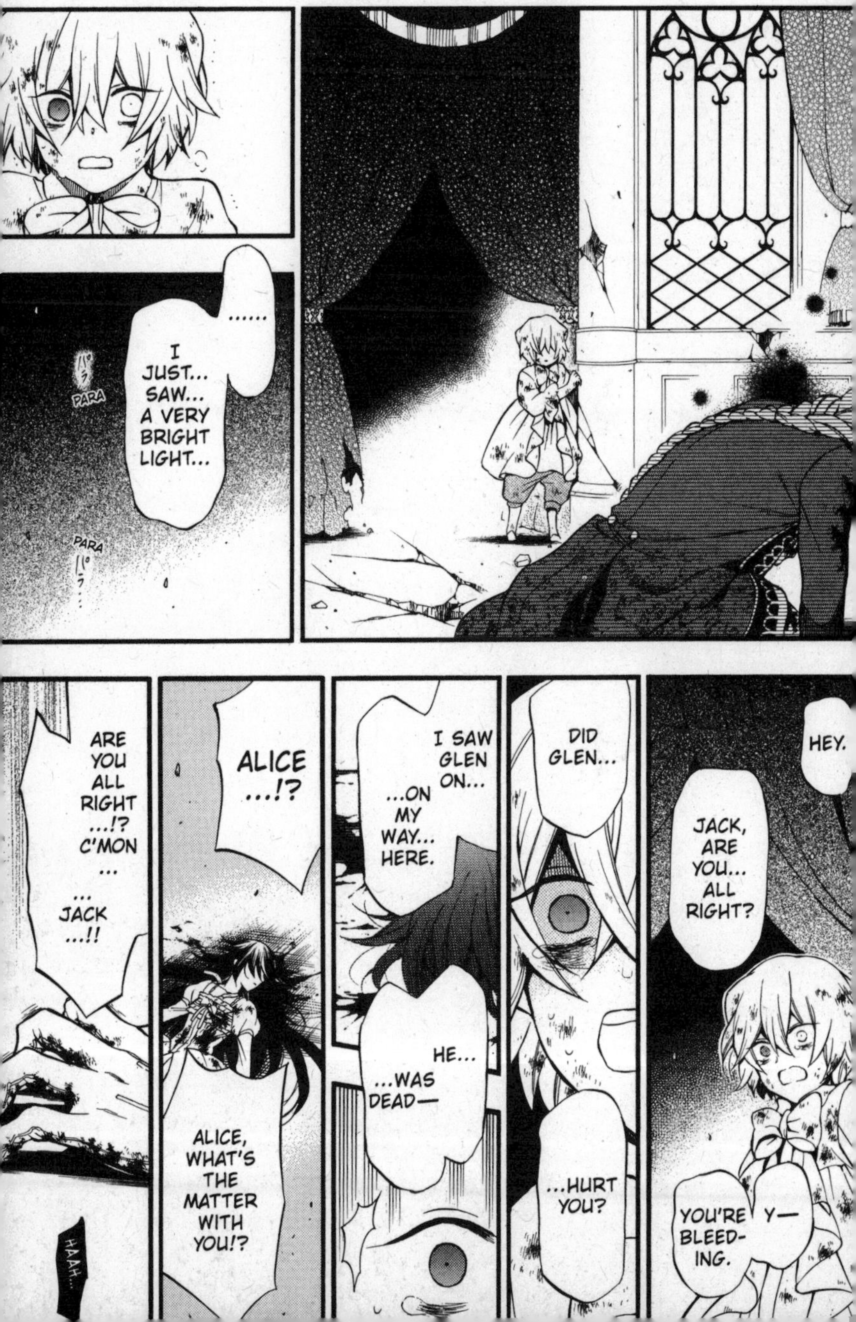
......
I JUST... SAW... A VERY BRIGHT LIGHT...
PARA
PARA
HEY.
JACK, ARE YOU... ALL RIGHT?
Y—
YOU'RE BLEEDING.
DID GLEN...
...HURT YOU?
I SAW GLEN ON...
...ON MY WAY... HERE.
HE...
...WAS DEAD—
ALICE ...!?
ALICE, WHAT'S THE MATTER WITH YOU!?
ARE YOU ALL RIGHT ...!? C'MON ... ... JACK ...!!
HAAH...

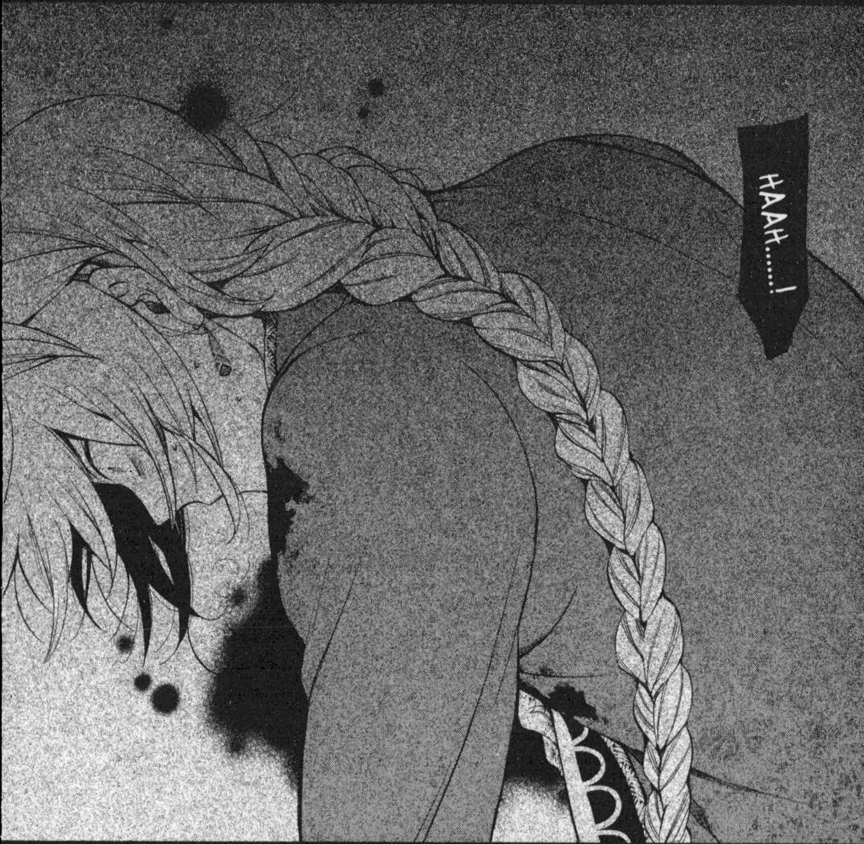
HAAH.....!

Retrace:LXXVII

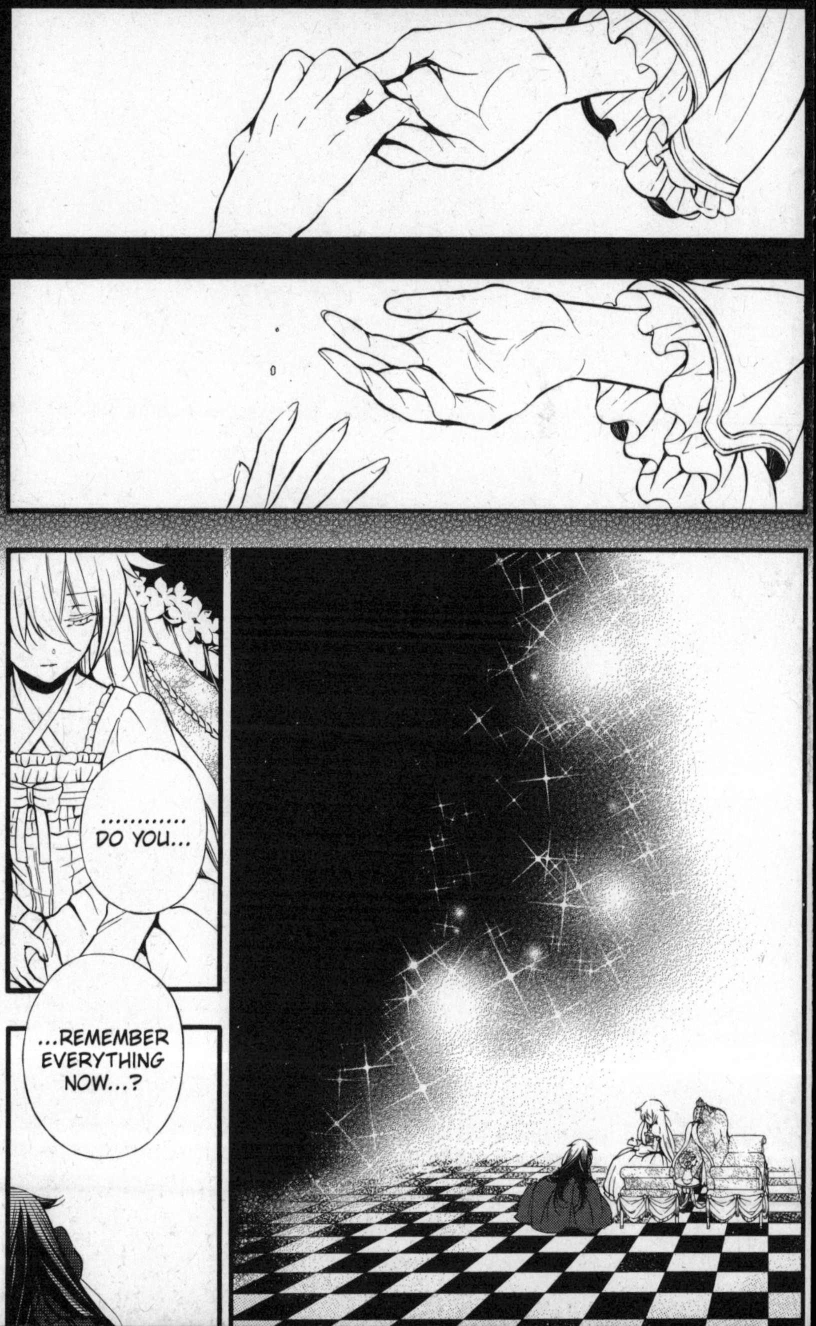
.... DO YOU...
...REMEMBER EVERYTHING NOW...?

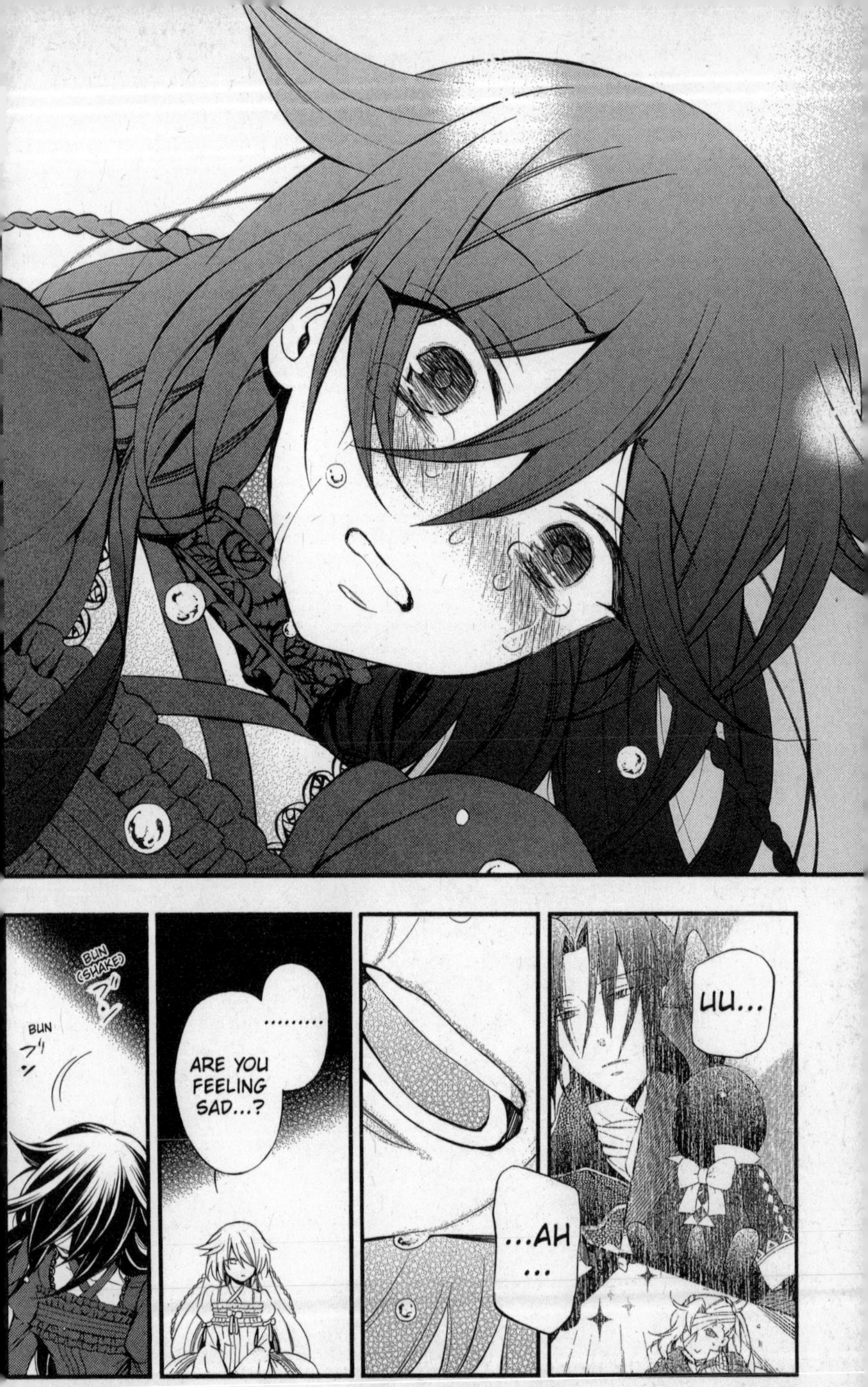
UU...
...AH ...
....
ARE YOU FEELING SAD...?
BUN (SHAKE)
BUN

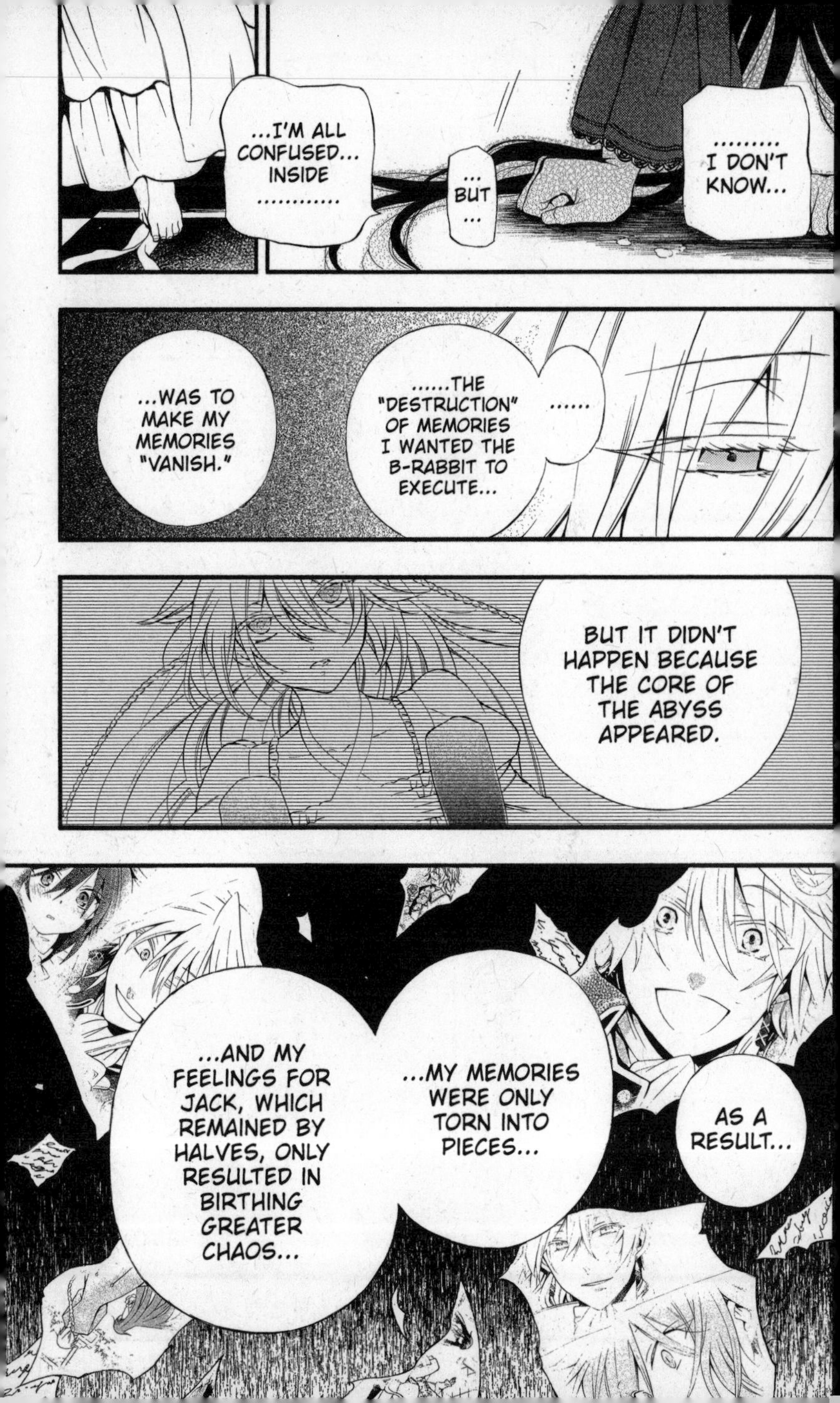
....
I DON'T KNOW...
... BUT ...
...I'M ALL CONFUSED... INSIDE ....
......
......THE "DESTRUCTION" OF MEMORIES I WANTED THE B-RABBIT TO EXECUTE...
...WAS TO MAKE MY MEMORIES "VANISH."
BUT IT DIDN'T HAPPEN BECAUSE THE CORE OF THE ABYSS APPEARED.
AS A RESULT...
...MY MEMORIES WERE ONLY TORN INTO PIECES...
...AND MY FEELINGS FOR JACK, WHICH REMAINED BY HALVES, ONLY RESULTED IN BIRTHING GREATER CHAOS...

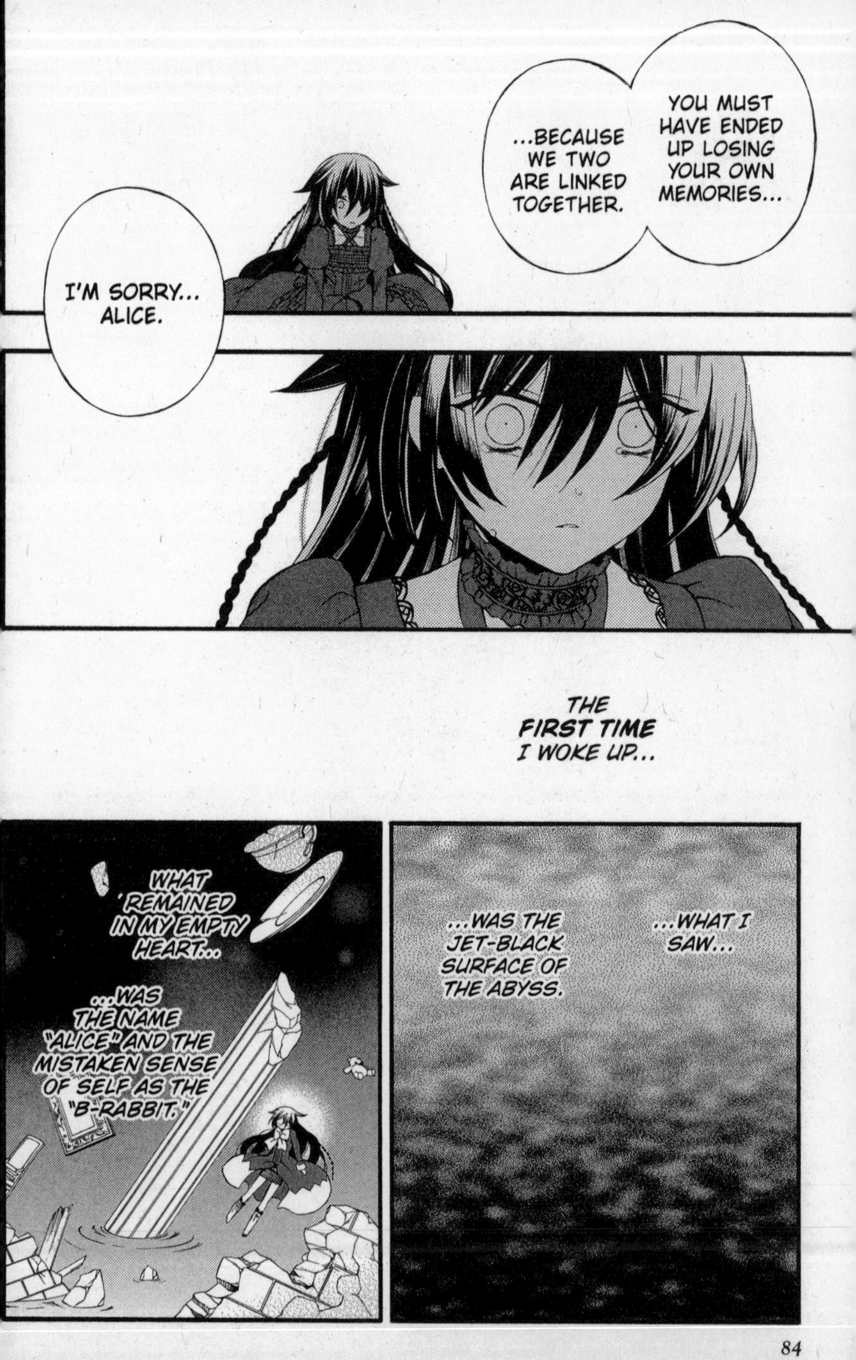
YOU MUST HAVE ENDED UP LOSING YOUR OWN MEMORIES...
...BECAUSE WE TWO ARE LINKED TOGETHER.
I'M SORRY... ALICE.
THE FIRST TIME I WOKE UP...
...WHAT I SAW...
...WAS THE JET-BLACK SURFACE OF THE ABYSS.
WHAT REMAINED IN MY EMPTY HEART...
...WAS THE NAME "ALICE" AND THE MISTAKEN SENSE OF SELF AS THE "B-RABBIT."

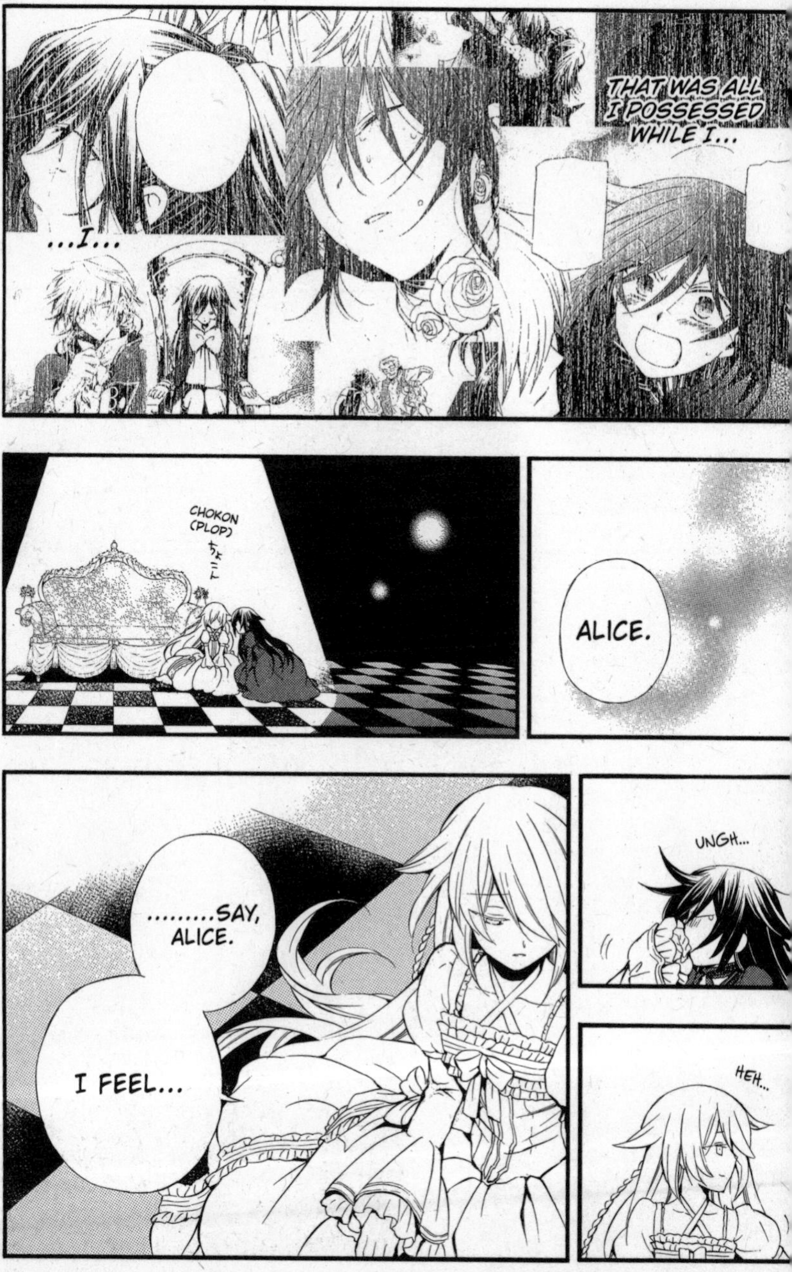
THAT WAS ALL I POSSESSED WHILE I...
...I...
ALICE.
CHOKON (PLOP)
ちょこん
UNGH...
HEH...
.........SAY, ALICE.
I FEEL...

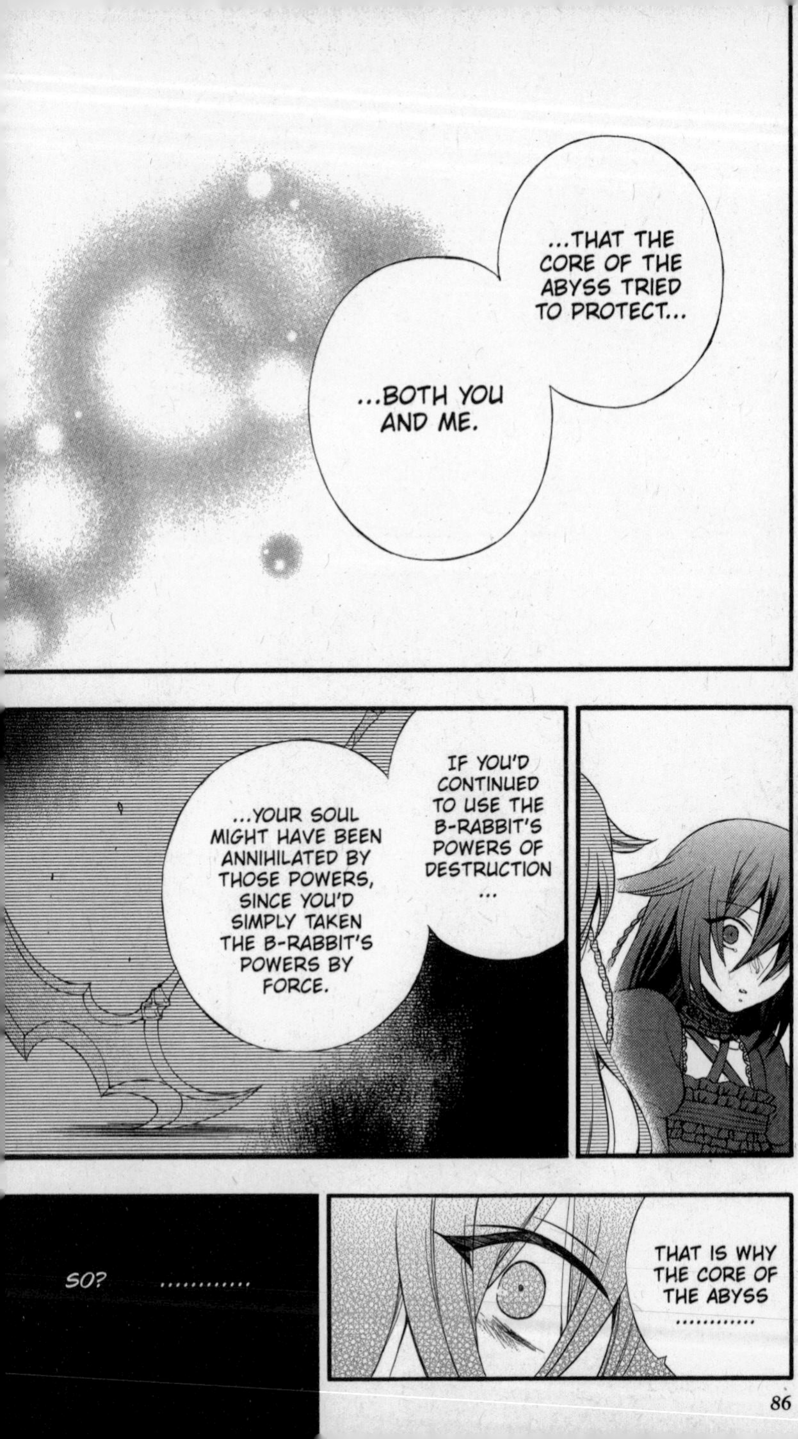
...THAT THE CORE OF THE ABYSS TRIED TO PROTECT...
...BOTH YOU AND ME.
IF YOU'D CONTINUED TO USE THE B-RABBIT'S POWERS OF DESTRUCTION ...
...YOUR SOUL MIGHT HAVE BEEN ANNIHILATED BY THOSE POWERS, SINCE YOU'D SIMPLY TAKEN THE B-RABBIT'S POWERS BY FORCE.
THAT IS WHY THE CORE OF THE ABYSS ....
....
SO?

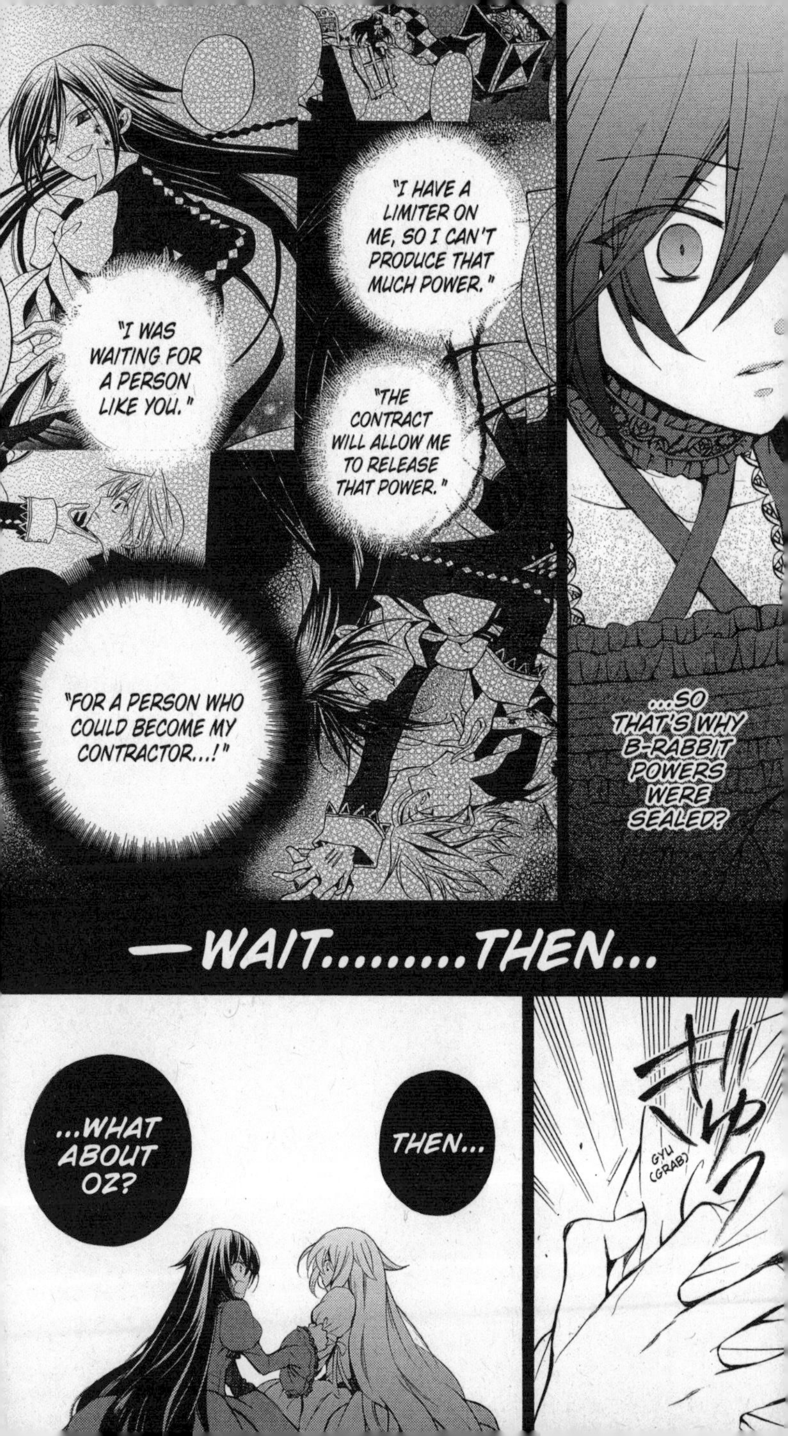
...SO THAT'S WHY B-RABBIT POWERS WERE SEALED?
"I HAVE A LIMITER ON ME, SO I CAN'T PRODUCE THAT MUCH POWER."
"I WAS WAITING FOR A PERSON LIKE YOU."
"THE CONTRACT WILL ALLOW ME TO RELEASE THAT POWER."
"FOR A PERSON WHO COULD BECOME MY CONTRACTOR...!"
—WAIT.........THEN...
GYU (GRAB)
THEN...
...WHAT ABOUT OZ?

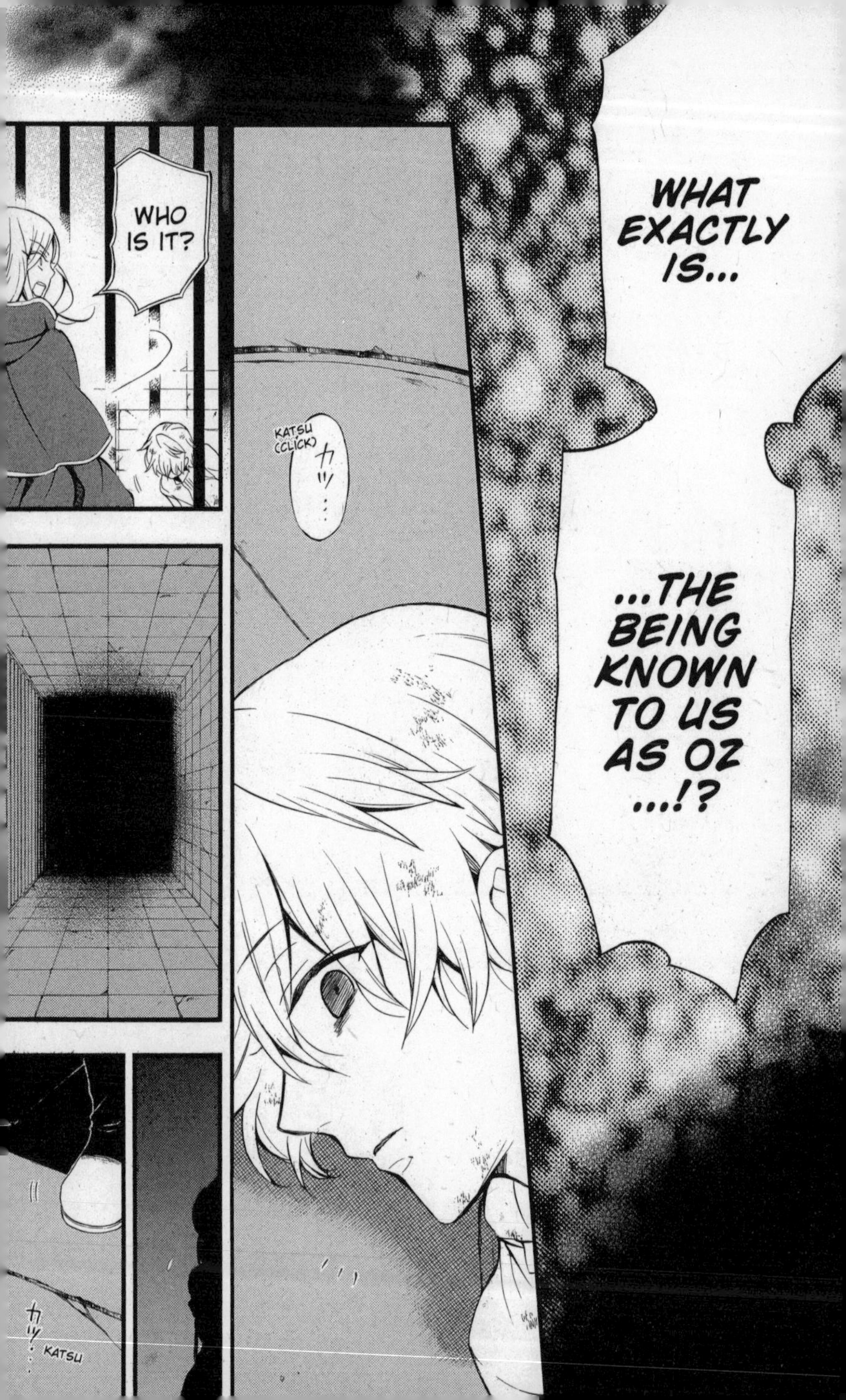
WHAT EXACTLY IS...
...THE BEING KNOWN TO US AS OZ ...!?
KATSU (CLICK)
カッ…
WHO IS IT?
カッ…
KATSU

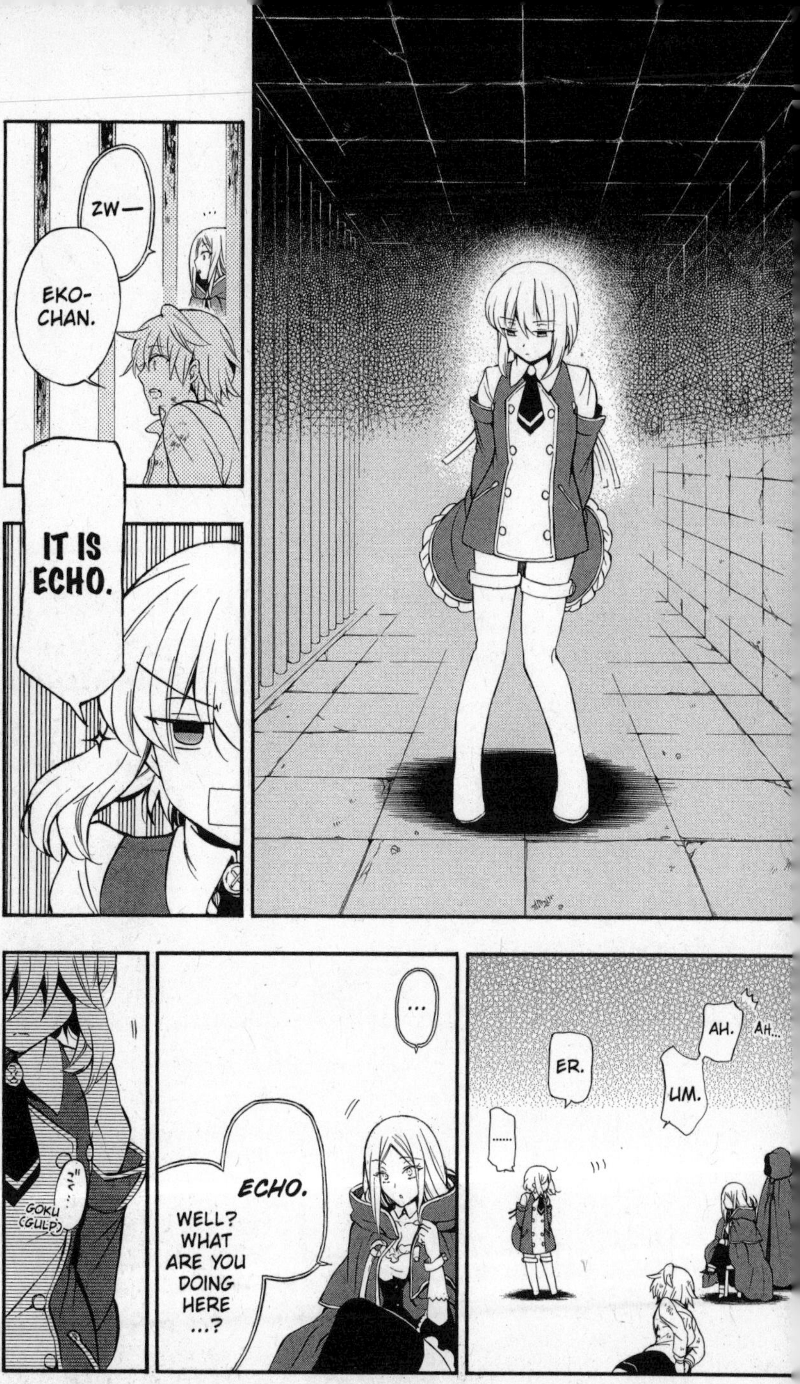
...
ZW—
EKO-CHAN.
IT IS ECHO.
AH...
AH.
UM.
ER.
......
...
ECHO.
WELL? WHAT ARE YOU DOING HERE ...?
GOKU (GULP)

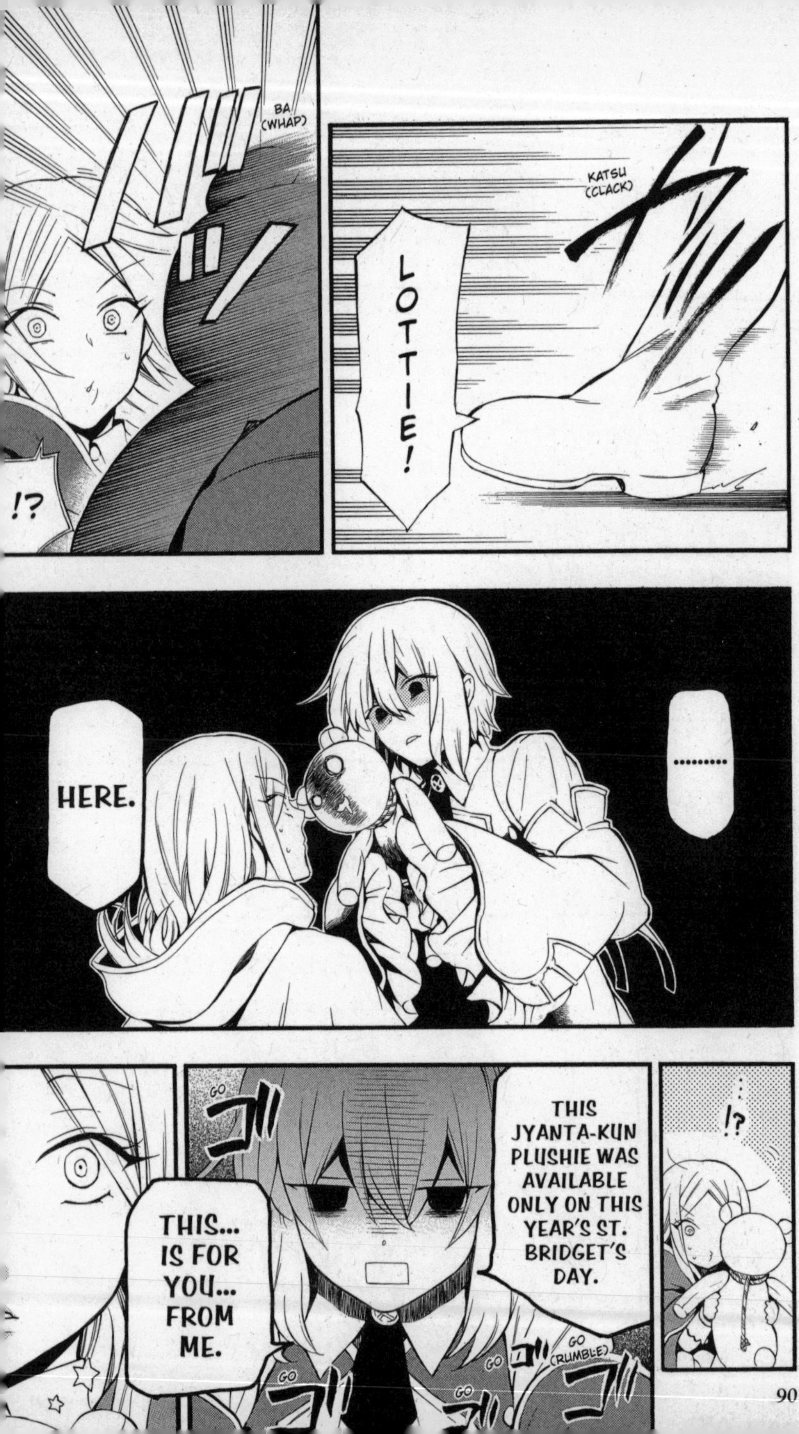
KATSU (CLACK)
LOTTIE!
BA (WHAP)
!?
....
HERE.
...
!?
THIS JYANTA-KUN PLUSHIE WAS AVAILABLE ONLY ON THIS YEAR'S ST. BRIDGET'S DAY.
GO
GO (RUMBLE)
GO
GO
GO
THIS... IS FOR YOU... FROM ME.

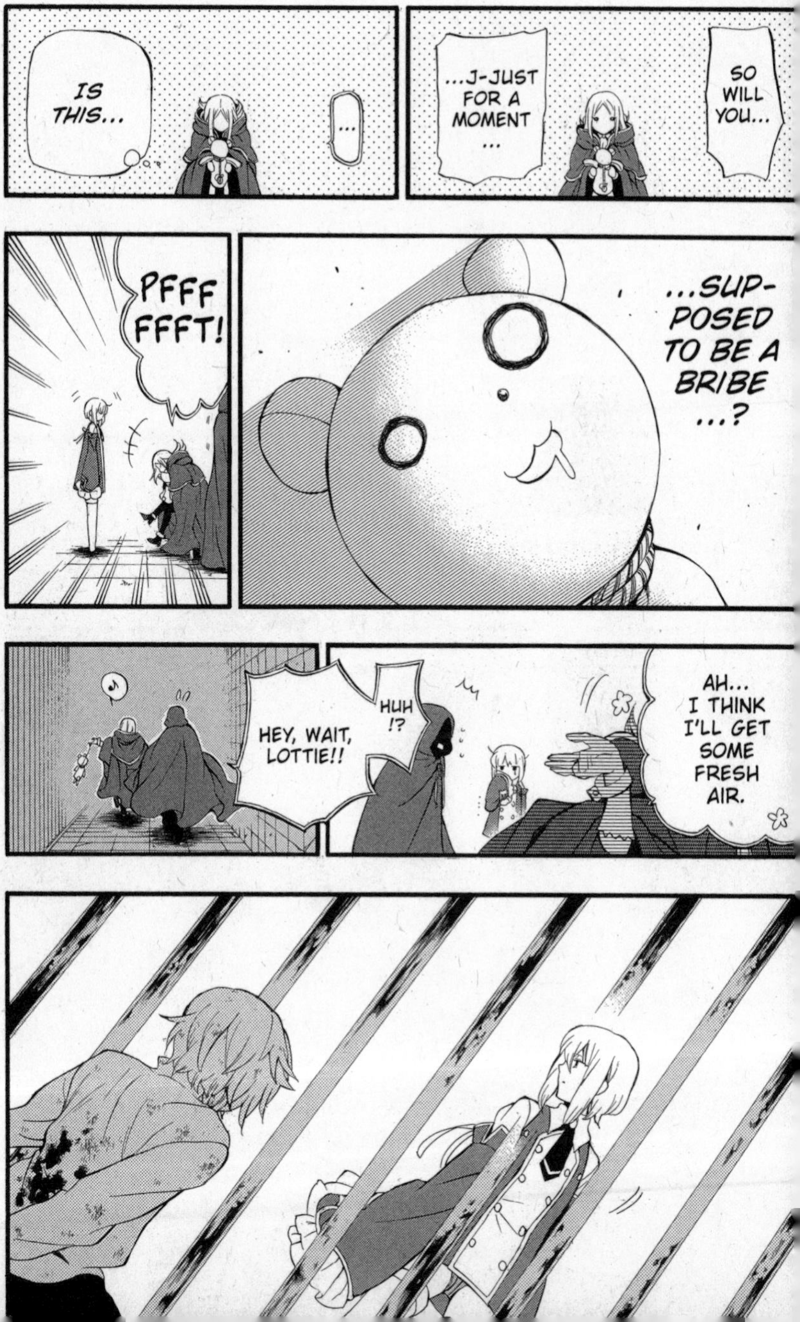
SO WILL YOU...
...J-JUST FOR A MOMENT ...
...
IS THIS...
...SUP-POSED TO BE A BRIBE ...?
PFFF FFFT!
AH... I THINK I'LL GET SOME FRESH AIR.
HUH !?
HEY, WAIT, LOTTIE!!

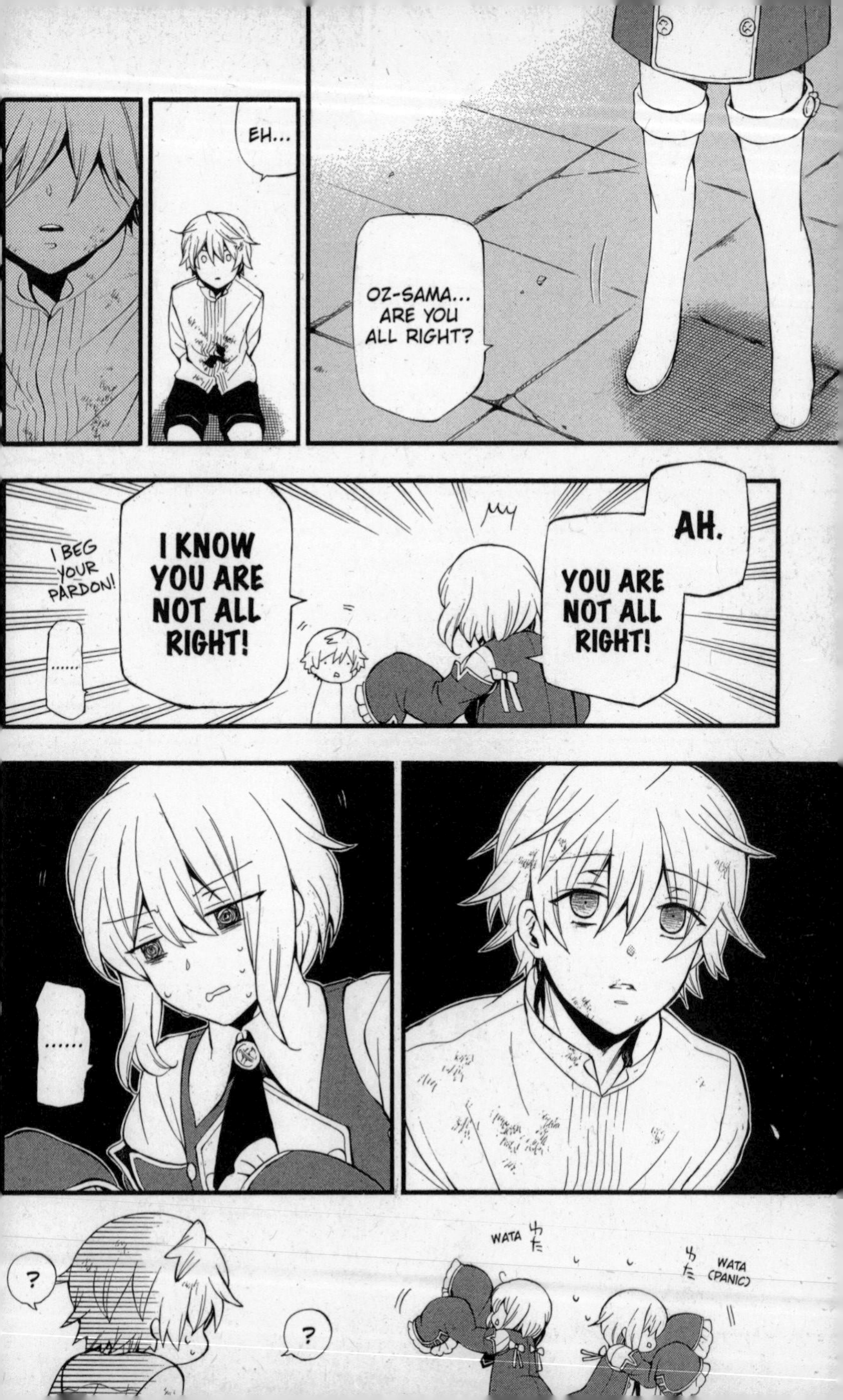

OZ-SAMA... ARE YOU ALL RIGHT?
EH...
AH. YOU ARE NOT ALL RIGHT!
I KNOW YOU ARE NOT ALL RIGHT!
I BEG YOUR PARDON!
......
......
わた
WATA (PANIC)
わた
WATA
?
?

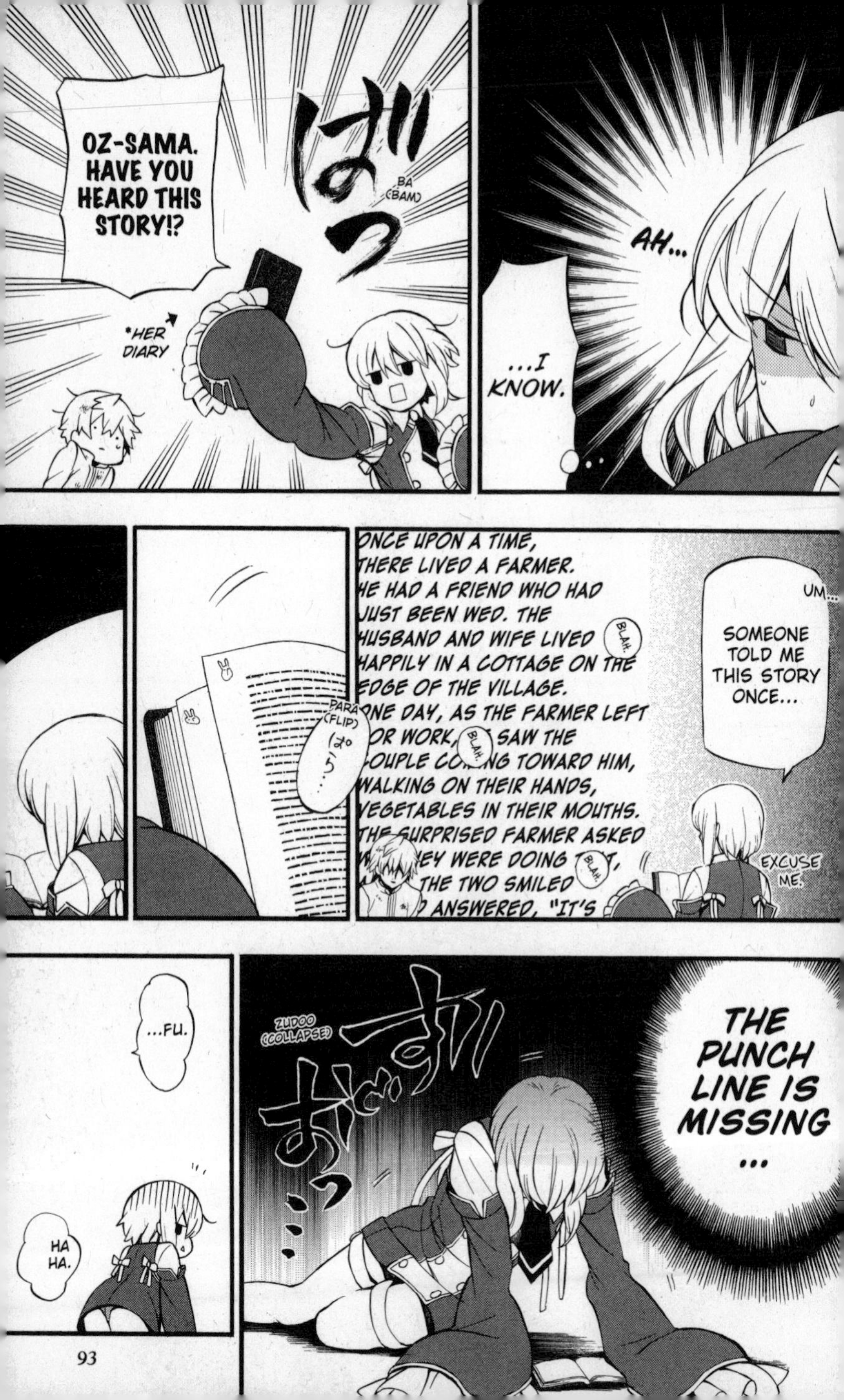
AH...
...I KNOW.
OZ-SAMA. HAVE YOU HEARD THIS STORY!?
ばっ
BA (BAM)
*HER DIARY
UM...
SOMEONE TOLD ME THIS STORY ONCE...
EXCUSE ME.
ONCE UPON A TIME, THERE LIVED A FARMER. HE HAD A FRIEND WHO HAD JUST BEEN WED. THE HUSBAND AND WIFE LIVED HAPPILY IN A COTTAGE ON THE EDGE OF THE VILLAGE. ONE DAY, AS THE FARMER LEFT FOR WORK, SAW THE COUPLE CO NG TOWARD HIM, WALKING ON THEIR HANDS, VEGETABLES IN THEIR MOUTHS. THE SURPRISED FARMER ASKED EY WERE DOING THE TWO SMILED ANSWERED, "IT'S
BLAH.
BLAH.
BLAH.
PARA (FLIP)
ぱら…
ZUDOO (COLLAPSE)
ずぅん
THE PUNCH LINE IS MISSING...
...FU.
HA HA.

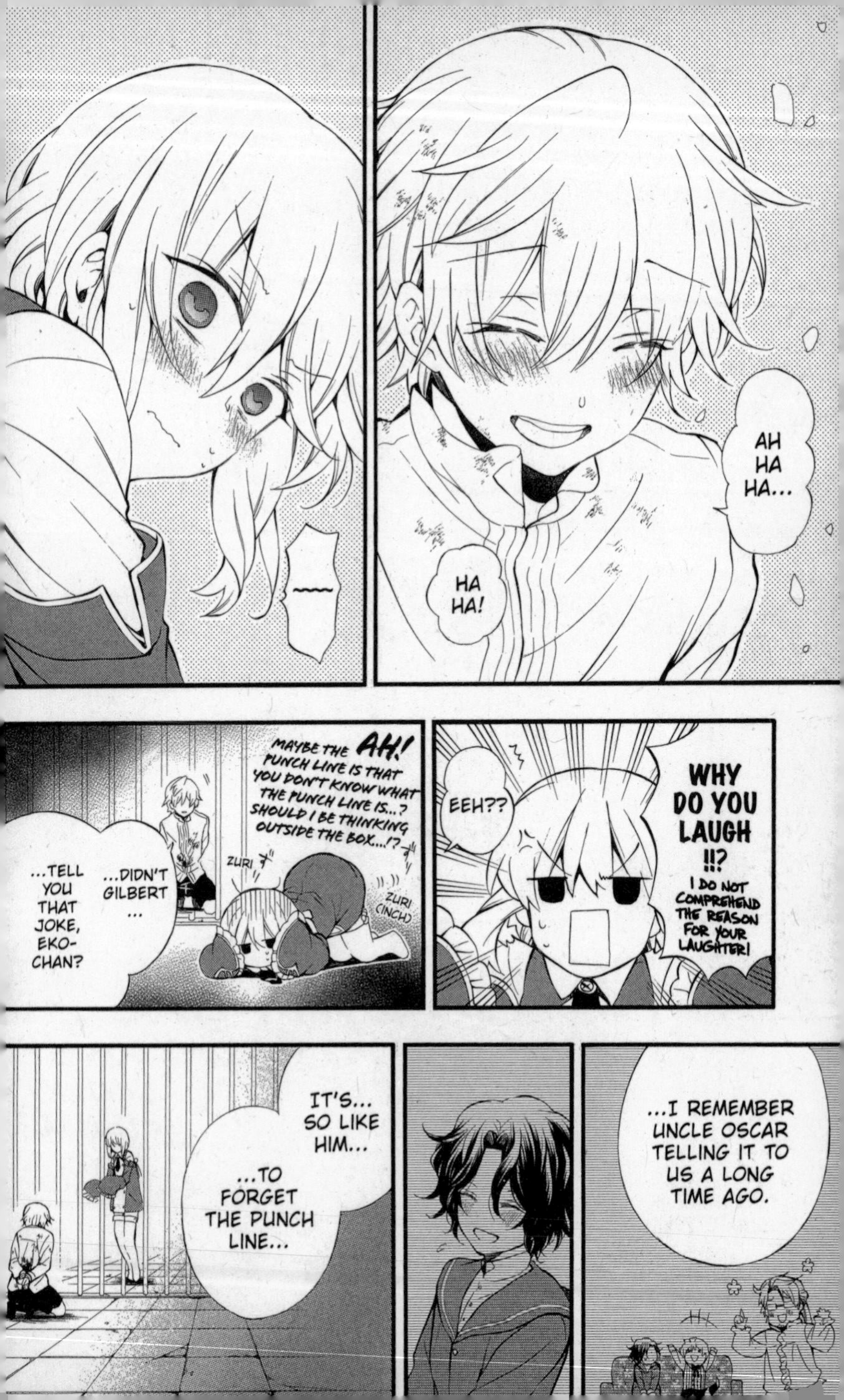
AH HA HA...
HA HA!
~~~
EEH??
WHY DO YOU LAUGH!!?
I DO NOT COMPREHEND THE REASON FOR YOUR LAUGHTER!
AH!
MAYBE THE PUNCH LINE IS THAT YOU DON'T KNOW WHAT THE PUNCH LINE IS...? SHOULD I BE THINKING OUTSIDE THE BOX...!?
ZURI
ZURI (INCH)
...DIDN'T GILBERT...
...TELL YOU THAT JOKE, EKO-CHAN?
...I REMEMBER UNCLE OSCAR TELLING IT TO US A LONG TIME AGO.
IT'S... SO LIKE HIM...
...TO FORGET THE PUNCH LINE...
~~~

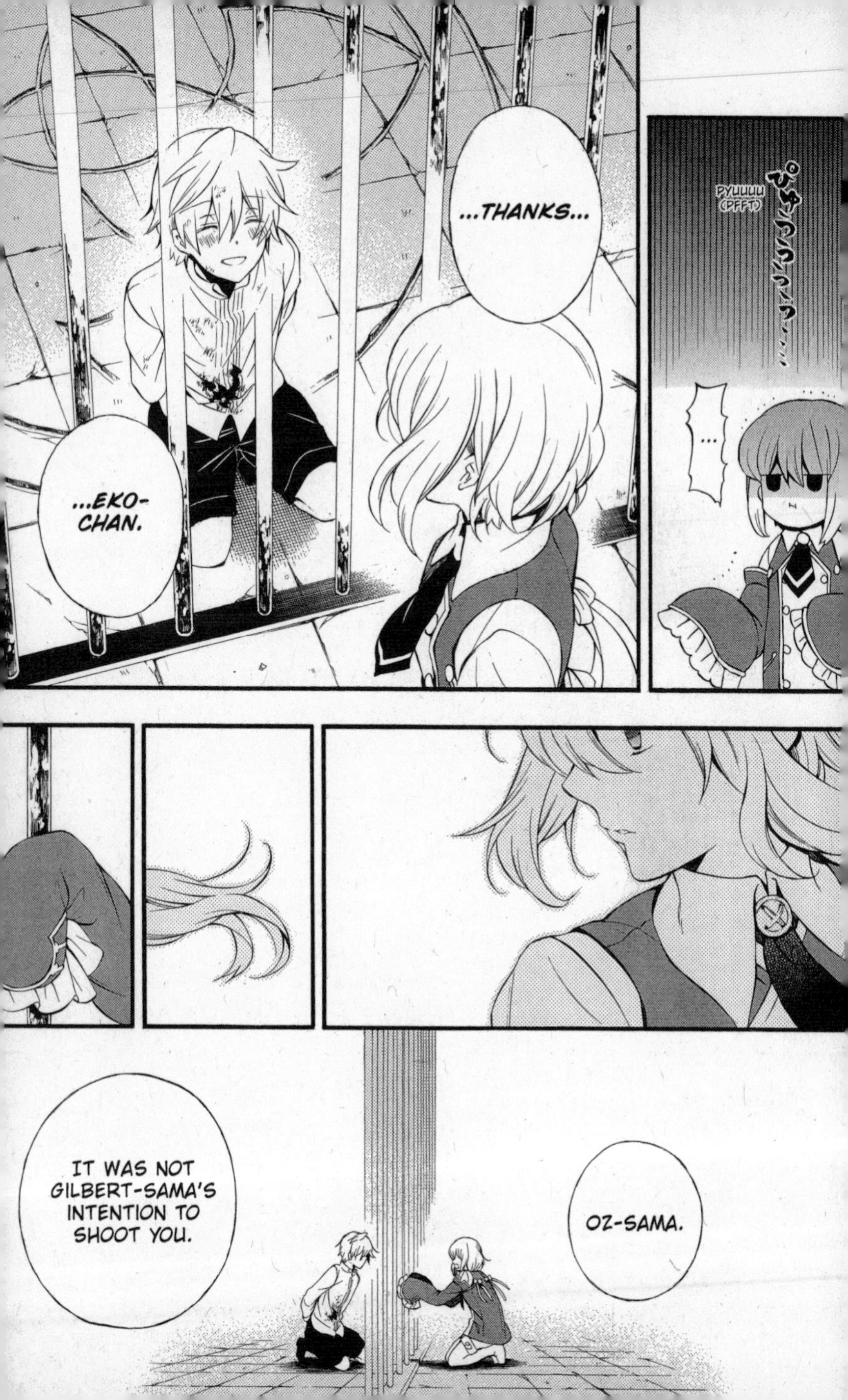
PYUUUU (PFFT)
...
...THANKS...
...EKO-CHAN.
OZ-SAMA.
IT WAS NOT GILBERT-SAMA'S INTENTION TO SHOOT YOU.

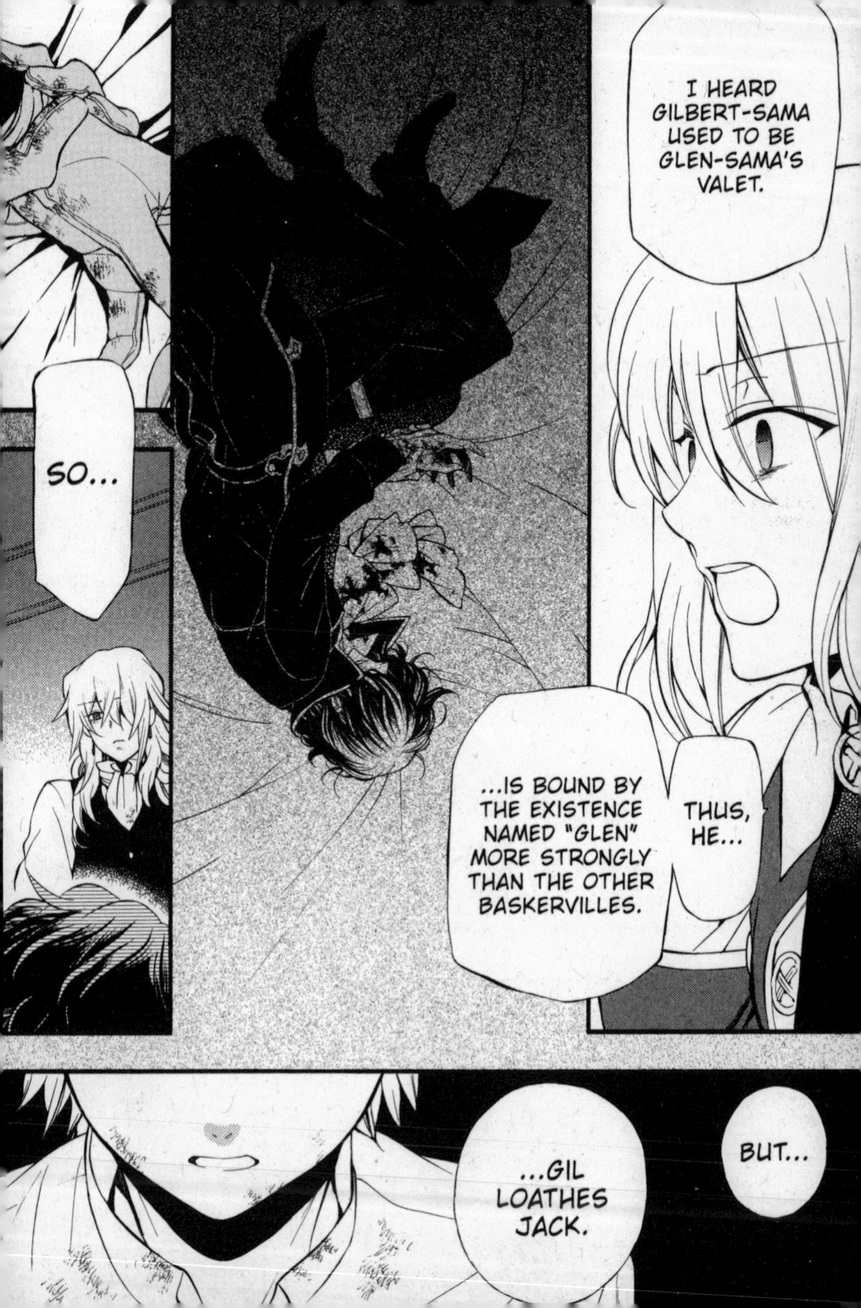
I HEARD GILBERT-SAMA USED TO BE GLEN-SAMA'S VALET.
THUS, HE...
...IS BOUND BY THE EXISTENCE NAMED "GLEN" MORE STRONGLY THAN THE OTHER BASKERVILLES.
SO...
BUT...
...GIL LOATHES JACK.

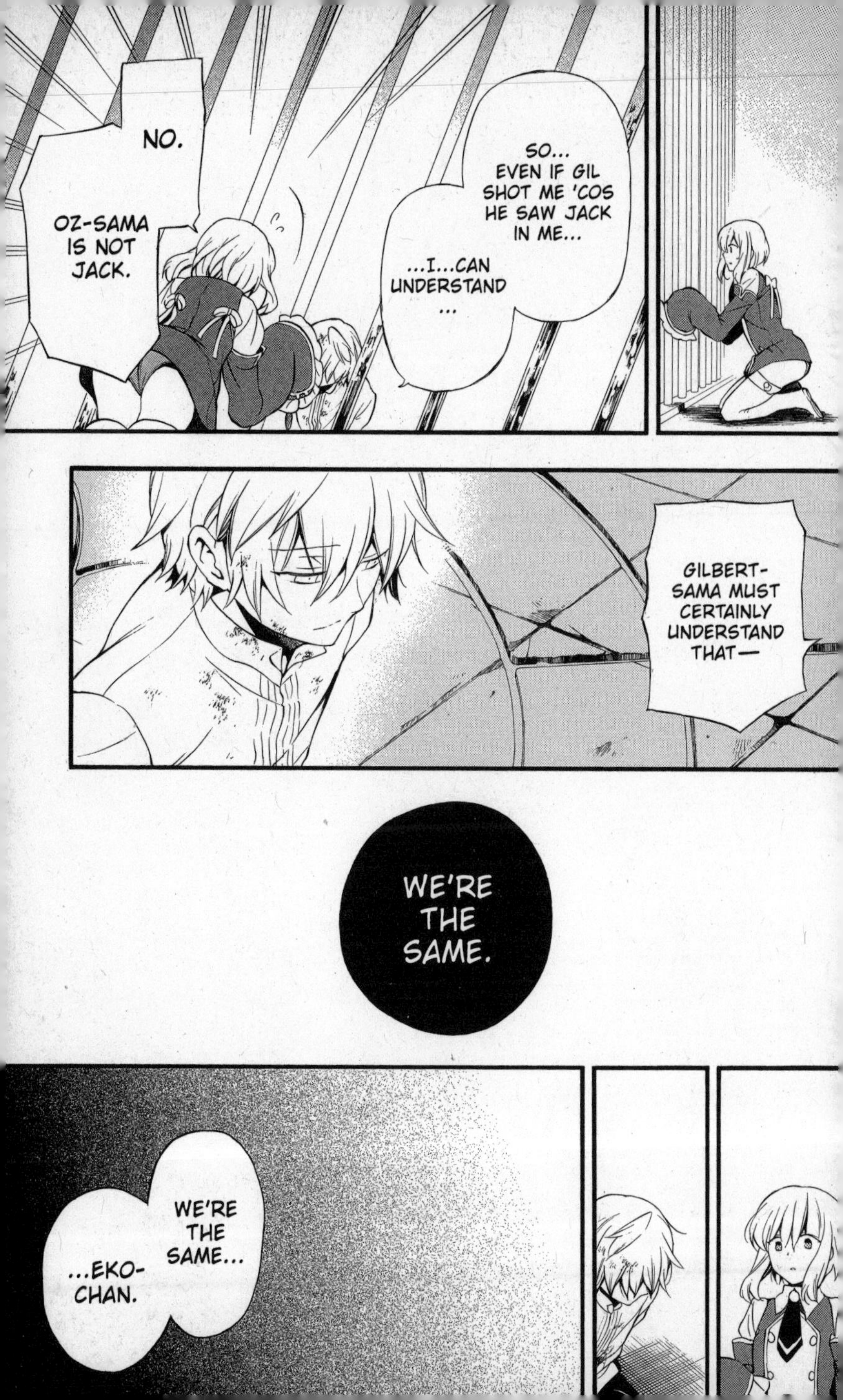
SO... EVEN IF GIL SHOT ME 'COS HE SAW JACK IN ME...
...I...CAN UNDERSTAND ...
NO.
OZ-SAMA IS NOT JACK.
GILBERT-SAMA MUST CERTAINLY UNDERSTAND THAT—
WE'RE THE SAME.
WE'RE THE SAME...
...EKO-CHAN.

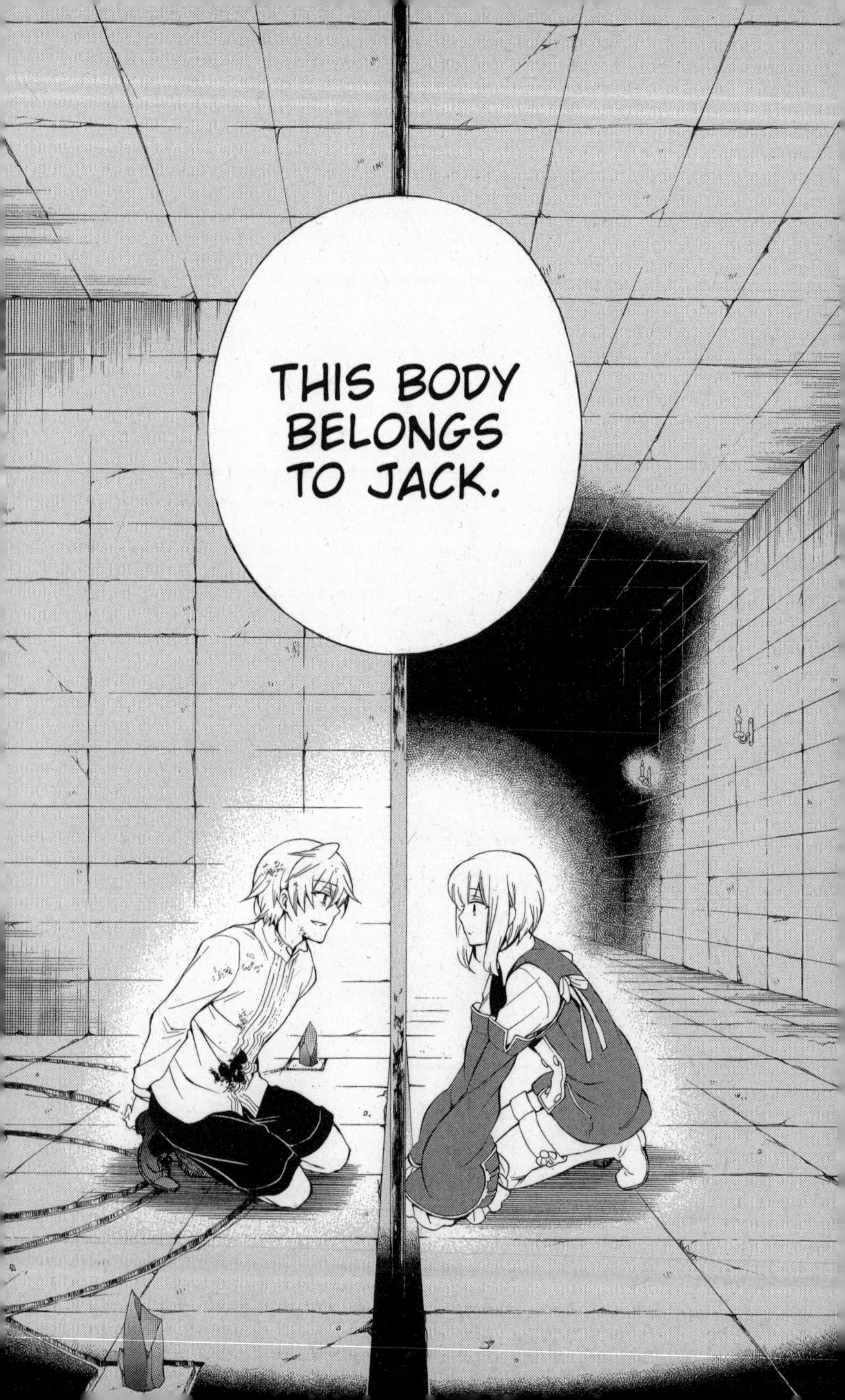
THIS BODY BELONGS TO JACK.

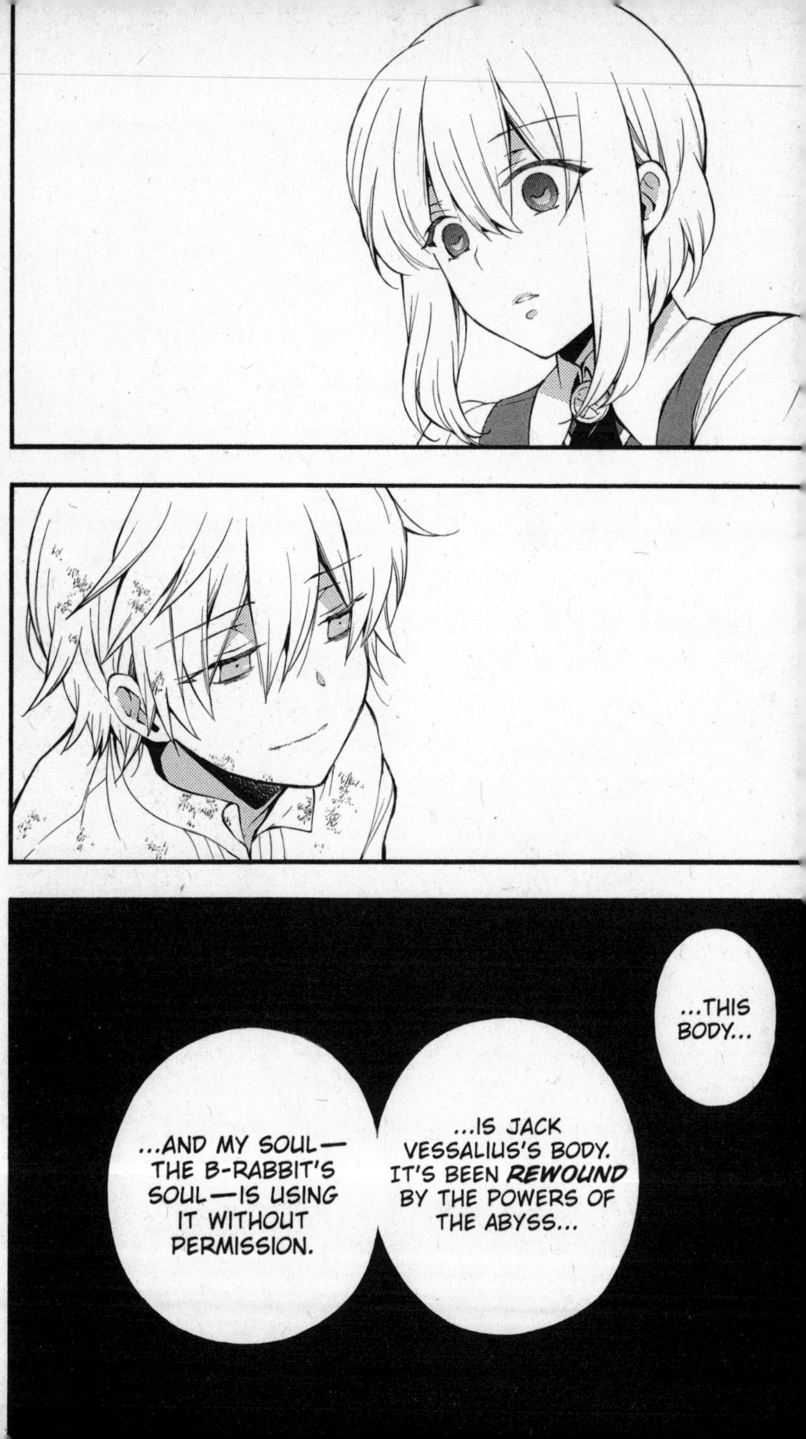
...THIS BODY...
...IS JACK VESSALIUS'S BODY. IT'S BEEN *REWOUND* BY THE POWERS OF THE ABYSS...
...AND MY SOUL—THE B-RABBIT'S SOUL—IS USING IT WITHOUT PERMISSION.

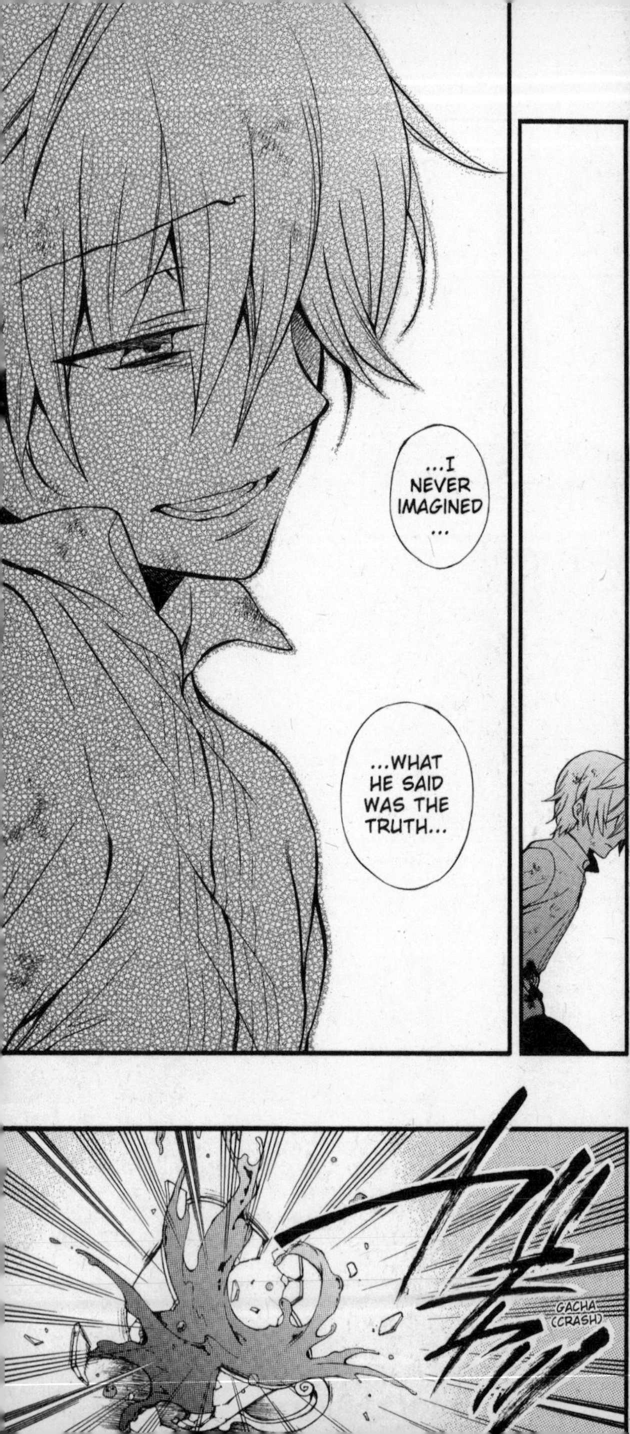
...I NEVER IMAGINED ...
...WHAT HE SAID WAS THE TRUTH...
GACHA (CRASH)

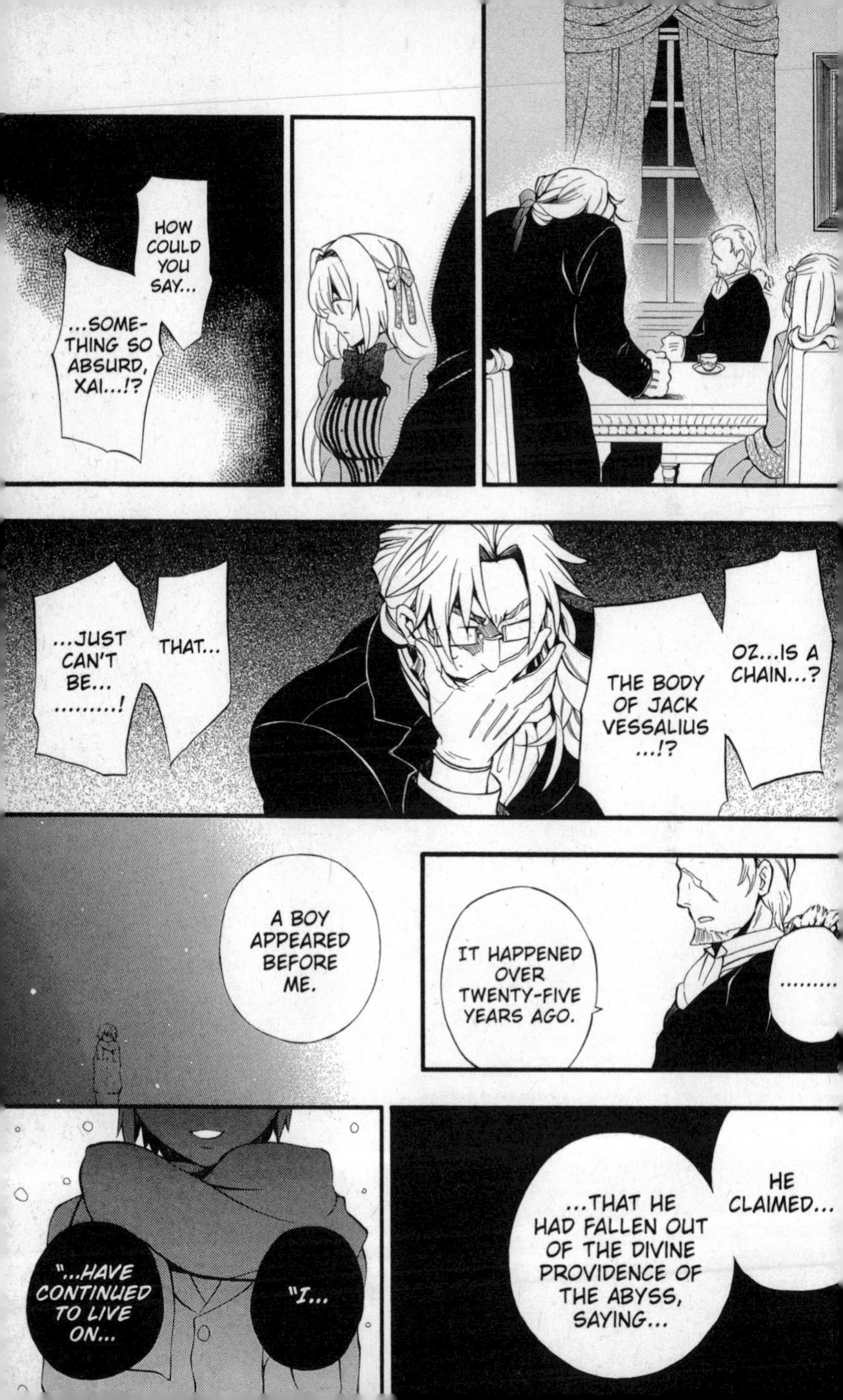
HOW COULD YOU SAY...
...SOMETHING SO ABSURD, XAI...!?
OZ...IS A CHAIN...?
THE BODY OF JACK VESSALIUS ...!?
THAT...
...JUST CAN'T BE... ....!
....
IT HAPPENED OVER TWENTY-FIVE YEARS AGO.
A BOY APPEARED BEFORE ME.
HE CLAIMED...
...THAT HE HAD FALLEN OUT OF THE DIVINE PROVIDENCE OF THE ABYSS, SAYING...
"I...
"...HAVE CONTINUED TO LIVE ON...

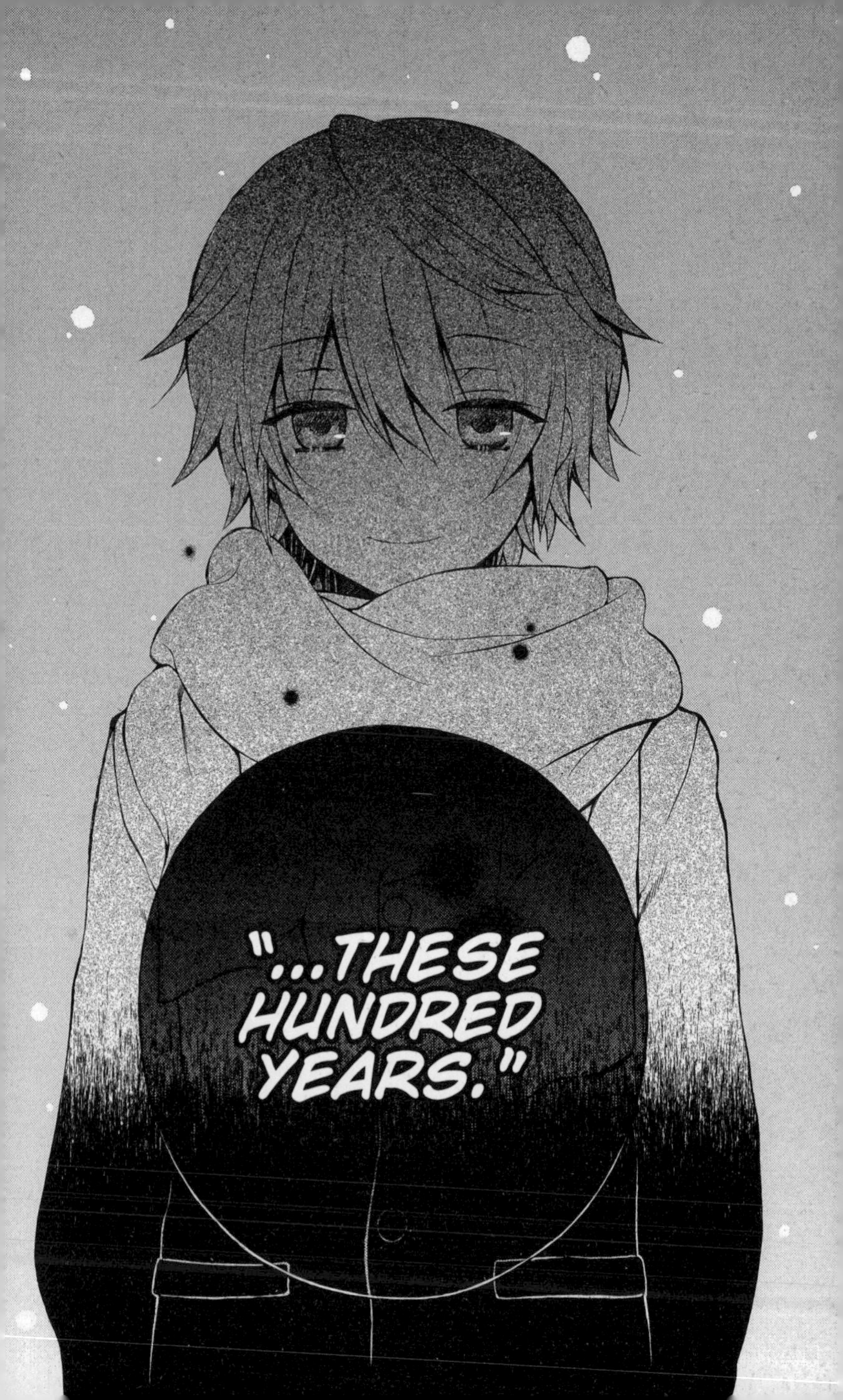
"...THESE HUNDRED YEARS."

Retrace:LXXVII Vacant

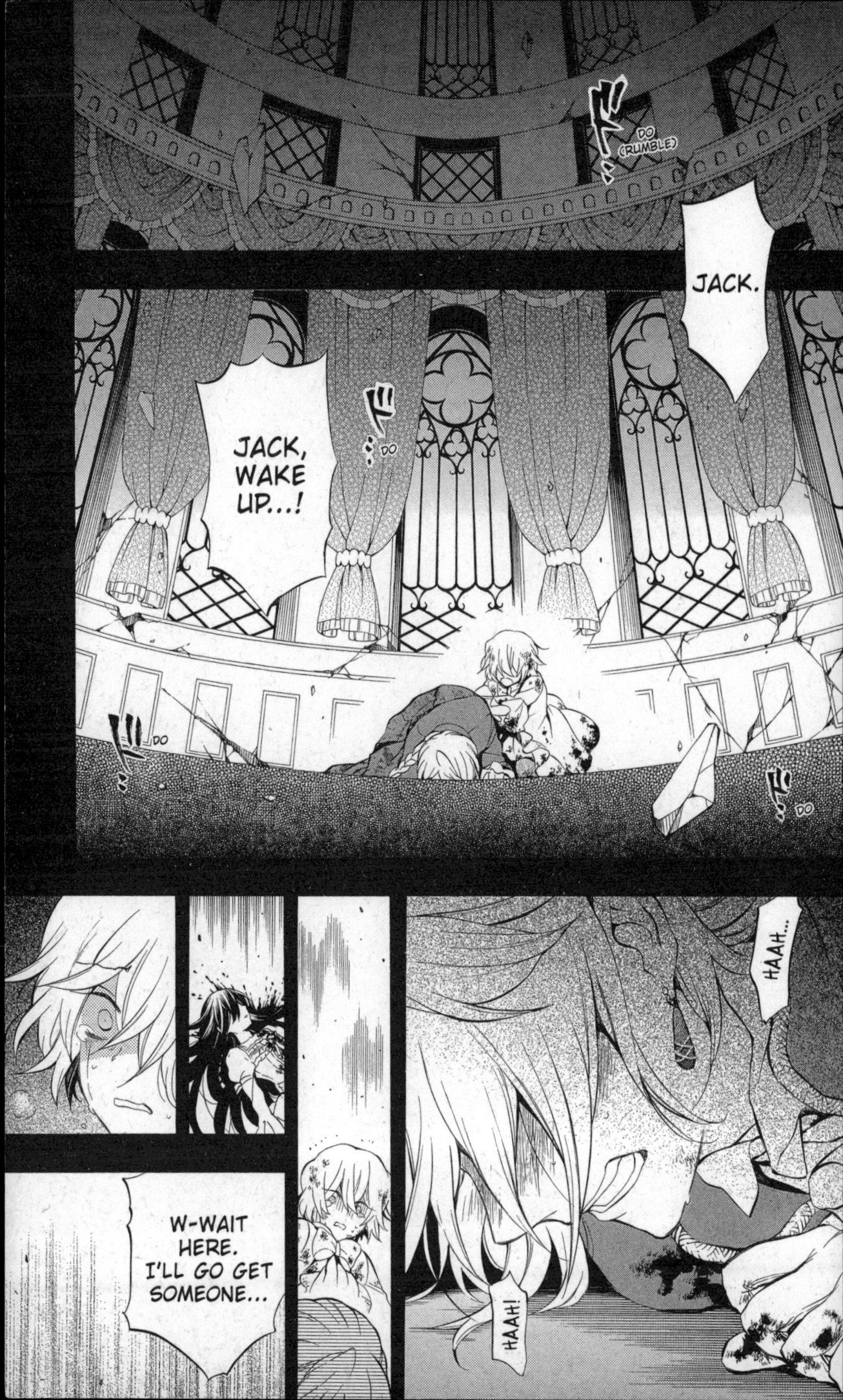
DO (RUMBLE)
JACK.
DO
JACK, WAKE UP...!
DO
DO
HAAH...
HAAH!
W-WAIT HERE. I'LL GO GET SOMEONE...

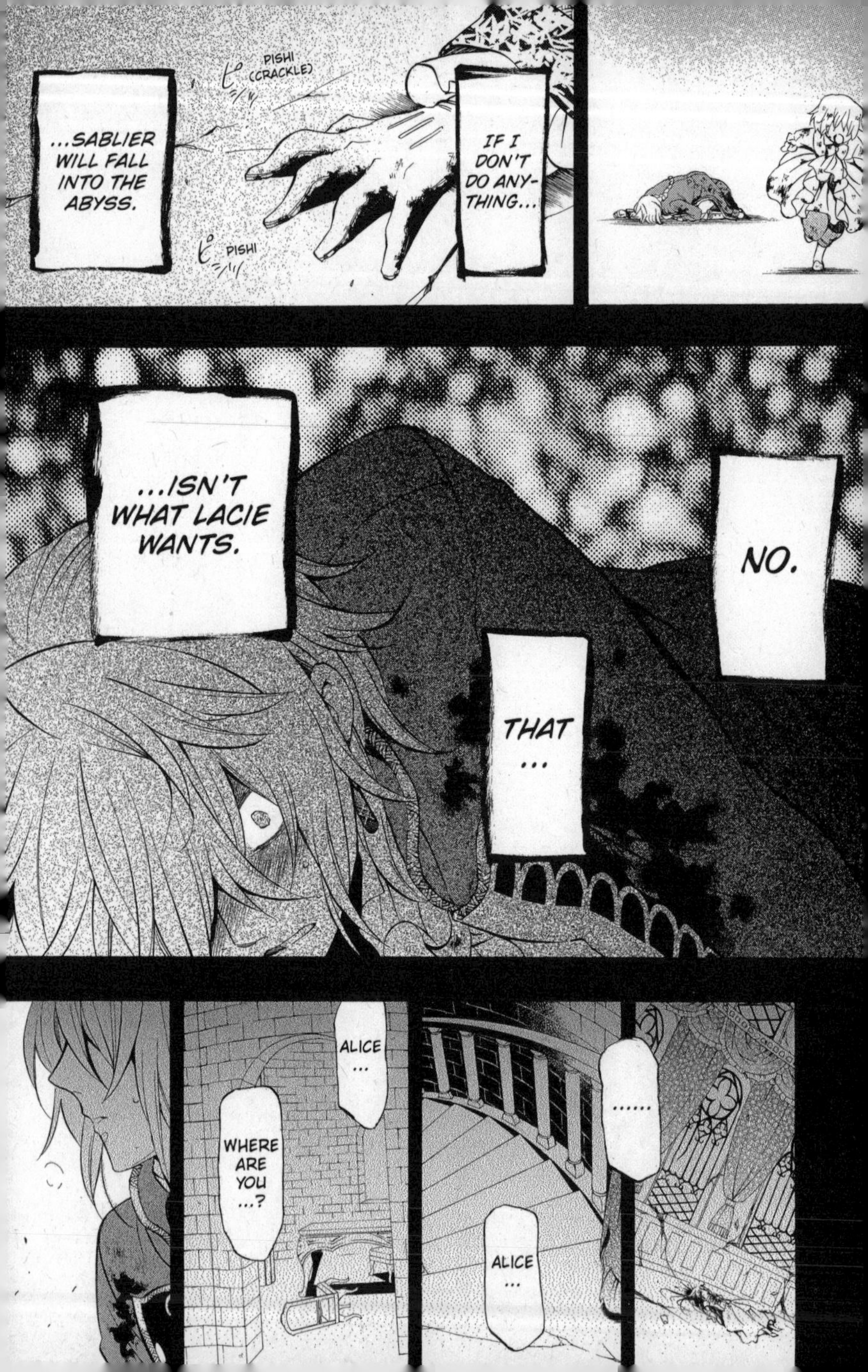
IF I DON'T DO ANY-THING...
PISHI (CRACKLE)
PISHI
...SABLIER WILL FALL INTO THE ABYSS.
NO.
THAT...
...ISN'T WHAT LACIE WANTS.
......
ALICE...
ALICE...
WHERE ARE YOU...?

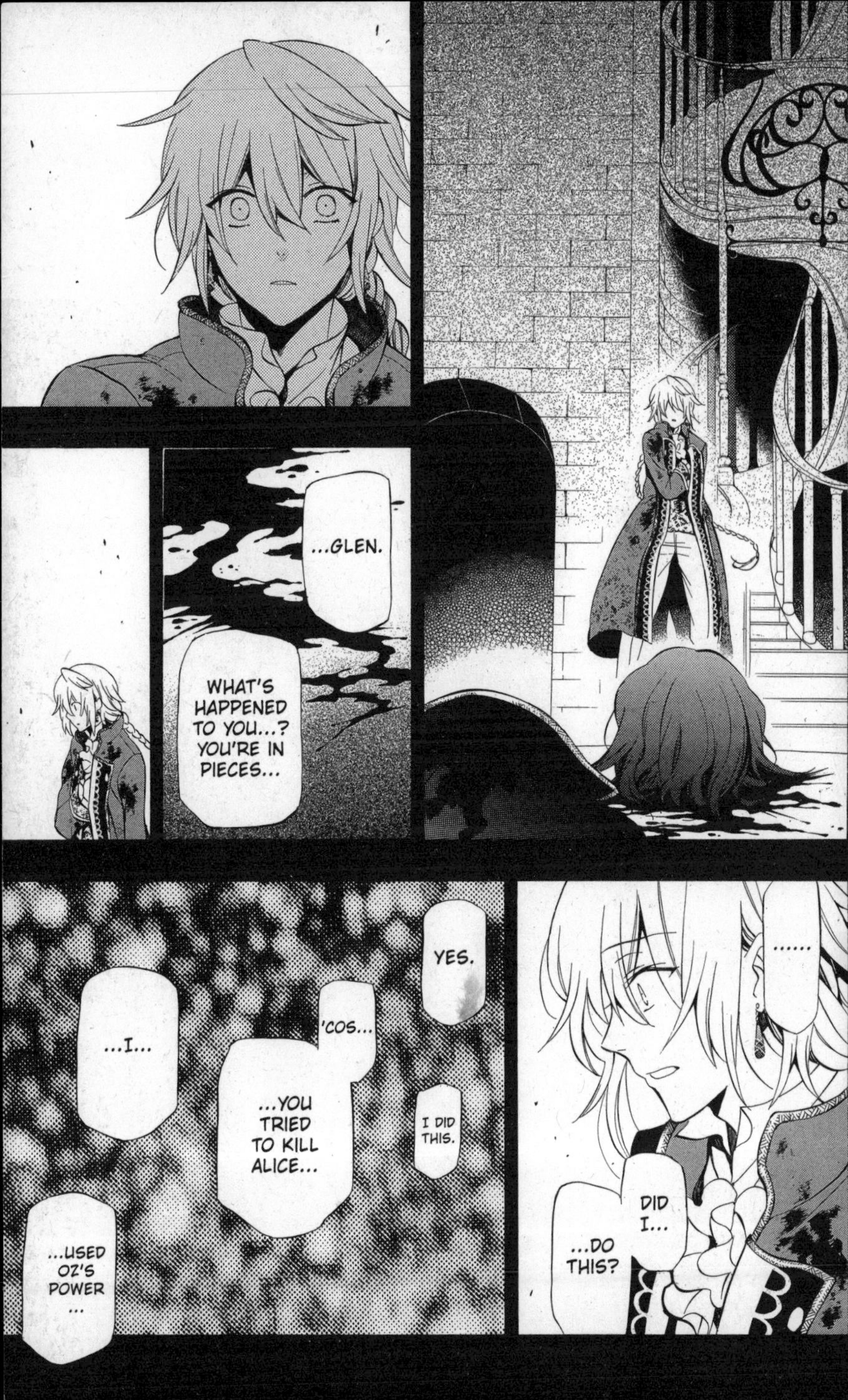
...GLEN.
WHAT'S HAPPENED TO YOU...? YOU'RE IN PIECES...
......
DID I...
...DO THIS?
YES.
I DID THIS.
'COS...
...YOU TRIED TO KILL ALICE...
...I...
...USED OZ'S POWER ...

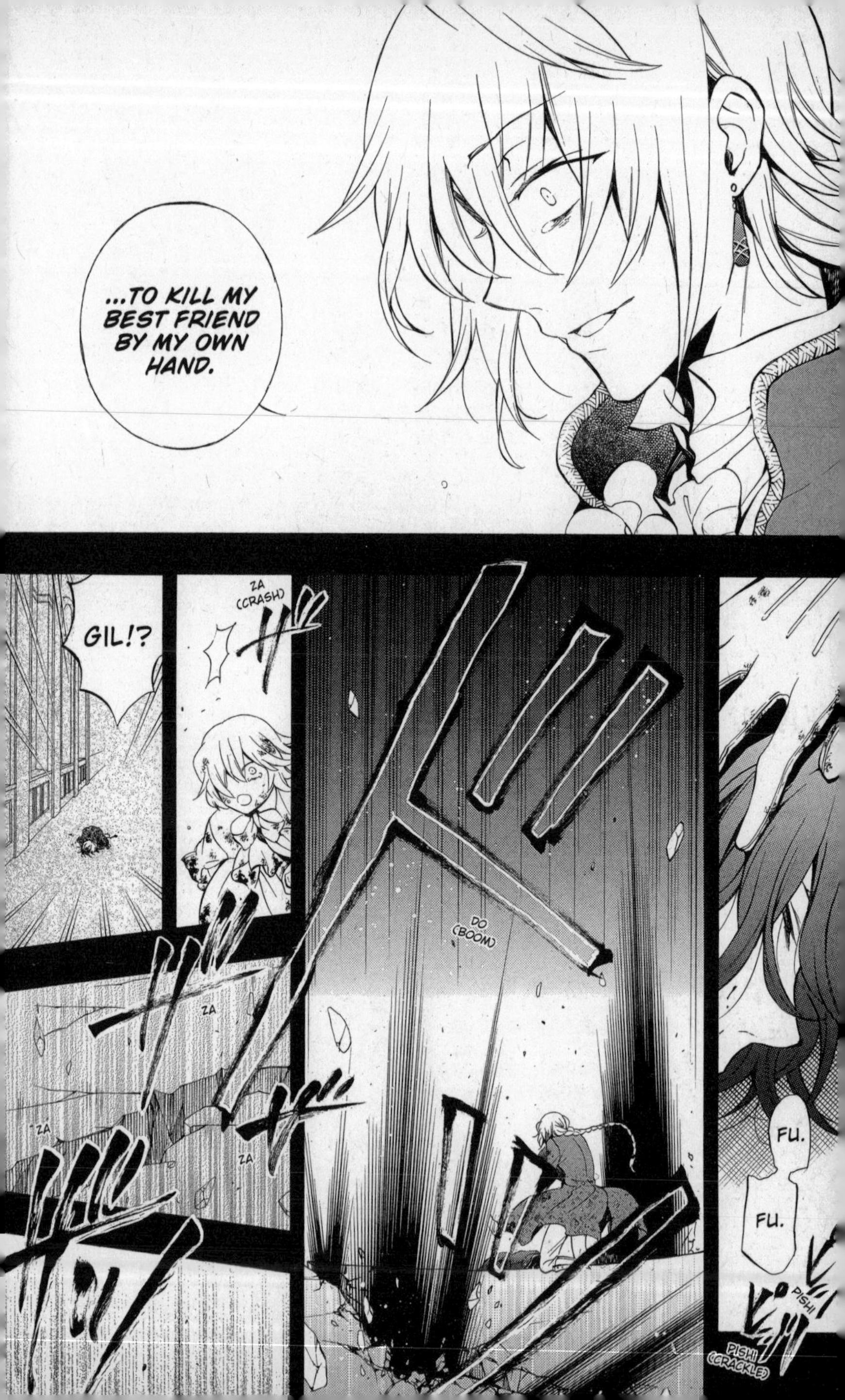
...TO KILL MY BEST FRIEND BY MY OWN HAND.
FU.
FU.
PISHI
PISHI (CRACKLE)
DO (BOOM)
ZA (CRASH)
GIL!?
ZA
ZA
ZA

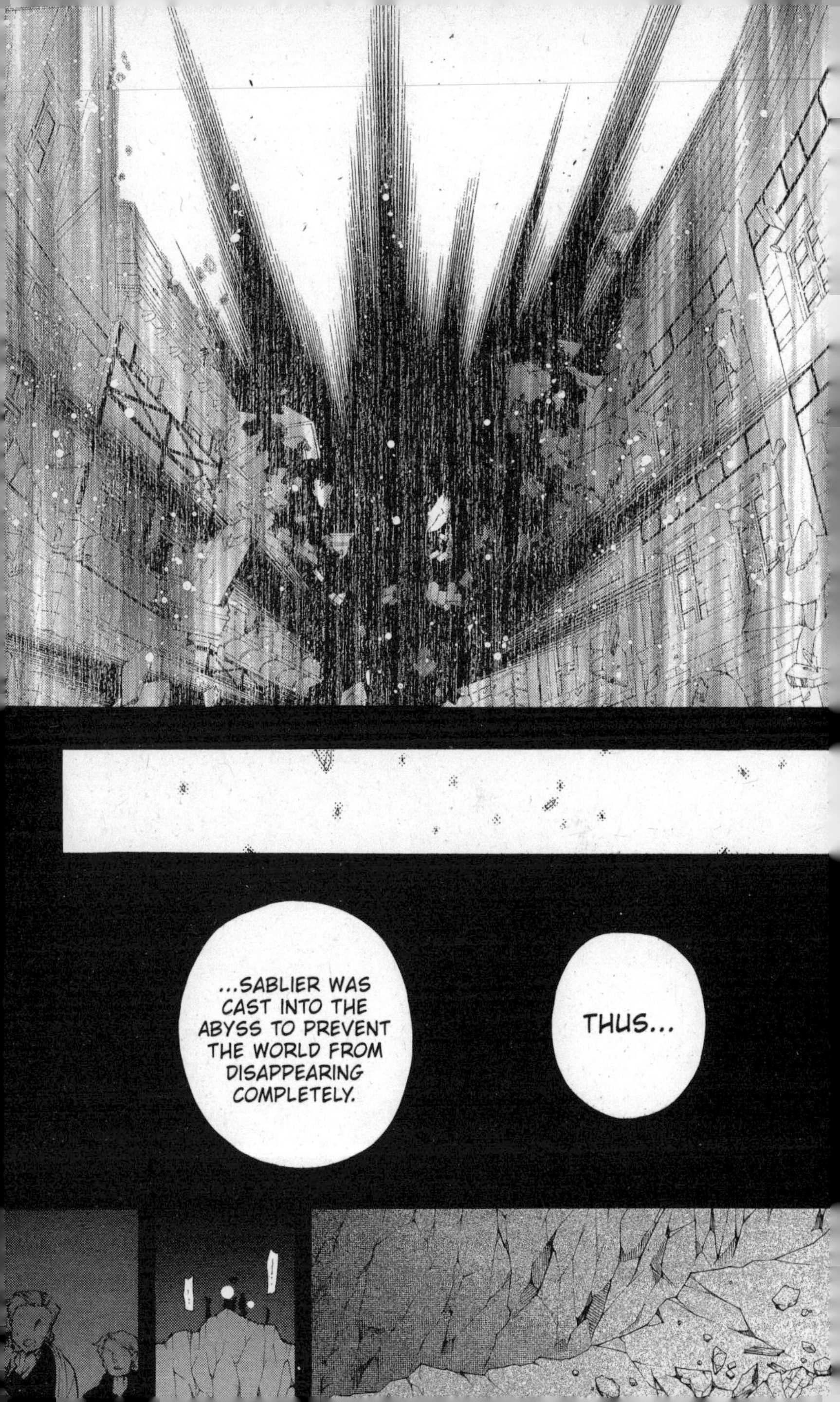
THUS...
...SABLIER WAS CAST INTO THE ABYSS TO PREVENT THE WORLD FROM DISAPPEARING COMPLETELY.

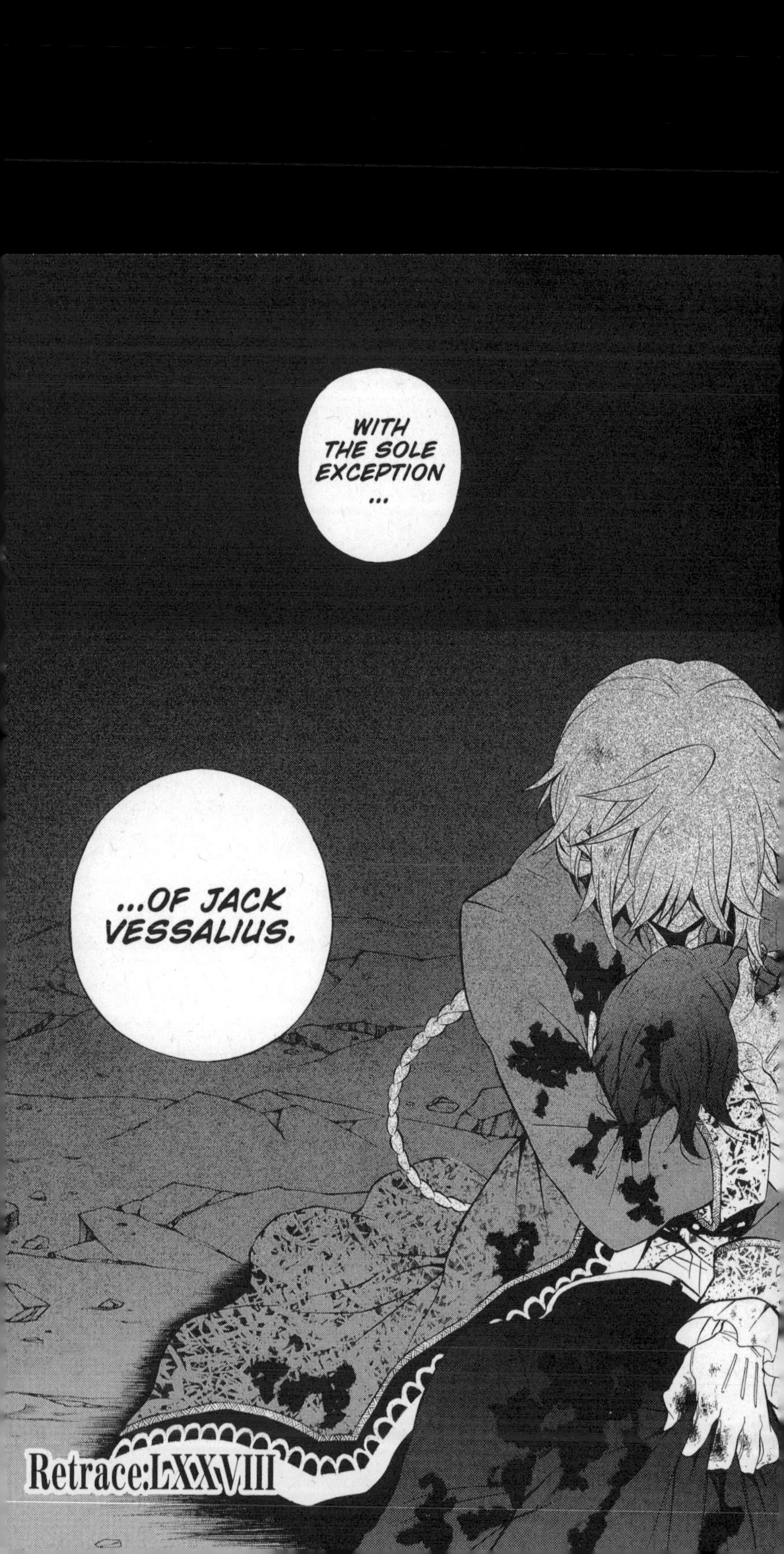
WITH THE SOLE EXCEPTION ...
...OF JACK VESSALIUS.
Retrace:LXXVIII

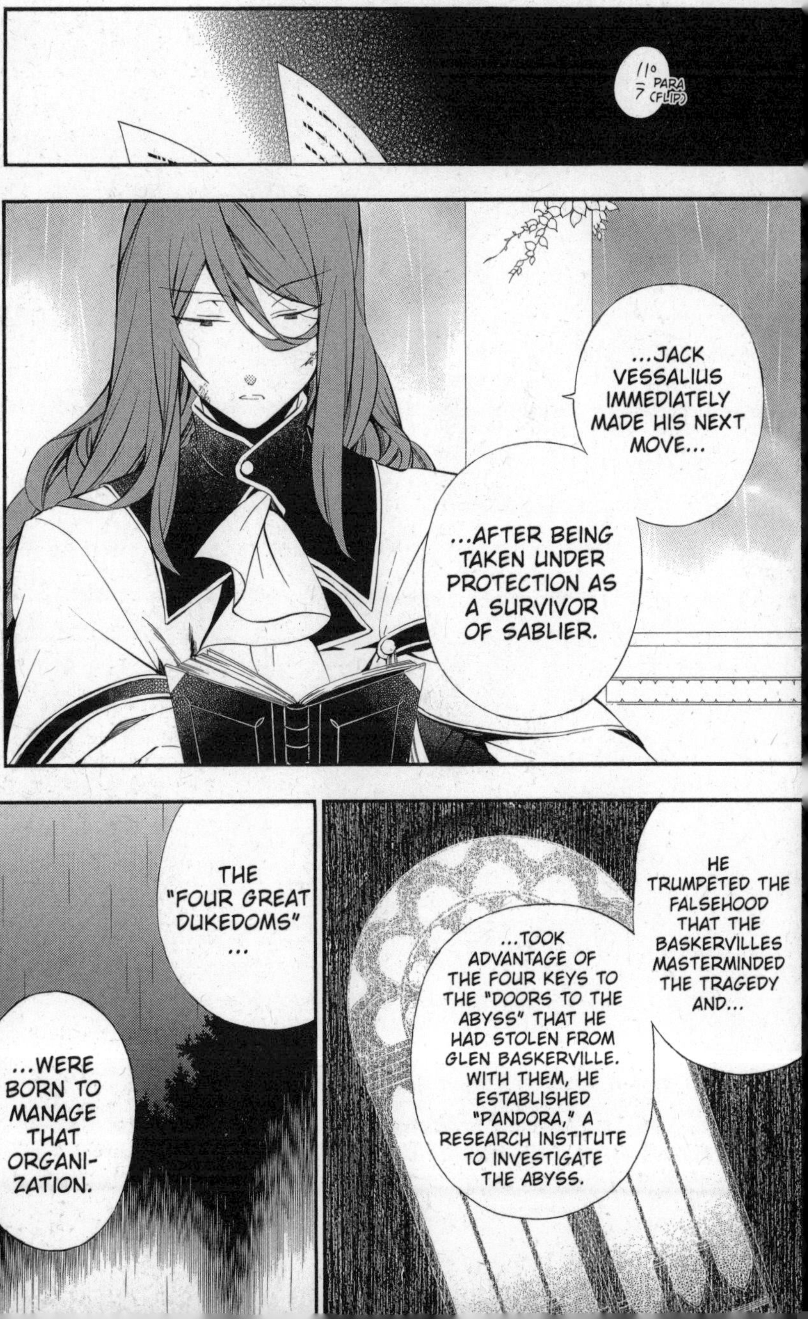
PARA (FLIP)
...JACK VESSALIUS IMMEDIATELY MADE HIS NEXT MOVE...
...AFTER BEING TAKEN UNDER PROTECTION AS A SURVIVOR OF SABLIER.
HE TRUMPETED THE FALSEHOOD THAT THE BASKERVILLES MASTERMINDED THE TRAGEDY AND...
...TOOK ADVANTAGE OF THE FOUR KEYS TO THE "DOORS TO THE ABYSS" THAT HE HAD STOLEN FROM GLEN BASKERVILLE. WITH THEM, HE ESTABLISHED "PANDORA," A RESEARCH INSTITUTE TO INVESTIGATE THE ABYSS.
THE "FOUR GREAT DUKEDOMS" ...
...WERE BORN TO MANAGE THAT ORGANI-ZATION.

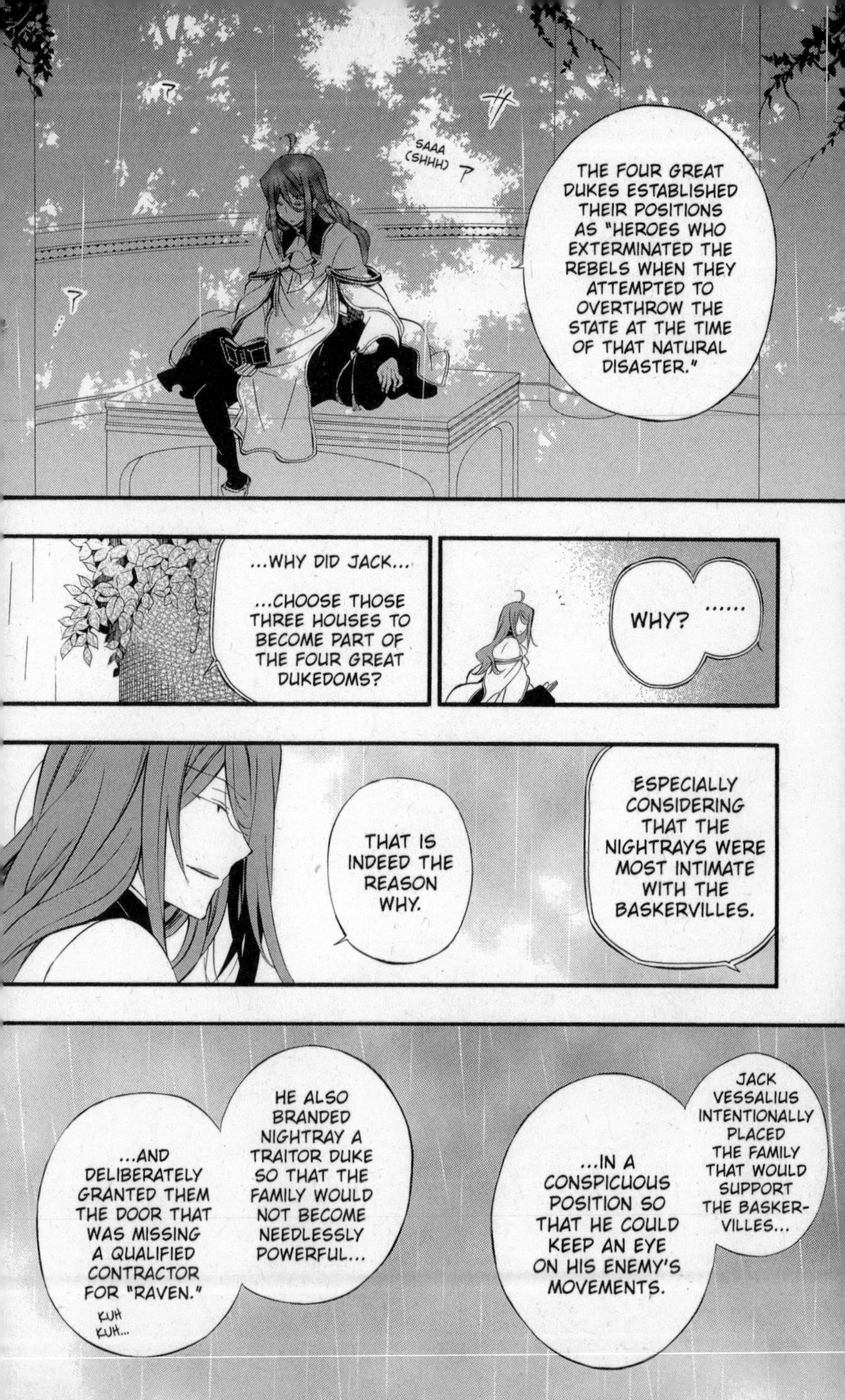
SAAA (SHHH)
THE FOUR GREAT DUKES ESTABLISHED THEIR POSITIONS AS "HEROES WHO EXTERMINATED THE REBELS WHEN THEY ATTEMPTED TO OVERTHROW THE STATE AT THE TIME OF THAT NATURAL DISASTER."
WHY? ......
...WHY DID JACK...
...CHOOSE THOSE THREE HOUSES TO BECOME PART OF THE FOUR GREAT DUKEDOMS?
ESPECIALLY CONSIDERING THAT THE NIGHTRAYS WERE MOST INTIMATE WITH THE BASKERVILLES.
THAT IS INDEED THE REASON WHY.
JACK VESSALIUS INTENTIONALLY PLACED THE FAMILY THAT WOULD SUPPORT THE BASKER-VILLES...
...IN A CONSPICUOUS POSITION SO THAT HE COULD KEEP AN EYE ON HIS ENEMY'S MOVEMENTS.
HE ALSO BRANDED NIGHTRAY A TRAITOR DUKE SO THAT THE FAMILY WOULD NOT BECOME NEEDLESSLY POWERFUL...
...AND DELIBERATELY GRANTED THEM THE DOOR THAT WAS MISSING A QUALIFIED CONTRACTOR FOR "RAVEN."
KUH KUH...

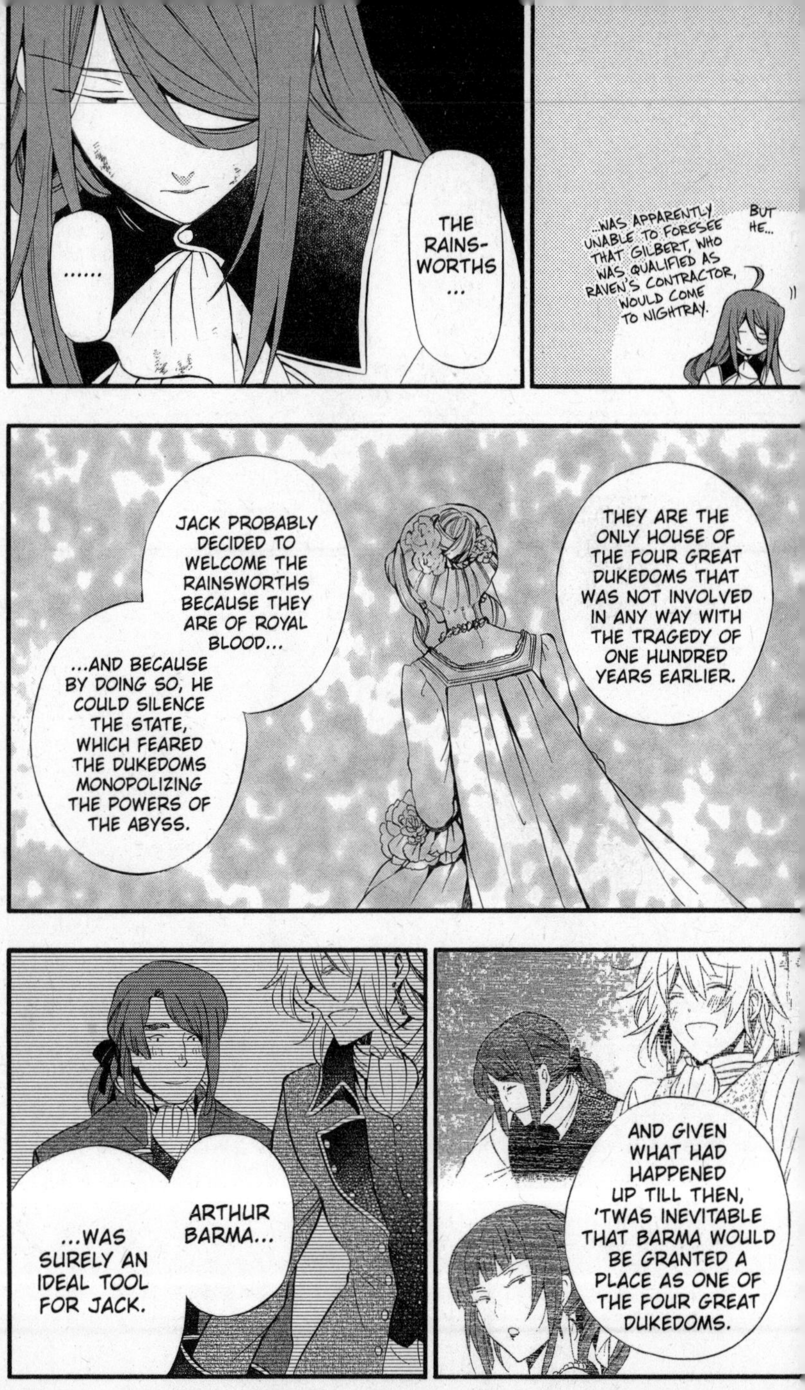
BUT HE...
...WAS APPARENTLY UNABLE TO FORESEE THAT GILBERT, WHO WAS QUALIFIED AS RAVEN'S CONTRACTOR, WOULD COME TO NIGHTRAY.
THE RAINSWORTHS...
......
THEY ARE THE ONLY HOUSE OF THE FOUR GREAT DUKEDOMS THAT WAS NOT INVOLVED IN ANY WAY WITH THE TRAGEDY OF ONE HUNDRED YEARS EARLIER.
JACK PROBABLY DECIDED TO WELCOME THE RAINSWORTHS BECAUSE THEY ARE OF ROYAL BLOOD...
...AND BECAUSE BY DOING SO, HE COULD SILENCE THE STATE, WHICH FEARED THE DUKEDOMS MONOPOLIZING THE POWERS OF THE ABYSS.
AND GIVEN WHAT HAD HAPPENED UP TILL THEN, 'TWAS INEVITABLE THAT BARMA WOULD BE GRANTED A PLACE AS ONE OF THE FOUR GREAT DUKEDOMS.
ARTHUR BARMA...
...WAS SURELY AN IDEAL TOOL FOR JACK.

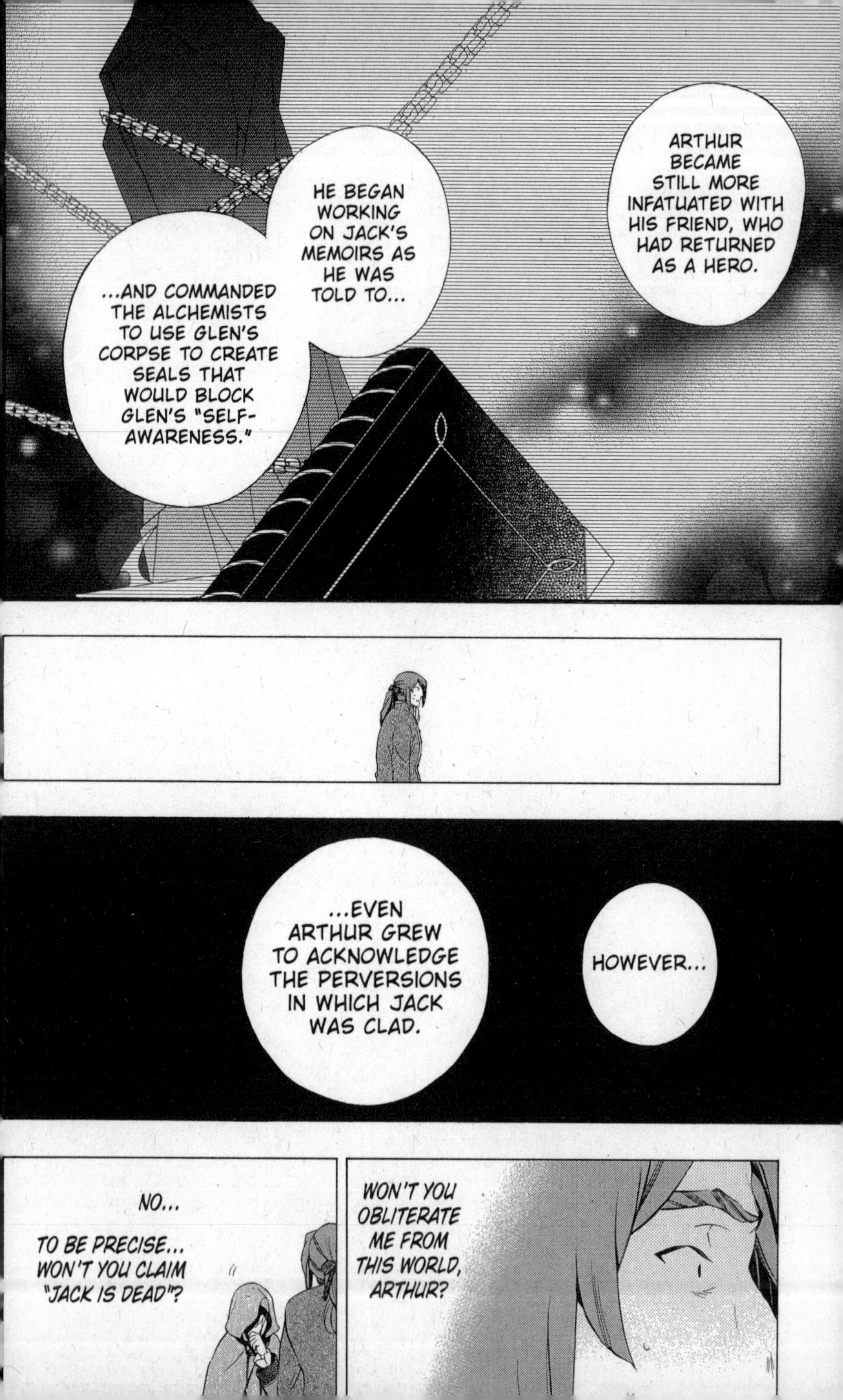
ARTHUR BECAME STILL MORE INFATUATED WITH HIS FRIEND, WHO HAD RETURNED AS A HERO.
HE BEGAN WORKING ON JACK'S MEMOIRS AS HE WAS TOLD TO...
...AND COMMANDED THE ALCHEMISTS TO USE GLEN'S CORPSE TO CREATE SEALS THAT WOULD BLOCK GLEN'S "SELF-AWARENESS."
HOWEVER...
...EVEN ARTHUR GREW TO ACKNOWLEDGE THE PERVERSIONS IN WHICH JACK WAS CLAD.
WON'T YOU OBLITERATE ME FROM THIS WORLD, ARTHUR?
NO...
TO BE PRECISE... WON'T YOU CLAIM "JACK IS DEAD"?

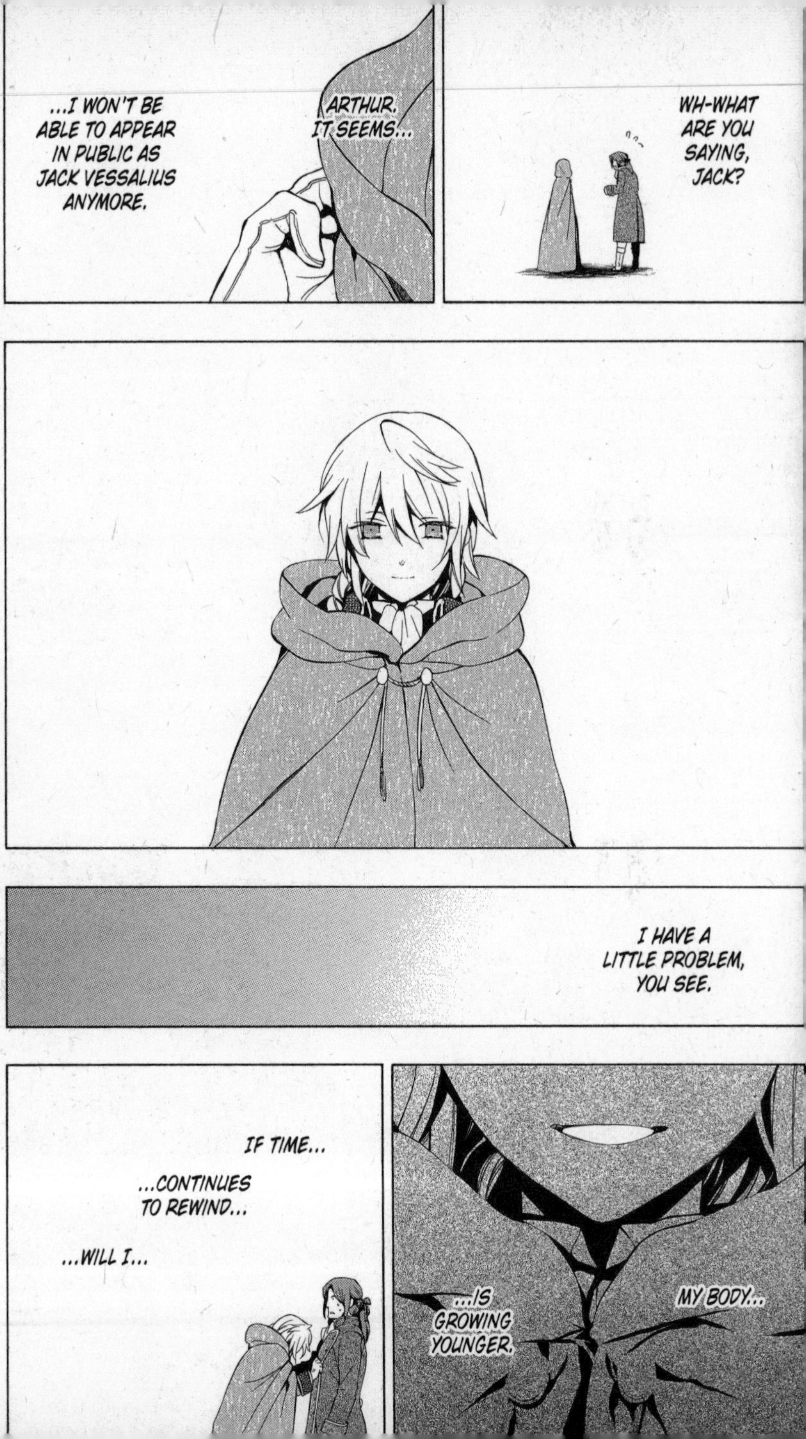
WH-WHAT ARE YOU SAYING, JACK?
ARTHUR. IT SEEMS...
...I WON'T BE ABLE TO APPEAR IN PUBLIC AS JACK VESSALIUS ANYMORE.
I HAVE A LITTLE PROBLEM, YOU SEE.
MY BODY...
...IS GROWING YOUNGER.
IF TIME...
...CONTINUES TO REWIND...
...WILL I...

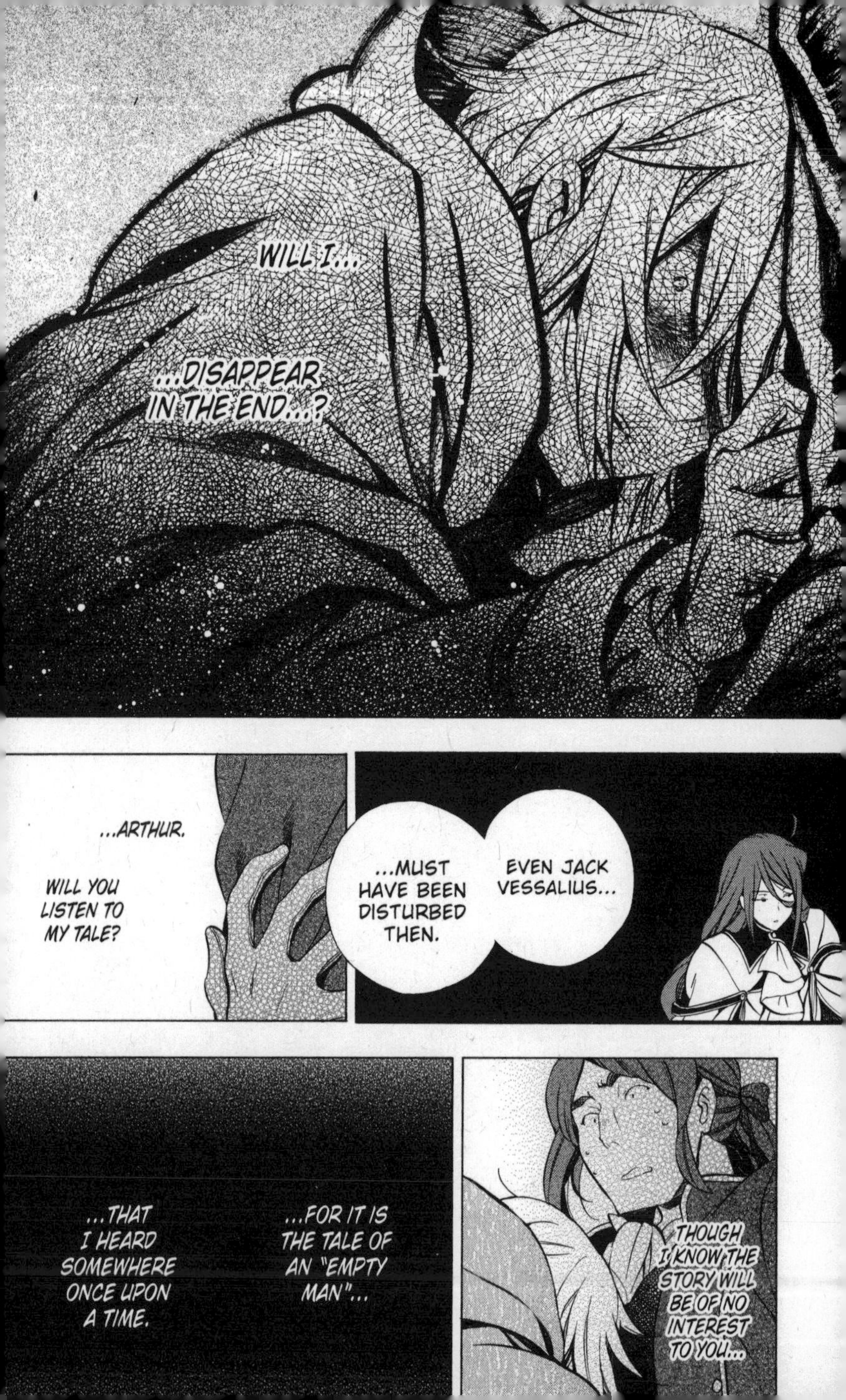
WILL I...
...DISAPPEAR IN THE END...?
EVEN JACK VESSALIUS...
...MUST HAVE BEEN DISTURBED THEN.
...ARTHUR.
WILL YOU LISTEN TO MY TALE?
THOUGH I KNOW THE STORY WILL BE OF NO INTEREST TO YOU...
...FOR IT IS THE TALE OF AN "EMPTY MAN"...
...THAT I HEARD SOMEWHERE ONCE UPON A TIME.

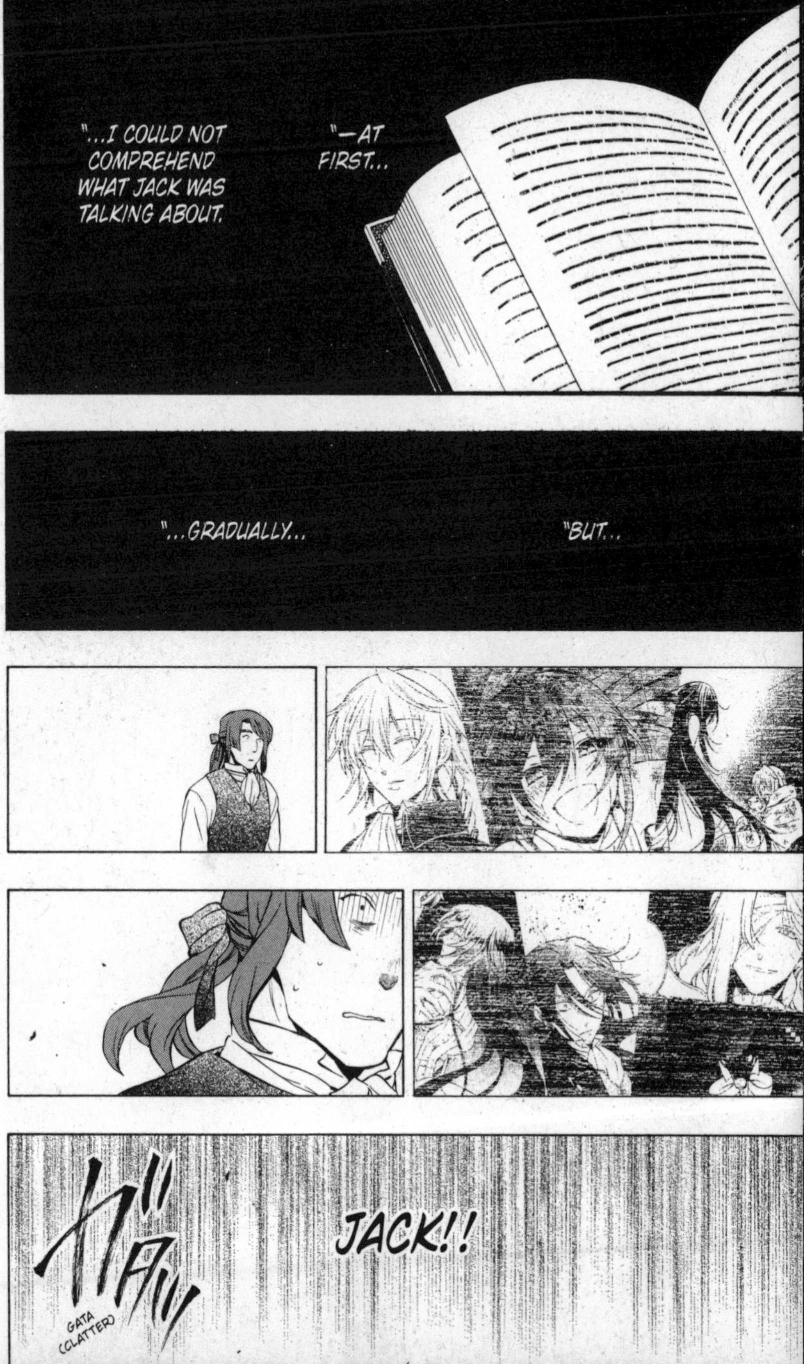
"—AT FIRST...
"...I COULD NOT COMPREHEND WHAT JACK WAS TALKING ABOUT.
"BUT...
"...GRADUALLY...
JACK!!
GATA (CLATTER)

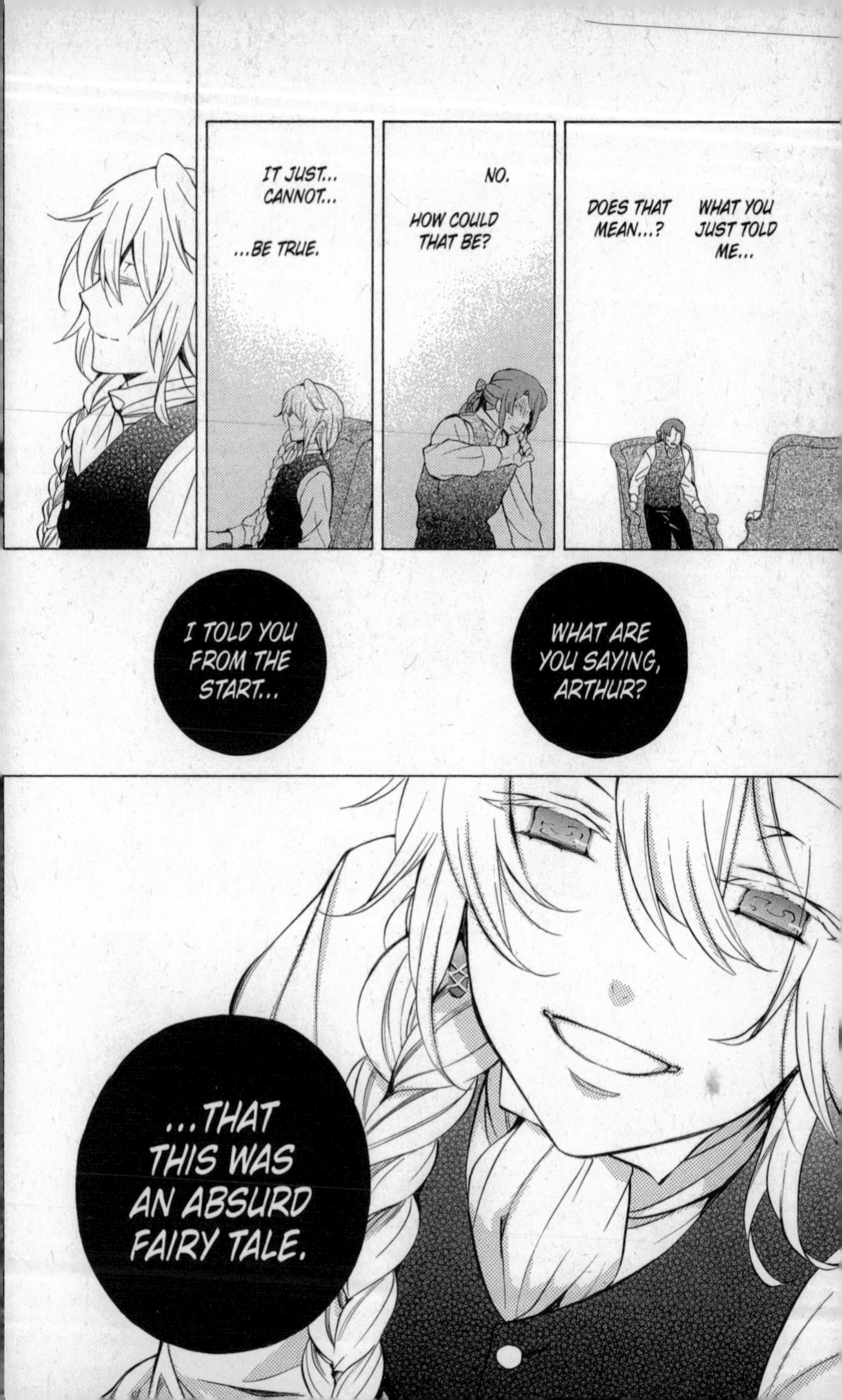
WHAT YOU JUST TOLD ME...
DOES THAT MEAN...?
NO.
HOW COULD THAT BE?
IT JUST... CANNOT...
...BE TRUE.
WHAT ARE YOU SAYING, ARTHUR?
I TOLD YOU FROM THE START...
...THAT THIS WAS AN ABSURD FAIRY TALE.

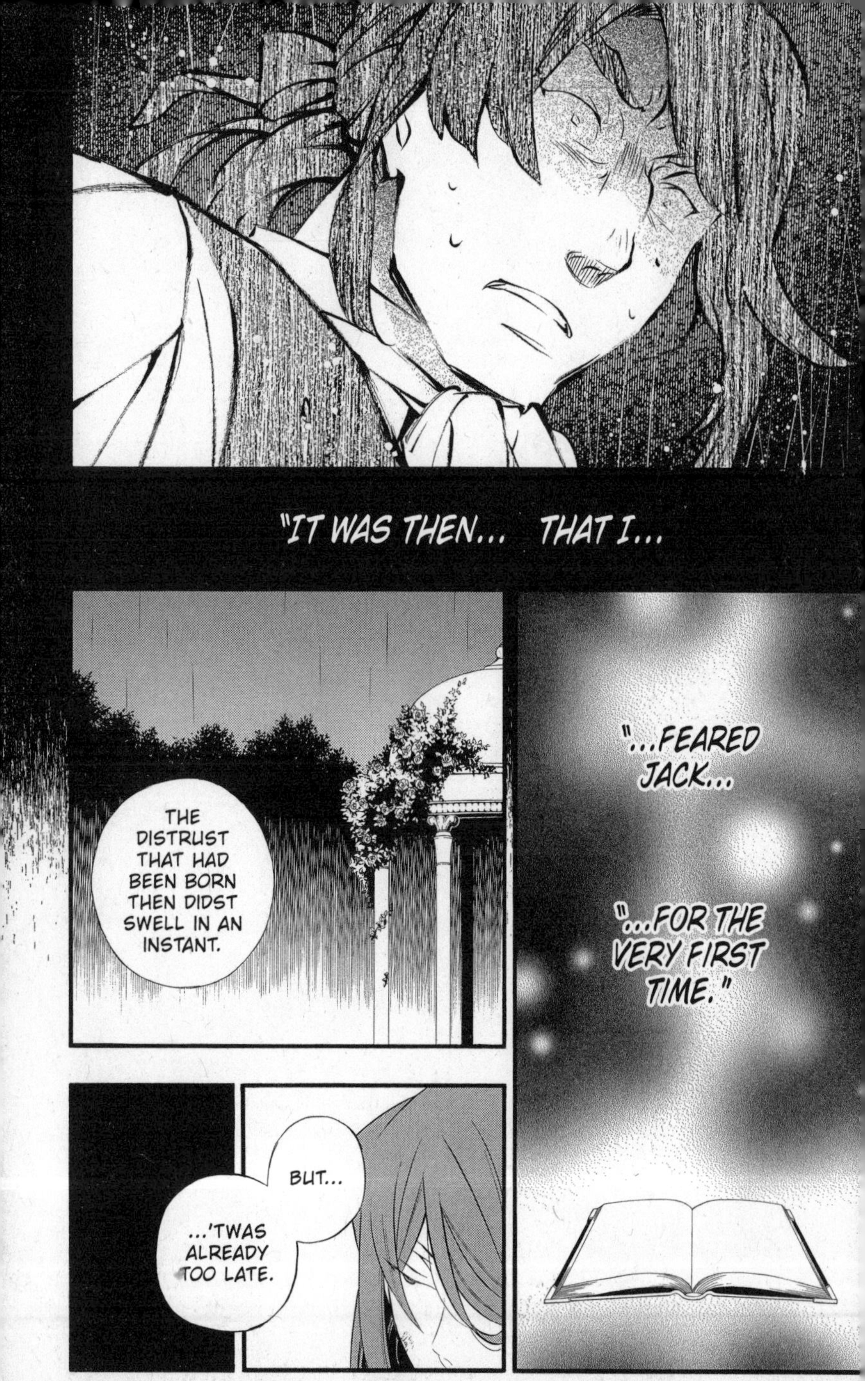
"IT WAS THEN... THAT I...
"...FEARED JACK...
"...FOR THE VERY FIRST TIME."
THE DISTRUST THAT HAD BEEN BORN THEN DIDST SWELL IN AN INSTANT.
BUT...
...'TWAS ALREADY TOO LATE.

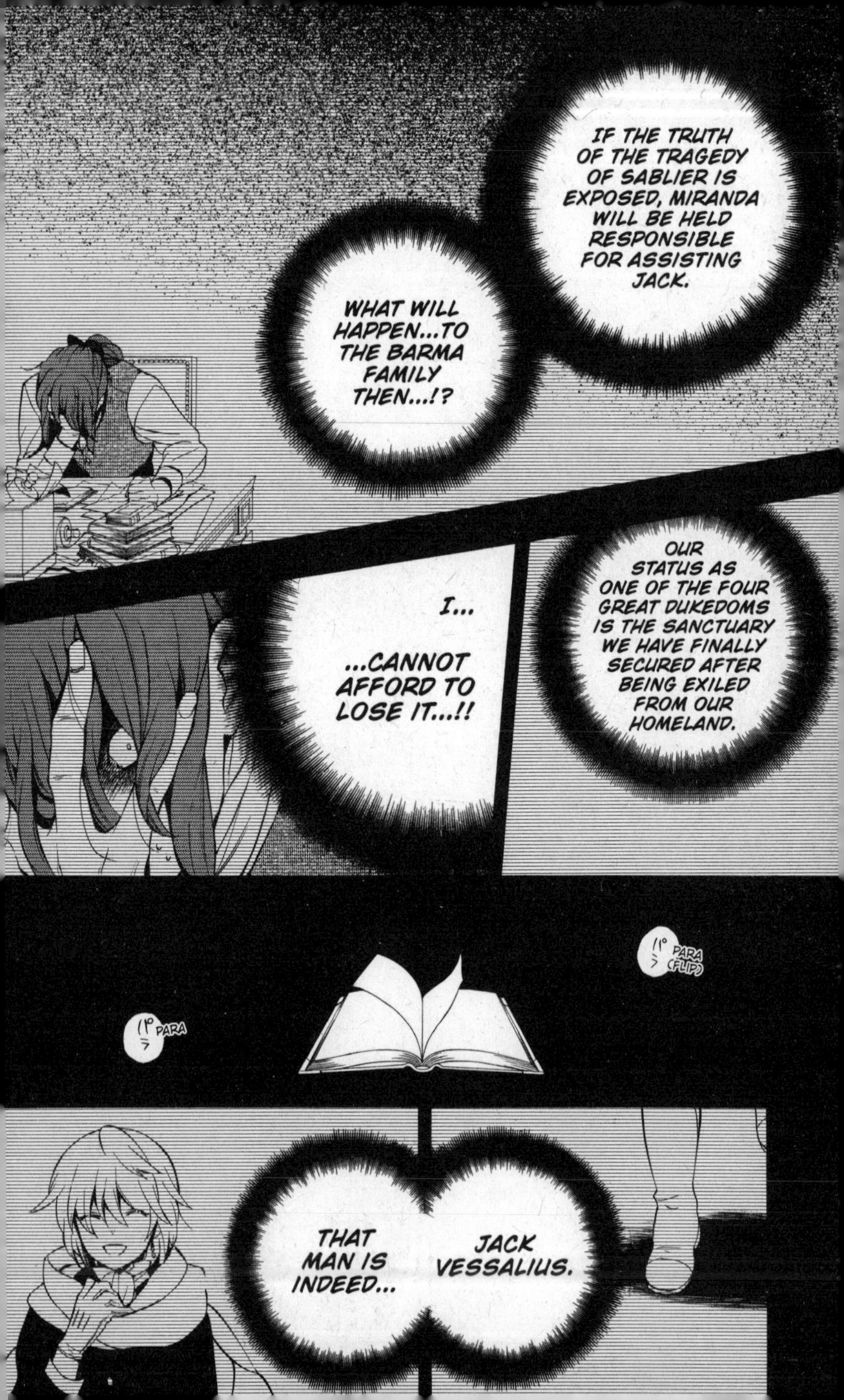
IF THE TRUTH OF THE TRAGEDY OF SABLIER IS EXPOSED, MIRANDA WILL BE HELD RESPONSIBLE FOR ASSISTING JACK.
WHAT WILL HAPPEN...TO THE BARMA FAMILY THEN...!?
OUR STATUS AS ONE OF THE FOUR GREAT DUKEDOMS IS THE SANCTUARY WE HAVE FINALLY SECURED AFTER BEING EXILED FROM OUR HOMELAND.
I...
...CANNOT AFFORD TO LOSE IT...!!
パラ
PARA (FLIP)
パラ
PARA
THAT MAN IS INDEED...
JACK VESSALIUS.

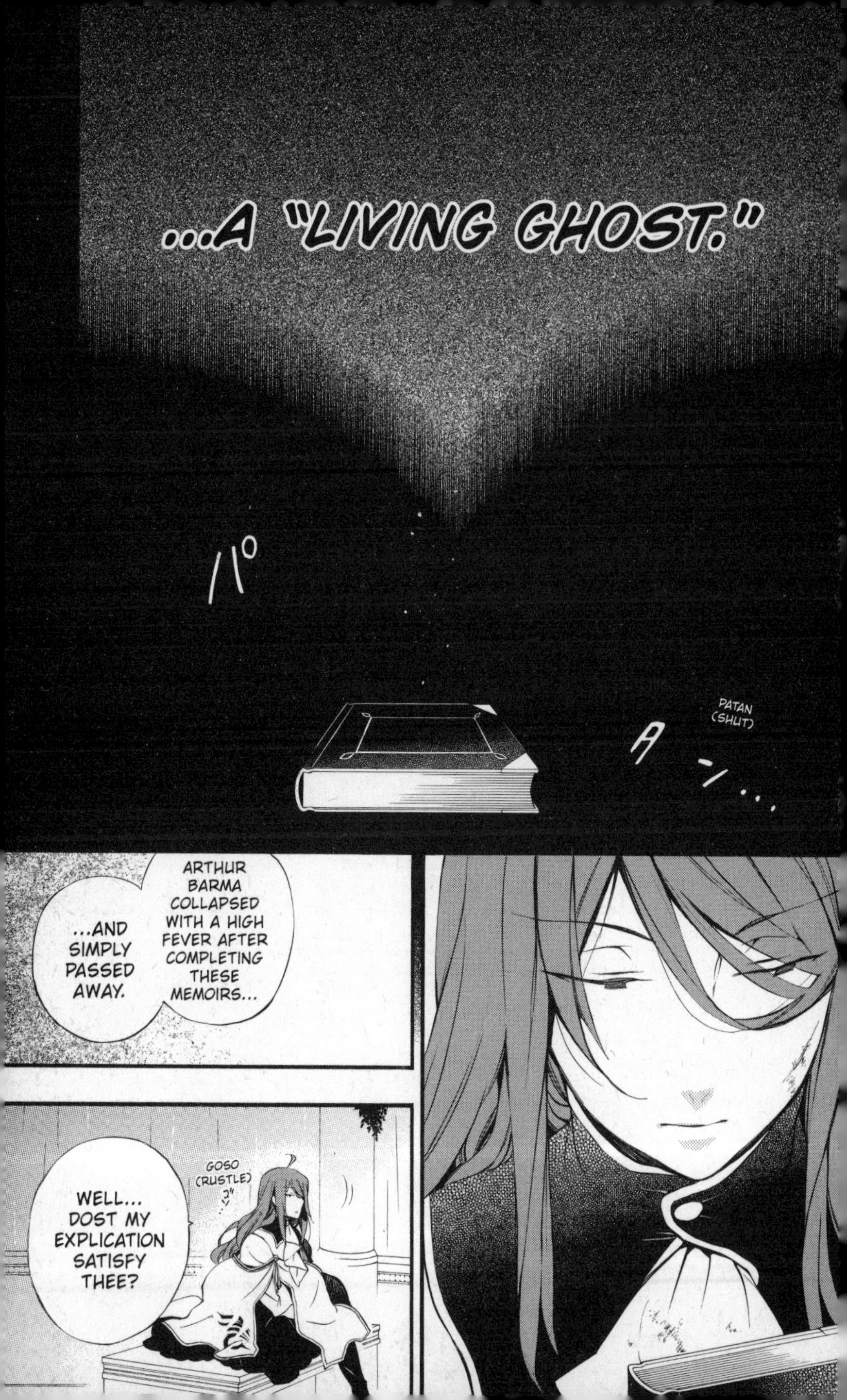
...A "LIVING GHOST."
PATAN (SHUT)
ARTHUR BARMA COLLAPSED WITH A HIGH FEVER AFTER COMPLETING THESE MEMOIRS...
...AND SIMPLY PASSED AWAY.
GOSO (RUSTLE)
WELL... DOST MY EXPLICATION SATISFY THEE?

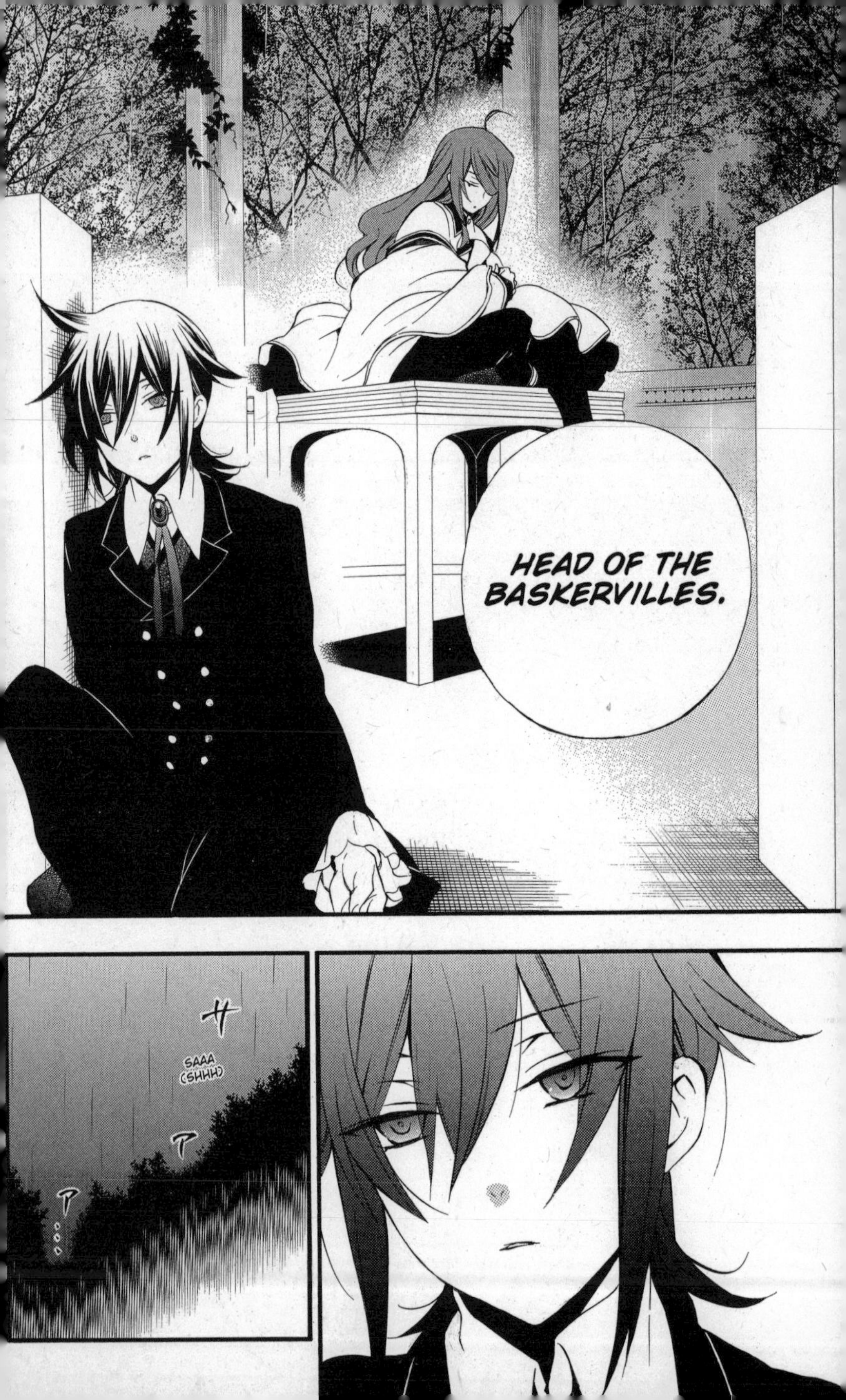
HEAD OF THE BASKERVILLES.
SAAA (SHHH)

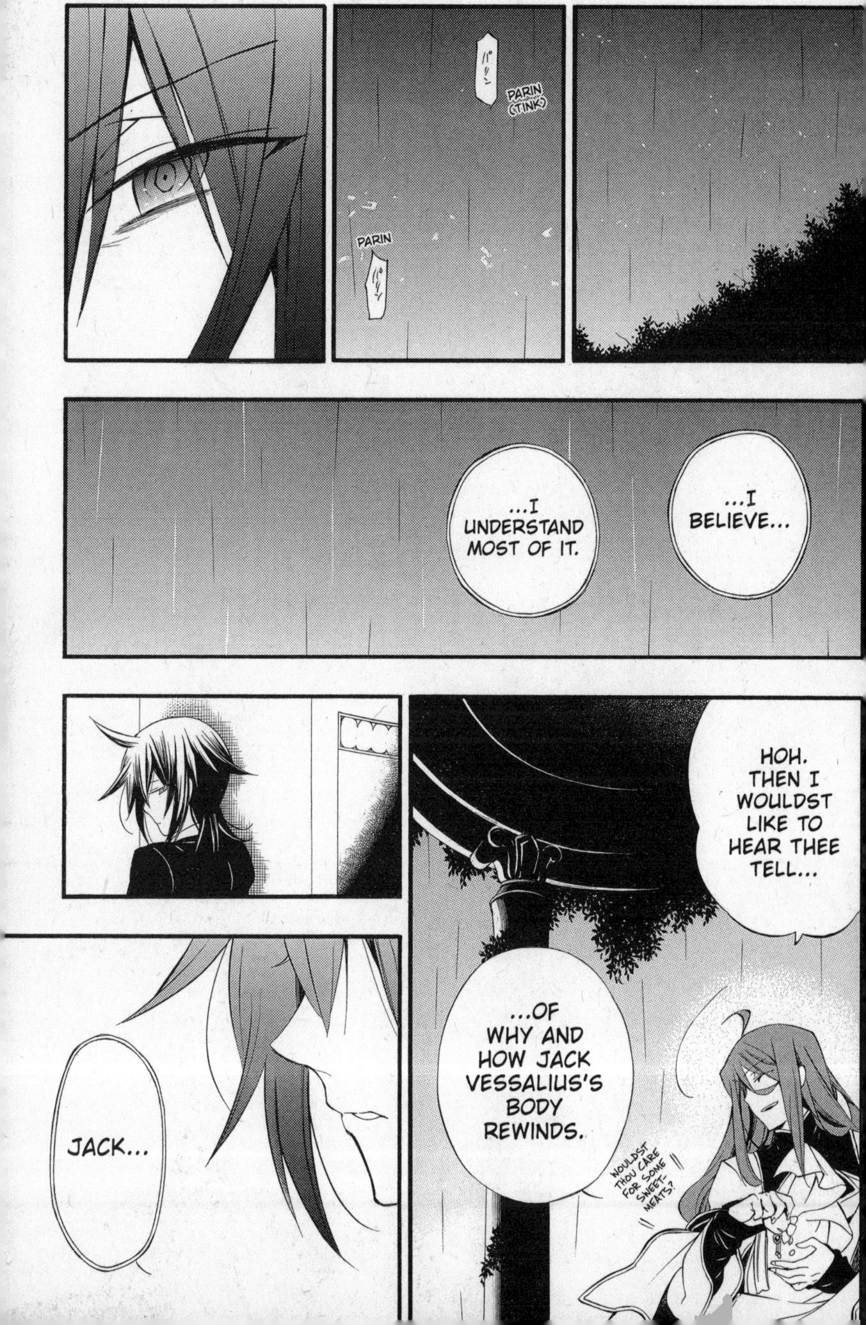
パリン
PARIN (TINK)
PARIN
パリン
...I BELIEVE...
...I UNDERSTAND MOST OF IT.
HOH. THEN I WOULDST LIKE TO HEAR THEE TELL...
...OF WHY AND HOW JACK VESSALIUS'S BODY REWINDS.
WOULDST THOU CARE FOR SOME SWEET-MEATS?
JACK...

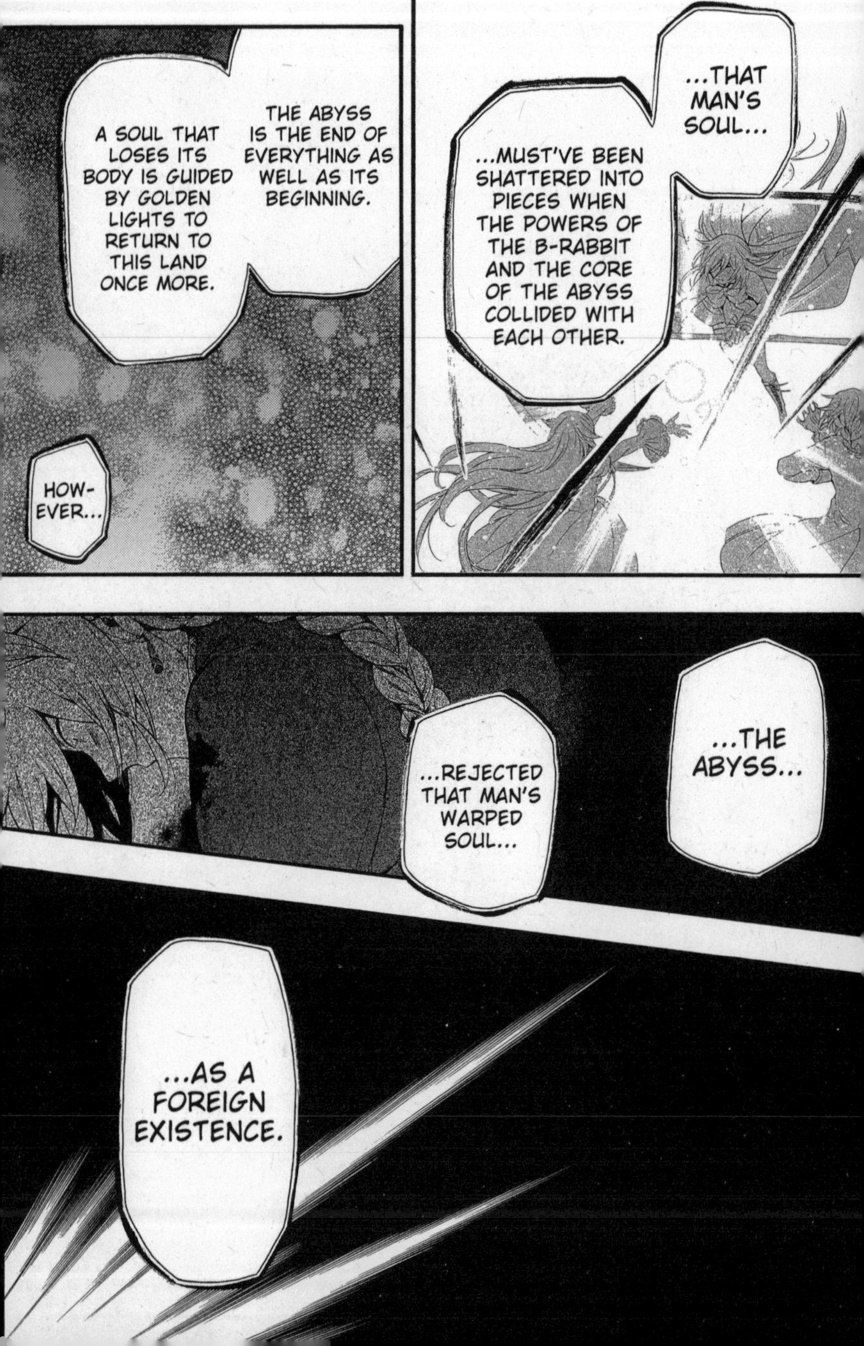
...THAT MAN'S SOUL...
...MUST'VE BEEN SHATTERED INTO PIECES WHEN THE POWERS OF THE B-RABBIT AND THE CORE OF THE ABYSS COLLIDED WITH EACH OTHER.
THE ABYSS IS THE END OF EVERYTHING AS WELL AS ITS BEGINNING.
A SOUL THAT LOSES ITS BODY IS GUIDED BY GOLDEN LIGHTS TO RETURN TO THIS LAND ONCE MORE.
HOW-EVER...
...THE ABYSS...
...REJECTED THAT MAN'S WARPED SOUL...
...AS A FOREIGN EXISTENCE.

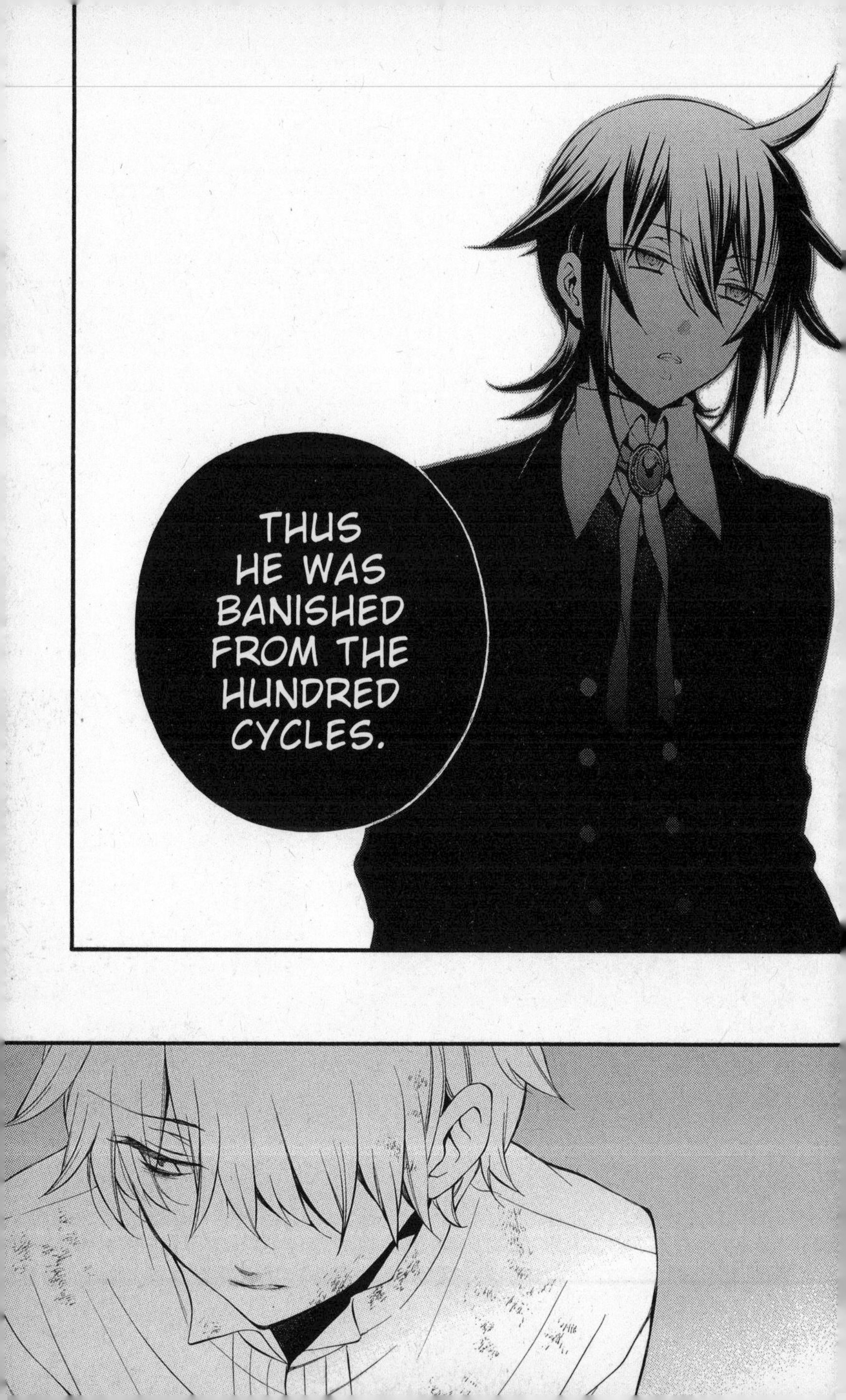
THUS HE WAS BANISHED FROM THE HUNDRED CYCLES.

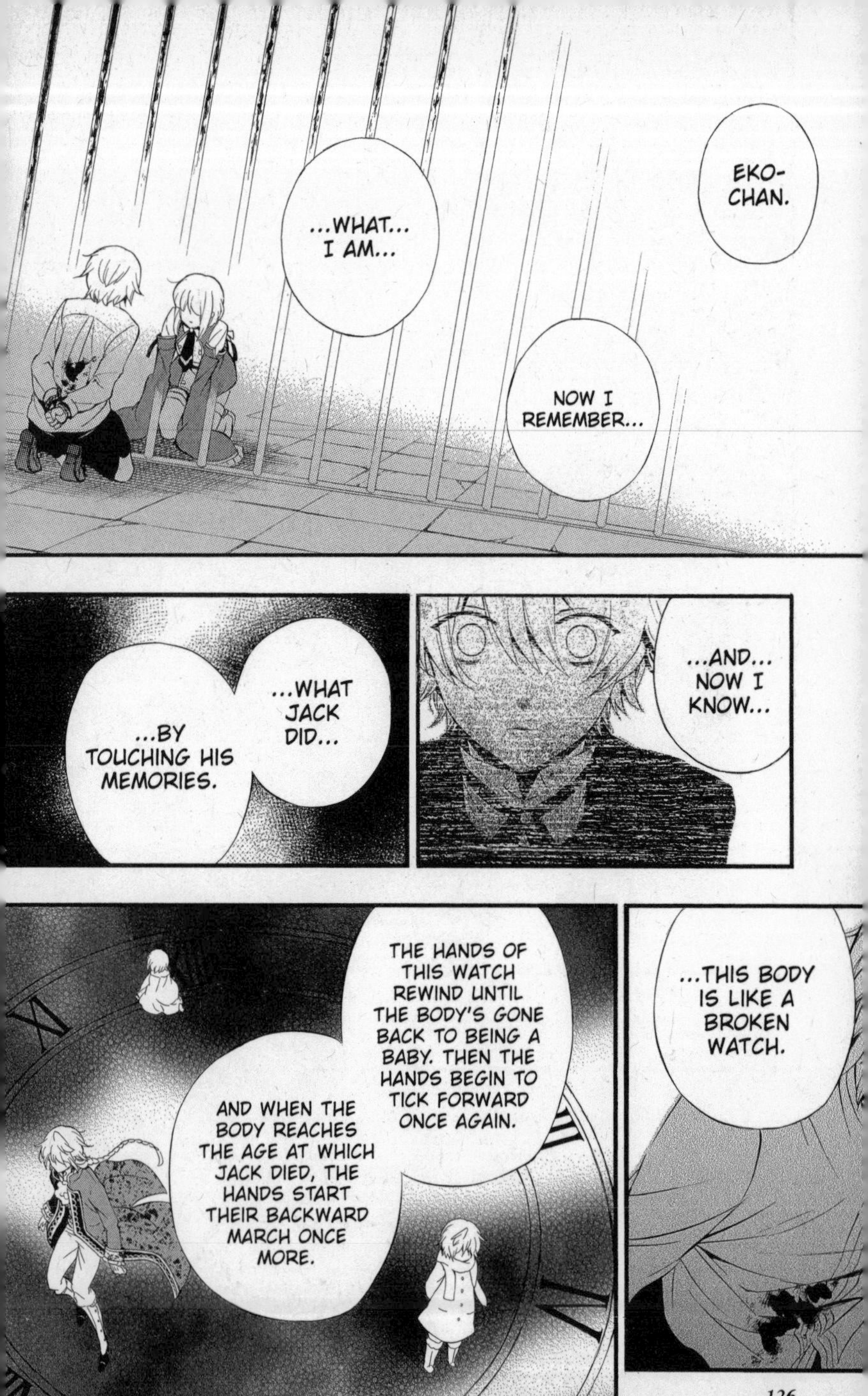
EKO-CHAN.
NOW I REMEMBER...
...WHAT... I AM...
...AND... NOW I KNOW...
...WHAT JACK DID...
...BY TOUCHING HIS MEMORIES.
...THIS BODY IS LIKE A BROKEN WATCH.
THE HANDS OF THIS WATCH REWIND UNTIL THE BODY'S GONE BACK TO BEING A BABY. THEN THE HANDS BEGIN TO TICK FORWARD ONCE AGAIN.
AND WHEN THE BODY REACHES THE AGE AT WHICH JACK DIED, THE HANDS START THEIR BACKWARD MARCH ONCE MORE.

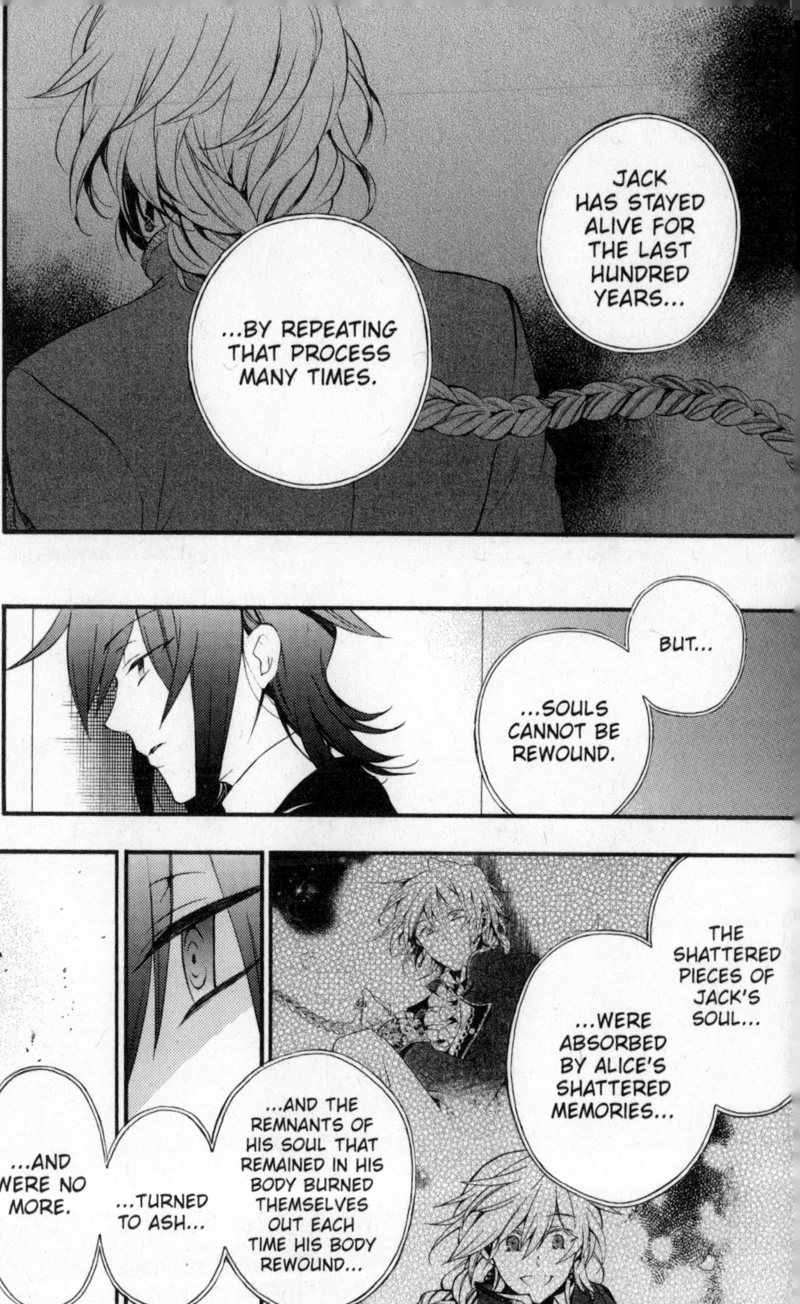
JACK HAS STAYED ALIVE FOR THE LAST HUNDRED YEARS...
...BY REPEATING THAT PROCESS MANY TIMES.
BUT...
...SOULS CANNOT BE REWOUND.
THE SHATTERED PIECES OF JACK'S SOUL...
...WERE ABSORBED BY ALICE'S SHATTERED MEMORIES...
...AND THE REMNANTS OF HIS SOUL THAT REMAINED IN HIS BODY BURNED THEMSELVES OUT EACH TIME HIS BODY REWOUND...
...TURNED TO ASH...
...AND WERE NO MORE.

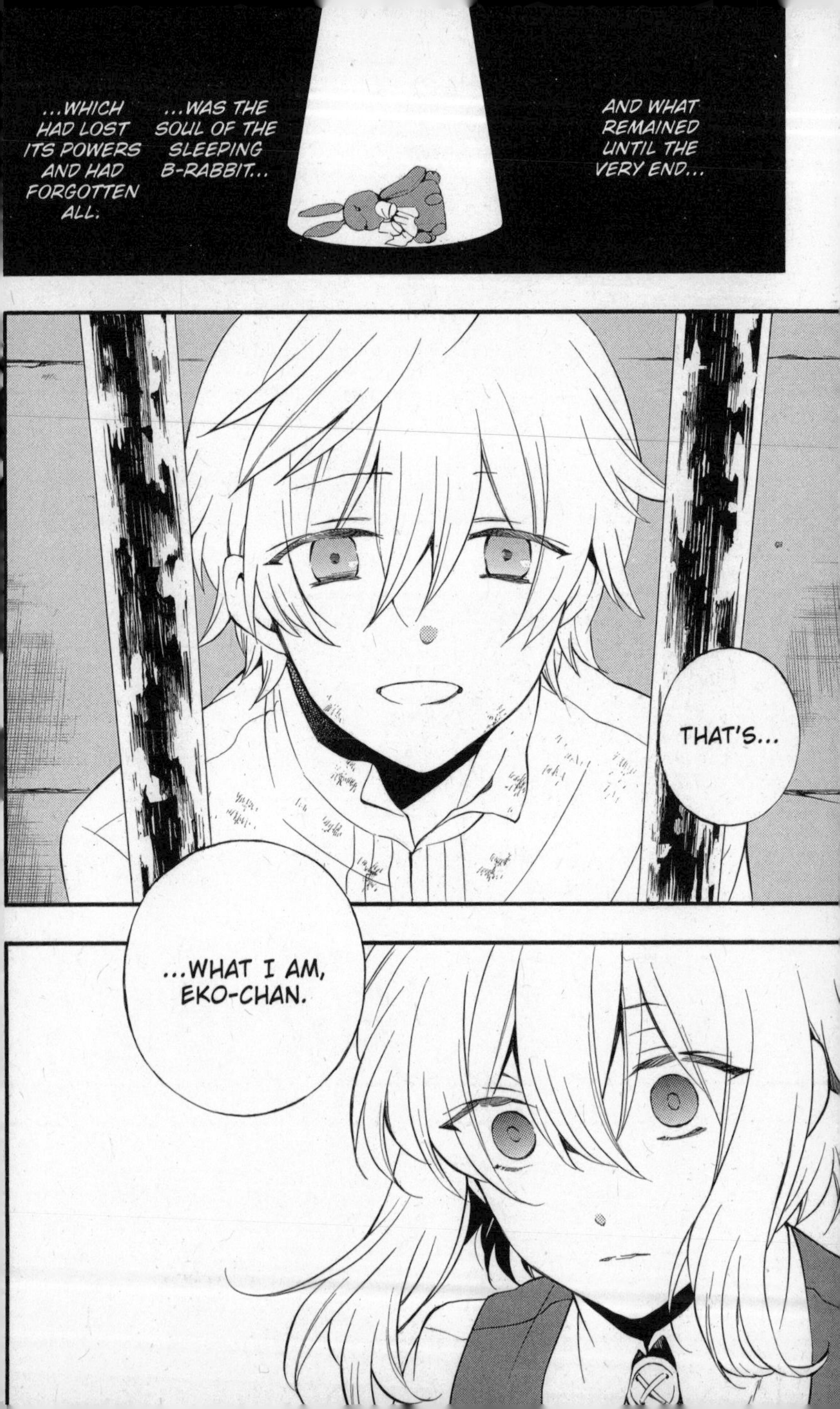
AND WHAT REMAINED UNTIL THE VERY END...
...WAS THE SOUL OF THE SLEEPING B-RABBIT...
...WHICH HAD LOST ITS POWERS AND HAD FORGOTTEN ALL.
THAT'S...
...WHAT I AM, EKO-CHAN.

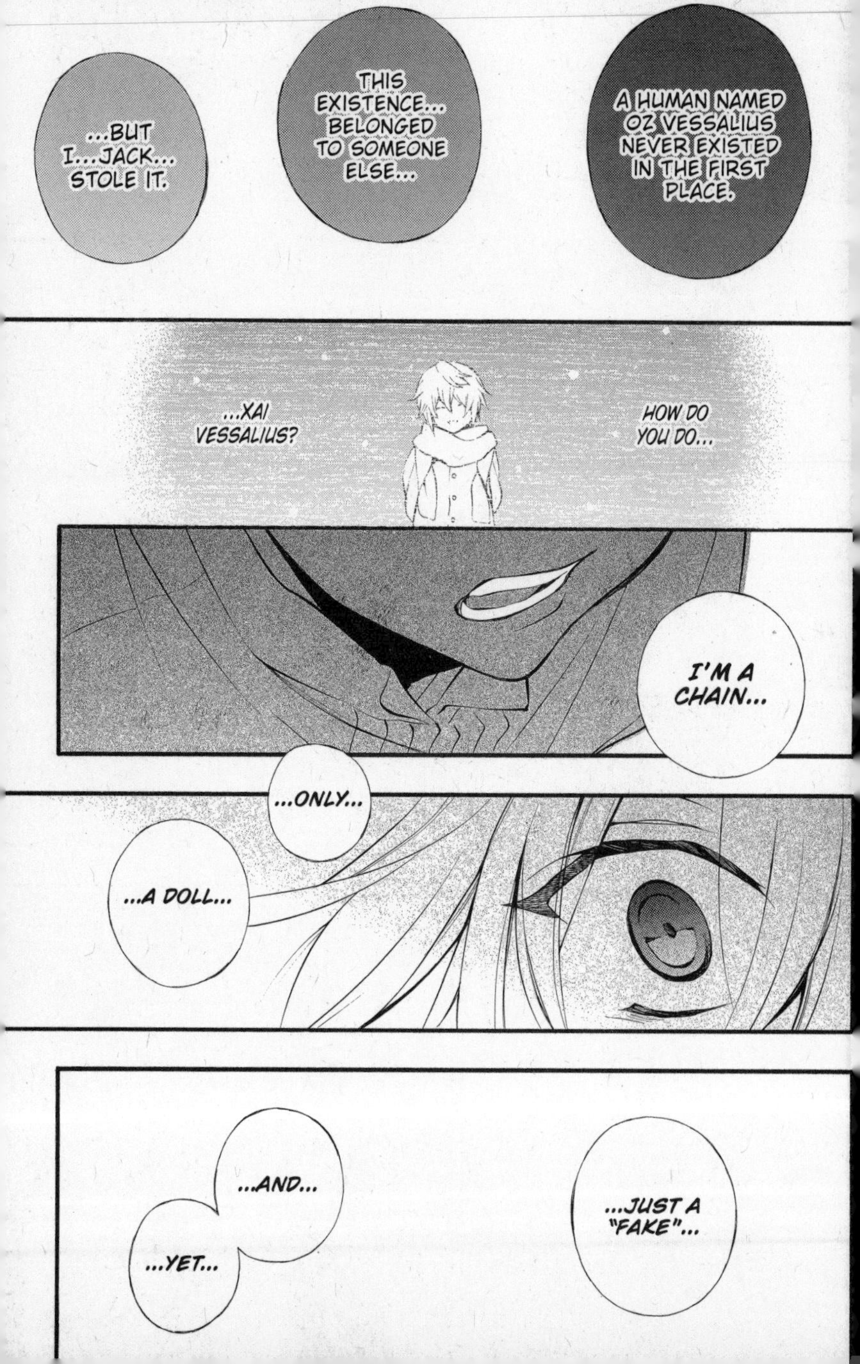
A HUMAN NAMED OZ VESSALIUS NEVER EXISTED IN THE FIRST PLACE.
THIS EXISTENCE... BELONGED TO SOMEONE ELSE...
...BUT I...JACK... STOLE IT.
HOW DO YOU DO...
...XAI VESSALIUS?
I'M A CHAIN...
...ONLY...
...A DOLL...
...JUST A "FAKE"...
...AND...
...YET...

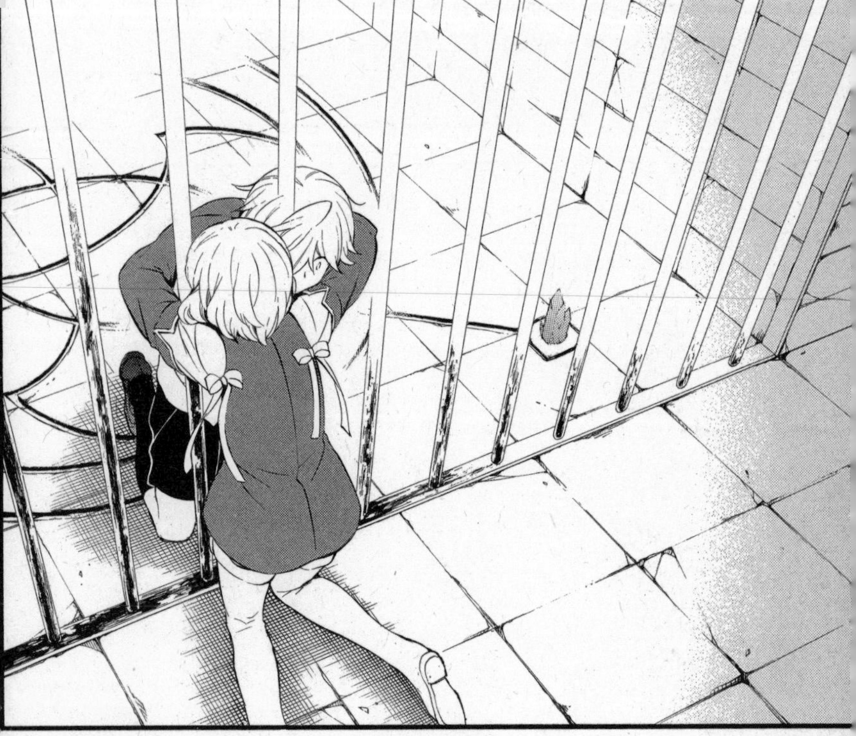

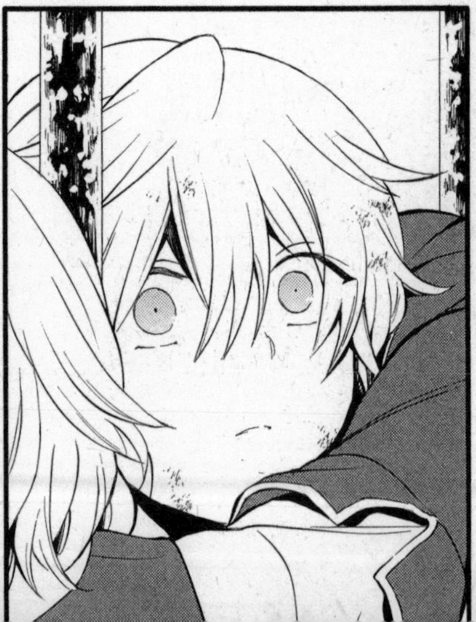

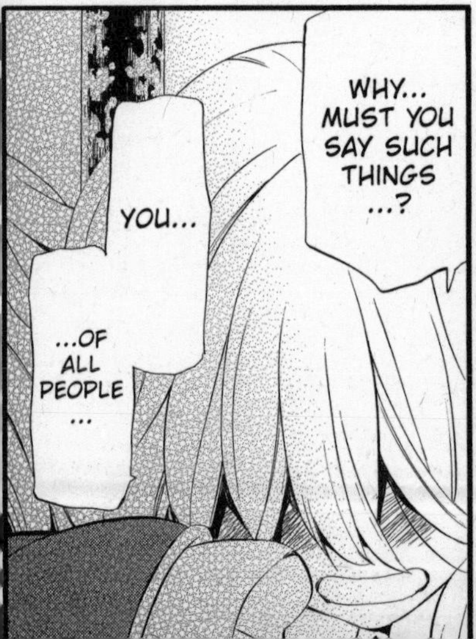
WHY... MUST YOU SAY SUCH THINGS ...?
YOU...
...OF ALL PEOPLE ...

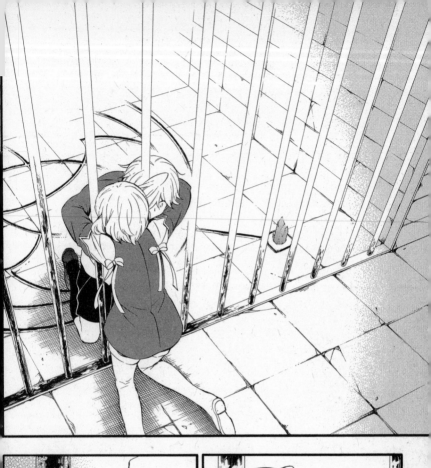

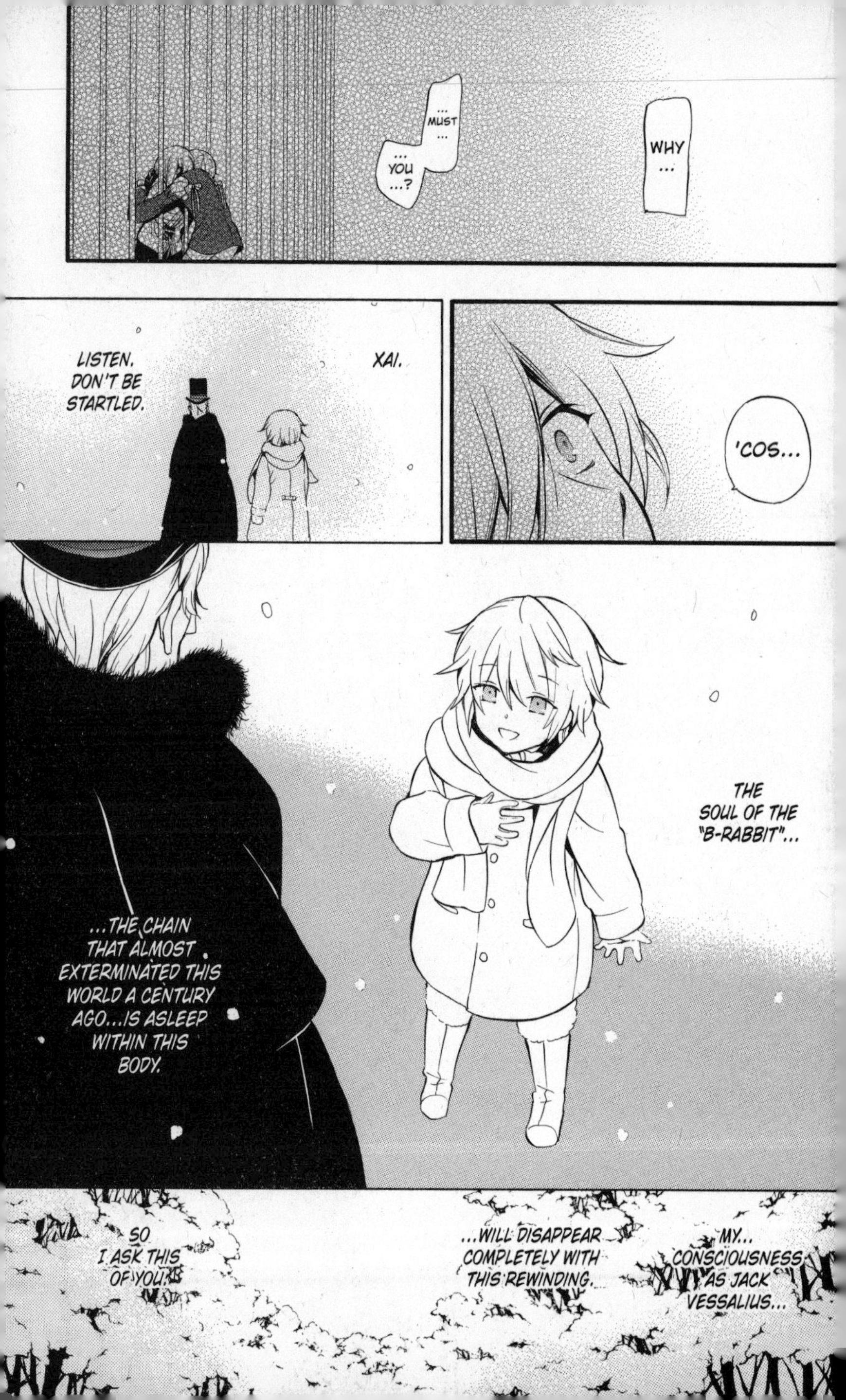
WHY ...
... MUST ...
... YOU ...?
'COS...
XAI.
LISTEN. DON'T BE STARTLED.
THE SOUL OF THE "B-RABBIT"...
...THE CHAIN THAT ALMOST EXTERMINATED THIS WORLD A CENTURY AGO...IS ASLEEP WITHIN THIS BODY.
MY... CONSCIOUSNESS AS JACK VESSALIUS...
...WILL DISAPPEAR COMPLETELY WITH THIS REWINDING.
SO I ASK THIS OF YOU.

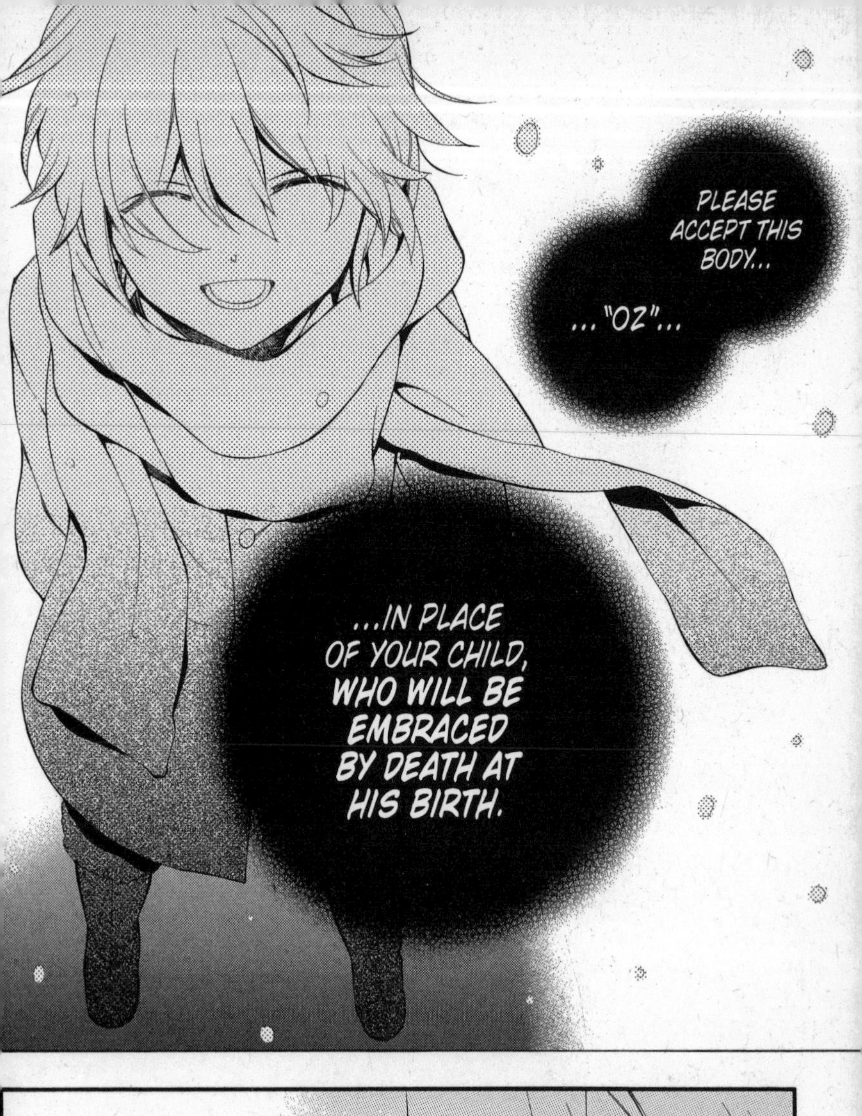
PLEASE ACCEPT THIS BODY...
..."OZ"...
...IN PLACE OF YOUR CHILD, WHO WILL BE EMBRACED BY DEATH AT HIS BIRTH.

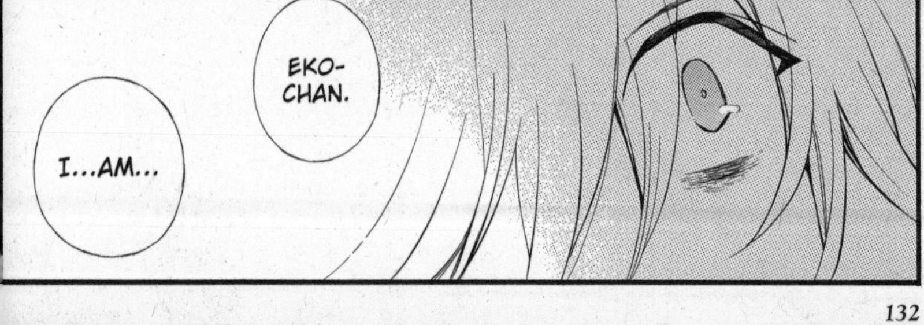
EKO-CHAN.
I...AM...

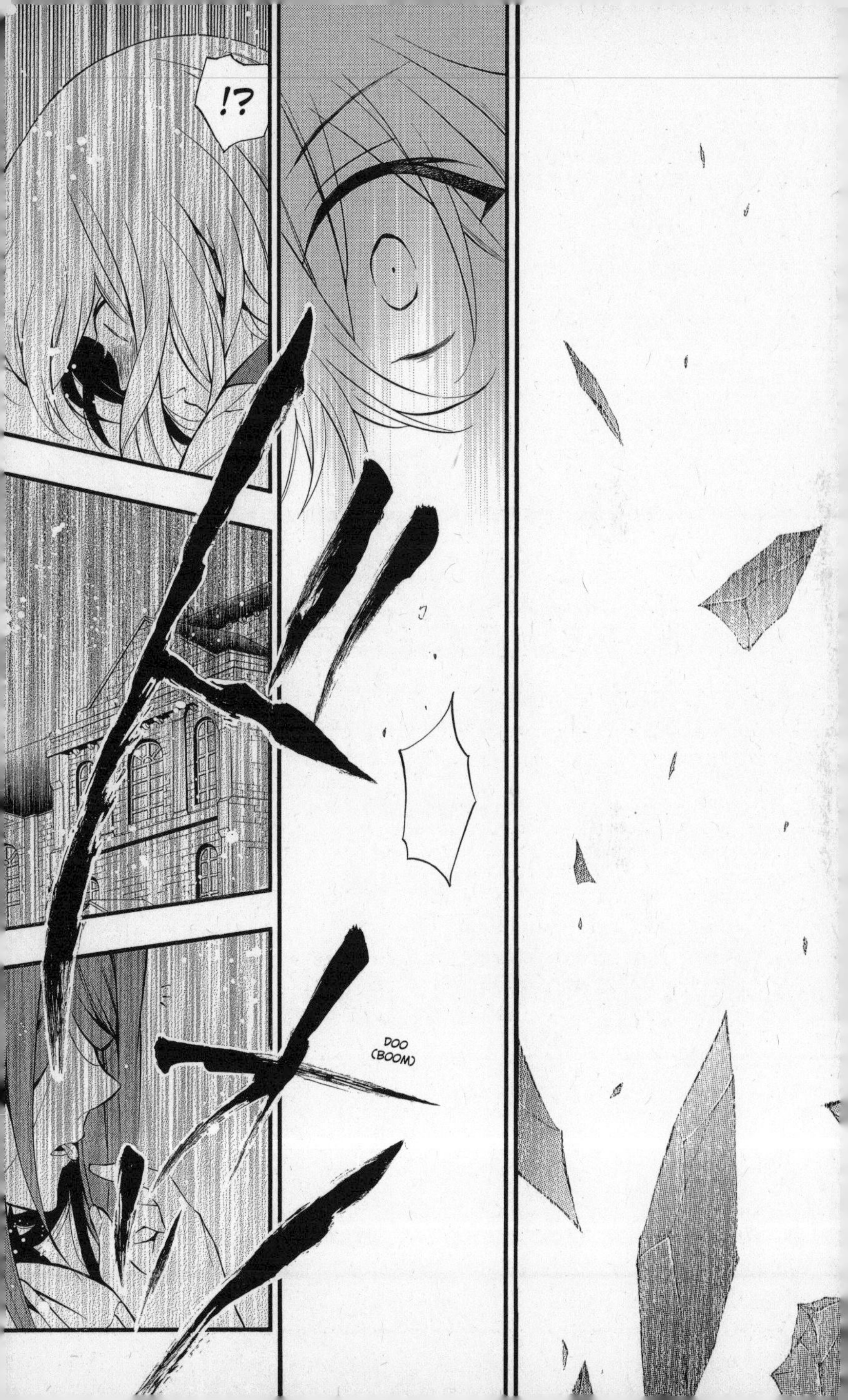
!?
DOO
(BOOM)

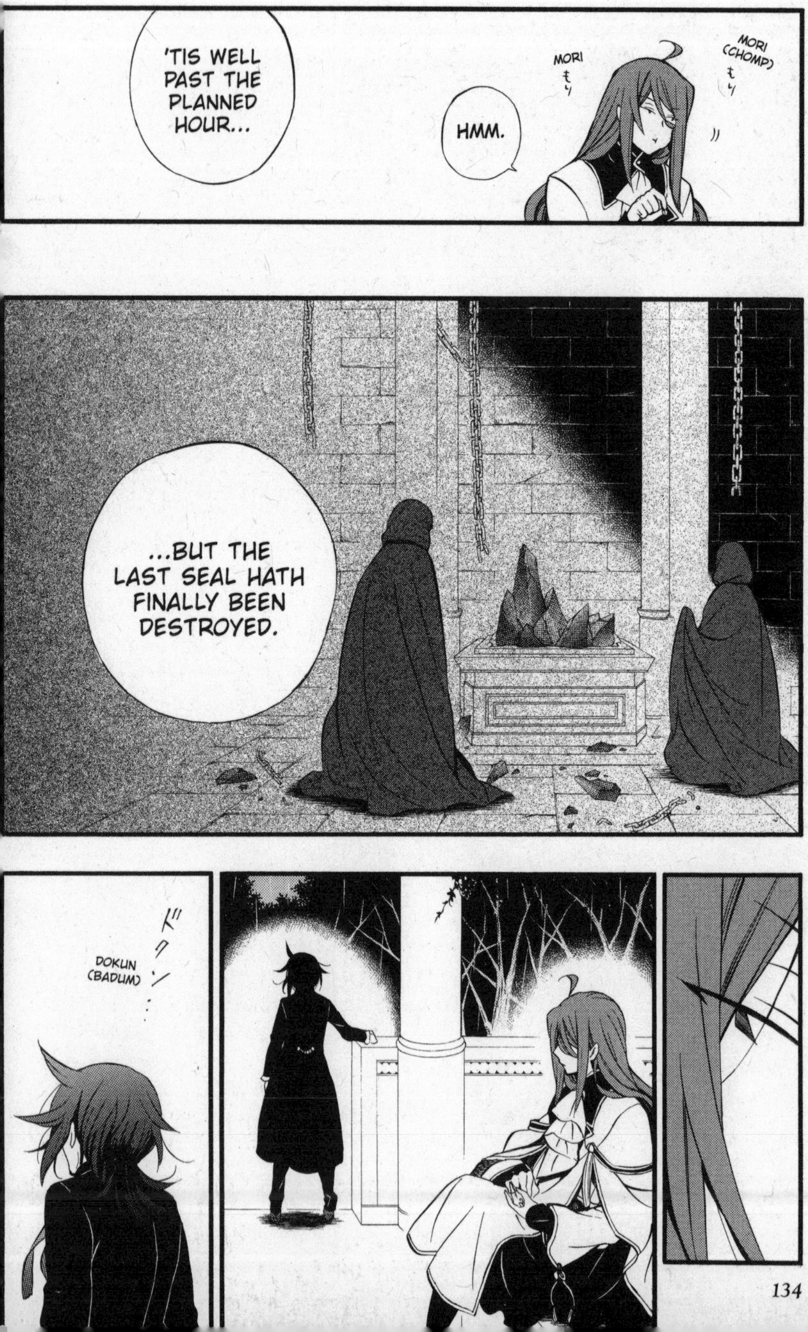
もり
MORI (CHOMP)
もり
MORI
HMM.
'TIS WELL PAST THE PLANNED HOUR...
...BUT THE LAST SEAL HATH FINALLY BEEN DESTROYED.
ドクン
DOKUN (BADUM)

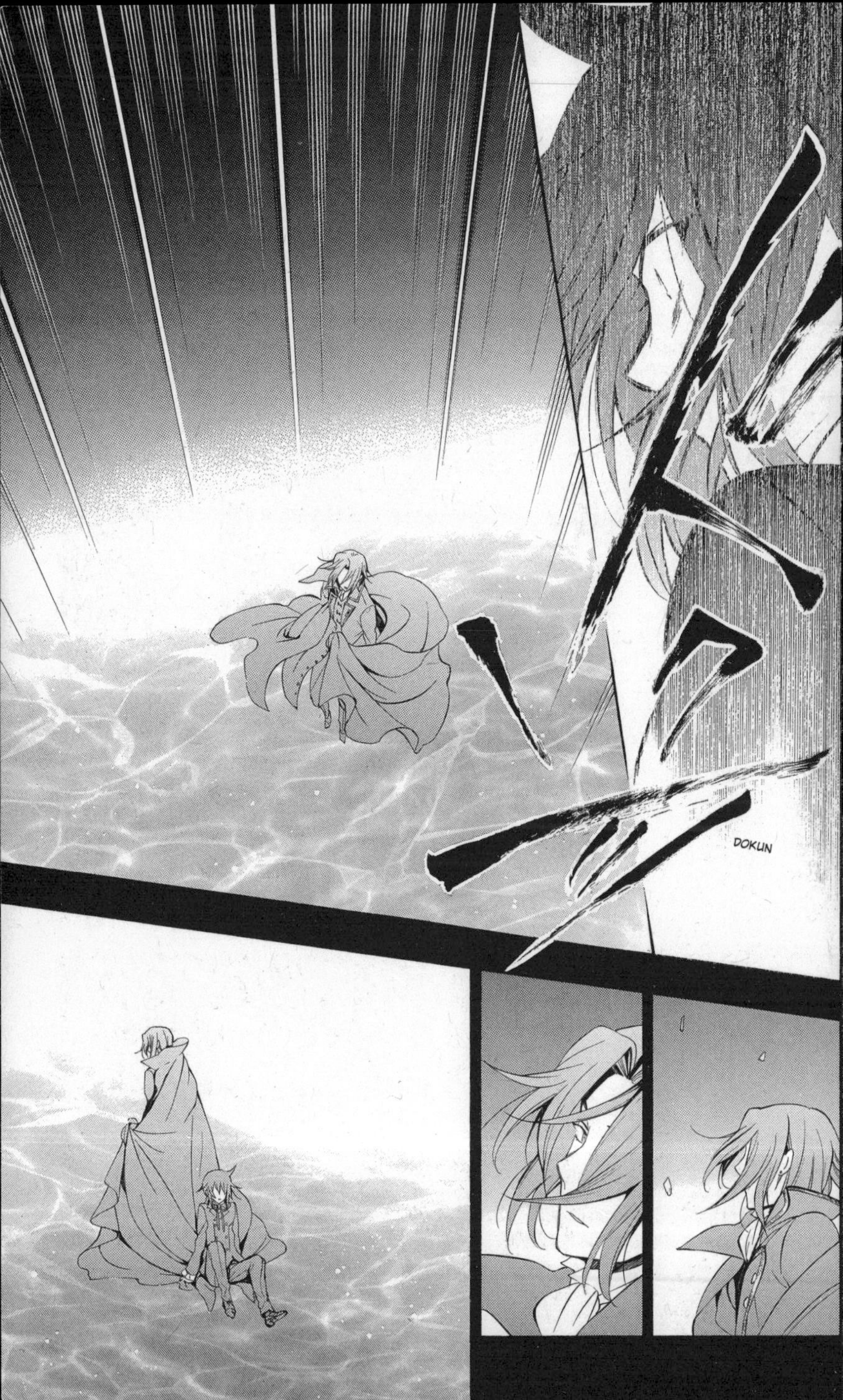
DOKUN

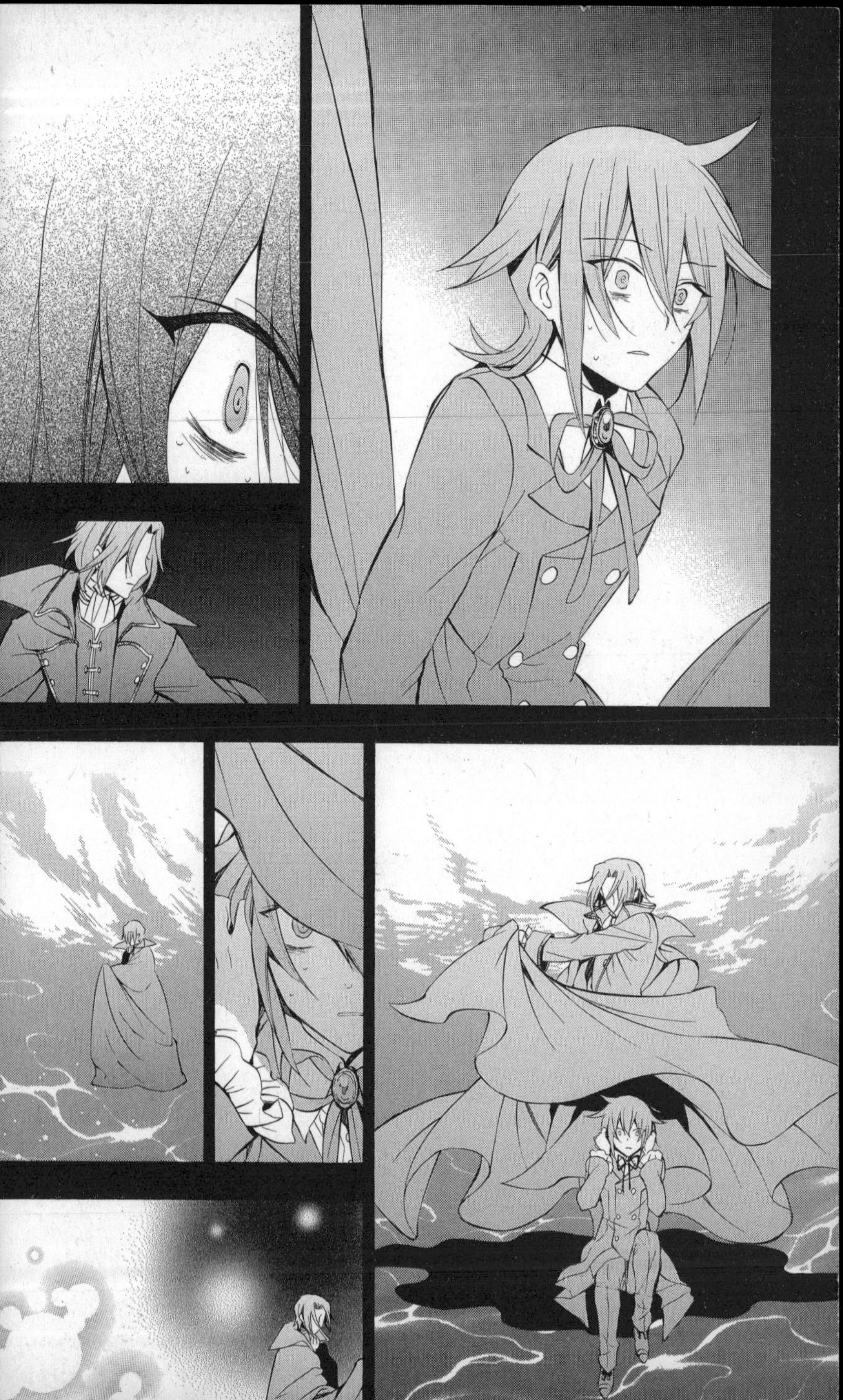

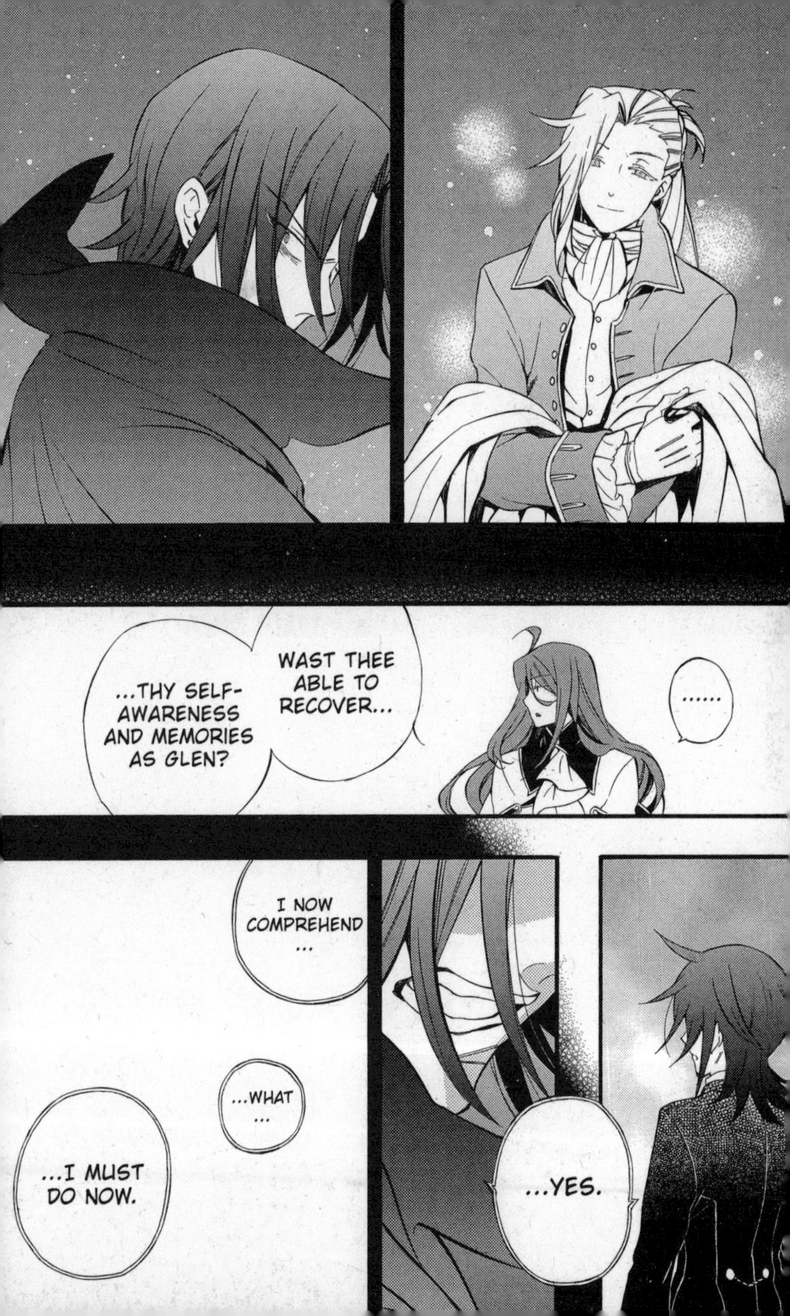
......
WAST THEE ABLE TO RECOVER...
...THY SELF-AWARENESS AND MEMORIES AS GLEN?
...YES.
I NOW COMPREHEND ...
...WHAT ...
...I MUST DO NOW.

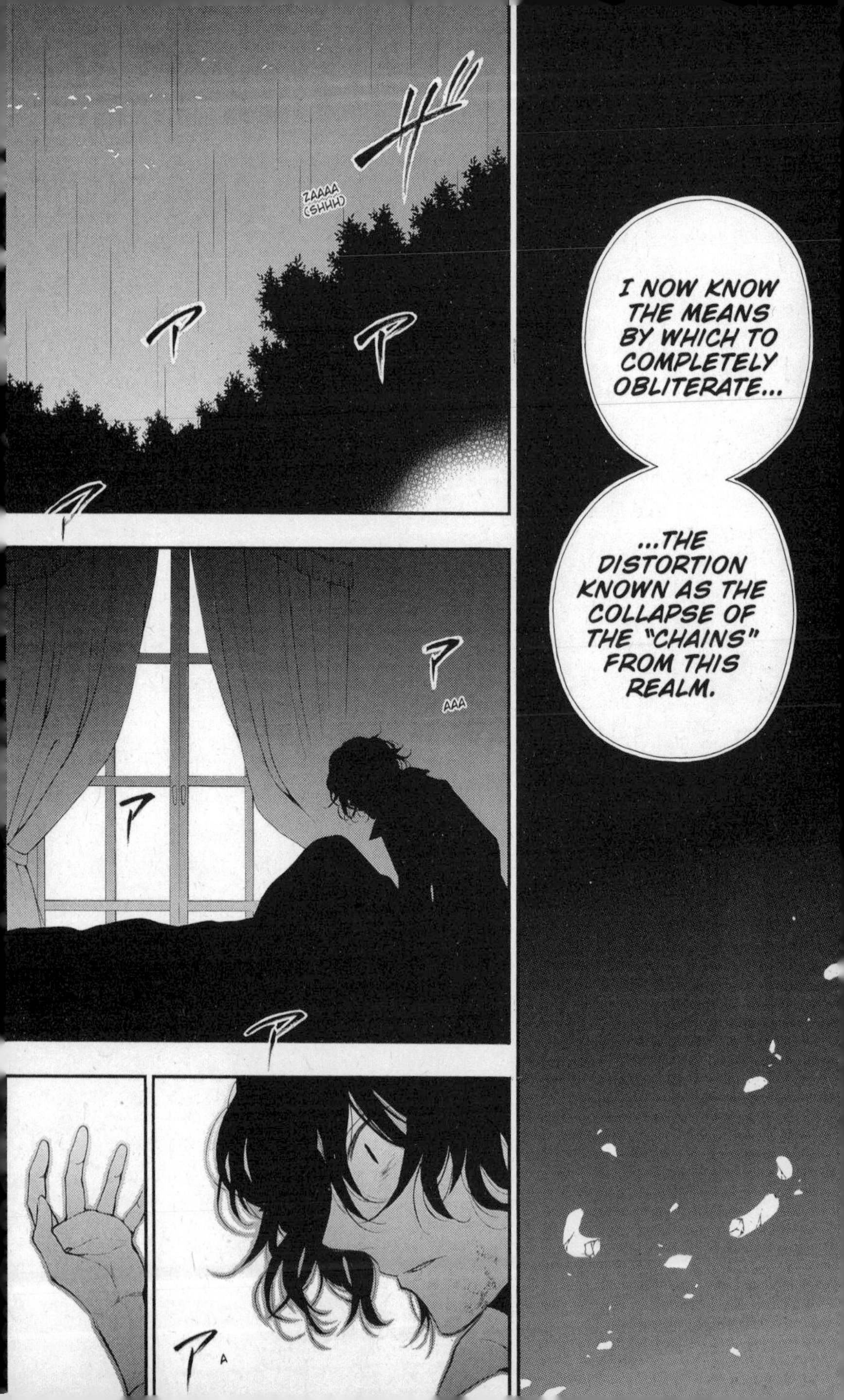
I NOW KNOW THE MEANS BY WHICH TO COMPLETELY OBLITERATE...
...THE DISTORTION KNOWN AS THE COLLAPSE OF THE "CHAINS" FROM THIS REALM.
ZAAAA (SHHH)
AAA
A

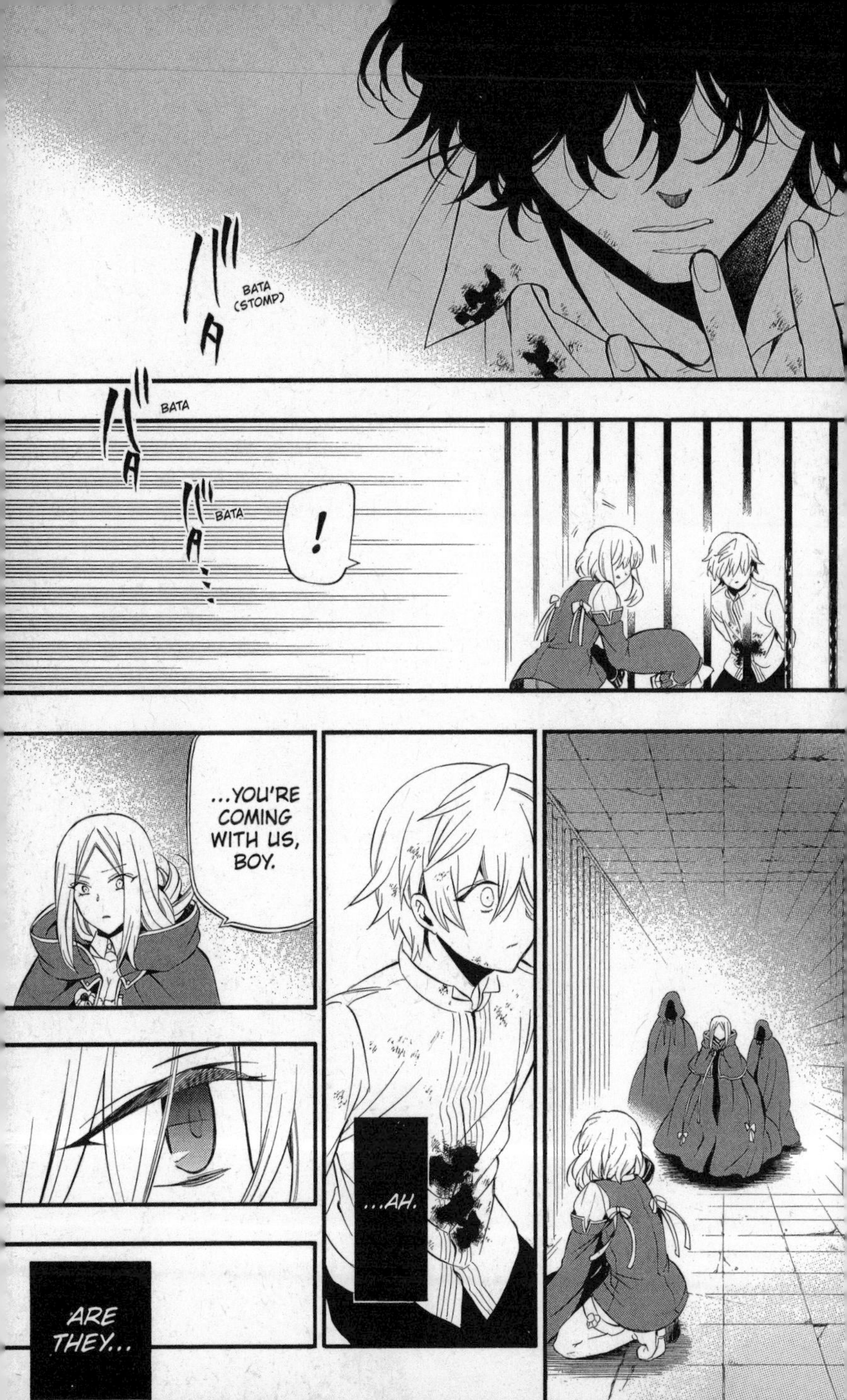
BATA (STOMP)
BATA
BATA
!
...AH.
...YOU'RE COMING WITH US, BOY.
ARE THEY...

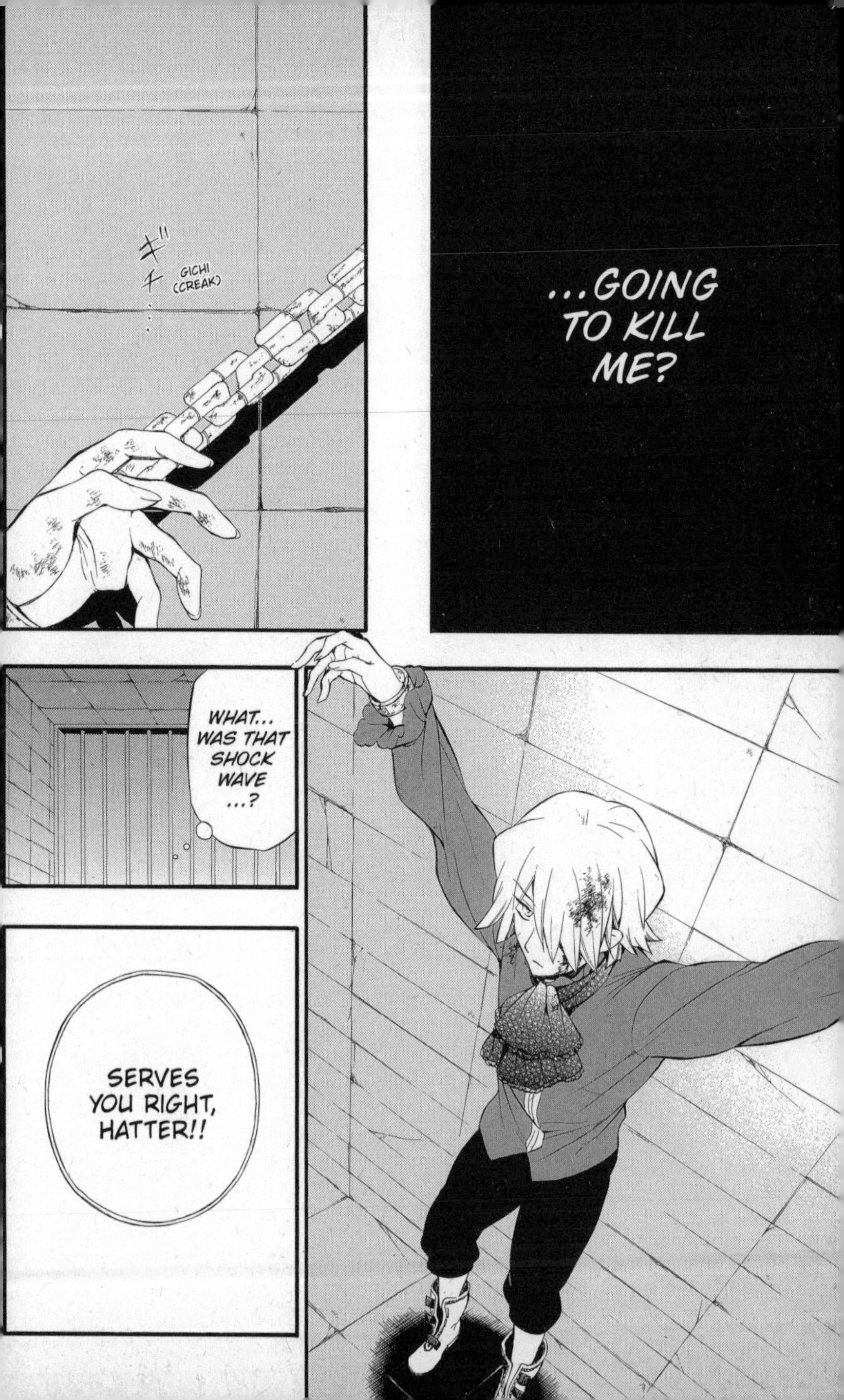
...GOING TO KILL ME?
ギチ…
GICHI (CREAK)
WHAT... WAS THAT SHOCK WAVE ...?
SERVES YOU RIGHT, HATTER!!

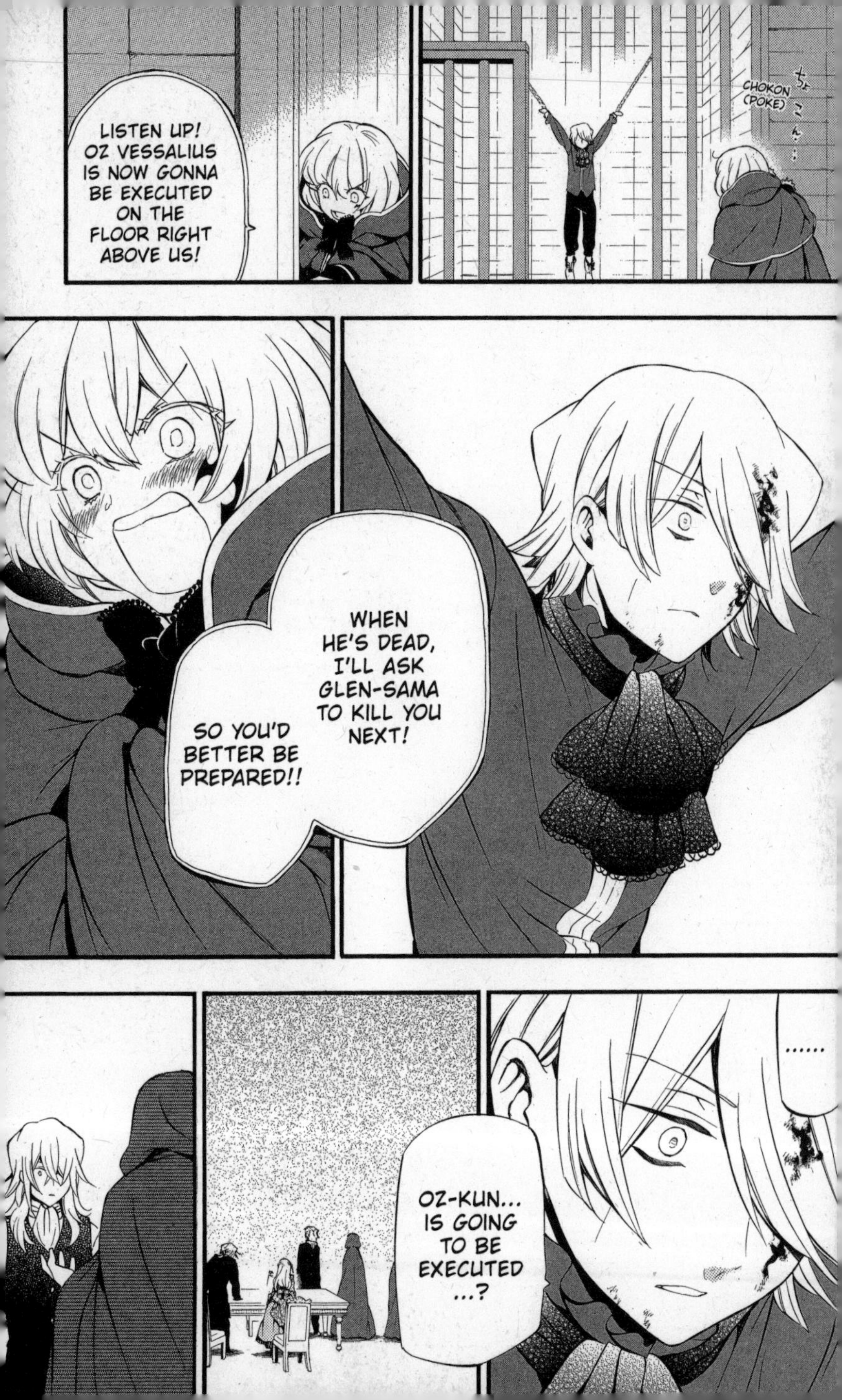

CHOKON (POKE)
ちょこん
LISTEN UP! OZ VESSALIUS IS NOW GONNA BE EXECUTED ON THE FLOOR RIGHT ABOVE US!
WHEN HE'S DEAD, I'LL ASK GLEN-SAMA TO KILL YOU NEXT!
SO YOU'D BETTER BE PREPARED!!
......
OZ-KUN... IS GOING TO BE EXECUTED ...?

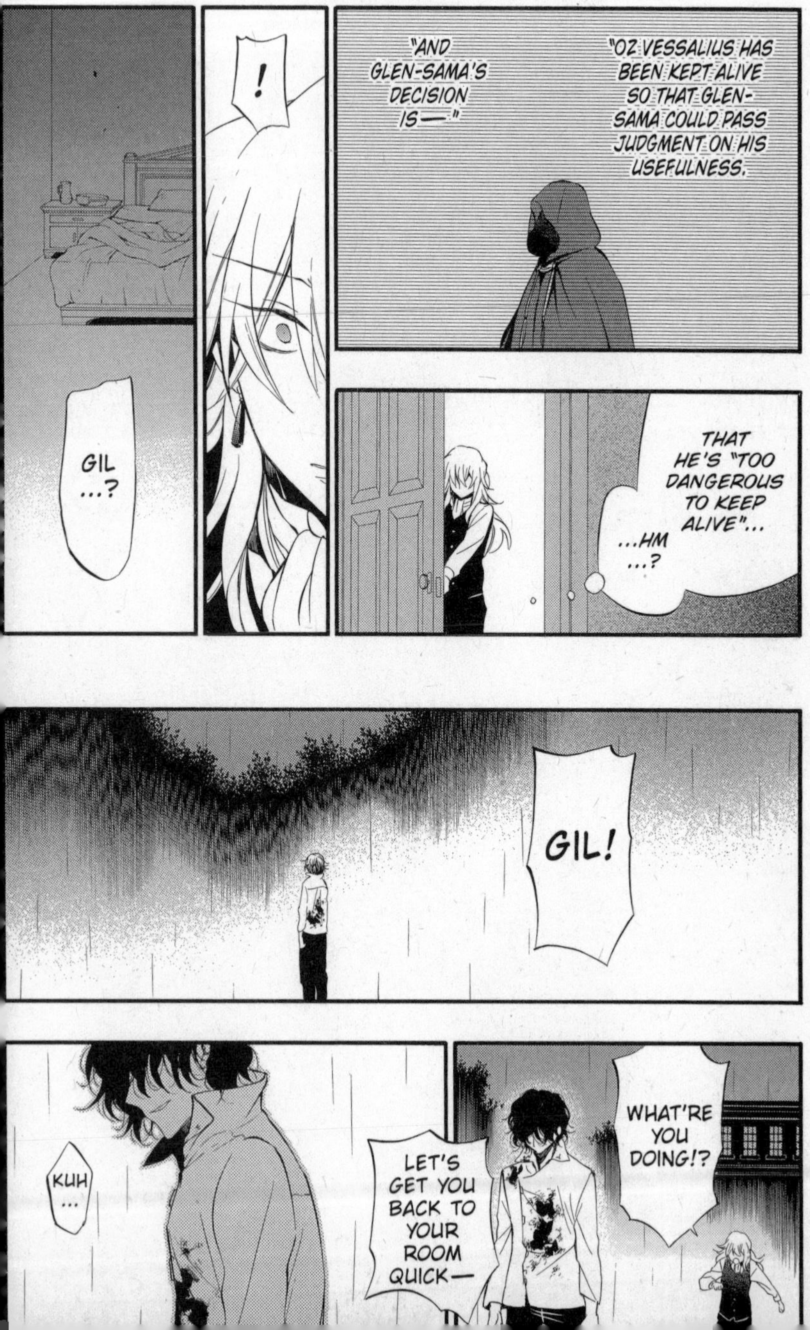
"OZ VESSALIUS HAS BEEN KEPT ALIVE SO THAT GLEN-SAMA COULD PASS JUDGMENT ON HIS USEFULNESS.
"AND GLEN-SAMA'S DECISION IS—"
THAT HE'S "TOO DANGEROUS TO KEEP ALIVE"...
...HM ...?
!
GIL ...?
GIL!
WHAT'RE YOU DOING!?
LET'S GET YOU BACK TO YOUR ROOM QUICK—
KUH ...

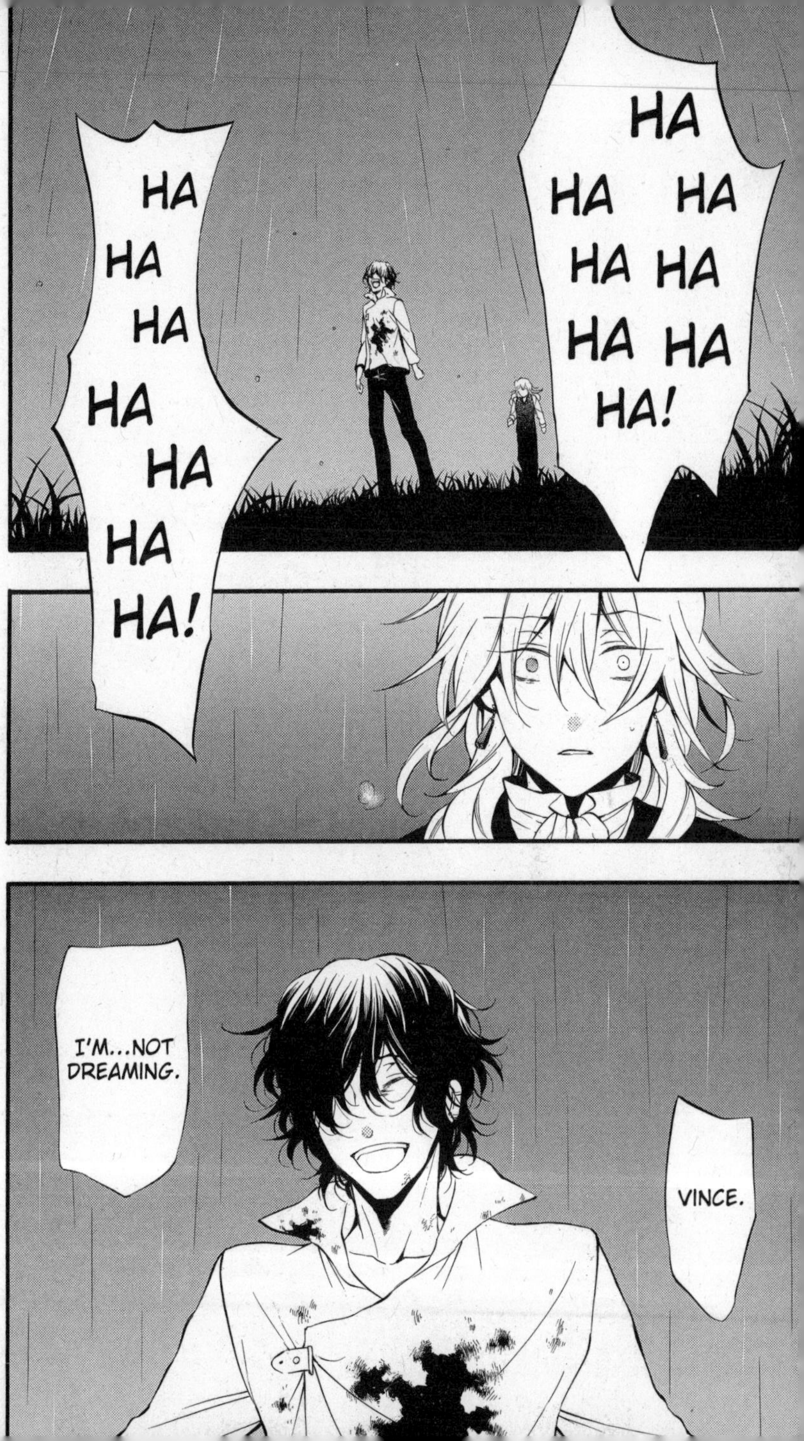
HA HA HA HA HA HA HA HA HA!
HA HA HA HA HA HA HA!
I'M...NOT DREAMING.
VINCE.

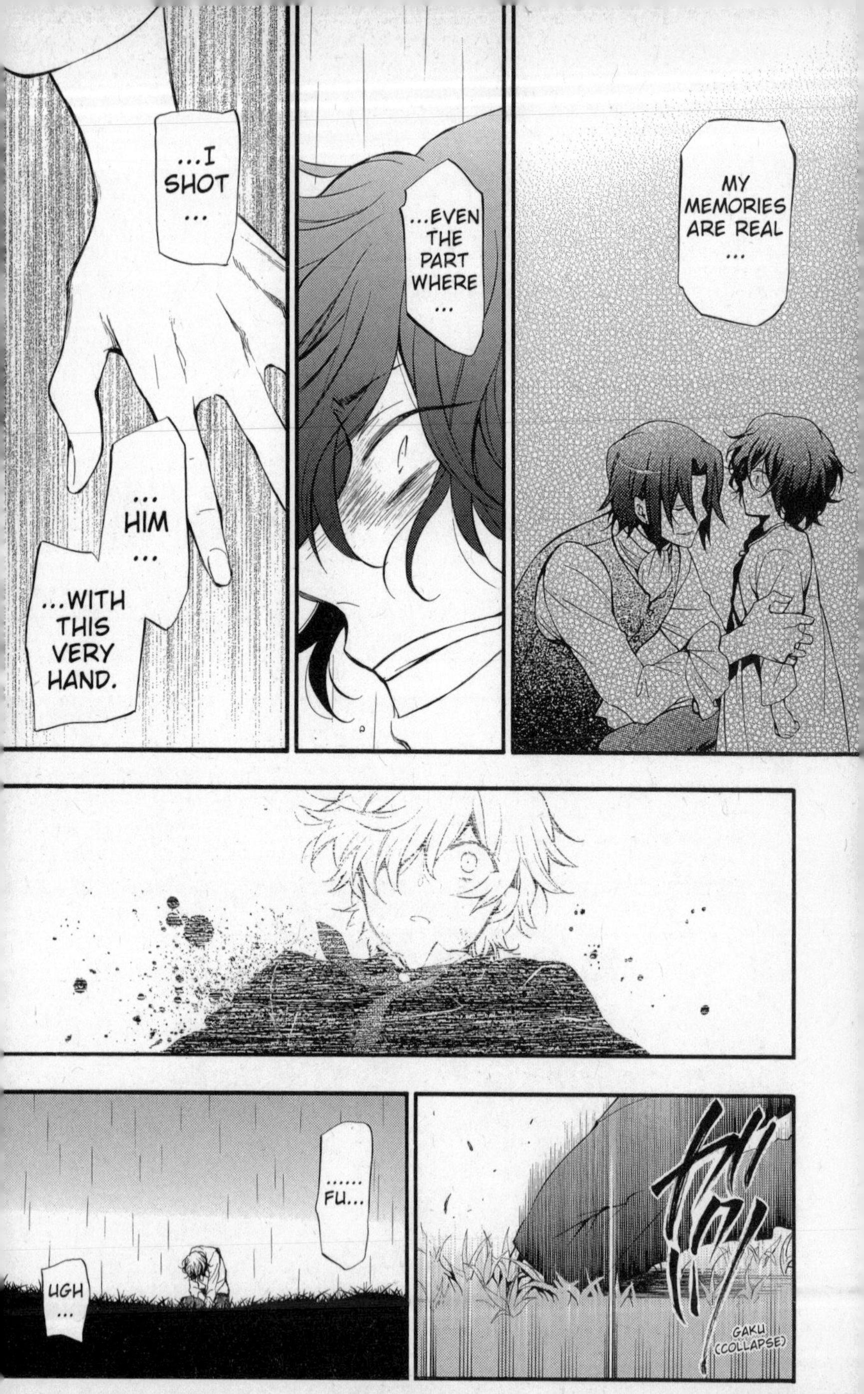
MY MEMORIES ARE REAL ...
...EVEN THE PART WHERE ...
...I SHOT ...
... HIM ...
...WITH THIS VERY HAND.
GAKU (COLLAPSE)
......FU...
UGH ...

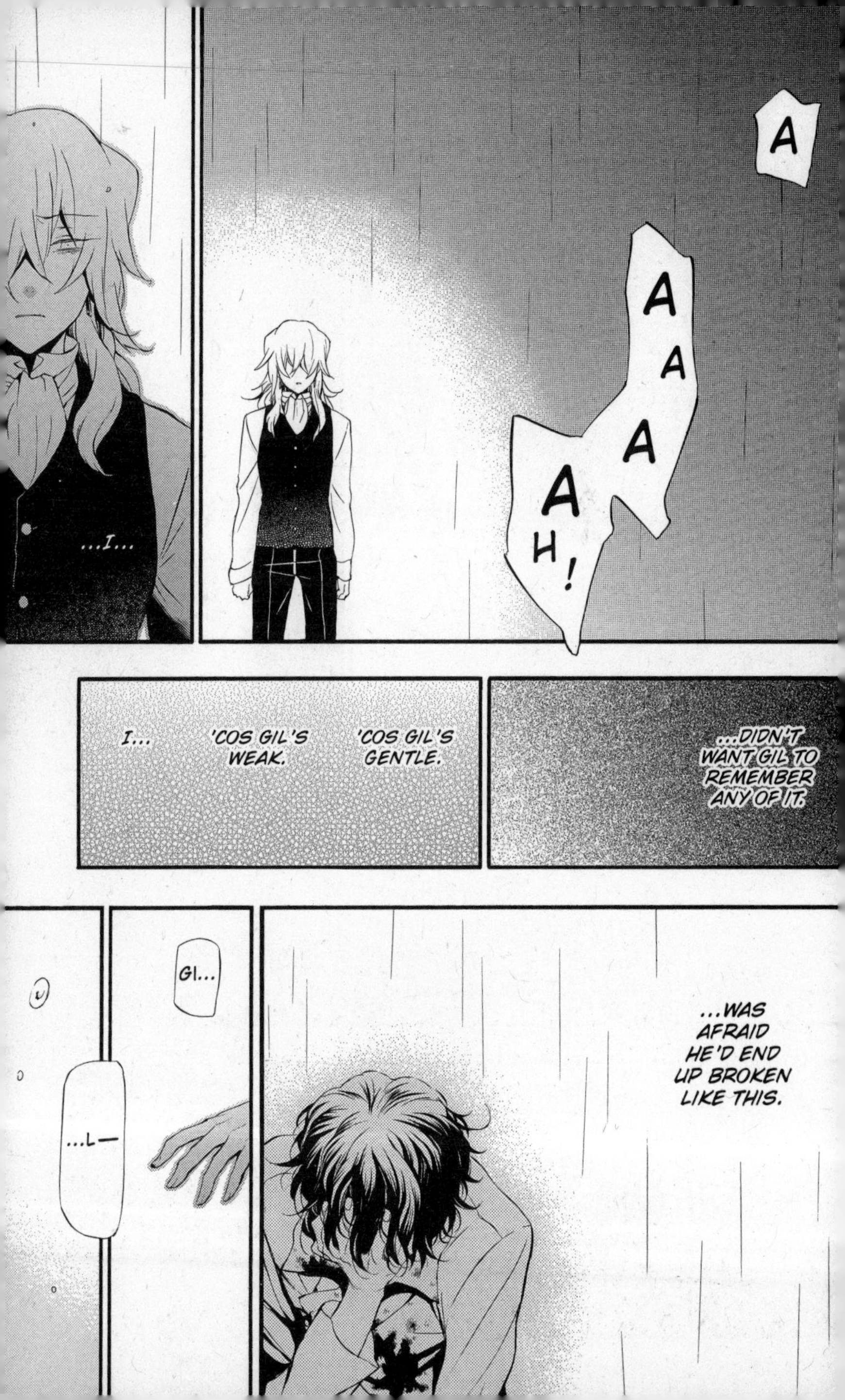
AAAAAH!
...I...
...DIDN'T WANT GIL TO REMEMBER ANY OF IT.
'COS GIL'S GENTLE.
'COS GIL'S WEAK.
I...
...WAS AFRAID HE'D END UP BROKEN LIKE THIS.
GI...
...L—

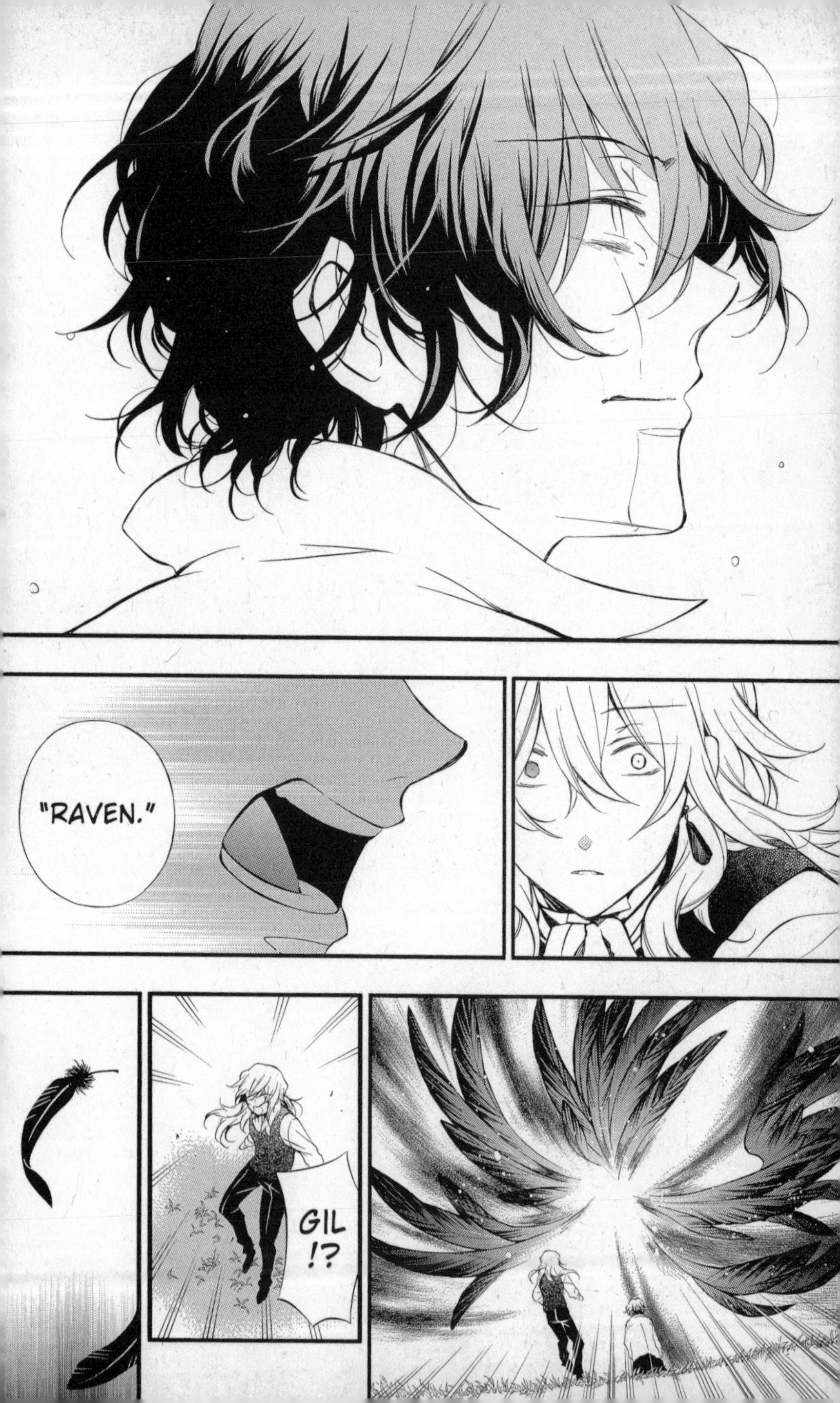
"RAVEN."
GIL !?

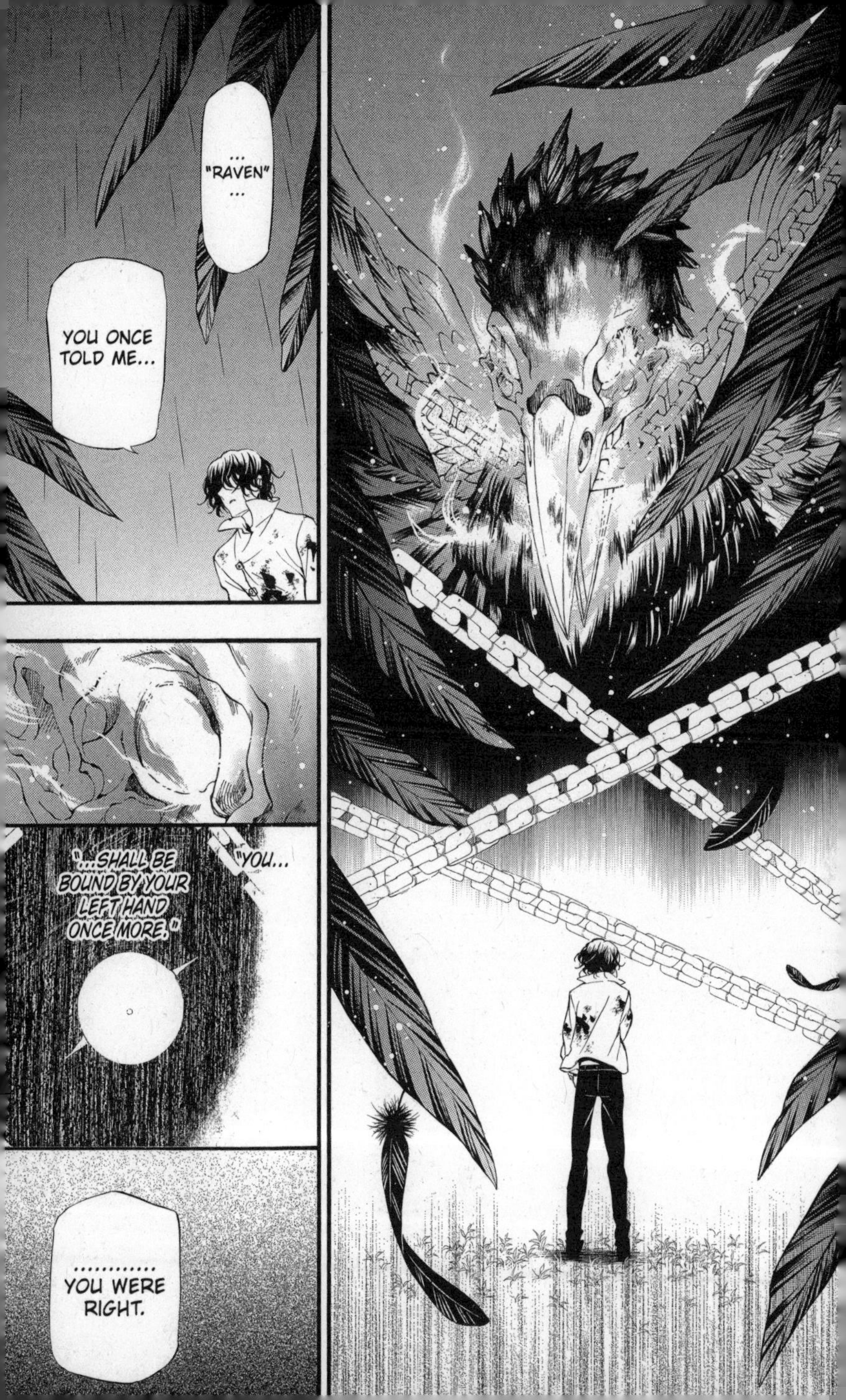
... "RAVEN" ...
YOU ONCE TOLD ME...
"YOU...
"...SHALL BE BOUND BY YOUR LEFT HAND ONCE MORE."
.... YOU WERE RIGHT.

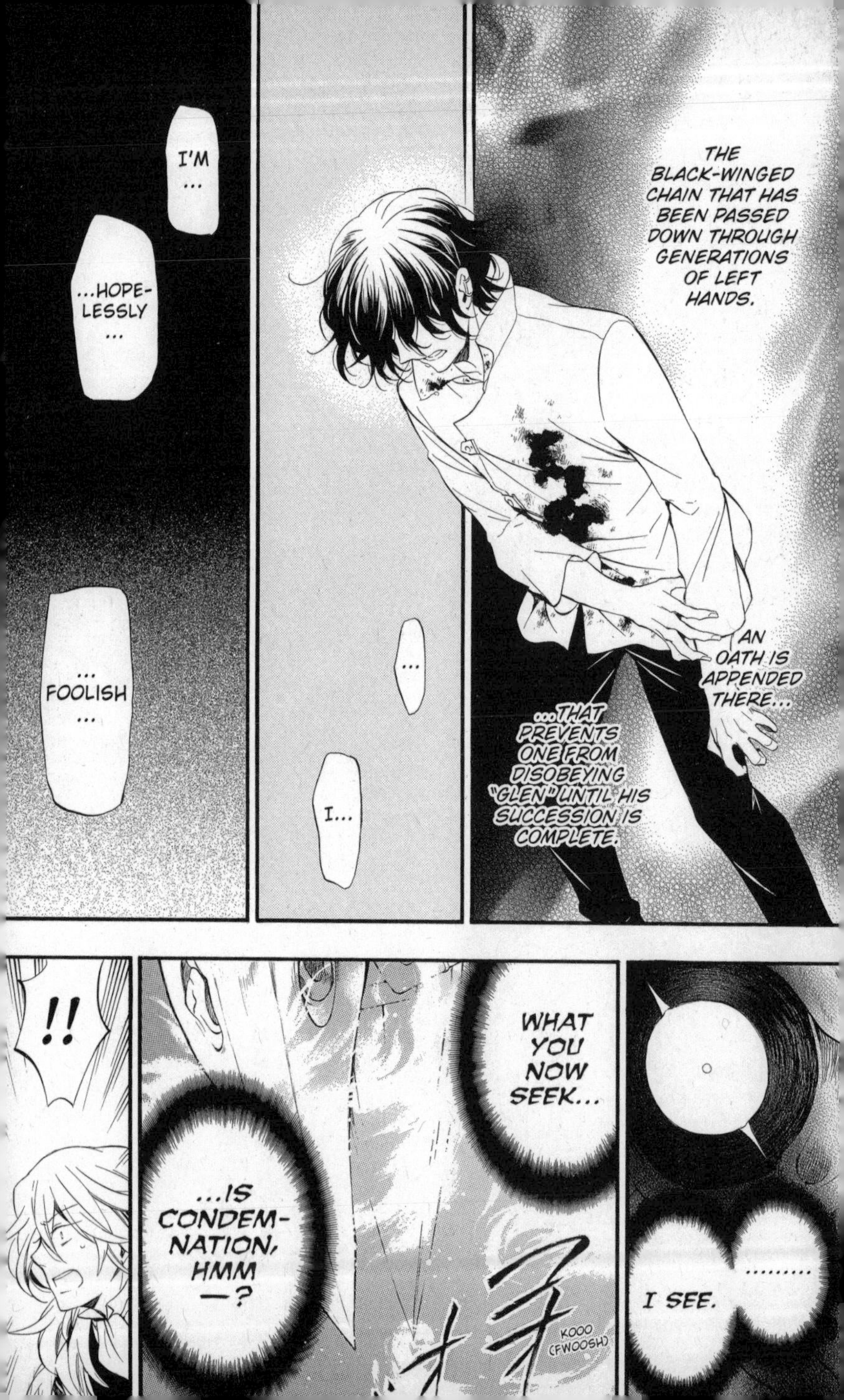
THE BLACK-WINGED CHAIN THAT HAS BEEN PASSED DOWN THROUGH GENERATIONS OF LEFT HANDS.
AN OATH IS APPENDED THERE...
...THAT PREVENTS ONE FROM DISOBEYING "GLEN" UNTIL HIS SUCCESSION IS COMPLETE.
...
I...
I'M ...
...HOPELESSLY ...
... FOOLISH ...
....
I SEE.
WHAT YOU NOW SEEK...
...IS CONDEMNATION, HMM—?
KOOO (FWOOSH)
!!

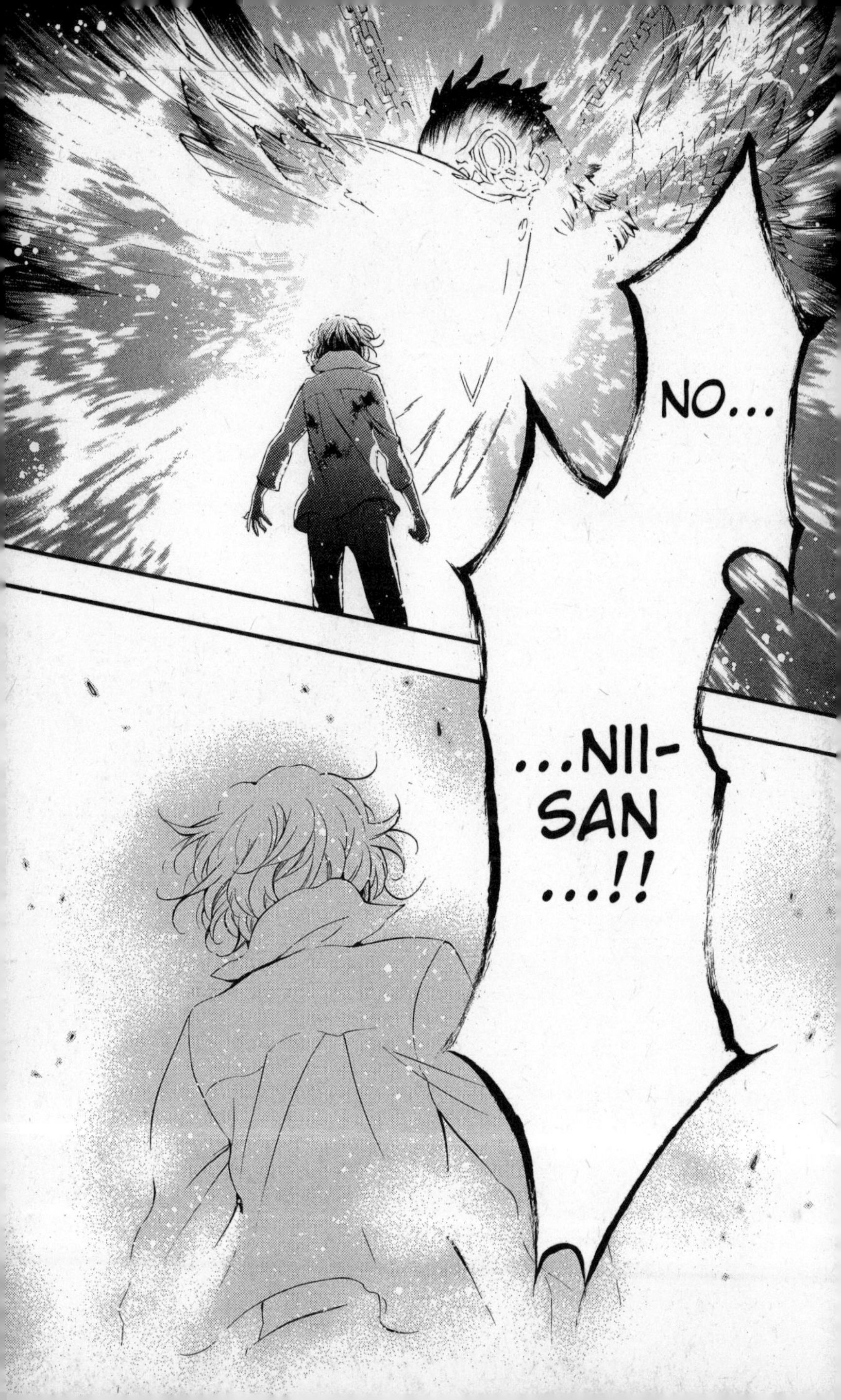
NO...
...NII-SAN...!!

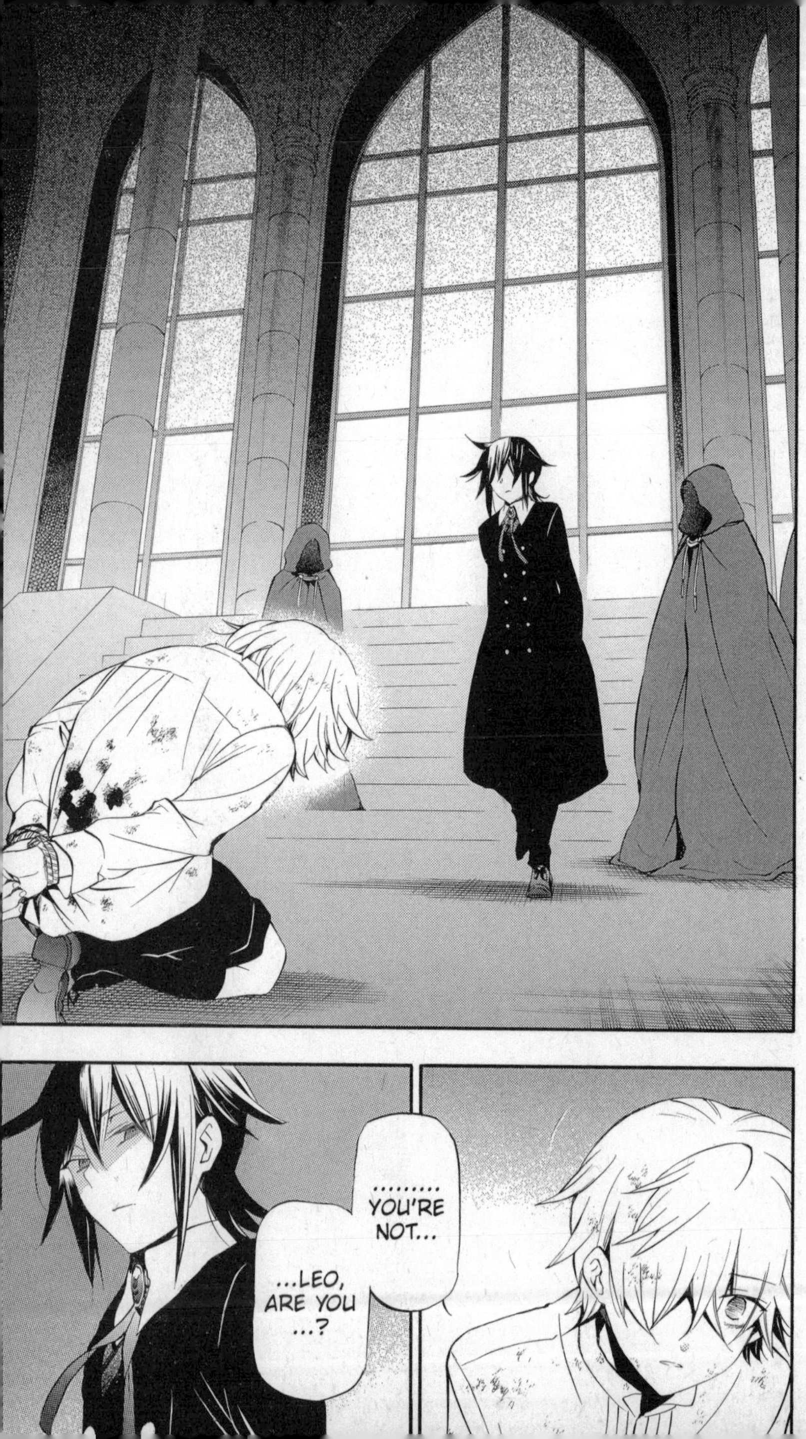
....
YOU'RE NOT...
...LEO, ARE YOU ...?

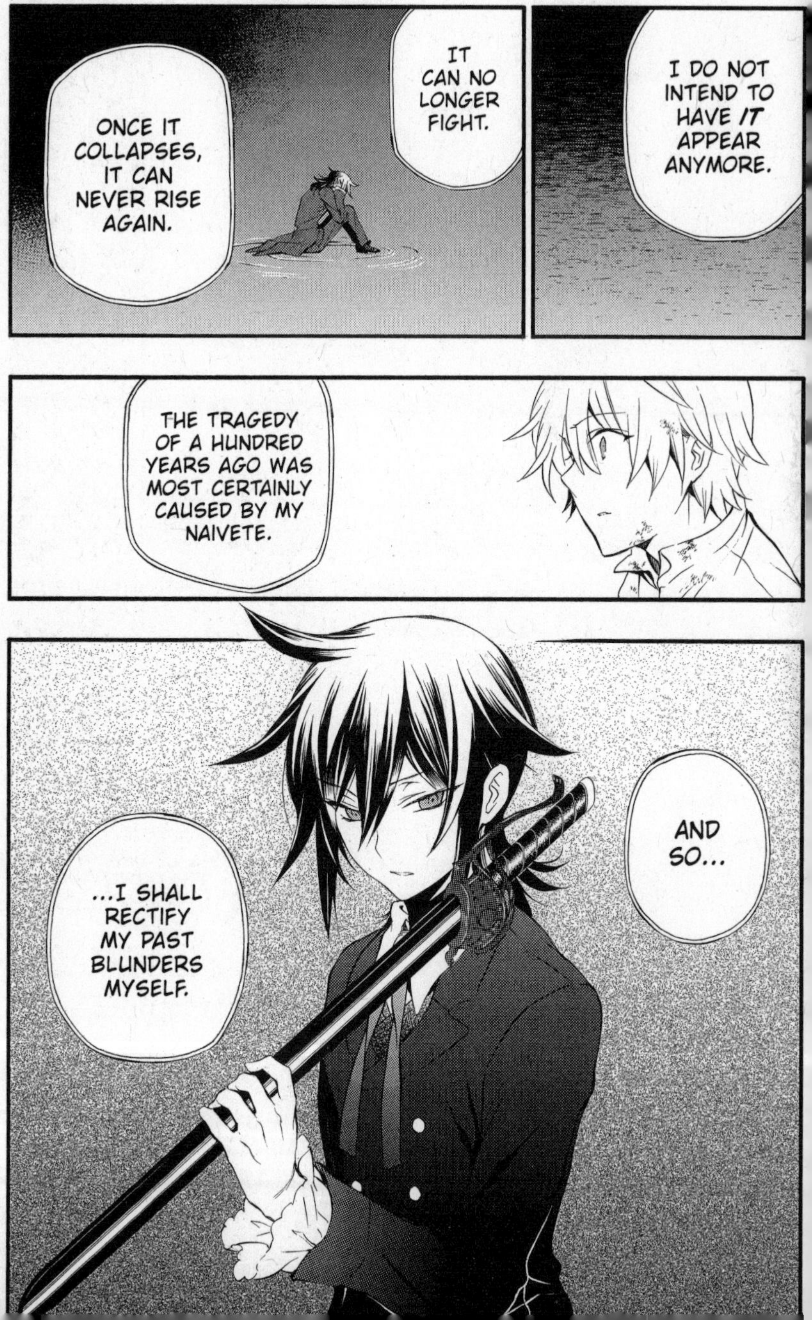
I DO NOT INTEND TO HAVE *IT* APPEAR ANYMORE.
IT CAN NO LONGER FIGHT.
ONCE IT COLLAPSES, IT CAN NEVER RISE AGAIN.
THE TRAGEDY OF A HUNDRED YEARS AGO WAS MOST CERTAINLY CAUSED BY MY NAIVETE.
AND SO...
...I SHALL RECTIFY MY PAST BLUNDERS MYSELF.

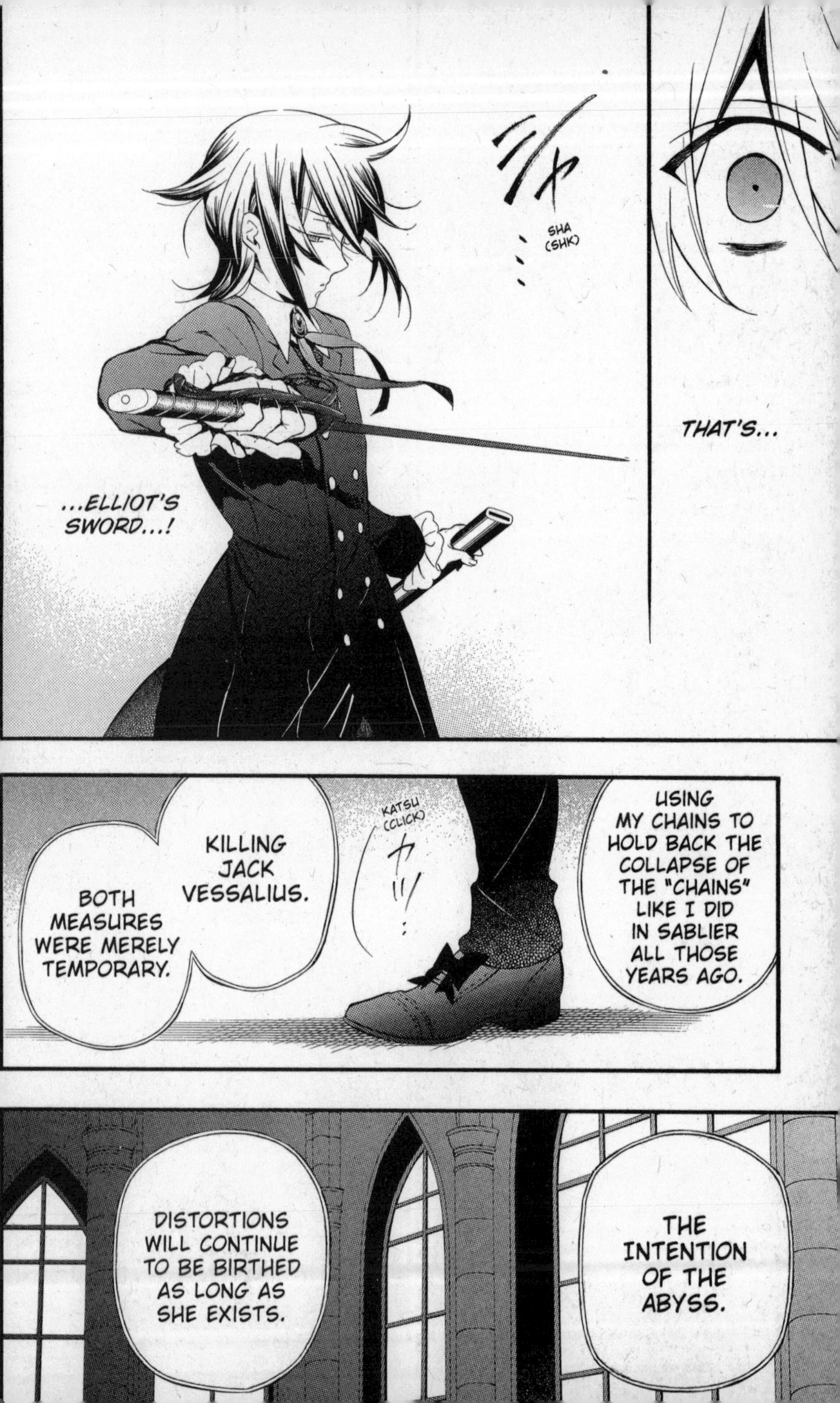
THAT'S...
SHA (SHK)
...ELLIOT'S SWORD...!
USING MY CHAINS TO HOLD BACK THE COLLAPSE OF THE "CHAINS" LIKE I DID IN SABLIER ALL THOSE YEARS AGO.
KATSU (CLICK)
KILLING JACK VESSALIUS.
BOTH MEASURES WERE MERELY TEMPORARY.
THE INTENTION OF THE ABYSS.
DISTORTIONS WILL CONTINUE TO BE BIRTHED AS LONG AS SHE EXISTS.

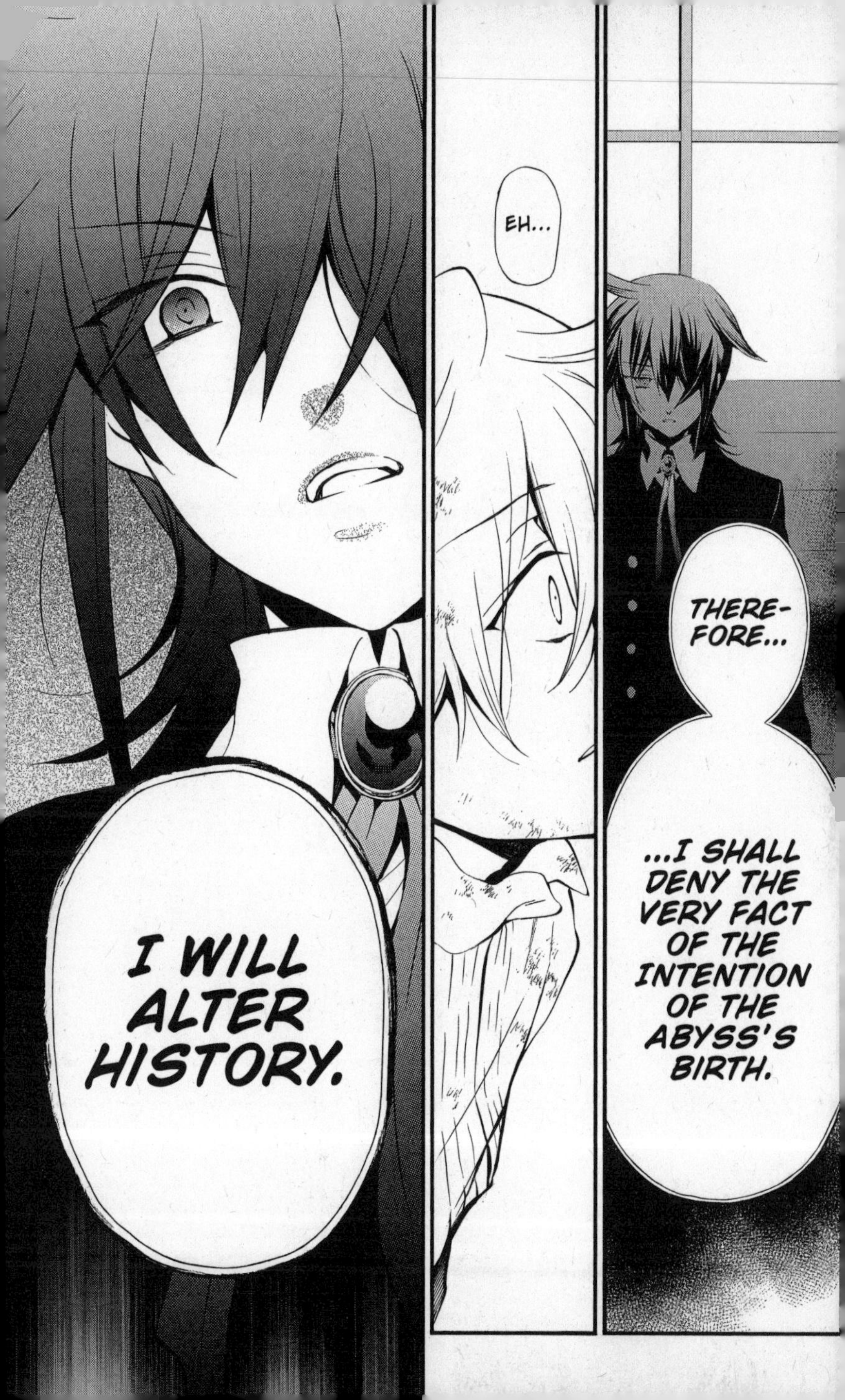
THERE-FORE...
...I SHALL DENY THE VERY FACT OF THE INTENTION OF THE ABYSS'S BIRTH.
EH...
I WILL ALTER HISTORY.

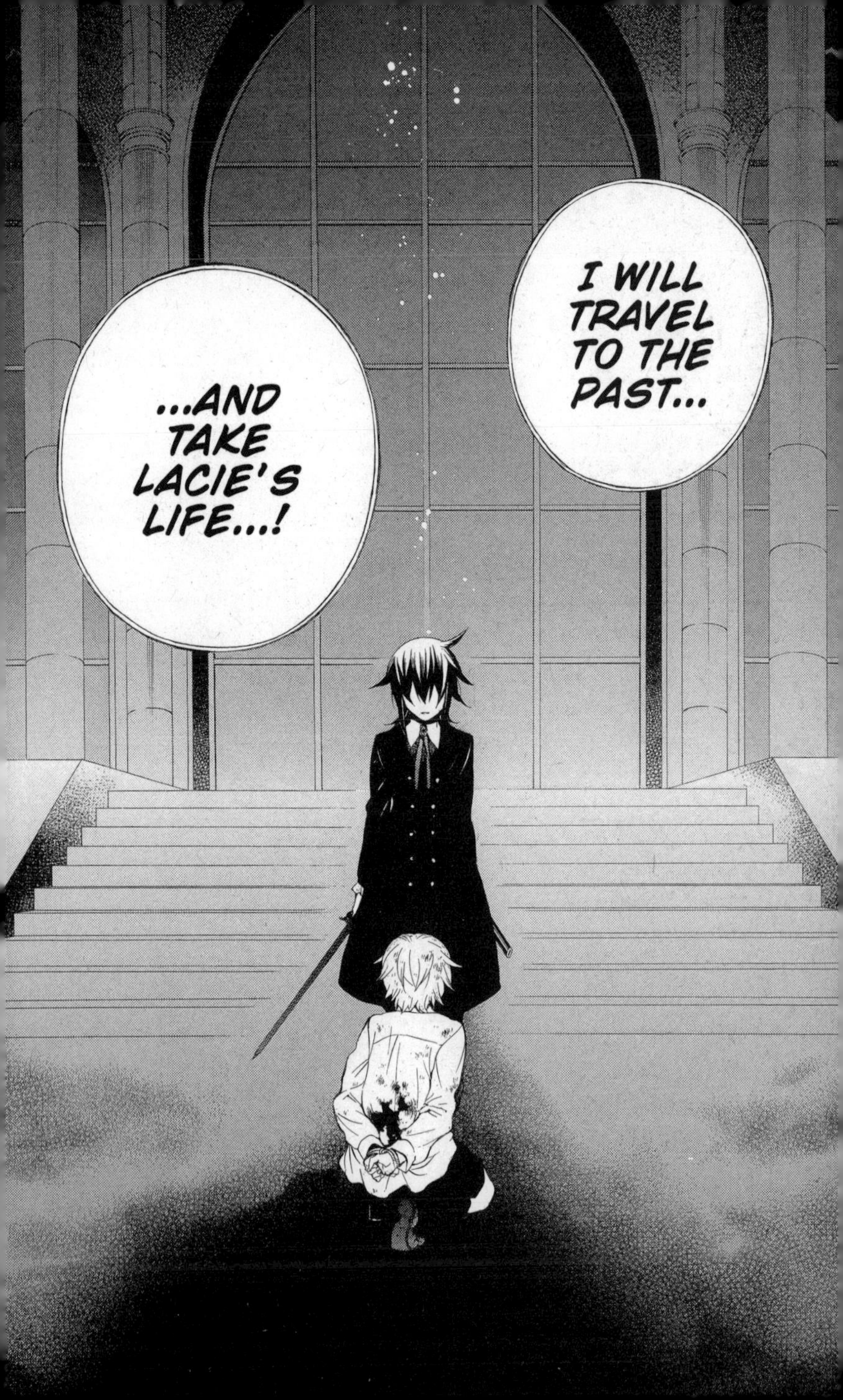
I WILL TRAVEL TO THE PAST...
...AND TAKE LACIE'S LIFE...!

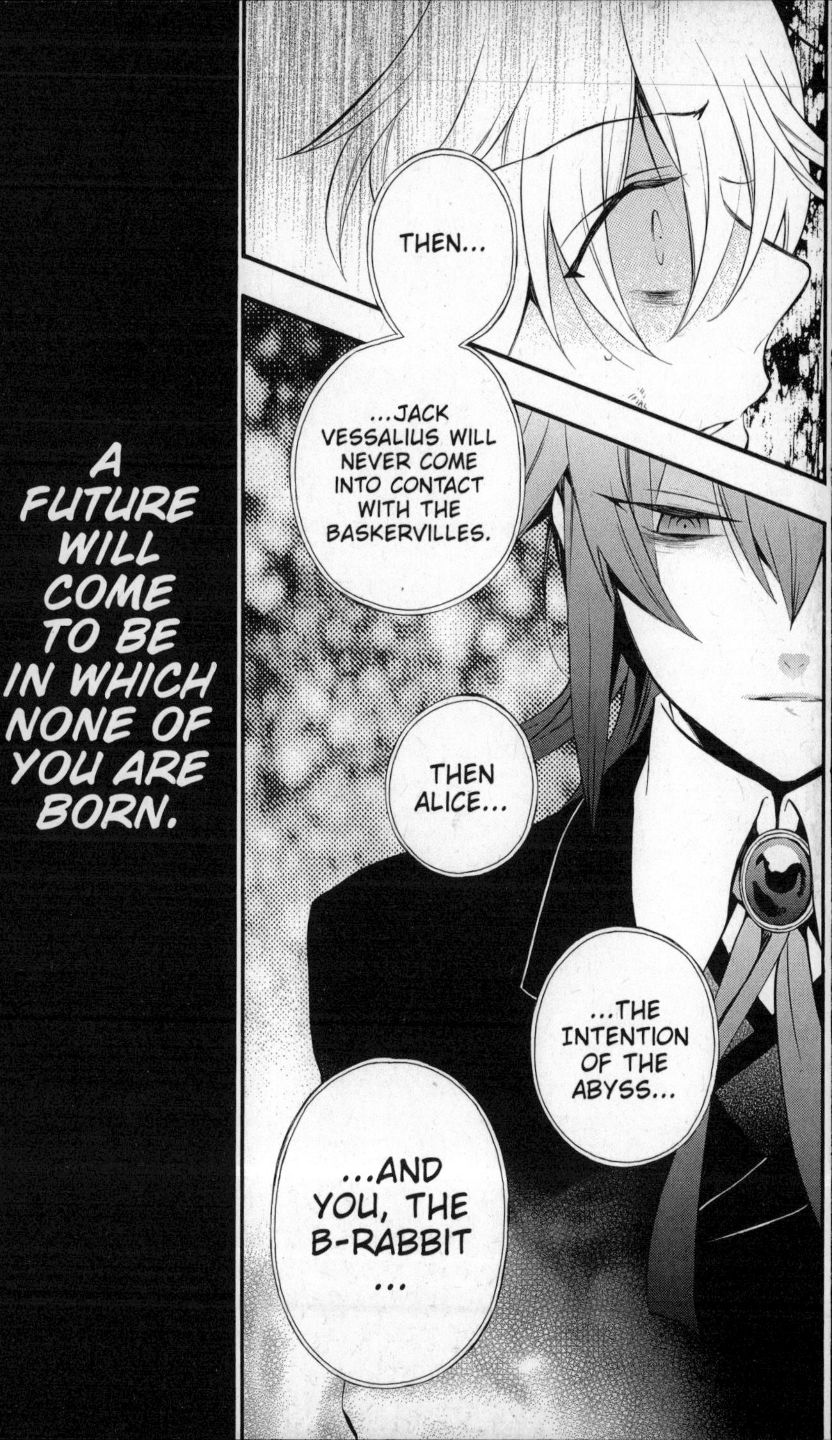
THEN...
...JACK VESSALIUS WILL NEVER COME INTO CONTACT WITH THE BASKERVILLES.
THEN ALICE...
...THE INTENTION OF THE ABYSS...
...AND YOU, THE B-RABBIT ...
A FUTURE WILL COME TO BE IN WHICH NONE OF YOU ARE BORN.

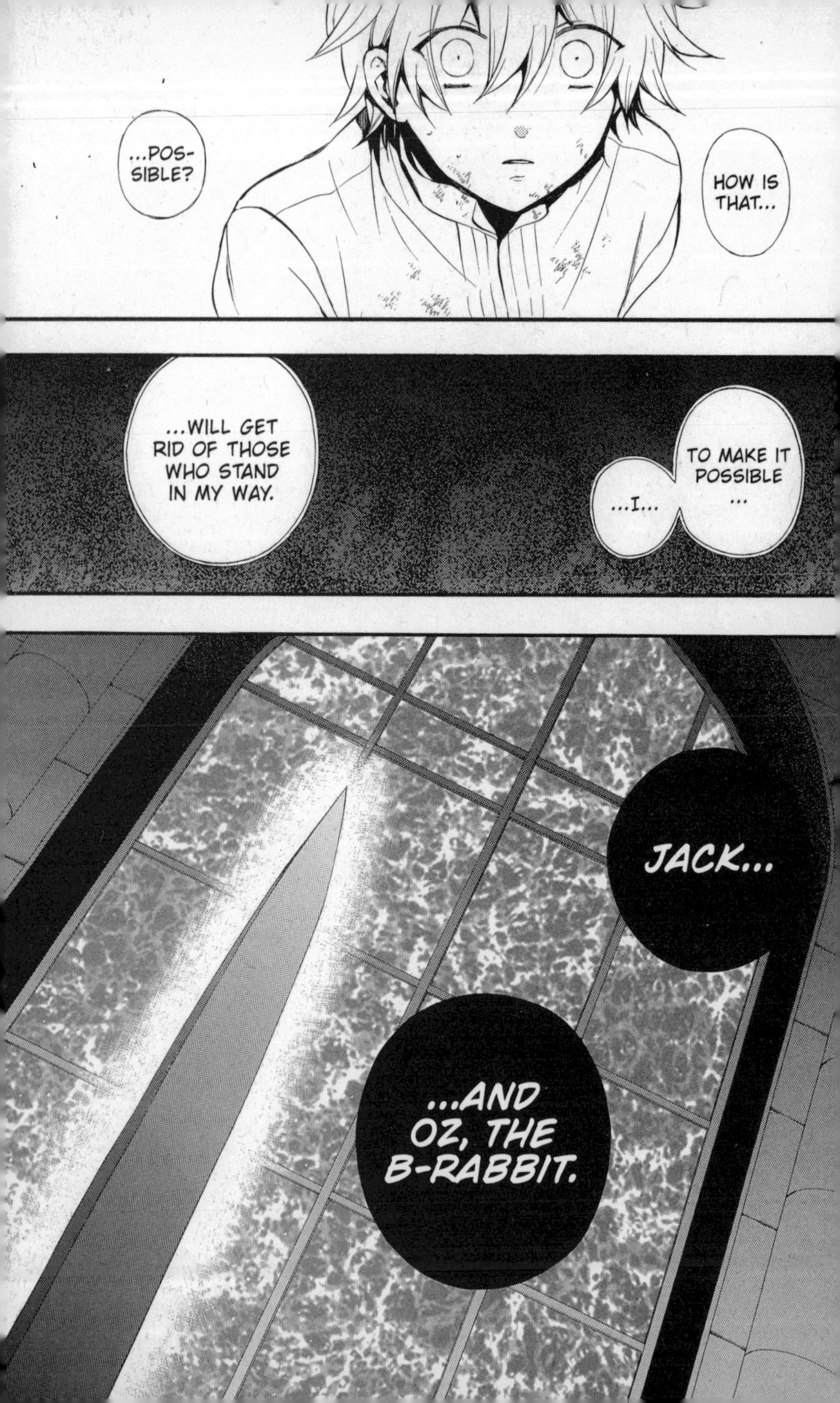
HOW IS THAT...
...POS-SIBLE?
TO MAKE IT POSSIBLE ...
...I...
...WILL GET RID OF THOSE WHO STAND IN MY WAY.
JACK...
...AND OZ, THE B-RABBIT.

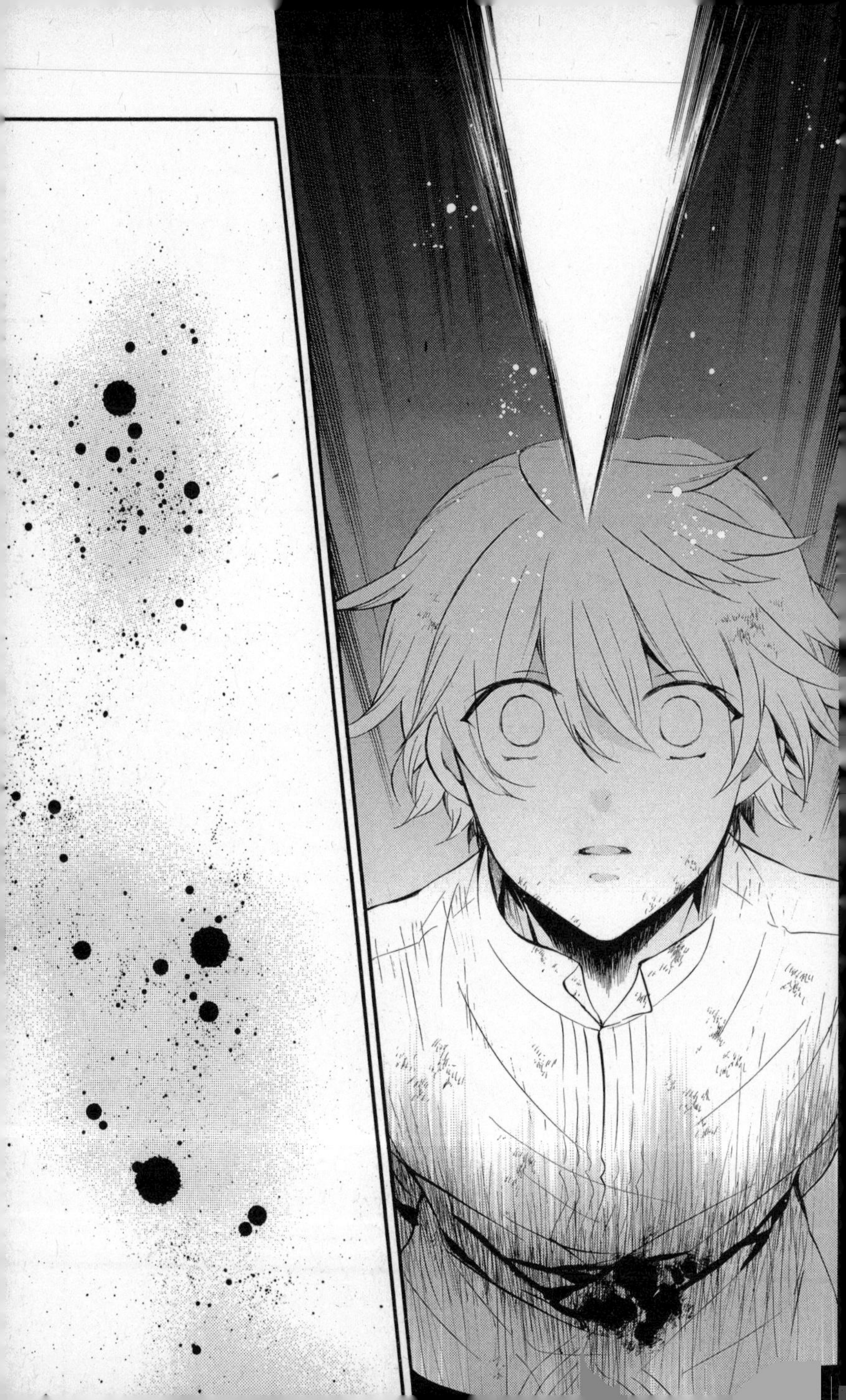

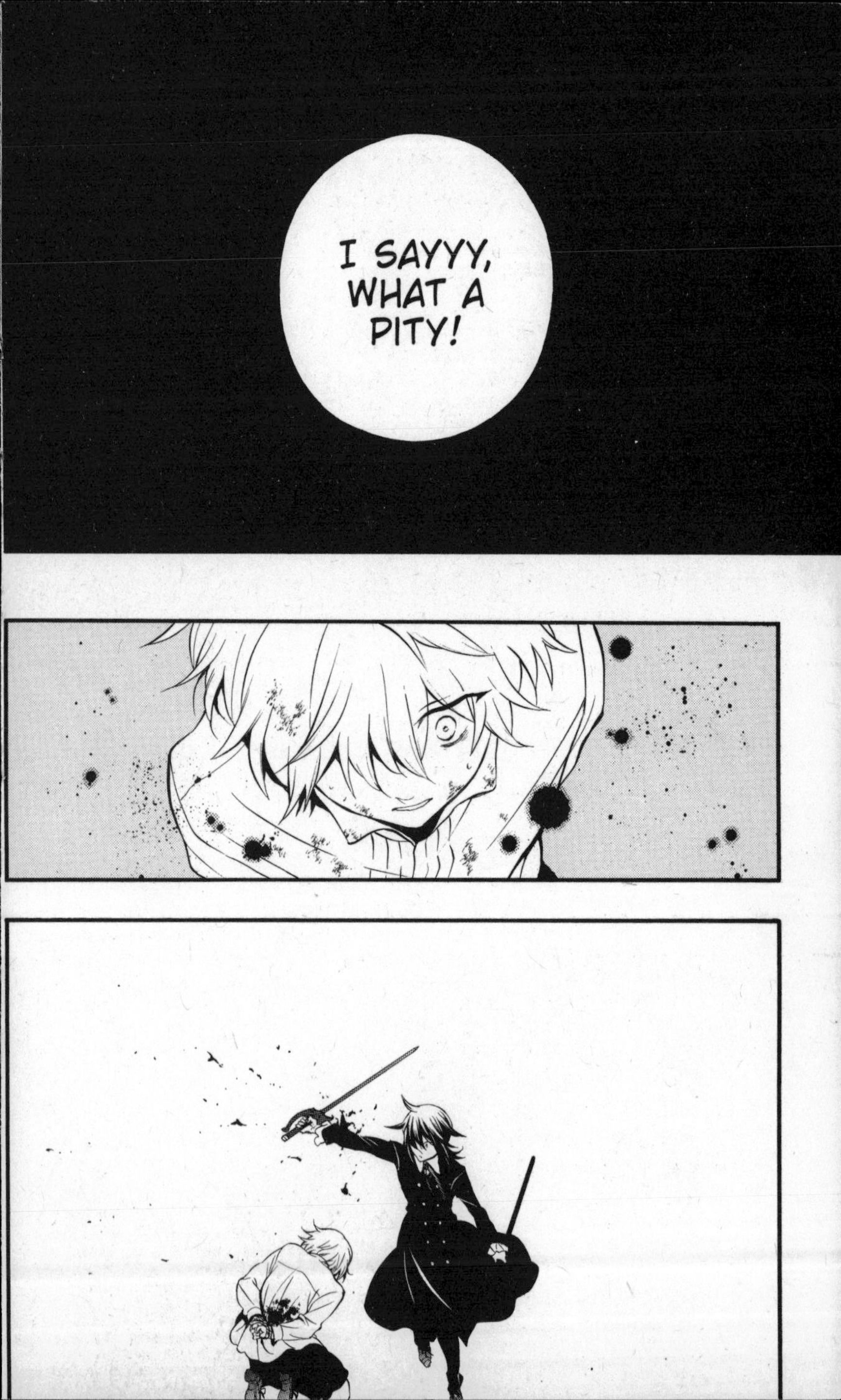
I SAYYY, WHAT A PITY!

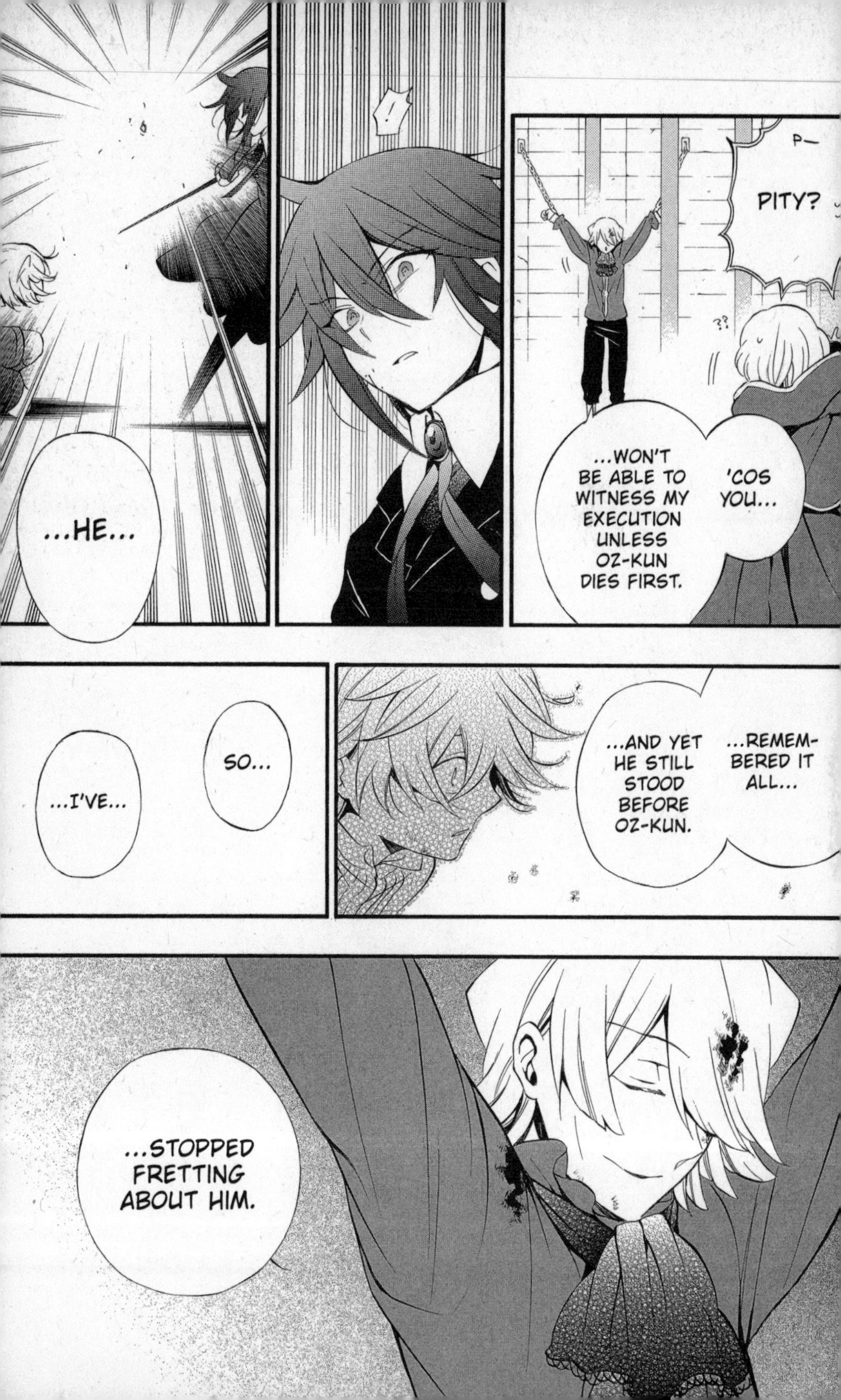
P—
PITY?
??
'COS YOU...
...WON'T BE ABLE TO WITNESS MY EXECUTION UNLESS OZ-KUN DIES FIRST.
!
...HE...
...REMEM-BERED IT ALL...
...AND YET HE STILL STOOD BEFORE OZ-KUN.
SO...
...I'VE...
...STOPPED FRETTING ABOUT HIM.

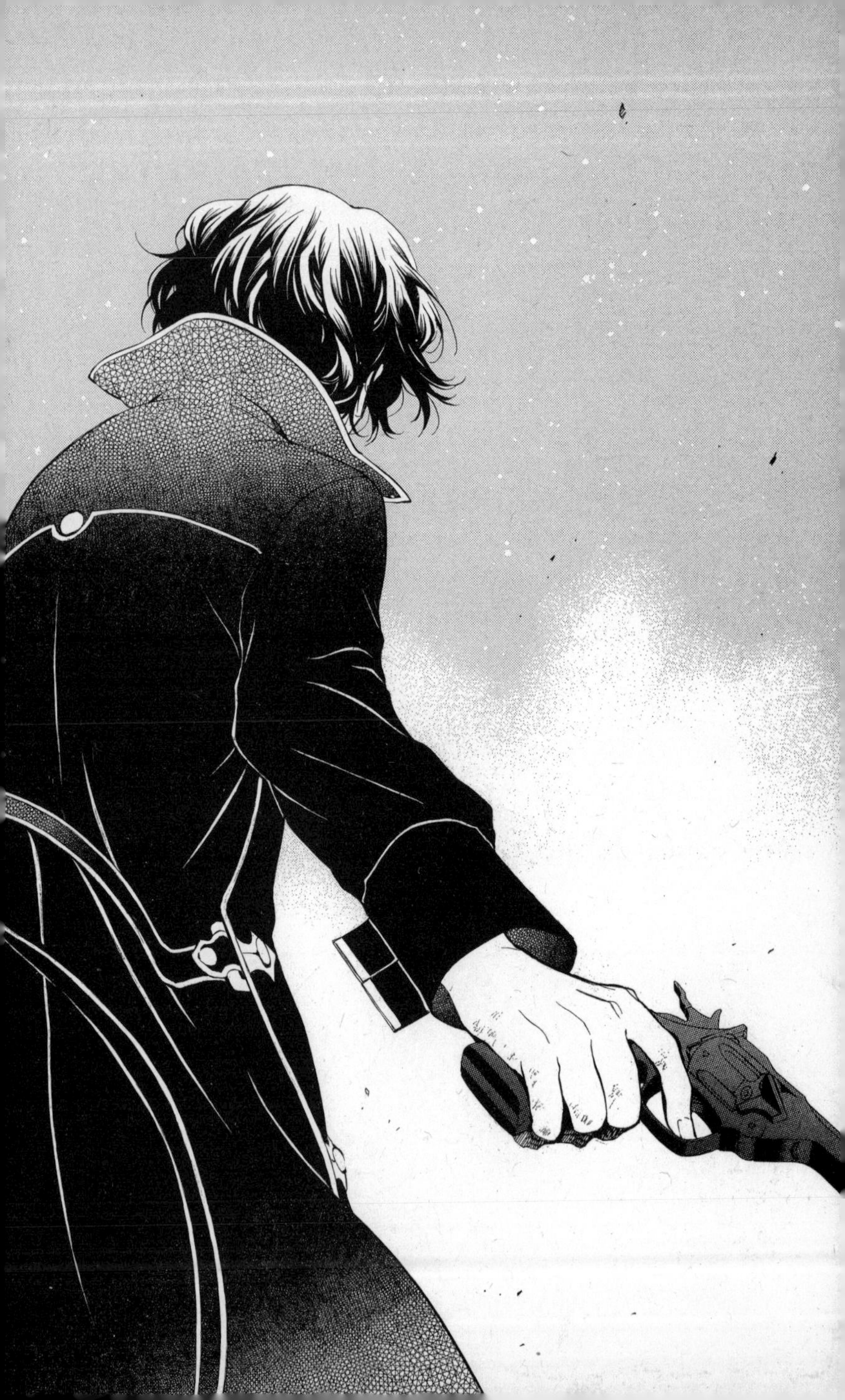

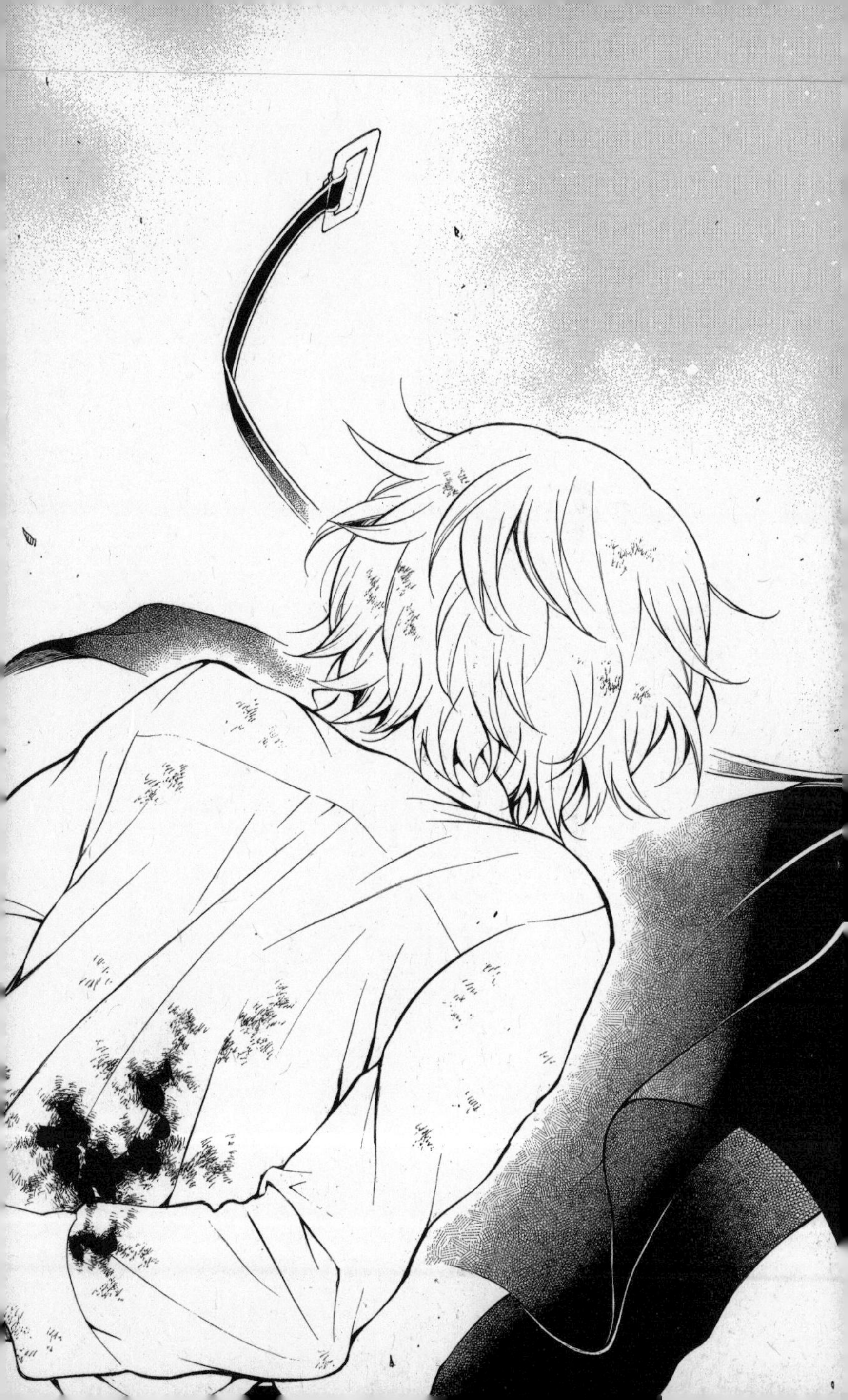

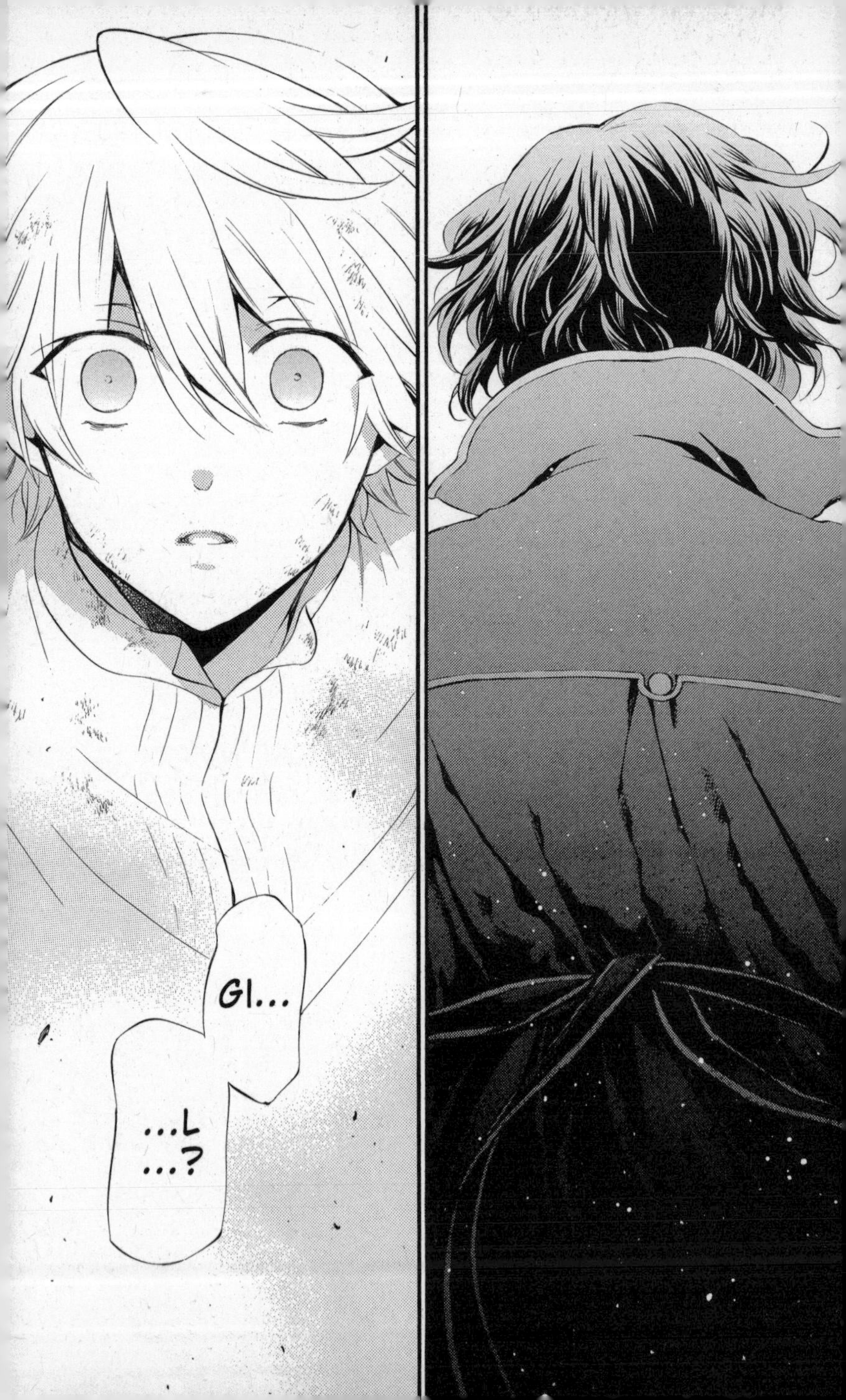
Gl...
...L
...?

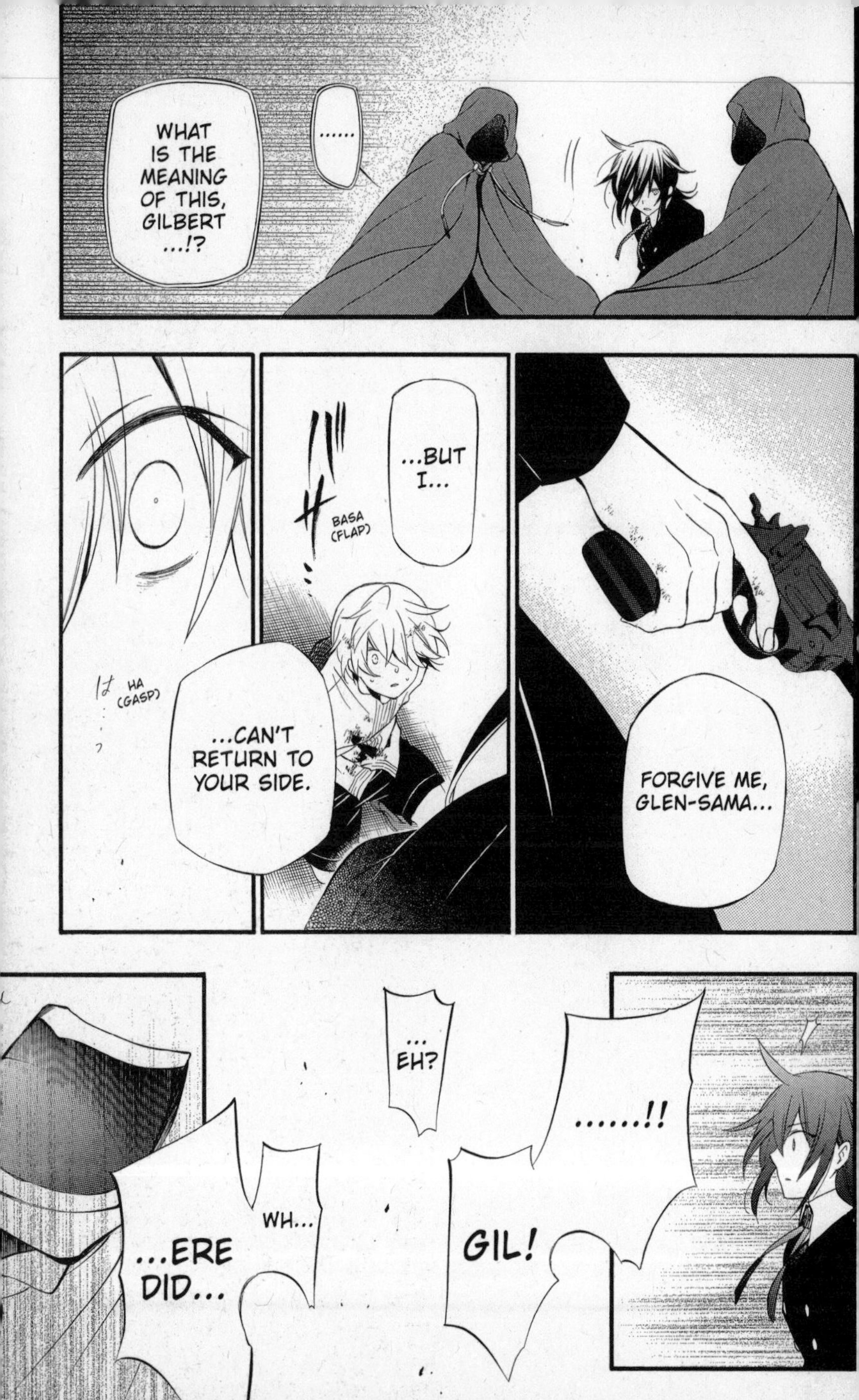
......
WHAT IS THE MEANING OF THIS, GILBERT ...!?
FORGIVE ME, GLEN-SAMA...
...BUT I...
BASA (FLAP)
...CAN'T RETURN TO YOUR SIDE.
HA (GASP)
......!!
GIL!
... EH?
WH...
...ERE DID...

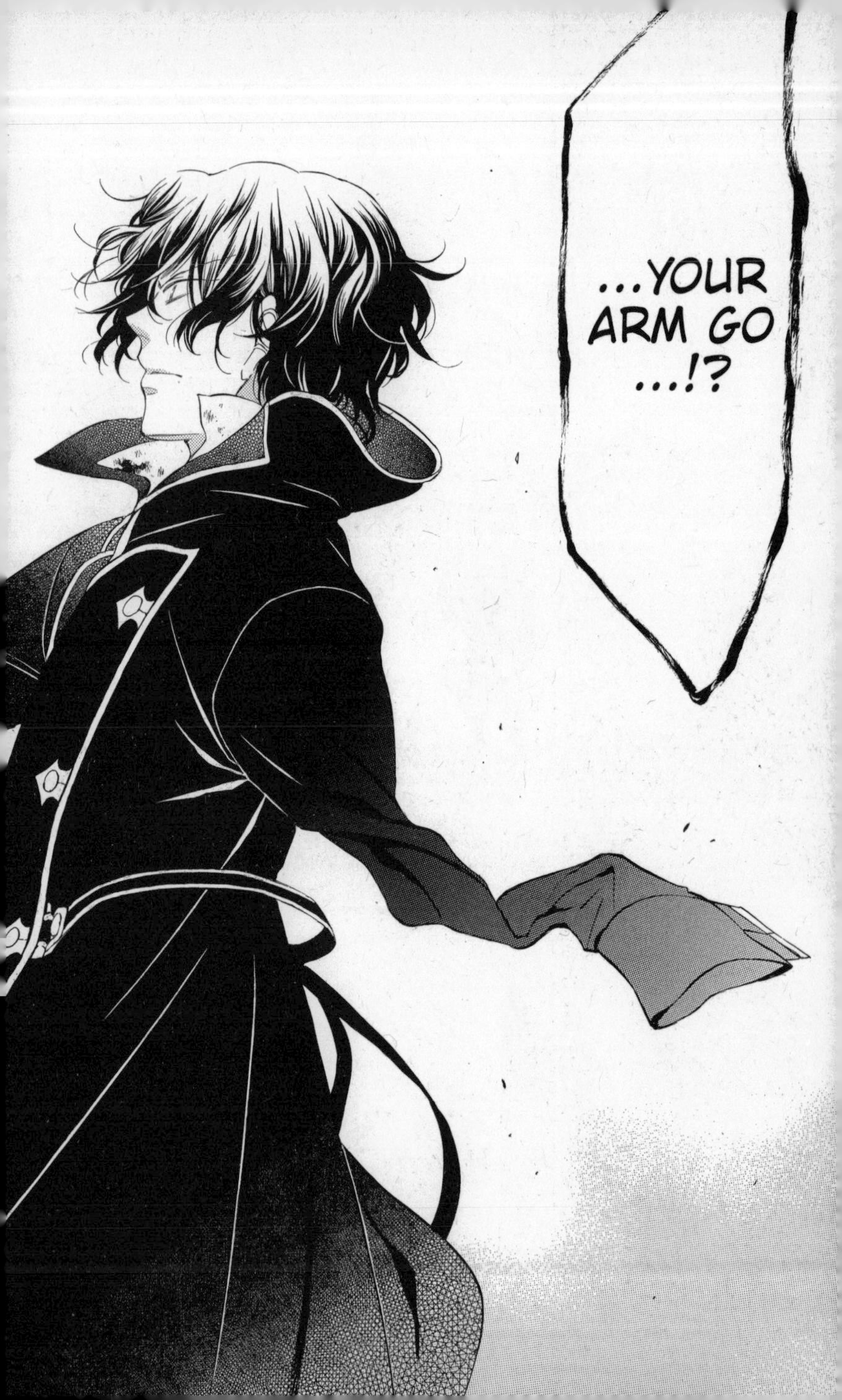
...YOUR ARM GO ...!?

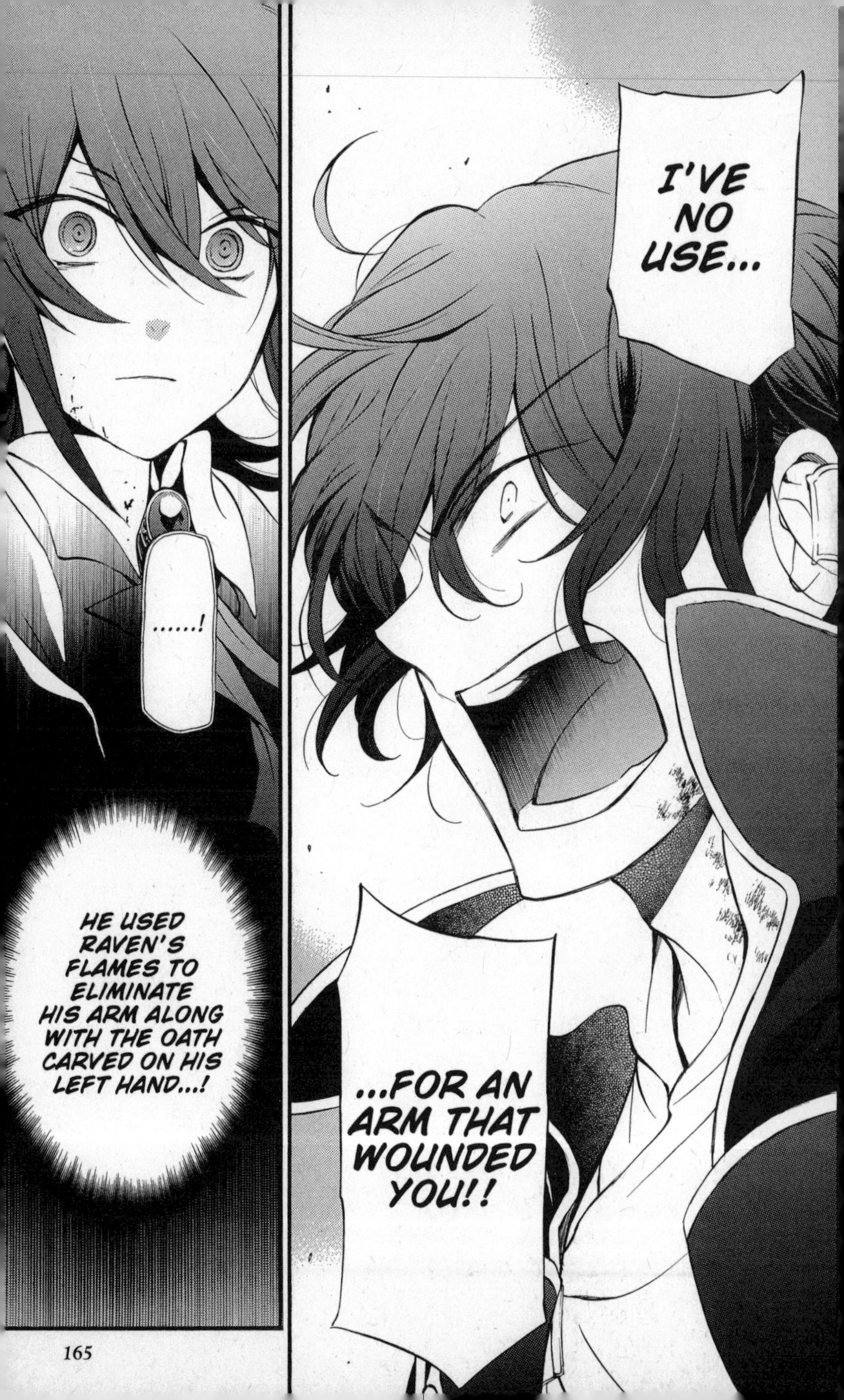
I'VE NO USE...
...FOR AN ARM THAT WOUNDED YOU!!
......!
HE USED RAVEN'S FLAMES TO ELIMINATE HIS ARM ALONG WITH THE OATH CARVED ON HIS LEFT HAND...!

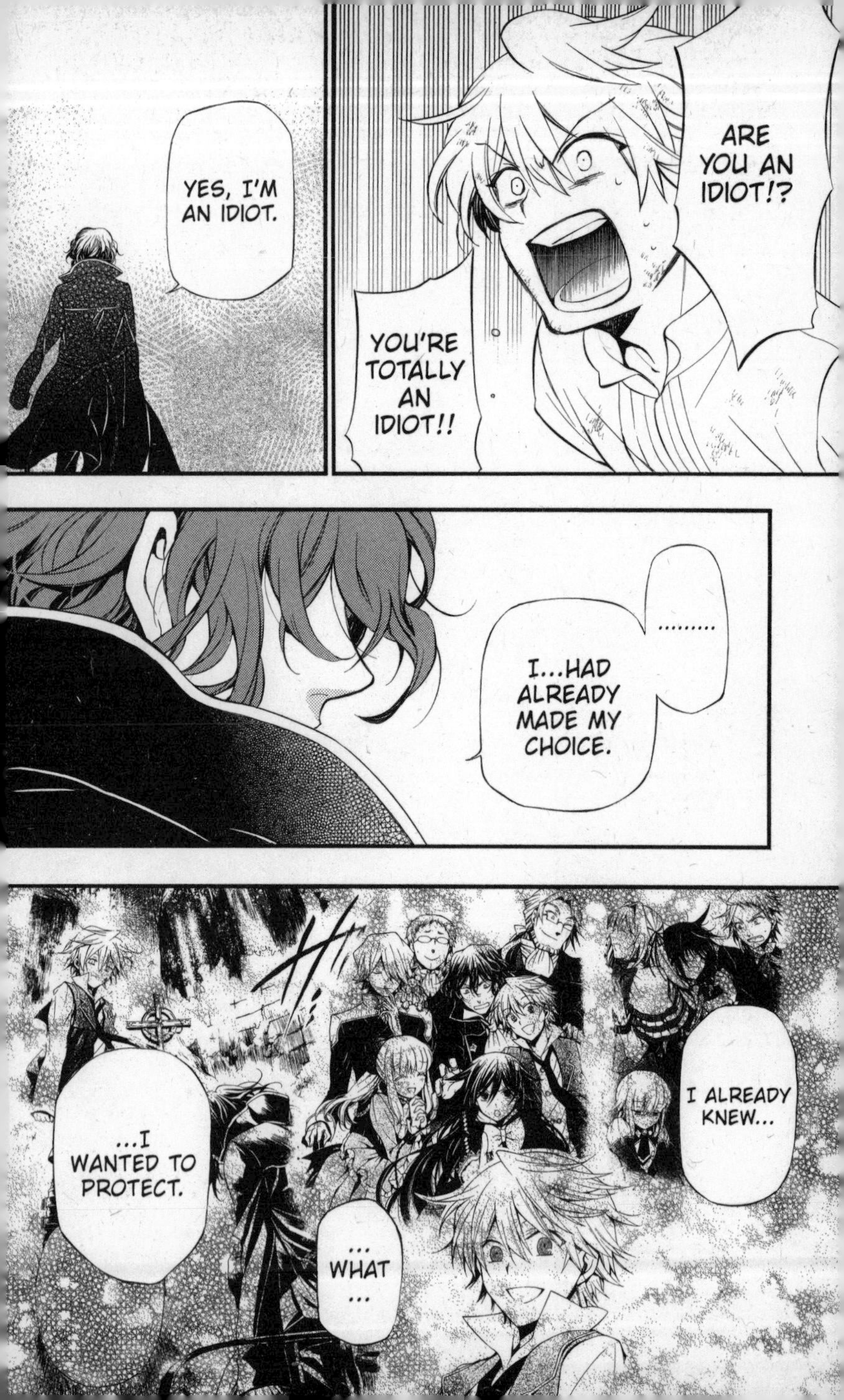
ARE YOU AN IDIOT!?
YOU'RE TOTALLY AN IDIOT!!
YES, I'M AN IDIOT.
....
I...HAD ALREADY MADE MY CHOICE.
I ALREADY KNEW...
...WHAT...
...I WANTED TO PROTECT.

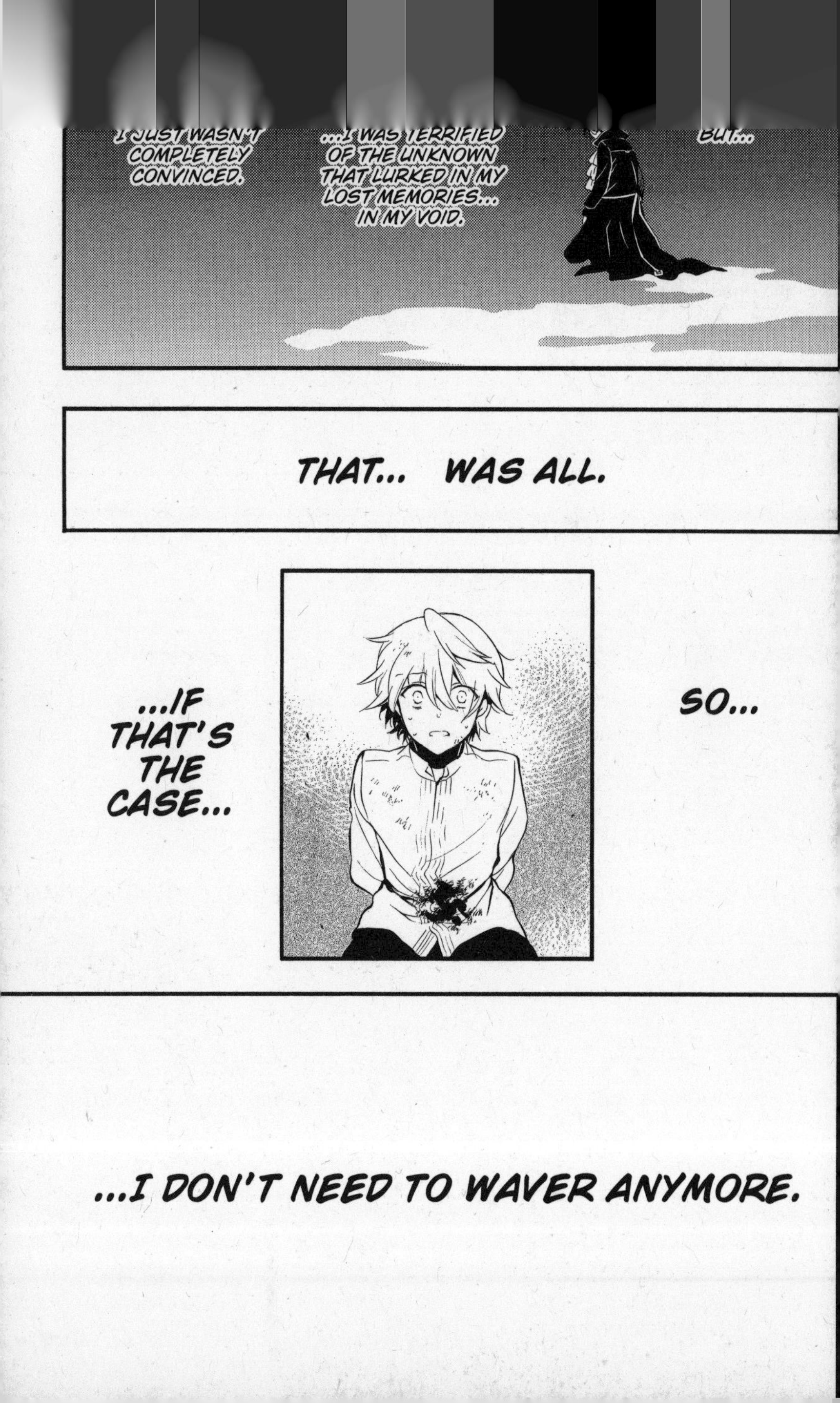
BUT...
...I WAS TERRIFIED OF THE UNKNOWN THAT LURKED IN MY LOST MEMORIES... IN MY VOID.
I JUST WASN'T COMPLETELY CONVINCED.
THAT... WAS ALL.
SO...
...IF THAT'S THE CASE...
...I DON'T NEED TO WAVER ANYMORE.

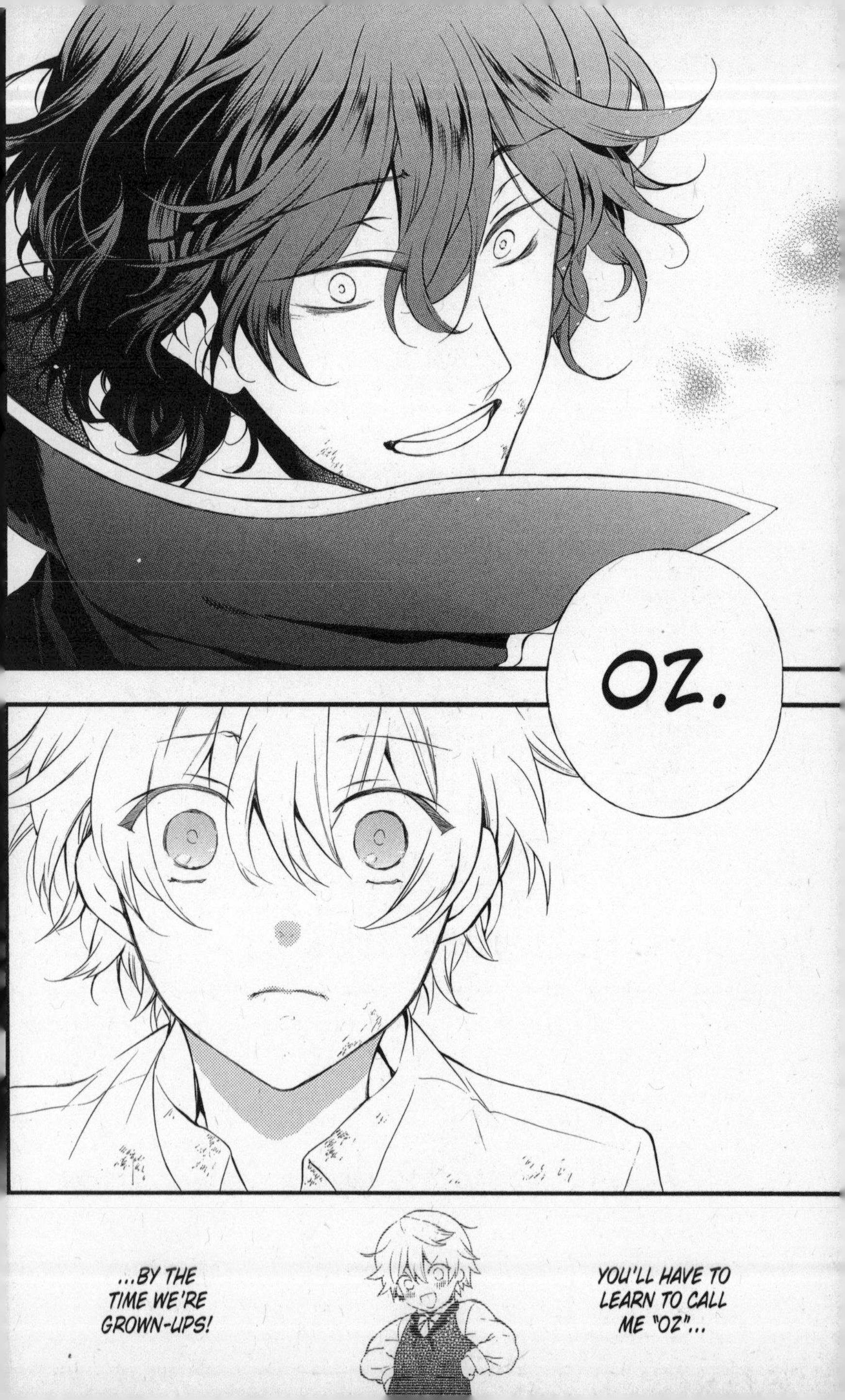
OZ.
YOU'LL HAVE TO LEARN TO CALL ME "OZ"...
...BY THE TIME WE'RE GROWN-UPS!

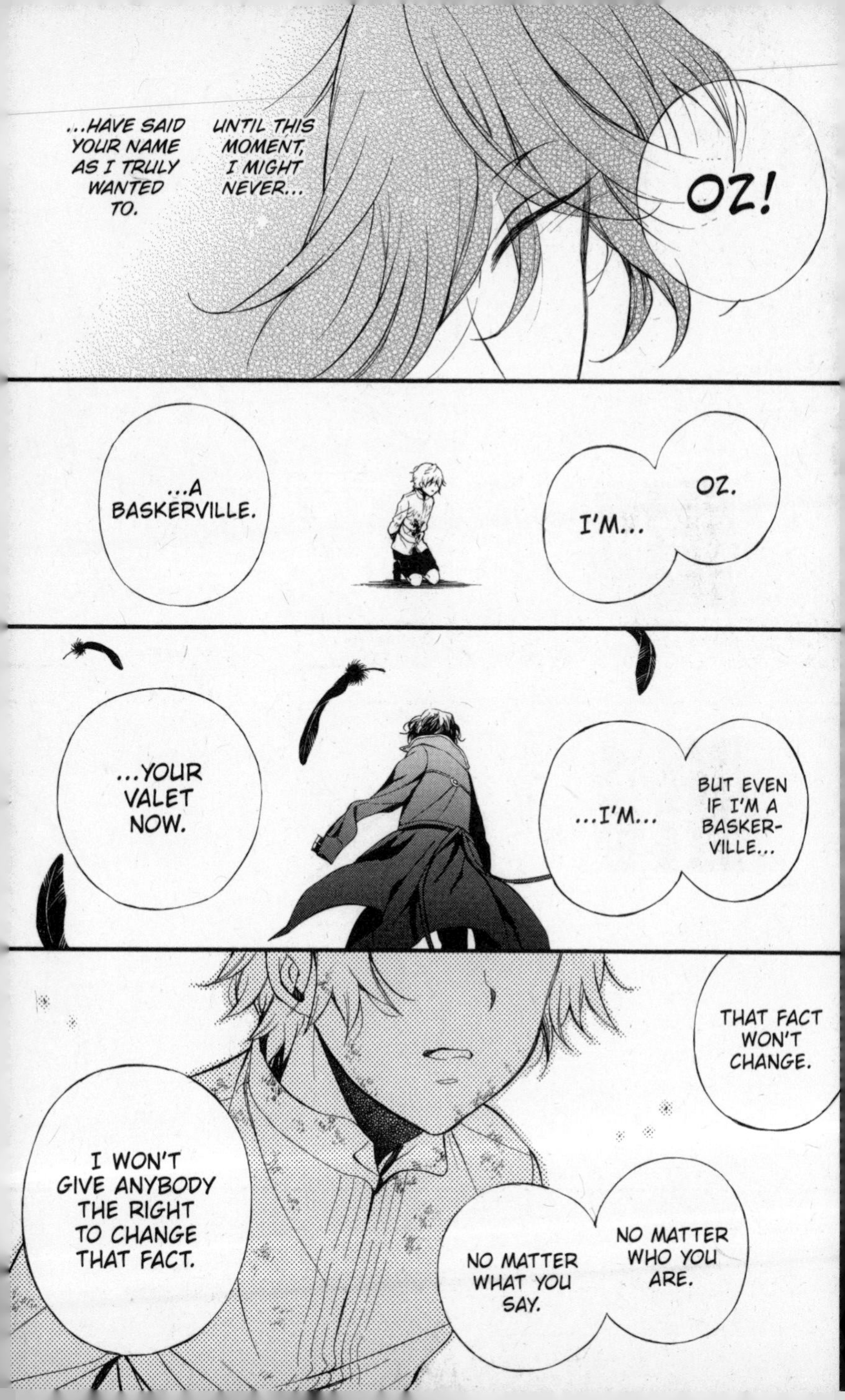
OZ!
UNTIL THIS MOMENT, I MIGHT NEVER...
...HAVE SAID YOUR NAME AS I TRULY WANTED TO.
OZ.
I'M...
...A BASKERVILLE.
BUT EVEN IF I'M A BASKER-VILLE...
...I'M...
...YOUR VALET NOW.
THAT FACT WON'T CHANGE.
NO MATTER WHO YOU ARE.
NO MATTER WHAT YOU SAY.
I WON'T GIVE ANYBODY THE RIGHT TO CHANGE THAT FACT.

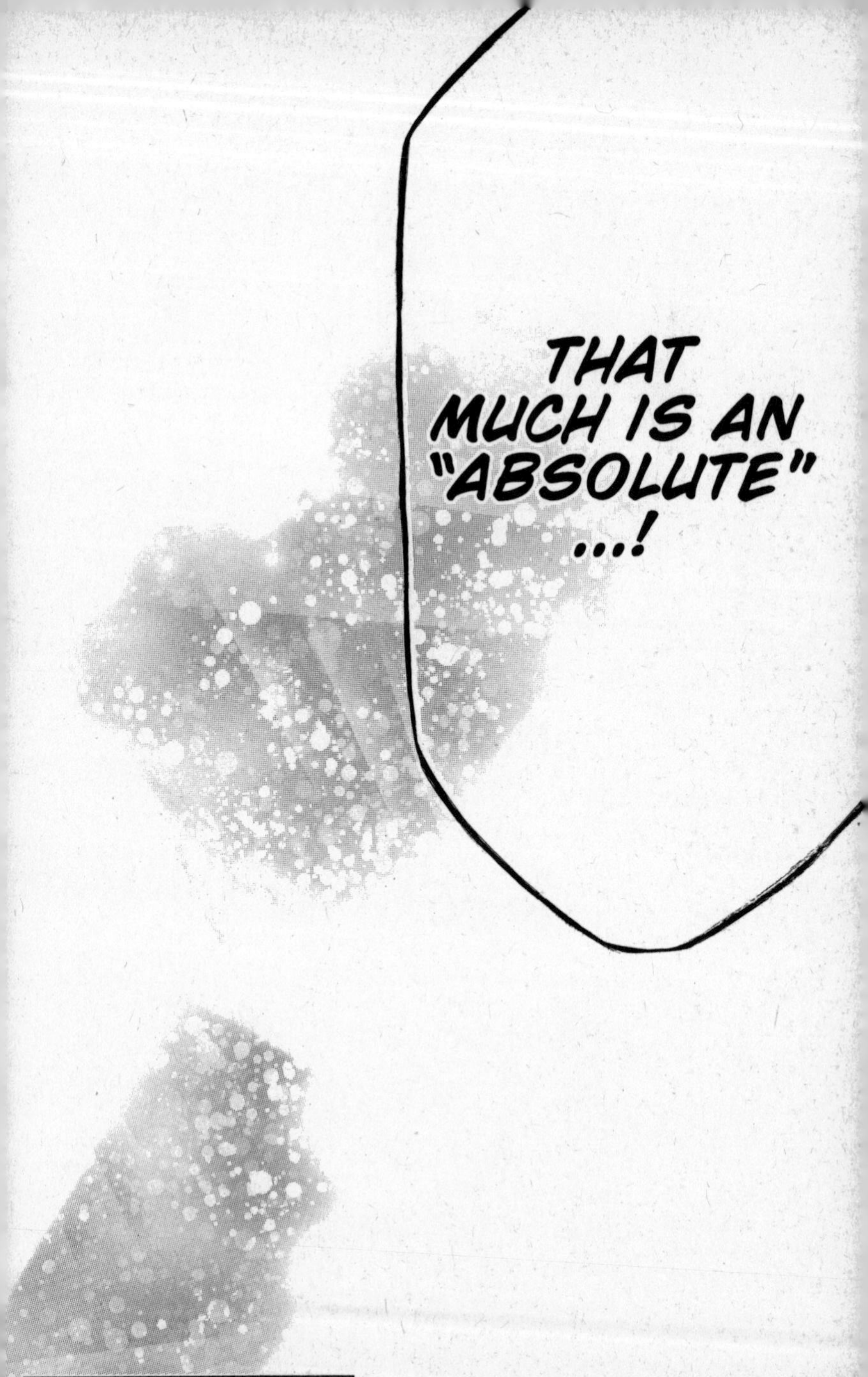
THAT MUCH IS AN "ABSOLUTE" ...!

TO BE CONTINUED IN PANDORA HEARTS 20

Retrace:LXXVIII Decision

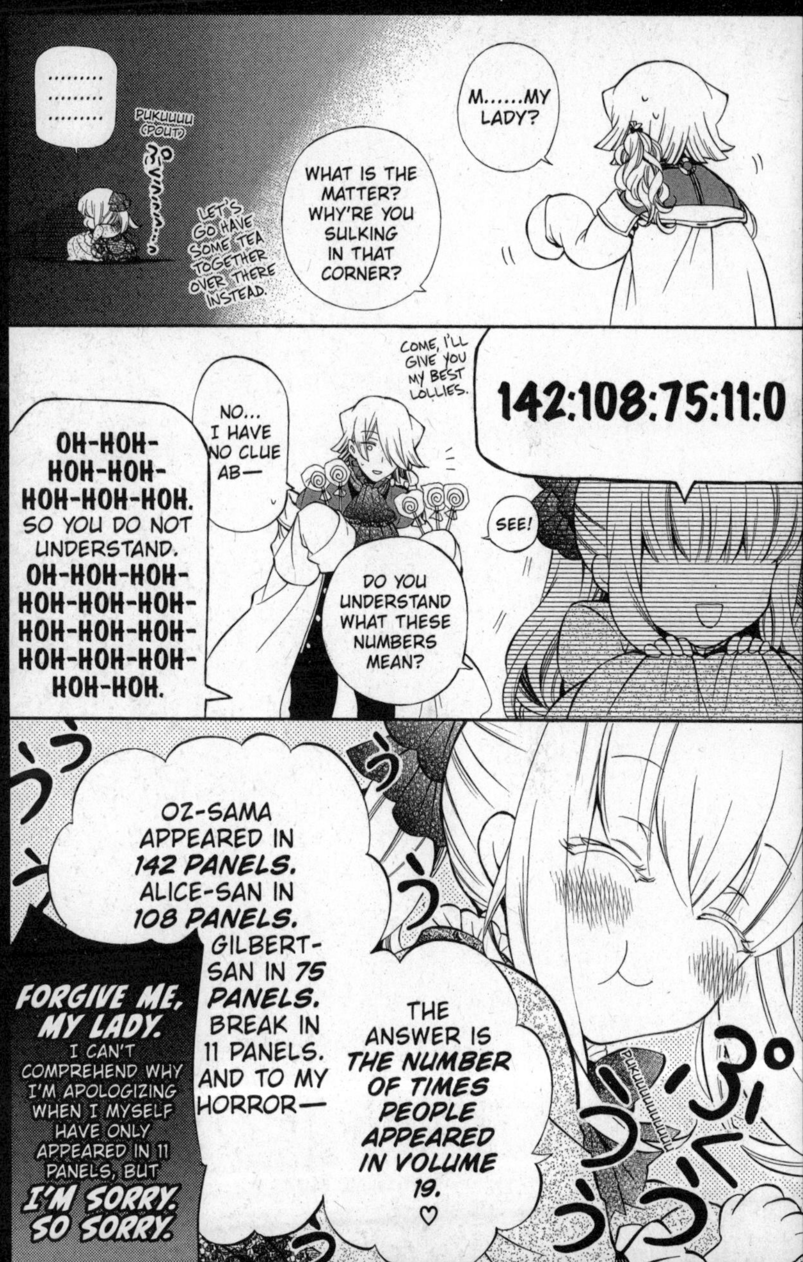
M......MY LADY?
WHAT IS THE MATTER? WHY'RE YOU SULKING IN THAT CORNER?
LET'S GO HAVE SOME TEA TOGETHER OVER THERE INSTEAD.
PUKUUUUU (POUT)
....
....
....
142:108:75:11:0
COME, I'LL GIVE YOU MY BEST LOLLIES.
SEE!
DO YOU UNDERSTAND WHAT THESE NUMBERS MEAN?
NO... I HAVE NO CLUE AB—
OH-HOH-HOH-HOH-HOH-HOH-HOH. SO YOU DO NOT UNDERSTAND. OH-HOH-HOH-HOH-HOH-HOH-HOH-HOH-HOH-HOH-HOH-HOH-HOH-HOH.
PUKUUUUUUUUUU
THE ANSWER IS THE NUMBER OF TIMES PEOPLE APPEARED IN VOLUME 19. ♡
OZ-SAMA APPEARED IN 142 PANELS. ALICE-SAN IN 108 PANELS. GILBERT-SAN IN 75 PANELS. BREAK IN 11 PANELS. AND TO MY HORROR—
FORGIVE ME, MY LADY. I CAN'T COMPREHEND WHY I'M APOLOGIZING WHEN I MYSELF HAVE ONLY APPEARED IN 11 PANELS, BUT I'M SORRY. SO SORRY.

I APOLOGIZE IF THE NUMBERS ARE WRONG, BUT SHARON'S 0 IS INDISPUTABLE.

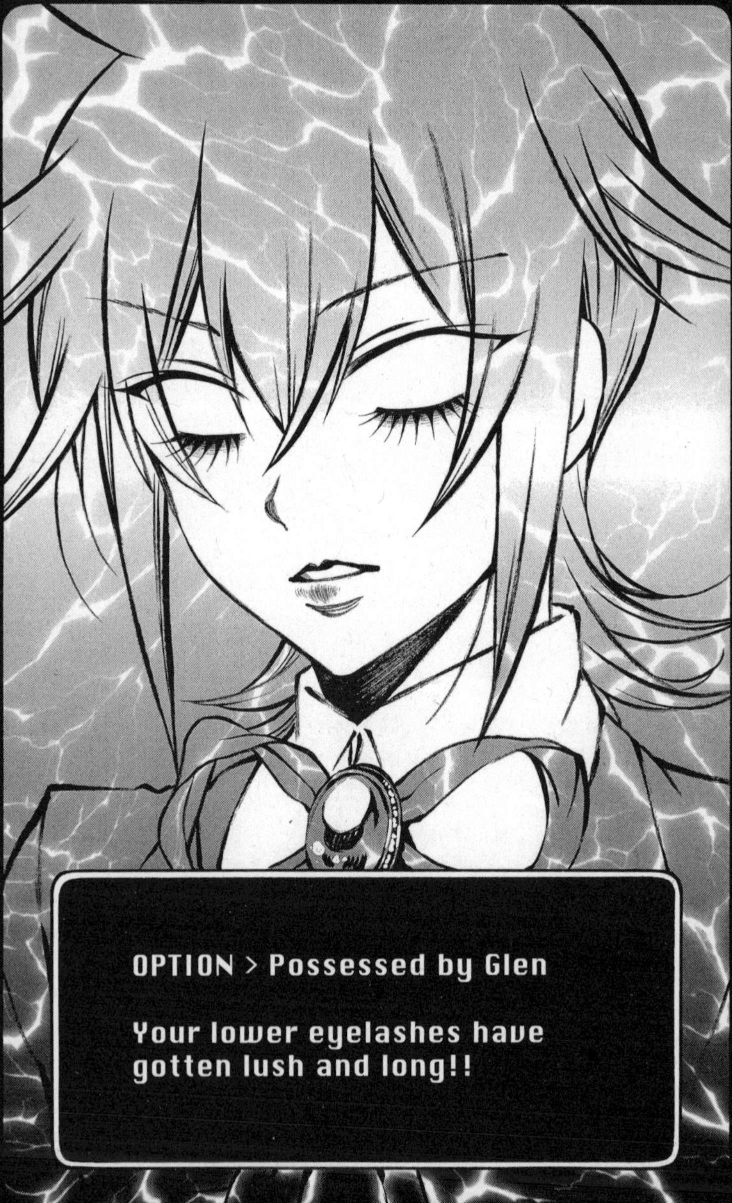
OPTION > Possessed by Glen
Your lower eyelashes have gotten lush and long!!

BONUS: "OSWALD SNAPS."

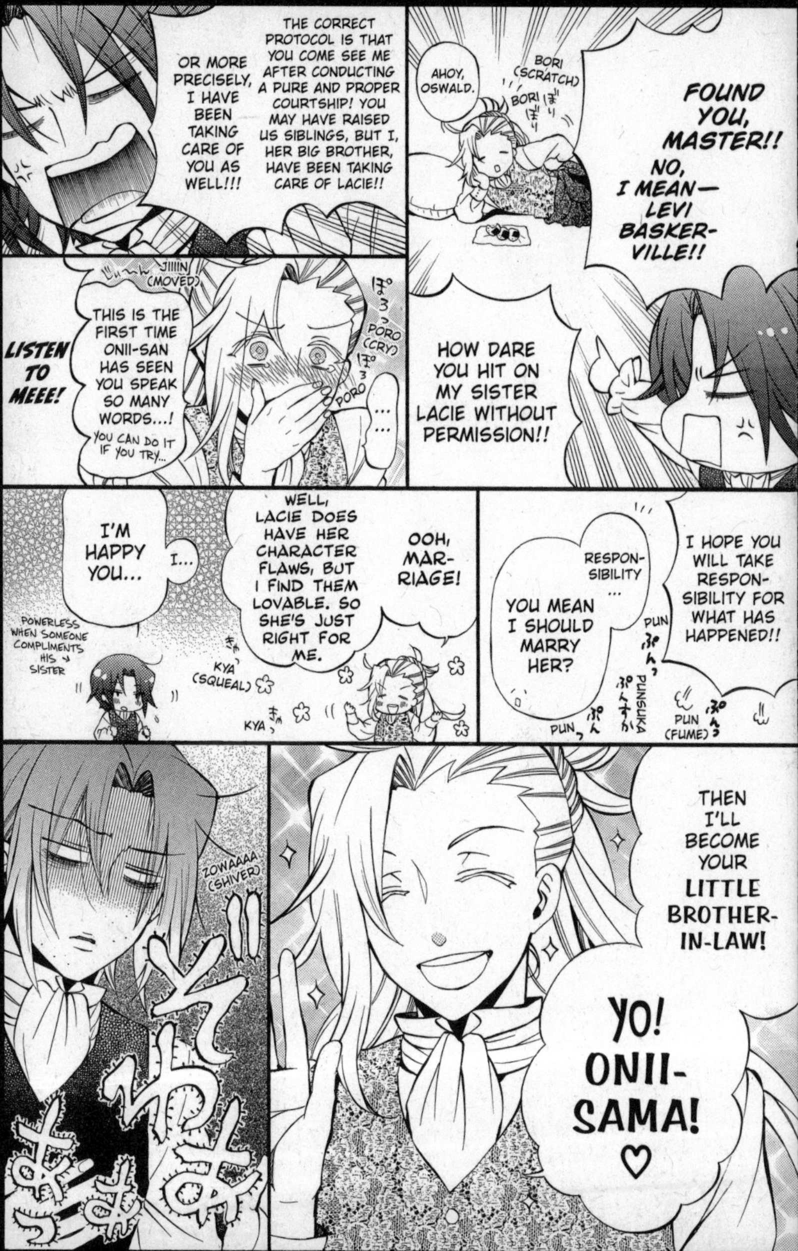
AHOY, OSWALD.
BORI (SCRATCH)
BORI
FOUND YOU, MASTER!! NO, I MEAN—LEVI BASKERVILLE!!
HOW DARE YOU HIT ON MY SISTER LACIE WITHOUT PERMISSION!!
THE CORRECT PROTOCOL IS THAT YOU COME SEE ME AFTER CONDUCTING A PURE AND PROPER COURTSHIP! YOU MAY HAVE RAISED US SIBLINGS, BUT I, HER BIG BROTHER, HAVE BEEN TAKING CARE OF LACIE!!
OR MORE PRECISELY, I HAVE BEEN TAKING CARE OF YOU AS WELL!!!
PORO (CRY)
PORO
JIIIIN (MOVED)
THIS IS THE FIRST TIME ONII-SAN HAS SEEN YOU SPEAK SO MANY WORDS...!
YOU CAN DO IT IF YOU TRY...
LISTEN TO MEEE!
......
I HOPE YOU WILL TAKE RESPONSIBILITY FOR WHAT HAS HAPPENED!!
PUN (FUME)
PUN
PUNSUKA
RESPONSIBILITY...
YOU MEAN I SHOULD MARRY HER?
PUN
OOH, MARRIAGE!
WELL, LACIE DOES HAVE HER CHARACTER FLAWS, BUT I FIND THEM LOVABLE. SO SHE'S JUST RIGHT FOR ME.
KYA (SQUEAL)
KYA
I...
I'M HAPPY YOU...
POWERLESS WHEN SOMEONE COMPLIMENTS HIS SISTER
THEN I'LL BECOME YOUR LITTLE BROTHER-IN-LAW!
YO! ONII-SAMA! ♡
ZOWAAAA (SHIVER)
SO LEVI DID NOT MARRY LACIE.

BONUS: "HE CAN DO GOOD WORK."

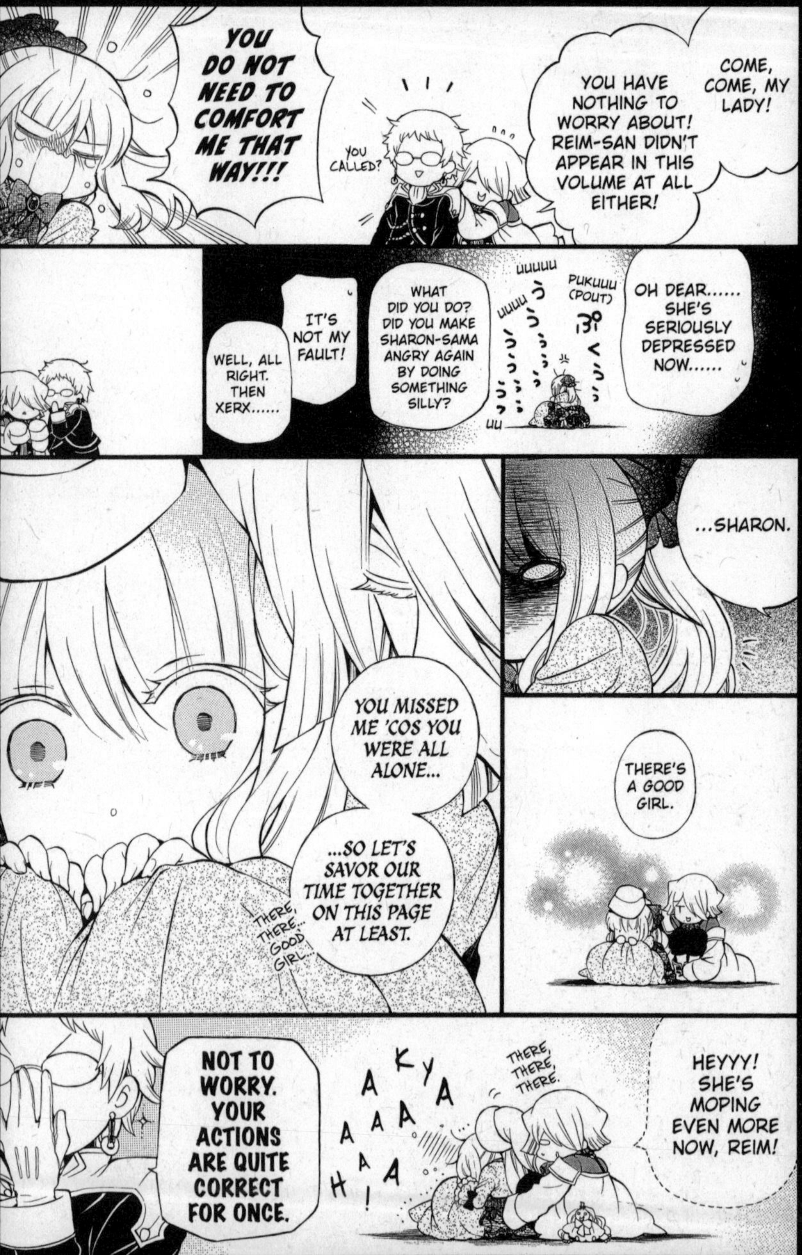
COME, COME, MY LADY!
YOU HAVE NOTHING TO WORRY ABOUT! REIM-SAN DIDN'T APPEAR IN THIS VOLUME AT ALL EITHER!
YOU DO NOT NEED TO COMFORT ME THAT WAY!!!
YOU CALLED?
OH DEAR...... SHE'S SERIOUSLY DEPRESSED NOW......
PUKUUU (POUT)
UUUUU
UUUU
UU
WHAT DID YOU DO? DID YOU MAKE SHARON-SAMA ANGRY AGAIN BY DOING SOMETHING SILLY?
IT'S NOT MY FAULT!
WELL, ALL RIGHT. THEN XERX......
...SHARON.
THERE'S A GOOD GIRL.
YOU MISSED ME 'COS YOU WERE ALL ALONE...
...SO LET'S SAVOR OUR TIME TOGETHER ON THIS PAGE AT LEAST.
THERE, THERE... GOOD GIRL...
HEYYY! SHE'S MOPING EVEN MORE NOW, REIM!
THERE, THERE, THERE.
NOT TO WORRY. YOUR ACTIONS ARE QUITE CORRECT FOR ONCE.

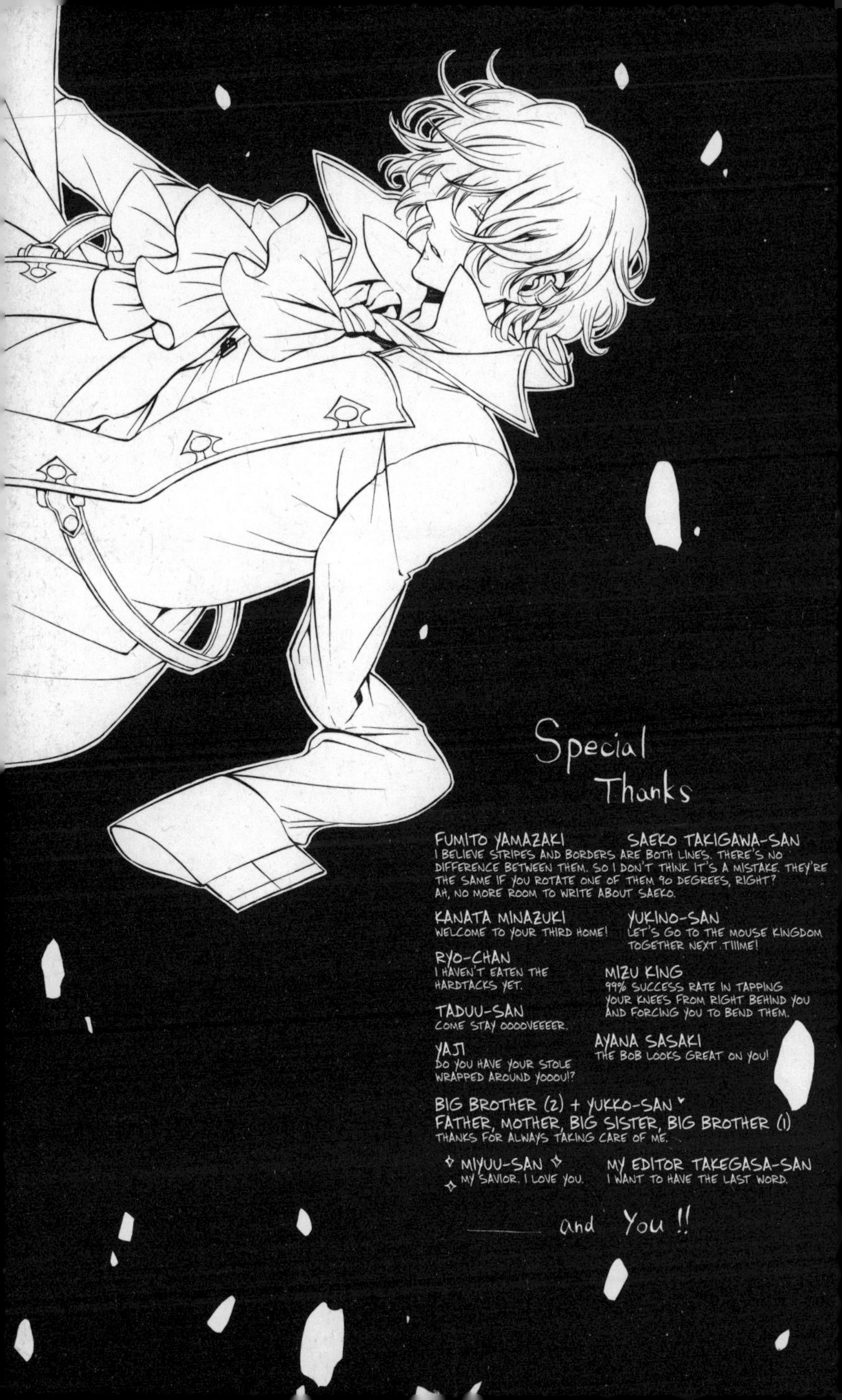

Special Thanks

FUMITO YAMAZAKI **SAEKO TAKIGAWA-SAN**
I BELIEVE STRIPES AND BORDERS ARE BOTH LINES. THERE'S NO DIFFERENCE BETWEEN THEM. SO I DON'T THINK IT'S A MISTAKE. THEY'RE THE SAME IF YOU ROTATE ONE OF THEM 90 DEGREES, RIGHT? AH, NO MORE ROOM TO WRITE ABOUT SAEKO.

KANATA MINAZUKI
WELCOME TO YOUR THIRD HOME!

YUKINO-SAN
LET'S GO TO THE MOUSE KINGDOM TOGETHER NEXT TIIIME!

RYO-CHAN
I HAVEN'T EATEN THE HARDTACKS YET.

MIZU KING
99% SUCCESS RATE IN TAPPING YOUR KNEES FROM RIGHT BEHIND YOU AND FORCING YOU TO BEND THEM.

TADUU-SAN
COME STAY OOOOVEEEER.

YAJI
DO YOU HAVE YOUR STOLE WRAPPED AROUND YOOOU!?

AYANA SASAKI
THE BOB LOOKS GREAT ON YOU!

BIG BROTHER (2) + YUKKO-SAN ♥
FATHER, MOTHER, BIG SISTER, BIG BROTHER (1)
THANKS FOR ALWAYS TAKING CARE OF ME.

✧ **MIYUU-SAN** ✧
✧ MY SAVIOR. I LOVE YOU.

MY EDITOR TAKEGASA-SAN
I WANT TO HAVE THE LAST WORD.

—— and You !!

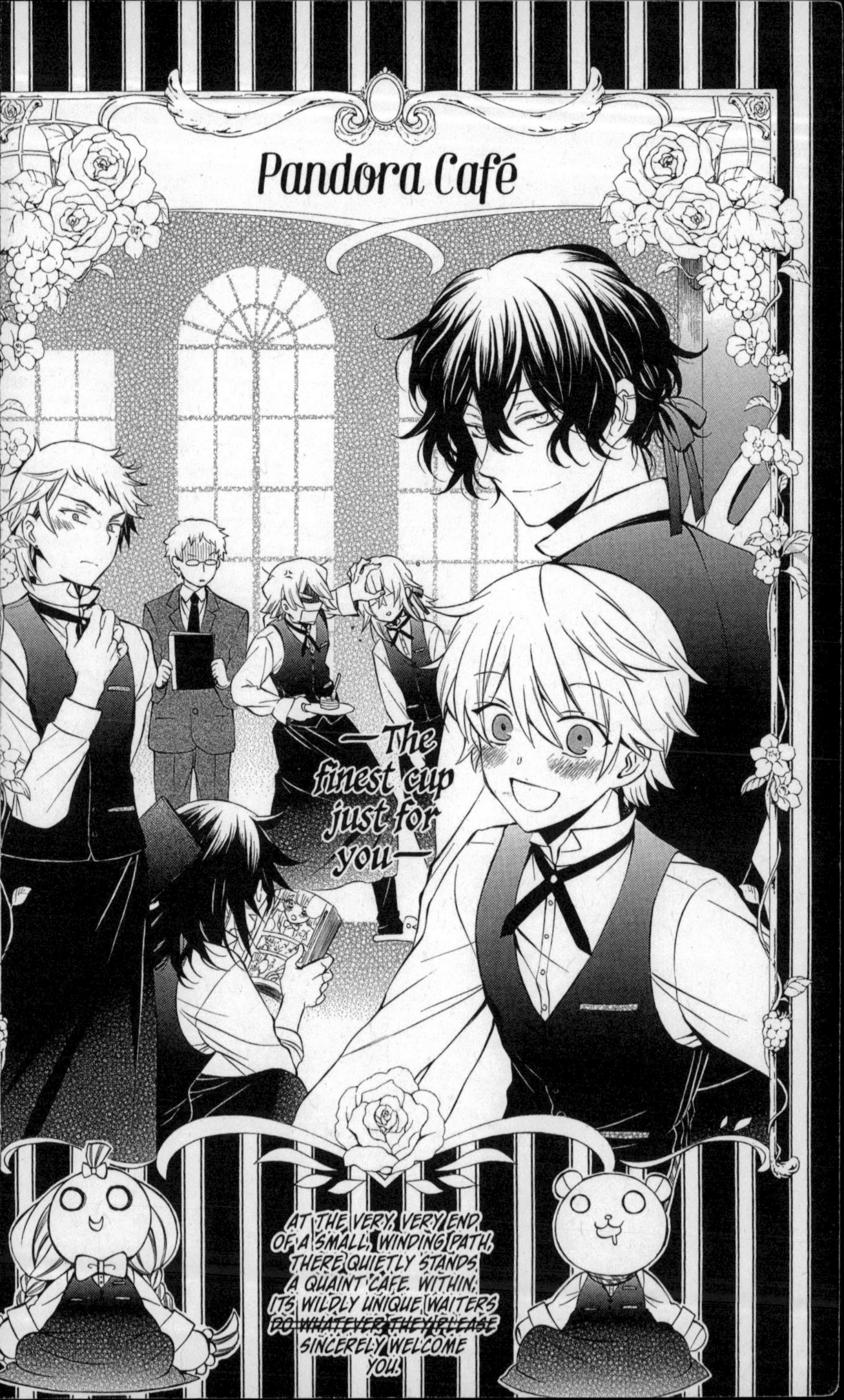
Pandora Café
—The finest cup just for you—
AT THE VERY, VERY END OF A SMALL, WINDING PATH, THERE QUIETLY STANDS A QUAINT CAFÉ. WITHIN, ITS WILDLY UNIQUE WAITERS ~~DO WHATEVER THEY PLEASE~~ SINCERELY WELCOME YOU.

Menu

Drink menu

Hot

GIL'S SUNNY COFFEE ········ 400

GIL'S DEVIL-MAY-CARE COFFEE ········ 450

GIL'S BASHFUL COFFEE ········ 600

REIM-SAN'S OH-SO-SERIOUS COFFEE ··· 800

REIM-SAN'S SURPRISE ATTACK COFFEE ·· 800

OZ'S TEE-HEE AND STICKING-HIS-TONGUE-OUT COFFEE ········ 350

Cold

ELLIOT'S PROUD CAFE LATTE ········ 400

ELLIOT'S **HOLD YOUR TONGUE, BOOR! HAVE YOU NO SHAME!? I SHALL JUDGE YOU!** MASALA CHAI TEA ········ 500

LEO'S SHUT-IN FRUIT PUNCH ········ 600

PLAIN, OLD ORANGE JUICE ········ 700

OZ'S LITTLE DEVIL ICED TEA ········ 500

EMILY'S LEAFY-GREEN SMOOTHIE ······ 900

Food menu

BREAK'S WHIMSICAL NAPOLITAN ······· 900

GIL'S SINCERE GRATIN ········ 800

GIL'S LONELY RICE DORIA ········ 800

OZ'S NONSENSE SANDWICH ········ 550

ELLIOT'S **I-IT'S NOT LIKE I MADE IT FOR YOU!** ONIGIRI ········ 600

LEO'S BOOKWORM TOAST ········ 700

REIM-SAN'S OVERTIME FULL-COURSE MEAL ········ 1200

Dessert menu

VINCENT'S HEART-RACING FRENCH TOAST ········ 500

BREAK'S PLEASE, WON'T YOU LET ME HAVE SOME TOOOO?♡ CHOCOLATE CAKE ········ 600

STRAWBERRY CAKE FOR OZ ········ 600

PAY GIL BACK APPLE PIE ········ 400

UNDER-THE-EYE MOLE PANCAKE (GARNISHED WITH A VAMPIRE TOOTH) ········ 700

—We're waiting for your visit.

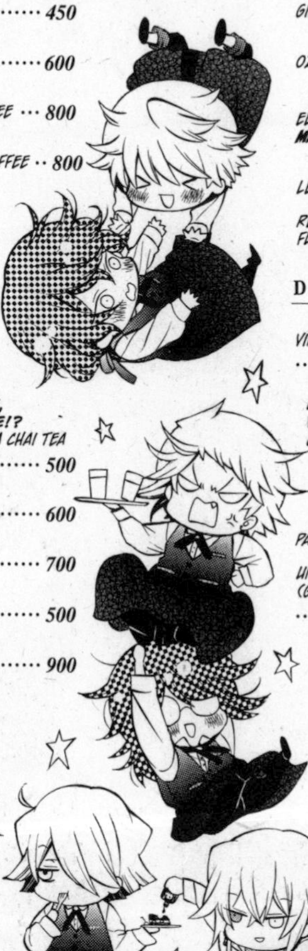

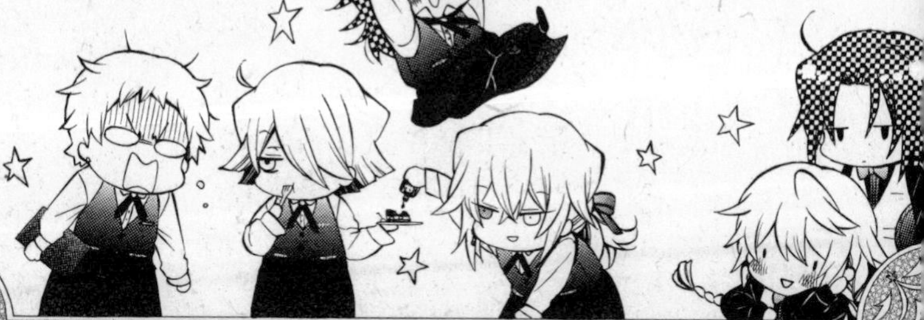

COMMON HONORIFICS
no honorific: Indicates familiarity or closeness; if used without permission or reason, addressing someone in this manner would constitute an insult.
-san: The Japanese equivalent of Mr./Mrs./Miss. If a situation calls for politeness, this is the fail-safe honorific.
-sama: Conveys great respect; may also indicate that the social status of the speaker is lower than that of the addressee.
-kun: Used most often when referring to boys (though it can be applied to girls as well), this indicates affection or familiarity. Occasionally used by older men among their peers, but it may also be used by anyone referring to a person of lower standing.
-chan: An affectionate honorific indicating familiarity used mostly in reference to girls; also used in reference to cute persons or animals of either gender.

tee-hee & sticking-his-tongue-out coffee   *page 178*

The Japanese word for this coffee is *tehepero*, which suggests an embarrassed laugh accompanied by sticking one's tongue out. It is often used when the speaker makes a mistake or wants to soften the other person's reaction.

Napolitan   *page 178*

A Japanese pasta dish made with spaghetti and ketchup in place of spaghetti sauce. Onions, green peppers, and meats such as ham, sausage, or bacon are other common ingredients, and the dish is typically topped with powdered cheese and tabasco.

doria   *page 178*

A Japanese comfort food dish of Italian heritage that is somewhat like a baked casserole made with chicken or seafood, rice, and vegetables and doused in bechamel/white sauce and cheese.

under-the-eye mole   *page 178*

Nakibokuro in Japanese, or literally, "crying mole." In fortune-telling, one characteristic attributed to people with these moles is that they are easily moved to tears and will often encounter events in life that will make them cry.

AUTHOR NOTE

I'm becoming more and more of an expert on various energy drinks these days. They only work for a limited time, though!

MOCHIZUKI'
MUSINGS

VOLUME

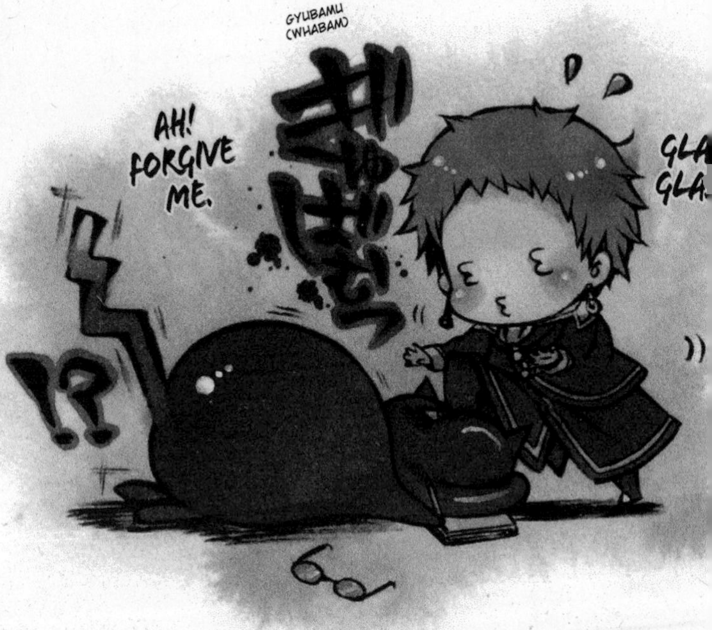
GYUBAMU
(WHABAM)
AH! FORGIVE ME.
!?

MOCHIZUKI

Translation: Tomo Kimura • Lettering: Alexis Eckerman

PandoraHearts Vol. 19 © 2012 Jun Mochizuki / SQUARE ENIX CO., LTD. All rights reserved. First published in Japan in 2012 by SQUARE ENIX CO., LTD. English translation rights arranged with SQUARE ENIX CO., LTD. and Hachette Book Group through Tuttle-Mori Agency, Inc.

Translation © 2013 by SQUARE ENIX CO., LTD.

Yen Press
Hachette Book Group
237 Park Avenue, New York, NY 10017

www.HachetteBookGroup.com
www.YenPress.com

Yen Press is an imprint of Hachette Book Group, Inc. The Yen Press name and logo are trademarks of Hachette Book Group, Inc.

First Yen Press Edition: December 2013

ISBN: 978-0-316-24037-6

10 9 8 7 6 5 4 3 2 1

BVG

Printed in the United States of America